ESCAPE FROM APARTHEID
A Novel

By: **FRANK R. SOUTHERS**

frs@southers.com

Copyright © 2018

Cover Photo: Shutterstock—by Tony Campbell, South Africa 2015

Cover Design: Patricia Hamilton, Pacific Grove, CA

ISBN # 13: 978-1985622067

ISBN # 10: 1985622068

Library of Congress # Pending

Printed in the United States of America

ESCAPE FROM APARTHEID

Escape from Apartheid, a novel, is a work of fiction and is a product created by the author's imagination. While the novel may refer to historical events, organizations, places, or people, the use therein of any actual person (living or dead), or actual names, or actual proceedings, or actual organizations, or actual places, or actual events, and/or actual quotations or speech or publication is entirely fictitious and entirely coincidental. Any reference to historical events, to real people, or to real places is a fictitious reference. Any resemblance to persons (living or dead), or names, or lyrics, or characters, or groups, or organizations, or businesses, or entities, or places, or locales, or cases, or incidents, or proceedings, or trials, or events, and/or quotations (whether actual or not) is entirely coincidental and is purely fictitious.

NOVELS BY FRANK R. SOUTHERS

The Grievance Committee—Book One

A Serious Mistake

To Get Even, a Novel

Lawyer Magic

Senator White

All novels are available in paperback and kindle at Amazon.com or on order from your favorite Bookseller

ACKNOWLEDGEMENTS

Writing a historical novel requires historical research of people and events occurring in another time and, perhaps, in another country.

While true history buffs can correctly criticize an author's misstating in a historical novel a sequence of events, a person's words, or an actual quotation, remember, please, that the historical novel is a work of fiction and the author is the creator of the story. So, remember that *Escape from Apartheid* is a mixture of fact and fiction. Nonetheless, without the dedicated work of many historians freely making their research available, few historical novels would be written.

Escape from Apartheid owes its very existence to the incredible work of innumerable historians and storytellers and their publishers. To name just a few, please allow me to recognize and thank:

Google; Wikipedia; Leonard Thompson, *A History of South Africa, 3rd Edition* (Yale University Press); *South African History On-Line*; Nelson Mandela, *Long Walk to Freedom* with connections by Richard W. Kelso (Holt, Rinehart & Winston-Harcourt Brace & Co); *The Mandela Foundation*; Alan Paton, *Cry, The Beloved Country* (Scribner); Janet Cherry, *Spear of the Nation* (Ohio University Press); Lindy Wilson, *Steve Biko* (Ohio University Press); The O'Malley Archives; Trevor Noah, *Born A Crime* (Spiegel & Grau)

ESCAPE FROM APARTHEID

Prologue

The six-member Grievance Committee Panel is deliberating privately as to whether Attorney Betty Sue Meadowlake violated the Texas Disciplinary Rules of Professional Conduct and should be disciplined.

Accused of releasing information to a San Antonio television station about her lawsuit against a corporate defendant in retaliation for the defendant's refusal to pay her pre-suit settlement demand, the corporate complainant contends the attorney's conduct constitutes Extortion, a felony under the Texas Penal Code.

Most of the Grievance Committee Panel Members appear to be agreeing with the corporate complainant that Betty Sue Meadowlake should be disbarred.

But Panel Member Tyrone Washington is arguing to excuse the accused lawyer's conduct because the United States Supreme Court has ruled in a similar case in Arizona that the federal constitutional right of free speech overrides any State's Lawyer Disciplinary Rules.

Tyrone reveals, "Perhaps some of you didn't know that as a youngster I was raised as a Black, or rather as a Colored, in South Africa during part of the Apartheid years. With that background, I favor the protection of every individual's rights, especially the right of free speech."

Tyrone pauses to let that sink in, especially to the two non-lawyers on the Grievance Committee Hearing Panel.

"In my personal experience and my family's experience under Apartheid in South Africa, any minority group

1

with the legal trappings of power can easily become terribly oppressive. A small group with the awesome power of government can impose its own rule of law as to what's right and what's fair on an overwhelming majority of the people. That small group becomes a dictator and can even decide what's legal and what's not. It can decide what is true and what is not. It can make people afraid to speak out. It can even control the media.

"Does that remind anyone of the Nazis in Germany under Hitler or fascists under Mussolini?

He watches to assure himself everyone is listening and then continues.

"That actually happened in South Africa and it can happen anywhere, even here in the United States of America. It doesn't take a lifetime to legally seize power."

His presence commands the Panel Members' attention. He continues.

"And, it can happen in the blink of an eye, even with just the next election. Legal oppression isn't always far away when a small group obtains control of the government; or obtains control of a part of the government; or obtains control of the legislature and marginalizes the majority of the people. That's what created Apartheid in South Africa."

He reaches for a glass of water and watches the five faces of the other members of the Hearing Panel.

"When a political candidate overrides the popular vote through legalities and through archaic means, that politician or his party can take control of the government.

"Then, that politician or political party can self-interpret the law, reward friends and pardon co-conspirators, punish adversaries, self-deal, and manipulate the media.

"That happened not only in South Arica but in other countries and, if we're not careful, that can happen here in the United States."

The lawyers on the Committee quickly connect Tyrone's comments about the overriding of the popular vote to the controversy between the popular presidential vote and the vote in the Electoral College enshrined in the United States Constitution.

The lawyers recognize the way legal control can be stolen from the majority of the people by a minority. But, they remain silent as Tyrone continues.

"So, people's rights are very sacred to me, even when I don't condone or agree with that person's conduct. That's right. I don't agree with Ms. Meadowlake's conduct. But, the United States Constitution and the U.S. Supreme Court guarantee our free speech rights even if we attack our own government with words or symbols."

Tyrone takes another sip of water and then raises his hand in the stop position. His smile doesn't diminish his seriousness as he adds, "But, even if we have free speech as written in the Constitution and in the law books, that right is worth nothing if the government doesn't actually enforce our right of free speech."

Tyrone sees that the other three lawyers on the Panel are listening, with one actually shaking his head affirmatively. Now, Tyrone knows he must convince the two non-lawyer-members on the Panel—a man of Hispanic heritage and an Anglo woman.

"In America, we even have the right to sue God, without being arrested by the religious police and taken before some Court of Inquisition as happened in Spain long ago.

"And we can criticize our local government officials, our Governor, our Legislators, our Judges, and yes, even our President, without being hauled in by the state or federal police and subjected to waterboarding, clubbing, teeth or fingernail extraction, amputation of some fingers, or some other torture.

"We can criticize our police, our local sheriff, or even the FBI or CIA without fear of retribution. And, we even can burn our precious flag without being jailed or deprived of our citizenship.

"We can even kneel during the playing of the National Anthem during a football game without arrest.

"That's what makes America great. Yes, that's what makes America great!"

He sees that the telling smiles on the lawyer's faces recognize the significance of his last remark. He continues, "Freedom of speech is nothing if we, the people and the government, don't guarantee enforcement and protection of those rights. We must do that today and not give just lip-service to the right of free speech, which is our savior against an oppressive government. Our right of free speech protects all of us, no matter our religion, no matter our gender, no matter our sexual preference, no matter our race, and no matter our national origin.

"That's why, my fellow Grievance Committee Members, I must vote for a dismissal of this grievance complaint."

After a lengthy discussion, the six Panel Members of the Grievance Committee in San Antonio, Texas unanimously dismiss the complaint.

4

"Excuse me," the staff investigator interrupts, "but our next case will be delayed for at least an hour, maybe two or three. So, we've got a lot of time on our hands.

"I didn't know Mr. Washington had spent his early years growing up during the Apartheid regime in South Africa. Since we have the time, Mr. Chairman, I suggest we ask him to tell us about it. I certainly would like to hear about it, especially from an African-American living and experiencing it firsthand. To confess, I myself don't know a whole lot about Apartheid or how it got control of South Africa. I remember that Nelson Mandela was imprisoned for many years because of Apartheid and there was a campaign in the United States to free Nelson Mandela. I sure would like to find out more about Apartheid."

Watching the affirmative head shakes, the Chairman asks, "Well, Tyrone?"

"Yes. To fully understand Apartheid you must have some major historical information. I hope that won't be too boring.

"I'll start the history lesson when the British finally beat the Dutch Afrikaners or Boers in 1902. A few years later, the British Parliament increased English territory by annexing the two remaining Dutch Colonies, leading to the adoption of a Constitution in South Africa and creating a unitary state with Parliament's oversight, similar to England's."

Watching their faces for attentiveness, Tyrone continues.

"The South African Constitution provided for no Bill of Rights and disenfranchised every Black except those Blacks in the Cape Colony. And, it eventually even disenfranchised those Blacks, too, along with Coloreds and Asians."

His audience is paying attention, he sees.

"It created a voting system which would favor political parties seeking voters in less populated rural districts to elect Members of Parliament. That means these elected Members of Parliament would win their office from a fewer number of voters in rural districts than would Members of Parliament elected in urban districts."

To the two non-lawyers' questioning faces, Tyrone says, "Later, you will understand the significance of winning the election to control Parliament without the most popular vote because that's how Apartheid happened.

"I know that you can identify that with our recent election in the United States."

He sees the recognizing smiles on the lawyers' faces.

"Then, in 1910 English King Edward VII proclaimed the creation of the Union of South Africa as part of the English Commonwealth, with the four Colonies now named Provinces."

Seeing no falling eyelids and no yawns, he continues.

"With the segregation groundwork already laid by the Dutch and English settlers, the Union of South Africa began a series of laws to segregate Blacks from Whites and to preserve the good life for Whites, mainly English and Dutch (now called Afrikaners), and to make cheap Black labor readily available."

As a means to guarantee the attention of his audience, he lowers his voice.

"Apartheid didn't actually begin until almost thirty years after the creation of the Union of South Africa by the British Crown. But a lot of racial segregation happened in South Africa leading up to Apartheid. That in itself is part of the story."

He pauses and asks, "Is everyone still with me? I hope I haven't bored you to death."

Tyrone hears a round of agreement that his story should continue.

"Fine. Now, as you follow my story, I hope you will understand a lot about Apartheid and what led up to its creation. I'll start the story in 1943 with my father, Charles Washington, and his parents, Sol and Alice. They lived in Durban, a big South African city bordering on the Indian Ocean."

Surveying his audience, Tyrone says, "I trust you'll find the story and the history very fascinating. I'll call the story 'Escape from Apartheid.' So, here we go. I hope you enjoy the story."

Chapter 1

Sixteen-year-old Charles Washington is running away from home for good. He quickly packs a few clothes in a small suitcase. His mother, Alice, has helped with his plan to escape from his father's abuse, but all the same Charles' fingers shake as he looks around.

Of course, his father, Sol, is totally in the dark about his son's plan to escape.

While Charles figures out what else to take, his father is completing his shift as a dockhand at the Durban city wharf. His knowing mother is conveniently shopping downtown at the Victoria Market across the street from St. Emmanuel's Catholic Church.

Before his father completes his shift, Charles intends to be gone for good. Otherwise, he can hardly imagine what his father would do to him.

* * *

Today, September 9, 1943, Charles' father will be late arriving home because of obvious excitement at the docks.

Like all the other cheering people in Durban, Sol feels the overwhelming joy of a smalltime victory over the Axis powers of Italy and Germany.

Today, the Italian submarine, *Ammiraglio Cagni,* and her crew of 85, surrendered to the British Navy in Durban, because there was no escape.

The *Ammiraglio Cagni*, a long-ranged raider, built in 1939 with 14 torpedo tubes and armed with extra torpedoes of 17.7 inch caliber, preyed on Allied merchant ships mainly in the South Atlantic. For these Italian sailors and their sub, the War is over.

Since the Durban harbor is now full of Allied ships which have escaped torpedoes from German, Italian, and even Japanese submarines during the World War, Sol is fully employed tying up ships and loading and unloading cargo. The main three South African ports of Durban, Port Elizabeth, and Cape Town have loaded tons of supplies onto Allied ships to and from Egypt after the Germans and Italians had closed the Mediterranean Sea to Allied shipping in 1941.

Twenty years ago, Sol fled to Durban, South Africa from Madras, (now Chennai) India. He arrived, along with several thousand other Indians, all indentured laborers secured by the Union of South African government to work on the sugar farms and in the coal, gold, and diamond mines. Several thousands of Asians from countries along the Pacific Rim also served as indentured laborers in South Africa.

All supplemented the laboring Natives, units of cheap labor, listed as assets on some bookkeeping ledgers.

When Sol's indenture contract had been completed, to assimilate easily and to gain his current employment, Sol changed his surname from Punjab to Washington. He held immense admiration for things American.

Sol knew the British and the Dutch had used laws to dis-criminate against Asians by employing special taxes—especially on Indians. The British and the Dutch had required the fingerprinting of Indians and segregated places of residences and businesses for Indians.

Many legislative bills in the 1920s were introduced by some of the more rabid dogs of segregation in the South African Parliament to limit the freedom of Indians and even require their deportation from the country. Some-times, even the Natal provincial government and the Durban city government joined in oppressive efforts against Indians, although Indians comprised the largest segment of the local city population. Of course, many Indians left the country rather than suffer this humiliation.

In the past, Sol's hero, Mohandas Gandhi has successfully fought some of these oppressive South African laws, by using his principle of non-violent resistance, namely, *Satyagraha.* The Gandhi method had worked in many instances.

Sol once held concerns that the local Whites, both British and Afrikaners, wouldn't work with Indians or even live next door to them.

But Sol's fears eventually lessen since, from the early part of World War II, these discriminatory laws relaxed in Durban in the Natal Province so that Indians had intermingled businesses and residences with Whites.

War and the threat of War always create new friends from old enemies, Sol reasons.

But in June of 1943 some things changed for the worse. To appease Whites afraid of business competition from Indians, the South African government led by Prime Minister Jan Smuts enacted *The Pegging Act of 1943* preventing Indians from owning property in areas reserved for Whites.

However, with the World War underway, enforcement is very slow. The trial of the first Indian arrested in June for non-compliance with the Pegging Act isn't even scheduled until October in 1943. While the government may yet crack down on Indians in South Africa and make Indians became persona non grata, Sol's world seems safe, at least for the present. Yet, he knows that if and when the government's policy speeds up, then

Sol's world will be threatened and will place fear on his economic table.

But that's not the only worry in Sol Washington's world because all is not well between Sol and his sixteen-year-old son.

Ever since Charles turned thirteen years of age, the boy and his father have been feuding over Charles' intention to become a Catholic priest. His mother is definitely in favor of his vocation and has even encouraged her son, who now has completed elementary school at St. Emmanuel's Catholic School.

While his wife and son are baptized Catholics, Sol proudly retains his Hindu religion.

To win Alice's hand, Sol had agreed reluctantly to raise their children as Catholic. But now he expects his only child to accept the hundreds of Hindu gods and to forego the one God in the Holy Trinity prevalent in Christianity.

While one may convert to Catholicism or some other form of Christianity, Sol knows that Hinduism doesn't generally accept converts. Since Charles carries his genes, his son is a born Hindu and always will be. The boy shouldn't even be a Christian.

On Charles' tenth birthday, Sol introduces his son to the Hindu temple in Durban, as part of his son's heritage. Much to the disdain of Alice, he begins his son's indoctrination of Hinduism by schooling him to count numbers in the Hindu language and comparing everyday Hindi words to everyday English words.

Indoctrination in religious theory soon follows. First, he tries reasoning with his wife and son.

Sol argues that of the three main Hindu gods, *Brahma* is the creator, while *Vishnu,* is the same as Jesus, but

Siva, the dealer of death and destruction in making rebirth occur, is unlike the Holy Spirit. Yet, he can't explain the reason for hundreds of other Hindu gods. His wife and son cannot comprehend that the Hindu gods have consorts. Alice and Charles consider these consorts as lovers for these gods, much like the ancient gods of pagan Rome and Greece.

He doesn't understand why his wife and his son will not believe in the Hindu theory of a series of rebirths or reincarnations through good *karma.* He says it's the same as living a good moral life under Christianity and getting a reward in heaven. The Hindu reward is a rebirth or reincarnation here on Earth.

Sol jokes, "You see, the soul doesn't have to travel so far up in the sky and through the whole universe in order to receive its reward from the Christian god in heaven. The soul is rewarded by *Siva* right here on Earth through rebirth, no travel required!"

No matter how much he tries to explain Hinduism to his wife and son, he can't make any headway.

Alice and Charles laugh when Sol explains one of the three basic principles of Hinduism, namely, *Puja,* or daily worship of a god for the granting of special favors, with the god represented by anything, whether it is a plant, an animal, or even any inanimate object possessed by the worshiper.

He still recalls the sarcastic remarks from Charles, "So, you just pray to a shovel, or a tree, or a car, or a cow? So, that's why we say, Holy Cow?"

Repressing his anger, Sol replies,

"Son, you know I don't eat meat. It's because we vener-ate cows and all animals. As babies, we live on mother's milk and the milk of cows, which nourishes us for life. Hinduism teaches us to live with a minimum of injury, cruelty, and violence to other beings. Meat eating preaches a mentality of violence and an absence of a peaceful and harmonious life."

Neither Alice nor Charles comments as Sol drones onward.

"Eating meat throughout one's life means that in the last breath of life, one's final vision will be one's rebirth in the animal kingdom instead of a birth of charity and generosity in perhaps one of the heavenly planets. As Lord Krishna said, 'The living entity in the material world carries different conceptions of life from one body to another as the air carries aromas. Thus, the soul takes one kind of body and again quits it to take another.' Please listen to what I'm saying, because all of our actions have consequences and the future brings like experiences to each of us. That is simply, *Karma*."

Sol thinks he has won the argument since neither his wife nor his son desires to continue the conversation.

For the life of him, Sol cannot see why his wife and his son don't see the similarity in the prayers when Catholics are asking some saint for favored intercession to the one Christian God containing three persons—that is, God the Father, His Son Jesus, and the Holy Spirit or Holy Ghost.

Sol jokes, "Well, really the Christian god containing three persons has just two heads because the third person doesn't even have a head, is invisible, and is portrayed as a white dove or a shining light. He is truly a holy ghost, one with holes in his sheets."

Neither his wife nor his son laughs.

His wife and son do not argue with him about the validity of Hindu cremation, one of the other basic

13

principles of Hinduism. While each prefers burial in the earth, nevertheless, the returning of the flesh to dust through ashes is acceptable.

But neither Alice nor Charles will accept the Hindi caste system, especially the part about the 'untouchables,' the caste idea being the third Hindu principal. Sol's efforts to explain the caste system failed miserably. He was not a happy man.

Black and from a Zulu tribe, Alice has experienced the horror of racial segregation from the British and the Dutch. She can remember the snubs and the put-downs and the anger and yes, even the threats.

With his golden tan, a dark bronze, Charles is considered as Colored under South African law, especially because his thick black hair isn't kinky. Although sheltered in Catholic school, he knows the pain of ostracism by Whites (both British and Afrikaners), by Blacks, by Asians, and by even pure-bred Indians disdainful of half-breeds.

Sol is deeply frustrated and now he wishes he'd put his foot down about allowing Charles to attend Catholic school at St. Emmanuel's. He agrees without any doubt that his son received a much better education at a Christian missionary school since the South African government contributes little funding for public education for non-White children (or in government-speak, Non-European children). Sol has seen the newspapers reports that more than 30% of Black children receive no schooling at all.

Yet, he's still angry about his son's desire to become a Catholic priest.

Sol's arguments against Catholicism have lately turned to threats. Last week, a heated argument ended with Sol slapping his son and ordering him to stay away from St. Emmanuel's Cathedral, just across the street from the busy Victoria Market in downtown Durban. After all, Sol knows the boy has completed his schooling at St. Emmanuel's and doesn't want his son hanging around Catholic institutions. He's threatened to remove all of his son's privileges for disobedience.

When Charles was a young boy, Sol punished his son by directing the boy to use the boy's right hand to pull the ear lobe on the left side of his head and for his son to use his left hand to pull the ear lobe on the right side of his head, while alternating between standing and squatting.

Sol's teachers in India proclaimed this maneuver as not only one of punishment but one which, thorough acupressure, activates the corresponding pituitary glands in the opposite sides of the student's brain. Indian scientists have declared the result from this traditional method improves the student's abilities for alertness, memory, and understanding.

But, now, losing his patience, Sol has grabbed both of his son's ears and pulled with such force as if the ear pulling will input understanding into his son's brain. Sol's jerking his son's ears made Charles cry out and raise his fists in self-defense. That defensive move causes Sol to whack his son on the head repeatedly.

When Alice tries to stop Sol, he smacks her hard with his closed fist and she falls to the floor. Charles is too little to stop his father.

Now, Charles knows he must escape his father's abuse.

Sol then orders Alice not to pay the balance of his son's tuition at St. Emmanuel's Catholic School, even threatening to smack her again if she disobeys.

He feels a lack of gratitude for what he's provided Alice, still working as a domestic for a White family.

Instead of living in a shack of mud, clapboard with a leaky tin roof, with an earth latrine, with a community water tap, and with a frequent lapse of electricity—as many Blacks do in several of the shanty towns outside of Durban, Sol has provided a two-bedroom red-brick house interspaced between a White and mixed neighborhood, within a mile of downtown Durban. Of the big cities, only in Cape Town do all the races intermingle, while in Durban, Whites and Indians at least—until recently—get along and generally tolerate Blacks, unlike much of the rest of the country.

Sol believes that the South African government with this kind of legislation is trying to purify skin color since Indians tend to have very dark brown skin pigment.

He thinks that the new Pegging law directed against Indians will upset the harmony between Whites and Indians in Durban.

Sol has read that when the Pegging law was proposed, the New Delhi government's response was the enactment of *The Indian Reciprocal Act.* This Indian law imposes the same restrictions on South African Whites in India as are imposed on South African Indians in South Africa. Of course, very few South Africans reside in India.

In this war of words between the two countries, Sol fears rioting by Indians in South Africa might occur and be met with like force from hooligans, especially Afrikaners. He knows that this time Gandhi's '*satyagraha*' will not stop the mutual bloodletting.

***

Before leaving the small house, Charles places the note on the kitchen table. He places the note in a spot his father will be sure to find it.

"Dear Mum & Dad: I love you both, but I am leaving for good and have taken my things. I am leaving Durban and I will not return. I will be all right. Don't try to find me. I love you both."

He signs the note, "Love, Charles, your son."

Charles sprints from the front door, suitcase in hand, and begins the long walk to the St. Emmanuel Cathedral in downtown Durban, away from the harbor. He has an appointment at the rectory with his friend, Father John O'Malley and another priest, who will decide if Charles has a true vocation for the priesthood. He knows Father John is on his side.

As he rounds the corner with a smile on his face, his thoughts are about dedicating his life to the service of God and saving the souls of everyone, especially the Natives, the Coloreds, and the Asians, including Indians. He knows he has the gift to persuade and convince these people to become Catholic, because he has already begun his missionary work with a few of the Indian boys in his neighborhood. He can hardly wait to meet with Father John.

But, then the thought strikes him. It's as if the devil is blocking him.

"What if, I mean, what if," he thinks, "Father John cannot convince the other priest that I have a true vocation to be a priest? Oh, my goodness, I cannot return home. My life would be miserable because of my father. Where would I go?"

"Yes, yes," he agrees with himself, as if an angel has planted in his brain the solution. He says aloud, "I'd join the army. During the War, they take everybody. But, don't worry, that's not going to happen, because I feel God wants me to be His faithful servant."

The smile spreads as he begins to run toward the safety of St. Emmanuel Cathedral, God's House.

He is wearing his school uniform consisting of black high-top leather shoes, khaki pants, a long sleeved white shirt, a light blue vest, a black tie, and a blue sport coat with four equally spaced golden buttons. His clothes are sparkling clean and his pants and shirt reveal careful hand ironing by his mother's love.

Charles has taken the money his Mother gave him for his journey and all the money he's saved, but he's taken nothing from the family treasure bowl hidden in a kitchen cabinet.

Chapter 2

Before Charles arrives at the rectory, Father John O'Malley is meeting with the former curator of St. Emmanuel's, Father Denis Hurley, an outspoken critic of the segregation practices of the government. Father Hurley is now the Superior of St. Joseph's Scholasticate in a suburb of Pietermaritzburg, the capital of the Natal Province.

Although Father Hurley has traveled to Durban for other reasons, while here he will help Father John evaluate Charles as an ultimate candidate for the priesthood.

The two priests are discussing the latest action by the African National Congress and that its new president, Dr. Alfred Xuma, has even allowed Black women to join the ANC in opposing policies of the South African government headed by Prime Minister Jan Smuts.

Both priests agree that women members in the ANC will help the organization prosper but hesitate in allowing women any leadership roles. One jokes as the other priest laughs, "What if we had women in the priesthood? We'd never get anything finished because we'd be arguing about it forever! But, that would be very interesting, I must confess, because some women are very bright. It's good progress."

Father Hurley asks, "Father John, did you hear that the ANC is working on the publication of a Bill of Rights for Africans, as founded on The Atlantic Charter as proposed by President Roosevelt and Prime Minister Churchill?"

"No, I hadn't heard about the ANC doing that. Say, wasn't Prime Minister Smuts himself involved in the drafting of the Atlantic Charter?"

"That's right. Well, it appears that Roosevelt and Churchill have laid the foundation for a United Nations and the fundamental rights of all people. Since our dear Prime Minister Smuts is involved in that, he'll have some tall explaining to his rabid segregationist dogs here in South Africa."

"Yes he will."

"He's still having trouble enunciating a clear policy dealing with Blacks and segregation. That radical Afrikaner group, *Ossewa Brandwag,* will spread their venom to every Afrikaner in the country with the hope that in the upcoming election of 1948, the Afrikaners and that crazy cleric from the Dutch Reformed Church, D. F. Malan, can take over the country. I've heard a few of Malan's speeches where he's preached that every Afrikaner has a sacred duty from God to make South Africa a White man's sacred republic."

"Say, wasn't Malan the man who urged Parliament to bar Africans from becoming full members of the Dutch Reformed Church?"

Father Hurley says, "I can't remember but that wouldn't surprise me. Well, to use the English word for *Ossewa Brandwag,* the Oxwagon Sentinel now claims its membership has grown to one-fourth of the one million Afrikaners in the country and the group now talks of using armed force to make South Africa a White man's Republic. One nut case even proposes the establishment of a new political party entitled the 'New Order' and patterned after Nazi fascism. Some of these Afrikaners are still in love with Hitler and his racial purity atrocities. And, sad to say, they simply hate the English."

Father John changes the subject.

"It looks like the ANC is keeping its protest rhetoric away from violence, although I've heard that the newly formed youth arm of the ANC is pushing for more aggressive action against the Smuts government. I hope the women members will tone down the violence talk. In my dealings with several of the locals in the Natal Province, elders of course, they seem to be true admirers of Gandhi's way to force change. What do you hear about it, Father Hurley?"

"No doubt, many of the young members want action now, since they don't see any concessions from the Smuts government. In fact, one young man at the Durbin meeting last evening argued strongly in favor of acts of sabotage. Naturally, he was shouted down with the stories about how Smuts, when he was a general in the South African army, brutally put down that insurrection in South West Africa against the imposition of segregation policies. You remember that our country in World War I invaded the Germany protectorate and annexed the country as South Africa's fifth Province. Smuts as an army general was unyielding in his viciousness!"

Father John comments, "I do have a question for you. Is the ANC making any inroads with the Zulu and Xhosa chiefs since the Smuts government's creation of the Reserves threatens all native South Africans? These African chiefs could be a big help in the struggle."

"Well, Father John, you are going to find out. Last week, I met Zulu Chief Albert Luthuli in Groutville. You may remember him as a former teacher at Adams College and a strong opponent of segregation and a devout Christian—although he is a blooming Methodist. Luthuli has spoken out very forcibly against using violence. He doesn't know if other Zulu chiefs will join him against the government since some chiefs and their counselors are totally beholden in power and money to the government. They bought the government's malarkey with their loyalty. I urged him to join the ANC with me and he is giving it his full consideration. Chief Luthuli is a natural leader."

"Father Hurley, what did you mean a while ago when you said that I was going to find out about the African Chiefs?"

"Since you are doing missionary work, particularly up north in Mpumalanga, and since the South African Police aren't watching you as they are me, I think you are the ideal person to find out. I've already obtained permission from Father Sean and the rest of your superiors."

"Are you kidding about the SAP watching you, Father Hurley?"

"Oh, it's just like a spy novel. You know, getting tailed and that kind of thing. I've seen them, the trench coats I call them, sometimes even at Mass. They may even read my mail or telegrams and listen in on my phone calls, if you can believe the movies. I guess I could be paranoid but I do see some strange signs."

"I didn't realize that, Father Hurley."

"Well, let's have a spot of tea before your young charge arrives to see if he has a real vocation for the priesthood. God knows we need plenty of Blacks and Coloreds to carry on the Lord's work in this country, full of *sangomas* able to cast a spell as witch doctors. These religious beliefs go back hundreds of years to the dark ages."

"Well, in my travels, Father Hurley, I've discovered that many of the Natives fear house-cats, or *heks,* as the Afrikaners call them. Since the Natives treat cats as voodoo creatures able to cast a spell, you will discover that there are no cats as pets in Native's houses—just dogs for warnings and protection."

"Well, only you would know that. Father O'Malley, those beliefs mean that we'll have to educate every Native since the government contributes so little to their education and doesn't want any Native to have a working brain. Then we have to convince the Natives to pray to a White Jesus."

Father John's face poses a question about what he is to discover on his trip.

Whispering, Father Hurley says, "Yes, Father John, now keep this to yourself. Here's what you are to do in your travels among the Natives."

***

Charles finally arrives at St. Emmanuel's Cathedral and goes straight to the church rectory. He says a silent prayer that the priests will accept him for study to the priesthood.

After a discussion with Father Hurley and Father O'Malley, Charles is elated that he has been considered as a candidate for priestly studies. First, however, Charles will board at St. Charles College, in reality a high school located in a suburb of Pietermaritzburg. The school, once owned by the Oblates of Mary Immaculate, Father John's religious order, is now run by the Marist Brothers who have agreed to accept Charles, tuition free.

Father John says, "Charles, you and I are on our way to your new home."

As Charles and Father John begin their travel to Pietermaritzburg, Father John tells him that he has been temporarily transferred to the north, to a mission in the Mpumalanga region.

"Yes, that was unexpected since we Oblates don't have a church there. But, it seems the people requested us to do the Lord's work, even though that the Benedictine Monks there have a long-established church in the main regional town of Nelspruit. I'll give you the address of St. Peter's in case you want to write me and eventually the letter will find me."

Sad to hear the priest will not be nearby, the sixteen-year-old boy nonetheless is glad to be on his way to the priesthood. He totally trusts Father John.

***

Charles mother had encouraged his leaving home. By saving part of her wages as a maid and saving part of her husband's wages, Alice has paid, with Sol's permission, a small bit of his tuition at the Catholic school in Durban. As for the conspiracy between her and her son, she prays that Sol is still in the dark.

Alice hopes that when her son completes school that he will be accepted at St. Joseph's Scholasticate in his ultimate study for the priesthood. She prays daily for this future event.

She will stay in touch with her son through an exchange of letters delivered at the rectory of St. Emmanuel's, but Alice will never disclose her son's letters or disclose Charles' whereabouts to her husband.

***

Later, after reading Charles' note, Sol cannot believe his son has run away. At Alice's insistence, they hurry to the nearest police station to report him missing. They expect help from the South African Police.

Providing the particular details to the White policeman, Sol and Alice are surprised by the man's attitude, especially since he speaks with a British accent.

He says, "Look at it. Your boy's gone, and he says he's not coming back. There's nothing we can do about that. Plenty of these runaways in these times join the army. You're just as well off without him, one less to feed, if you ask me. We have plenty to do without trying to find some runaway. Go and look at the train station or the bus station. No, we don't need his picture."

With that response, Sol and Alice realize that the government isn't going to help them. Fortunately, as they leave the office, they don't hear the two White policemen talking.

"Damn Indian! He married a Native and now they got a Colored. They're ruining our country! Maybe this new law that Smuts has passed will get rid of some of them Indians who think they own the country. Hell, they ought to send the Indians back to India. We need to take back our country!" one sitting policeman says, as he pounds his fist on his desk.

The standing policeman raises his fist in the Nazi salute and shouts, "Yes, send all these *kaffirs* to the Reserves and get these lazy bastards out of our country. Build a goddamn fence to keep 'em out! Make it thirty feet high! Put barbed wire on top! And just let in the ones who want to work the shit jobs, I say! The rest are all freeloaders and think they own the country! Thank goodness the damn government is again using the Pass Laws to force the Natives out of the cities. And don't let 'em ever come back unless they're willing to work without those damn boycotts and work stoppages! We've had enough of that shit! We need to end the threat of them taking over! After all, it's our country, by God!"

***

At Alice's suggestion, they walk to St. Emanuel's School for any sign of Charles. The registrar nicely reports that she has no information.

Betting that Sol will not get near the Catholic Church, Alice says, "Let's check with the rectory."

She wins because Sol replies, "I don't want anything to do with them stinking priests!"

A smiling Alice says, "Fine. You wait here and I'll check."

She reports truthfully, "They have no information to give us, Sol. Let's go home."

Returning home, Sol realizes he has lost his son and he tries to console Alice as best he can. She seems to have retreated inside herself, which, he reminds himself, is the Zulu way. He is thankful that she has cast no blame on him as the reason for his son's leaving home. He vows to be as kind, as caring, and as loving a husband as is possible. It's the Hindu way.

He must, especially during these times when the South African government is attacking all Non-Europeans with all sorts of discriminatory laws. The Pegging Law may just be the first against any foreigners, not just Indians.

Now when the Nazis are exterminating Jews—men, women, and children, the South African government is enforcing *The Aliens Act of 1937* prohibiting the entry of Jews or any foreigner who cannot assimilate as White into South Africa. Sol considers the South African law as an appeasement to the Afrikaners who favor the Nazis' rise to power under Hitler. He has often called that law as inhumane.

And the government is trying to disenfranchise all Non-European, especially Indians.

"It's downright disgraceful. What they are doing is turning this group of people against that group of people. They are trying to keep us separated into groups so they can control all of us," Sol says to himself.

He predicts that if the government persists in its segregation policies against Blacks and Indians in Durban, race riots will occur, since, when Blacks and Indians are counted together in Durban, the Whites are heavily outnumbered.

He muses, "I wonder if the government ever counts the numbers."

* * *

Of course, while at St. Charles College near Pietermaritzburg, Charles gets a dose of South African government and politics from his Catholic teachers.

Charles learns that in 1943 Jan Smuts of the United Party became Prime Minister and won control of the Parliament, with a victory over D.F. Malan and his Reunited National Party (later renamed the National Party) and its nationwide platform of total segregation. D. F. Malan, a religious cleric in the Dutch Reformed Church, still holds strong beliefs that God has placed Whites in charge of South Africa, a White man's Republic.

His teacher points out that the South African government under Smuts hadn't shifted away from racial segregation because of this election.

"You see, students, Prime Minister Smuts instead believed, and still does, the Natives are inferior to Whites, incapable of self-government. Mr. Smuts thinks Africans should live separately to preserve African cultures. But in reality, students, that means Mr. Smuts wants a separate area for Whites, to keep the Blacks out. In fact, according to the newspapers, Mr. Smuts has dismissed one of his cabinet ministers who lightened up on application of the Pass Laws to Blacks."

The teacher sees the students are listening.

"You know from your own eyes, even more Blacks than ever are now migrating to the urban areas, even here in Pietermaritzburg. Students, do you think that as the political winds shift, Prime Minister Smuts will relax the Pass Laws during the remainder of World War II?"

From his mixed class of Whites, Blacks, Coloreds, and Indians, the teacher hears, "No, sir!"

"Well, we shall see."

Chapter 3

In the South African summer of December, 1944, Father John returns from his mission and is meeting with Father Denis Hurley in Pietermaritzburg for a de-briefing. Now that Charles has completed a year at St. Charles College, Father John will gather Charles to accompany him tomorrow to villages on their way to Mpumalanga. Eventually, the priest will leave Charles with some monks in the town of Nelspruit as he continues his mission, as dictated by Father Denis Hurley.

But of course, the priest won't disclose to Charles his real mission to Mpumalanga.

Father John tells Charles of their new adventure to Mpumalanga and discloses that Mpumalanga in many Native languages means sunrise or east.

"Your sun also will be rising, Charles, as we visit the land of sunrise and many of the villages along the way."

The priest wants Charles to have a practical experience in understanding the true life of a priest, especially in the villages of South Africa, and also in truly examining Charles' own desire for a religious vocation.

Charles admits to the priest that he had flunked first-year Latin and barely passed the course the second time.

"Father John, I find myself wanting to be outside, away from the classroom, working in the garden. I don't espe-cially like being in the classroom, although I find some of the discussions very interesting, mostly about our country. I know my mother's dream is for me to be a priest, but now, I myself don't know it that's for me."

Citing his own indecision and doubts, Father John tells Charles, "Well, I know you've studied hard and been somewhat isolated from the world here at St. Charles College. Have you even been off campus, Charles?"

"Only once, Father. It's been a very sheltered life. And, truthfully, I'm tired of book-learning."

"I understand completely, Charles. When I was in your shoes, my advisor let me travel with him and exposed me to the world and its temptations. I then could make an honest evaluation of my planned vocation and whether that was what I really wanted."

Father John sees Charles is focused.

"Charles, you'll stay with me for a while and, besides helping me with my priestly duties, you'll get some exposure to the world. There's a lot of South Africa to see, though we will just be touching the surface. You'll see the real South Africa. When you aren't traveling with me, I've arranged for you to have a job in one of the towns. Hey, you'll even get paid for your work at that job. We'll find out what is right for you. I hope that meets with your approval, Charles."

"Oh, yes it does, Father and thank you! I'm very excited!"

They travel the grueling 500 kilometers from Pietermaritzburg to Nelspruit, stopping at several small towns or villages for Father John to hear confessions, baptize converts, both adults and children, perform a marriage, say Mass, and conduct one funeral. Charles serves as an altar boy, wearing a white surplice Father John has given him.

Father John's sermons at Mass with the villagers and townspeople are tame when compared to some Charles has heard from the priests in Mass in the school chapel.

Those sermons criticized the government's segregationist policies, while Father John's are about God's love for humanity. Actually, Charles tires of hearing Father John say over and over again that, "God loves you." But, of course, he says nothing.

Sometimes, Father John has late night meetings privately with some of the Natives. Charles wonders, "What's going on? Why does he have these late meetings? Why doesn't he invite me to come with him?"

At first, Charles thinks of spying on Father John, but his conscience gets the best of him and he doesn't.

Nonetheless, Charles is grateful to Father John for getting him out into the world and to experience its wonders and its treasures. It is freedom, an escape, and what he's daydreamed about in the classrooms, in the dormitory, and even during Mass in the chapel at St. Charles College.

As Charles travels with Father John, he sees the faces of the Natives and their clothes unmasking the Natives' poverty. When the priest and Charles are in a town or village in which vacationing European travelers are visiting, he sees the barefooted little Native children begging for pencils, and especially for coins and for candy. He hears that many White families—mostly the Afrikaners—use the Natives, men and young women, as farm laborers but sometimes as farm animals to work the land. He hears the Natives' pay is meager.

He's heard stories from the Africans about mistreatment from the South African Police—both White and Black. Some Africans are beaten or summarily taken to jail on trumped up charges and then force-labored as farmworkers for Whites as a means to pay off their fines.

Their stories scare him back to the safety and the secure isolation and sanctity of the priesthood.

At times, Charles feels he is ready to become a postulate and enter study at the seminary at St. Joseph's Scholasticate. But then, as he thinks about his future—when the time comes as a novitiate to get serious about making vows of obedience, poverty, and chastity—Charles wonders if he can really do it.

Finally, after a month of mostly visiting African villages and tribal camps and a few small towns, Father John and Charles arrive in Nelspruit, where Father John stops at the rectory of St. Peter's Church run by the Benedictine Monks. Greeting the superior, Father John introduces Charles and the welcoming monk gives Father John a key and directions to a small house on the church grounds. The priest and Charles walk with his suitcase to the house, key open the door, and walk to Charles' room.

"You'll be living here, Charles. You'll get breakfast and supper with the Monks in the main dining hall over there. The other two rooms in the house are for visiting guests. Let's see your room. Not bad, even if I say so—even your own bath and water-closet. You've everything you will need, even soap, towels, and some religious books. As you can see, you're just a short walk from the dining hall and the church."

"Yes, Father."

"Let's drop off your suitcase and we'll go to the store where you'll be working for my old friend, Jim Wright. It's just a short walk up the hill. You will be working there until I return from the mission. I suspect that'll be in about 3 months, but it could be longer. So let's head over to Mr. Wright's store."

As they trudge up the hill, Father John says, "If you need to contact me in an emergency, I can be reached by short wave radio contact, but not all the time. I do receive letters, including mail from St. Emmanuel's, eventually delivered to me. But don't hold your breath, Charles, for it might take weeks for a letter to reach me. Of course, you can give the monks your letters to your mother for delivery at St. Emmanuel's. Well, here we are."

He introduces Charles to Jim Wright, the White English owner of a small store which stocks everything imaginable, from food to fence posts to guns to sporting equipment to clothing. They shake hands as Jim says, "Welcome, Charles. Glad you're here. Father John tells me that you like working in the garden. Well, I grow a lot of good things in my garden behind the store. Now, during the War, some vegetables are scarce. And, I'd be much obliged for your assistance in the garden."

That pleases Charles, as Mr. Wright continues.

"Of course, you'll be working mostly in the store, but, I'm sad to say, it won't be in the front with the customers. In case you didn't know, the Smuts government has decreed that Whites have preferential hiring. As soon as someone sees you in the front, I'll have to argue with the authorities to hire a White guy to replace you. So, you'll be working in the back where I hope the customers won't see you or complain if they do. Of course, with your schooling, you could easily be in the front. We'll keep your job to ourselves. You understand, Charles?"

"Yes, sir, I do. I'll be glad to work wherever you tell me, Mr. Wright."

"That's great. Now, we do have a wide variety of customers—some Natives, some English, some Afrikaners, some Colored, even a stray Chinaman or Indian. By the way, do you speak any Afrikaans or Zulu or Xhosa or Swati, Charles?"

"No, I don't, Mr. Wright. Just English," Charles says, being careful to hide that he's part Indian so as to not provide a trail for his father to find him. He hears Mr. Wright.

"Every month, weather permitting, St. Peter's has a dance for young people, but mostly the Natives come. Most of the local young Afrikaners aren't Catholic, but are of the Dutch Reformed Church. The local Afrikaners don't come since their parents would be horrified if one of their children danced with a Native or, I dare say, even a Colored. Some of them don't even like sharing with a Native the same plate even after it's been washed. And, sad to say, some of the Brits fall in the same pit. Now, Charles, I will tell you that some of these girls are a real knock-out. Very pretty! Interested?"

Mr. Wright guffaws at his last word and repeats it. "Interested?"

Charles doesn't see any disapproval signs from Father John about meeting girls. In fact, Father John gives him a wink with his smile, saying, "Yes, you should meet a few girls. It's good thing, Charles. It's a good thing and I suggest you do it. But do remain silent about working for Mr. Wright, okay? You can say you are Mr. Wright's grandson if someone asks. I've already squared that with Mr. Wright."

Charles grins at the priest's suggestion for skirting the truth and that he, a Colored, is blood related to Jim Wright.

Handshakes and goodbyes all around as the priest enters his vehicle to complete his journey to the mission. Charles waves goodbye, as Father John drives north on his way into the hinterlands, but still Charles wonders about the mystery surrounding the priest.

**

Jim Wright and Charles hit it off immediately and, while Charles works away from any prying eyes, he welcomes his time working with his hands, digging, planting, trimming, and picking the produce behind the store. Since arriving, Charles' six-foot frame has filled out and all the lifting, carrying, pushing, pulling has toned and strengthened his muscles. Mr. Wright has given Charles a set of larger work clothes, a broad-brim straw hat, a pair of gloves, a pair of work boots, and a huge discount to purchase from his store some more dressy clothing. Thanks to Mr. Wright's kindness, Charles' easy selection now includes khaki pants, a brown tie, two long-sleeved white shirts, brown high-top leather shoes which match his brown sweater and sport coat.

He's heard Mr. Wright tell a customer that Charles is his grandson, explaining that his son married a Colored woman in Port Elizabeth. Later, a chuckling Mr. Wright confessed to Charles about the fabrication.

One day, in the back office, away from prying eyes and ears, Charles and Mr. Wright are having a friendly chat. When Mr. Wright notices Charles is looking at his desktop where a newspaper in English headlines that the South African Parliament in June of 1945 has enacted *The Natives (Urban Areas) Consolidation Act.*

"Excuse me, Mr. Wright, but what does that mean?"

"Charles, this legislation prohibits a Black man from residing in White metropolitan areas unless the Black man has had continuous residence there since birth or has had proof of continuous work there for ten years for any employer. This legislation also allows the government to deport Blacks if found to have been leading an idle or dissolute life or if guilty of certain offenses."

That has Charles' attention.

"Well, the new Pass Law doesn't apply to you since you're Colored. Any Black man in violation can be deported legally without any trial to one of those awful areas—the Reserves. You've heard about that, right?"

Shaking his head from side to side, Charles realizes that he hasn't been keeping up with politics. He hears Mr. Wright.

"Okay, a little history, if you're not bored. In 1913, the government enacted the *Natives Land Act* which set aside about 7% of the country's lands for Blacks and reserving 93% for Whites, but placing many restrictions on Black ownership and prohibiting Blacks from purchasing White lands or even share-cropping White lands. The so called Reserves largely contained infertile land and could never support the Black eighty percent of the country's population."

"Wasn't there protests about this, Mr. Wright?"

"Oh! Yes! The African National Congress protested and even went to England to seek assistance from the English Prime Minister, Lloyd George, but he deemed the problem not one for the Commonwealth to solve but one for a South African solution. There's no chance for this government to find any kind of solution! We just keep going on and on even though the ANC has been protesting for years!"

"Mr. Wright, forgive me for being so uninformed. But, what's the African National Congress or the ANC?"

"The ANC or the African National Congress is a political organization comprised of mostly Africans or Blacks, with a helping of some Coloreds, some Whites, and some Asians. It has been and is the main organized opposition to these horrible segregation laws. A few in the ANC believe in armed protest, but most believe in working within the system to overturn this oppression. It is my understanding that the ANC has prepared for South Africa a Bill of Rights patterned after the United Nations Charter."

Charles' face transmits his need for more information about the segregation and Mr. Wright obliges.

"Charles, these laws began way back in the 1920s as a sop to Whites, especially the Afrikaners, to limit the movement of Blacks, control Black urbanization, and allocate Blacks as migrant workers to Whites. But, you see, that wasn't enough, because the right-wing Afrikaner *Broederbond* and other radical segregationists elected a different political party and Jan Smuts as Prime Minister was replaced as Prime Minister in the 1924 election. The new Parliament enacted even more repressive laws against Blacks."

"What do you mean, Mr. Wright?"

"Well, just a few examples, Charles. White labor unions were legal, but not Black labor unions. The Minister of Labor could force the hiring of Whites over Blacks. That was true also for Blacks' employment in the mines. Except for eligible Blacks in the Cape Province, Blacks could no longer vote in the same

37

elections as Whites, while the voting qualifications for White men and White women were relaxed. But that wasn't the worse thing the new government wanted to control. Can you guess what that was, Charles?"

"No sir."

"Extra-marital sex between a European and a Native in 1927 became a criminal offense punishable with imprisonment! My God! The government wanted to peek inside our bedrooms! And that, Charles, is still the law today."

Still thinking of the priesthood, Charles declines comment about that subject, but instead asks, "You said Mr. Smuts was out but, as I understand it, now he's back in as the Prime Minister?"

"Yes, because of the Great Depression, all of South Africa was suffering, especially the Afrikaners. The Prime Minister at that time feared defeat and joined forces with Smuts in 1934. That continued until the Germans declared war on Britain. The old Prime Minister supported Germany and Smuts supported Britain, and there you go. Smuts is in again in '43. Clear?"

"Yes sir."

Changing the subject, Mr. Wright announces, "Well, this evening behind St. Peter's, the church is having that dance I told you about. Well, Charles, as I've mentioned, a lot of the young people from the town and all the surrounding area will come because the soda pop, fruit juice, and popcorn are all free. It'll be a lot of fun. Yes, Charles, it will be a lot of fun! And, there will be some pretty girls, especially the local Africans! I think you should go. Yes, my boy, you should go and have fun."

Reluctantly, Charles agrees to go. "Yes sir, I'll go for a little while."

He thinks, "After all, what's the harm?"

Chapter 4

Father John has returned from his missionary and special duties in the territory north of Nelspruit in June of 1945. First he stops at St. Peter's, retrieves his mail, and gets a great welcome from the Monks after catching up on local occurrences.

Afterwards, he drives up to Mr. Wright's store to greet Charles and Jim.

He bears news that Father Denis Hurley a frequent critic of the government's racial segregation policies, is being considered as the new Bishop in the Diocese of Durban.

Mr. Wright responds, "Well, if that rumor is true, then that is good news because Bishop Hurley will be a bigger thorn in the government's side."

After the priest has finished his travel stories, Jim excuses himself as Father John and Charles are starting a frank discussion about Charles' vocation.

After a while, Father John says, "Charles, you don't have to apologize. Honestly, one of the reasons for bringing you here to the land of sunrise was to determine if you truly had a vocation to become a priest. From my own personal experience, I know how hard it is to surrender one's self, to get away from all the corporeal desires existing in the world. Indeed, there is a lot of temptation."

"Yes. I understand, Father."

"Remember, Charles, the Good Lord also believes in love: He understands love of humanity, love of one's parents, love of one's neighbors, love of one's children, love of one's country, love of the Church, love of God, and certainly not the least, the love between a man and a woman. We are all made in His Image and Likeness, Charles."

"Yes, Father, I've heard your sermons from the pulpit and I know that God loves me," he says very humbly.

"Good. And, Charles, it's important that a person discover early that he cannot devote his life to the priesthood and all of its sacrifices. I know of a few priests who have a difficult time resisting temptation. They probably shouldn't be priests."

Charles eyes widen.

"Your dear mother wants you to become a man of God. She has shared her hopes with me on more than one occasion, Charles. But, you should yourself make this decision. You should not decide to become a priest just because it's your dear mother's dream. You should not decide to become a priest just because your dear mother will be disappointed if you don't. I hope I'm making myself clear."

Charles realizes he's not written his mother in almost a month, although he has received her two letters addressed to Father John but delivered through St. Emmanuel's and the monks at St. Peter's. She writes that his father is growing angry at the laws restricting the rights of Indians and his emotions may jeopardize his employment as a dockhand.

"Yes, Father. I understand that it's my own decision. I know my mother will be disappointed but I think she'll get over it. At least, I pray she will, Father. And, I've prayed very hard before making this decision."

"Good. I know you have. Well, tell me a little bit about this girl, Mary. And, by the way, just her name, Mary, is a good sign, since, as you know, I am an Oblate of Mary Immaculate, and we venerate the Mother of God.

I love the sound of her name—Mary! It is like the most wonderful sound to my ears. Well, go ahead."

After Charles informs Father John the details of his meeting and courtship of Mary, he reveals that Mary is the eighteen-year-old daughter of a local Zulu tribal chief and that Mary has been promised as the bride to one of the warriors in the tribe."

"I see," Father John contemplates, rubbing his forefinger to his chin. He realizes that this Zulu tribe has moved north, a long way from the area around Durbin and that the tribe is probably rather independent.

"Father John, Mary's betrothal has been sealed by the warrior's down payment to her father of her dowry with a goat and several chickens. I'm told that the chief and the warrior have sliced their wrists and exchanged blood. I guess that's some kind of blood oath between the two men."

The priest listens.

"Naturally, Mary wasn't asked if she wanted to marry the warrior and her protests mean nothing to the chief. He told her that his word is the law, that she is his daughter and must obey him. Mary says I should talk with the chief but the chief may want me to fight the warrior for Mary as if she is some property. I don't know what to do."

"I see. Well, Charles, you'll never win this battle with the chief. In Zulu, the chief is *inkosi,* which means he is the master. First of all, if Mary doesn't marry the warrior, the *inkosi* will be required to return the dowry offering and pay a penalty, which—at the very least— would be to pay the jilted bridegroom double—with two goats and twice as many chickens. And, if my

42

understanding of these things is accurate, the *inkosi* may also have to pay the warrior some money."

Charles' eyes widen.

"The *inkosi* isn't about to release his daughter from this contract so you two can marry. And, the *inkosi* would lose face with the tribe. He'll be considered as a weakling. That's the Zulu way.'

Charles nods.

"Worse, from your stand point, is that the warrior may challenge you to fight for Mary. While I see you've put on some muscle working for Mr. Wright, I don't think you've worked out with a knife or a spear."

The priest grins at the last statement.

"What do you suggest, Father John? I want to marry her!"

"First, I must ask if Mary realizes that this will mean a final separation from her family and her Bantu-speaking friends and relatives. Does she know that the two of you must flee this area, leave no trace, and never return? Does she know that she will surrender her lifestyle here and undertake a completely different life in a completely different world?"

He watches Charles' face.

"And, Charles, it's a world she's not used to. And, does she know that as the daughter of a Zulu chief, she is giving up the benefits of that life? Does she understand that her future life somewhere else will be uncertain? Will she be willing to work to help pay the everyday bills? Does she have the utmost faith in your ability to care for her?

"Does she know all that, Charles?"

"Father John, we've talked it over and she understands and agrees. She is very smart. But you can ask her yourself because she should be here at the store very shortly. When I heard you would arrive today, I asked her to come to the store because I wanted you to meet her. And, we agreed that we want your guidance."

"Yes," Father John says.

"In fact, here she is now."

As she walks toward them, Father John notices that she wears none of the traditional Zulu dress, no geometric jewelry, no neck rings, no Zulu facial makeup, and no traditional head covering, no bones protruding from her nose or ears.

Instead, she looks, well, he smiles, "Yes, Charles, she is lovely. I understand completely. And, like your own dear, sweet mother, she is also a Zulu princess. You are a lucky fellow, Charles."

Mary walks to the back of the store and sees Charles. She kisses him and tells him that she has gathered her possessions and crept away without anyone's discovery. She agrees that she is ready to leave with Charles.

The priest learns that Mary as the tribal chief's daughter has received not only Baptism from the Benedictine Monks at St. Peters but also schooling in the Catechism and in the English language.

He is impressed that she speaks English perfectly and easily grasps the problems of leaving her Zulu homeland. She's not just some uneducated Native girl looking for a way out of her tribal obligations by marrying upward. He is surprised that Mary even has a good grasp of what is happening against the Natives in

South Africa, although she has obviously never been far from home.

Father John counsels with Charles and Mary and, when satisfied, he says, "Charles and Mary, I think you should leave this area as soon as possible."

But the priest sidesteps thinking too deeply about the ethics of his recommendation.

"Where do you think we should go, Father?" Mary asks.

"Probably to one of the big towns where you will just melt into the population," the priest replies, as he rubs his chin. Then, without farther hesitation, he says, "Out of all the towns, I think Cape Town would be the safest for you. I doubt anyone from your tribe will follow that far. It's the most liberal and the races seem to get along well. Everyone—Black, White, or Colored—could ride the same buses and same trains, even frequent a few of the restaurants, and the like in Cape Town."

"That's a long way, almost the other side of the country, Father John. I bet it's over almost two thousand kilometers, at least," Charles volunteers.

"Yes it is. And you probably should get married before leaving, I think."

"Father John, will you marry us?" Charles pleads.

"I would, but under the circumstances, I won't. And, neither will any of the Monks at St. Peter's or any of the several Protestant ministers, because all of us missionaries will become persona non gratia in this whole area of Mpumalanga. All our efforts in baptizing the Natives and preaching the gospel will just go up in smoke. I'm sorry about that, Charles and Mary, and I hope you understand. I must think of the general good over the specific."

He remains silent about how his marrying the couple would compromise the other part of his mission, especially since he must meet with Mary's father, the local Zulu chief. To protect his mission, the priest must disassociate himself from Charles.

"Father John, what's the solution?" Charles ponders.

The priest rubs his chin as the mental light bulb illuminates the right answer.

"Let's talk to Jim Wright and see if Jim can get the local magistrate here in Nelspruit to perform a quick civil ceremony. He has a lot of pull with the locals."

Explaining the situation to Mr. Wright takes a few minutes, but Jim doesn't hesitate and immediately contacts the local magistrate who readily agrees to a wedding in an hour and reveals that the bride and groom must produce government-issued identity cards. Jim turns to Charles and Mary, "You do have your identification cards, correct?"

Examining their cards, Jim learns that Mary is truly the daughter of the local Zulu chief. Initially Jim fears a loss of business with the chief and his counselors should the chief discover Jim's involvement, but sensing the bravery of Father John, subject to the same rejection upon discovery by the Zulu chief, he doesn't hesitate. Besides, the magistrate won't publicize the wedding.

Father John questions, "Jim, are you certain the magistrate will perform the marriage, knowing that the bride is a chief's daughter?"

"Not a problem for the magistrate since he's owes his appointment to the government and he's an Afrikaner. Not a problem for him."

"That's good," the priest says.

Jim says, "Charles, I've got just what we need in my desk."

He produces a plain gold band.

"It was my late wife's and now it's yours, Mary."

Charles remembers that the picture of Mr. Wright's wife still resides in plain view on his office desk and notices that Mr. Wright's left ring finger still bears his own plain gold band. But, he immediately removes it and hands it to Charles.

Jim Wright asks, "I take it that you two will leave town, correct? You certainly can't stay here. I don't suppose either of you has a travel permit, correct?"

Father John interrupts, "Jim, they're excluded from the Pass Book law and they won't need one with me and when I get to Pretoria, I'll get travel permits for them to Cape Town."

Jim says, "Not true, Father. They will need a pass permit for Pretoria because there are now a lot of checkpoints on the main high road and even on some on the secondary roads. The government wants to limit the travel of Blacks and keep them out of the cities. But, wait a minute. Wouldn't it be quicker for them to catch the train here in Nelspruit and go all the way to Cape Town on the train? They could even get a sleeper since it'll take a day or two or maybe three to get there."

Before the priest can answer, both Charles and Mary can hardly wait for a train ride since neither has even ridden on a train, whether a steam-engine train, wood-burner, or an electric one.

The priest replies, "Of course, it'd be much quicker, but, Jim, you forget how much trouble these two would have with the South African Railway system of segregation of the races in this area. I've heard some

47

awful stories from people in the Natal Province about very unequal treatment by the authorities between White passengers and Black and Colored passengers. I understand that's true even in Pretoria and Johannesburg, Jim."

Before Father John can soften his words to appease the fear in Mary's eyes, Jim agrees, "Yes, you are right about unequal treatment in this area of the country. Why just last week, a young Black man, who had somehow found himself in the Whites-only car, was thrown from the moving train by the ticket checker and another White passenger. Worse, the police recorded the episode as if the fellow himself jumped from the train to avoid punishment for his trespass. They even labeled it as a suicide."

Father John winces at Jim's report, "Well, of course, that's not the case in Cape Town, where Blacks and Coloreds can even ride in the same passenger cars with Whites and that's also true about buses, taxis, and trams in Cape Town. You know I grew up there and my parents still live there. I also know that in other areas of the country, Blacks and Coloreds are treated very well by South African Railway staff and any enforcement is lax."

He hopes that melts the anxiety on Mary's face.

Jim says, "Father, I didn't know you were originally from the Cape. But, you're Irish. How in the world did that happen?"

"That's an easy answer, Jim. My folks emigrated from Ireland and started a business and I spent my earlier years there before I went to Johannesburg to university. And, I've returned to the Cape many times."

"Hey, I didn't know you were going to Pretoria, Father. Why there?"

Father John replies, "Yes, Jim, I was planning on leaving tomorrow morning on my way to Pretoria for any appointment with my old friend, Jan Hofmeyr. I picked up my invitation at St. Peter's, forwarded all the way from Durban. And, I've some other business, uh, uh, there."

Father John almost lets his trip post-Pretoria to Johannesburg slip from his lips.

Mr. Wright exclaims, "Hofmeyr, in the government—that Hofmeyr, the acting Prime Minister, when Smuts is out of the country? I remember that in August of 1944, Smuts attended the Dumbarton Oaks Conference in Washington, D.C. and was helping to write the Preamble to the United Nations Charter. The newspapers back then said he's hobnobbing with Roosevelt and Churchill. I guess he's returned again to England."

"No, Jim, Prime Minister Smuts is in San Francisco in the United States for the opening session of the General Assembly of the United Nations. It's quite an honor for him."

"I see. Well, Father John, what happened to St. Joseph's at Pietermaritzburg or St. Emmanuel's in Durban?"

Father John explains, "Jim, yes, I'm returning to St. Joseph's and to St. Emmanuel's after my business is finished in Pretoria. Well, Jan Hofmeyr was one of my favorite professors when he taught in Johannesburg at the old South African School of Mines. He used to make fun of my Irish brogue and did a funny imitation. When Mr. Hofmeyr was promoted and became

49

principal of the university, he changed the name of the School of Mines to the University of Witwatersrand. Of course, I lost track of Jan when I left for my priestly studies in Rome. But, since I've been back in South Africa, we stay in touch. Anyhow, I do have an appointment with him."

"Father John, I didn't know you, a man of the cloth, hung with the higher-ups," Mr. Wright says with that same guffaw, while shaking his head sideways.

Ignoring that remark, the priest adds, pointing to Charles and Mary, "But I can leave tomorrow morning and I can take you two as far as Pretoria. There, you can catch a quick bus to Johannesburg and then transfer to a long distance coach on the way to Cape Town. And I will secure the right travel documents or permits to Cape Town from my friend. At least, I hope I can."

To safeguard his contact, Father John remains at Jim Wright's store during the wedding ceremony. He explains to the wedding couple that he cannot risk the Chief discovering his involvement in helping them. But he doesn't disclose the real reason.

Although witnessing the marriage ceremony, Jim Wright is not an official witness, those being the magistrate's wife and one of the clerks in his office. The magistrate defers to Mr. Wright's request in Afrikaans to pronounce the wedding in English rather than in Afrikaans.

The magistrate and his wife produce some fresh bread cakes from maize and forth some *burukuta* to toast the wedding couple. Jim explains that this is a local brew from sorghum. They exchange toasts in English.

Pocketing the money from Jim, the magistrate produces a marriage license and enters the marriage of June 15,

1945 in the official registration book which Charles and Mary sign.

After the wedding, Jim Wright empties all the money from his pockets and in spite of the protests from Charles and Mary, insists that the couple consider the money as their wedding present. Thanking him, Charles pockets the coins and puts the bills in his wallet.

When they return from the Magistrate's office to meet the priest at the store, Jim asks, "Father, do you need any chits for petrol since we're still under rationing because of the War."

"Thanks, Jim, first for keeping me out of the limelight and safeguarding me with the Chief."

"No problem, Father."

"And, as to the petrol, thanks, I've plenty. That's one thing this government does right. It makes sure we religious can travel into the bush."

"Oh?"

"You know, Jim, my Anglican friend, Father David Russell, says we religious are the government's best friends. We help keep the Natives from getting restless and taking back their country. Or, at least the powers think so.

"As one of my superiors once said, very sad but also very true, "We gave the Natives our Jesus, the Bible, and the Catechism while the Natives gave us their land.

"We are the government's best barrier against any threat by the Natives."

Jim Wright agrees, "There's no doubt about that. And, that David Russell is quite the firebrand—a hell raiser against the government. Oops! Pardon my language! Forgive me, Father?"

"Certainly, Jim."

Touching his thumb and index finger of his right hand, extending the other three fingers, in the form of the Greek letters for Christ, and making the sign of the cross, Father John blesses the couple.

"May the Good Lord bless you, give you happiness throughout your lives, and deliver you from temptation, and keep you safe from all harm and evil, forever and ever. Amen."

Leaving Jim's store, Father John drives the newlyweds to Charles' place at the guest house at St. Peter's Church. He again thanks them for allowing him to remain hidden from the Magistrate's view.

Father John says, "I'll be right back with your supper since I know we couldn't celebrate in public with a wedding feast."

Returning with two plates of food and a small carafe of sacramental wine from the Monk's dining hall, Father John smiles, "Supper is served. No, I'll eat with the Monks. All right, Mary and Charles, I will come by tomorrow morning at five o'clock. Have your things ready. We'll go to the five-thirty Mass at St. Peter's, have a quick bite with the Monks, and then be on our way. Have a good night! Congratulations! And, may God bless you and your marriage. Amen."

Father John makes several phone calls before retiring.

That night, Charles and Mary consummate their marriage. When they are finished with their love-making, Charles is silent but pleased that Mary is a virgin.

Mary says, "Charles, my love, we will always remember this day, June 15th, when we married. I love you!"

Charles replies, "Yes, my love, and I love you, too!"

The next morning, they will leave with Father John to Pretoria, the administrative capital of the Union of South Africa.

Chapter 5

Before leaving for Pretoria, Father John stops the vehicle in front of the South African Police station in Nelspruit and says, "Let me have your identify cards so I can negotiate a travel permit for you two all the way to Pretoria."

Taking the cards, the priest enters the small building. After ten minutes, a smiling Father John returns, saying, "That was easy. It pays to get along with these fellows. The one I had to see was an Afrikaner; so, speaking Afrikaans with a big smile helps a lot. And while most of these Afrikaner police belong to the Dutch Reformed Church, this one was a parishioner of St. Peters and remembered me. He did tell me that on the way we must stop for inspections by the South African Police, but we should have no trouble. Off we go!"

No sooner does Father John clear the outskirts of Nelspruit, than Mary falls asleep in the back seat. Smiling, the priest with his forefinger gives Charles the whisper signal.

"Charles, our next town is Alkmaar and we should have no trouble there with any police. The last time I drove this road last July, there were a lot of potholes full of rain water on my side of the road and I had to cross the center line to avoid them. That was in the winter when we had all that rain. Frankly, I said a silent prayer to St. Christopher to keep me safe as I drove through the water at those fords. I see this time the road looks good, even though it's mid-June and the beginning of the wintery rainy season."

Since Charles has never been this way, he is watching the scenery sail by and simply shakes his head. Finally he asks, "Father, how far is it to Pretoria?"

"Roughly, from Nelspruit about 240 kilometers is my best guess."

"So we should be there in what—about four hours?"

Father John cautions, "I can't say, because there may be rocks on the road or some repair problems or even a bad accident. I recall one time when a coal truck overturned, dumping its load clean across the roadway; it took hours for the mess to be cleaned before the roadway was opened again. And, we may get stopped by the police at any of the many checkpoints along the way. Plus, sometimes there are robbers, real highway men, just like in Robin Hood, except they are Natives."

"You're kidding, right Father John?"

No, Charles, I'm not. Now, if we do get stopped by the police, let me do all the talking. You and Mary should try and remain silent. Just produce your identity cards and hopefully we won't have any trouble. I've got your travel permits. When I show this invitation from the acting Prime Minister to come to Pretoria, I don't expect any trouble, but with some of these Afrikaners, you just can't be certain. In case you didn't know, a lot of these Afrikaners in this part of the country don't care for the government which they think is too slanted toward the English. A lot of them wanted South Africa to remain neutral during the War instead of fighting Germany and some wanted to side with Germany. And, when the war started, some Afrikaners even broadcast radio programs of Nazi wartime victories."

"Yes, Father, Mr. Wright filled me in about the local Afrikaners' dislike of Blacks and Coloreds, too. At St.

Charles College, we learned how the government enacted laws favoring not just the Afrikaners, but also all Whites. These laws penalized Blacks, Coloreds, and even Indians, Asians, and Jews."

"Well, Charles, not all Afrikaners are bad people. But, by and large, many, many Afrikaners think that God has given them the best parts of Africa as their own special place and that the Good Lord expects all Africans to find their own land to preserve their own culture. The really radical Afrikaners want South Africa as strictly a land for Whites only. They see the British government as blocking their hopes and dreams."

"But, let me ask you a question, Father. Why do I see so many Afrikaners working for the government since they don't like the British, especially working as the police?"

"An excellent question, Charles; your teachers told me you are very bright. The South African government made Afrikaans and English as the two official languages. The government also opened up the civil service to Afrikaners, many of whom lived below the poverty line. So, it was a good opportunity for them even though in some areas the Afrikaners are still in the lower ranks of the police."

"Yes, that makes sense. When Mary awakens, we need to tell her about the police."

The priest nods agreement as the vehicle passes through Alkmaar.

Looking out the window, Charles sees many Blacks slowly walking along the roadway. Most of them, he assumes, are male workers, but every now and then, he sees a Black woman carrying a bundle on her head, a bag in one hand, a very small child in the other hand,

and with another two or three small children trudging behind, but no man in sight.

As the car progresses toward Pretoria, he expects a repetition of the same view of Blacks walking along the roadway.

Now and then he sees a mule or oxen pulling a plow with a Black man walking behind. And less frequently, he spies a lonesome tractor.

Once in a while, Charles notes a White man on horseback hollering at a Black man actually pulling a plow himself in the hardscrabble land, obviously in need of the winter rains of June, July, and August. Sometimes, when the road turns sharply and is close to the edge, Charles can see cracks mangling the reddish earth.

Father John interrupts, "Charles, look over there. See that ox wagon? Well, a little over a hundred years ago, the Afrikaners organized a great trek with many hundreds, maybe thousands of ox wagons, and moved inland, north and east away from the British."

Making certain Mary is still asleep, Father John continues.

"As you know, from your South African history lessons, the Afrikaners drove the Zulu and Xhosa tribes from their land. On every December 16th, there's a huge enactment of ox wagons on parade in Pretoria, a celebration of the battle of Blood River and the Afrikaners' defeat of the Zulu nation."

Charles remembers his history lesson also about the American Indians, just like the Africans, driven from their land and placed on reservations or reserves. He thinks that's what also happened to the native peoples in South America by the invading Europeans who swapped their religion for the Natives' lands, not a fair exchange. But he remains silent.

Father John interrupts his thoughts. "As my memory serves me, our next town is Elandshosek, and we should pass through it okay. Then, we hit Ngodwana. The last time through this next place, Panorama, I got stopped on the roadway by some Natives who tried to extort some money before letting me pass."

"You weren't kidding about the highwaymen."

"That's right," the priest says, "they cut down a large tree and pulled it across the roadway. But when they saw me raise Jesus' cross and bless them in Latin, they were afraid I'd put some hex on them. Three men pulled the large tree aside so I could drive on. I made it passed Panorama with no problem."

"Father, did they put the tree back across the road after letting you through?"

Suppressing a laugh, the priest says, "Yes, they did, waiting for some unlucky traveler, Black or White."

"Father John, are there a lot of these robbers?"

"Yes, sad to say, because the government's policies have driven many people into poverty and most of those are Africans, who have been driven from their land or relocated elsewhere and who can barely eke out a living in the Reserves, or in the mines, or in the cities, especially in Johannesburg. Lucky you are going to Cape Town, Charles, because the Cape Province is very liberal and tolerant of all people."

When Mary stirs and awakens, Charles repeats the priest's instructions about the police, but says nothing about robbers.

They sail through the next small town and avoid a herd of goats on the side of the roadway.

Mary and Charles look out and see, just over a fence, a tarp-covered housing with cardboard sides. A Black woman tends a small wood fire close by. Down the hillside, two small children play. Looking back toward Mary, Charles imagines he sees worry lines on her face, but he remains silent.

Near the town of Middenburg, they approach an orange barricade across the roadway and see a sign in English and Afrikaans, directing the vehicle to pull over and stop. A White policeman approaches Father John's side of the car and, in the Afrikancr language, asks for "Papers!"

Father John produces his own and hands him the travel permits and the identity cards from Charles and Mary. Without waiting for any questions, the priest responds first by saluting the policeman in Afrikaans, "Good day, young man." But then he turns to English, "We are on our way to see the acting Prime Minister in Pretoria. Here is our invitation, sir!"

Quickly looking at the documents and then casting a suspicious look at Mary in the back seat, he says, this time in English, "Wait, while I check this with the officer in charge."

Watching him enter the small hut and converse with another uniformed policeman, under his breath, Father John says, "Keep calm and don't say anything."

Five minutes pass.

Returning, the guard orders in Afrikaans, "All right, you can go."

As the car slowly returns to the roadway, Charles asks, "Father, I guess you had to learn to speak Afrikaans and some of the native African languages."

Father John answers, "Yes, I did and they're several *Bantu* languages, with Zulu being one of the most difficult. But, it goes with the territory. Well, that stop wasn't too bad, but I know we'll have another stop in the next town, which is bigger and I think there is a larger contingent of police there to check Pass Books and travel permits."

"What town is that, Father John?" Mary hesitates.

Father John momentarily looks toward the back seat and sees the anxiety and the fear of the unknown in her Zulu's eyes. He understands that this young girl has never been far from her home area surrounding Nelspruit. Rightly, he thinks, she is apprehensive about traveling so far from her comfort zone and scared of what the future brings.

"Mary, the town is Emalaheni to the Natives. The Afrikaners named the place as 'White Ridge' in Afrikaans but the English couldn't pronounce the Afrikaner word and instead call it 'Witbank.' So, on maps you will see both Emalaheni and Witbank. When we get there, check out that large sandstone white outcropping as its namesake. The town is now surrounded by a farming community but originally the place was a railway stop for the coal deposits."

Mary says, "Father John, as a European, you sure know a lot about the country."

Smiling, the priest adds, "Here's a bit of history: the town is famous for hiding Winston Churchill after his escape from a Boer prison in Pretoria. Yes, that Winston Churchill, the current Prime Minister of

England! Now, most people here in this area speak Afrikaans or Zulu. You would fit right in, Mary. And, by the way, young lady, I was born here in South Africa in Cape Town."

Finally, they reach the outskirts of Emalaheni and are immediately instructed by a large sign in English and Afrikaans (but not in Zulu) to pull off the roadway and stop in front of a small wooden building, the police checkpoint.

In a khaki uniform with a peaked hat sporting a polished black leather visor, a tall and muscular Afrikaner approaches the priest's vehicle, and opens the driver's door. In a commanding voice in Afrikaans, he orders everyone out.

Another policeman has a similar hat but also has a sour look on his face. He is smaller than the first one and stands on the other side of the vehicle.

Again, Father John is quick on the draw. First, he salutes a greeting in Afrikaans to the two men, "Good Day, my good men." Then, he quickly transfers to English, "I know you want to see our papers. I've saved you the trouble." He hands the documents, including the invitation from the Prime Minister, to the policeman standing next to the priest's side of the car.

Responding in English, the taller policeman says, "Yes, thank you. Now, all three of you, step away from the car. Have a seat on those wooden benches outside while we search the car. Give me the keys to the boot so I can see what's inside. After we check, my superior will confirm this is a legitimate invitation from the Prime Minister's office."

They watch as the small policeman copies the car's number plate on a form on a clipboard. He then demands the vehicle registration information before the three have exited the car.

Father John complies and hands him the car's paperwork. He says, "Well, inside you will find all my priestly things, some camping stuff, a sleeping bag, my suitcase, two boxes of ammunition, and a machete. In the glove box, I've a pistol. Be careful, sir, since the gun is loaded. The gun permit is with the paperwork I've just handed you. In the boot, you will also find one suitcase each for Charles and Mary."

"Why does a priest need a gun, sir?" the taller policeman asks. The smaller policeman answers, "Why? He needs it to shoot the devil, of course!"

"My good men, even a priest cannot reason with a lion, or a cheetah, or another unreasonable animal, or even a robber," Father John laughs but gets no response from either of the men who apparently miss the irony of the identity of an 'unreasonable animal.'

Mary interrupts, "And, yes, I have some things in a straw bag, which is my purse, as you can see."

She opens the bag so he can peer inside and says, "And I need to go to the ladies room, sir."

In English, the smaller policeman smirks, "No ladies room for you, Missy. Go into the bush over there behind the wooden fence. You, Colored boy, can do the same. The priest can use the inside toilet. We don't have one for you people. It's not surprising that you people can't read either English or Afrikaans. The sign on the WC door says 'Whites Only'!"

After an hour passes, the two policemen return and the taller one asks, "Tell me, Father, what kind of a car is this? I've never seen one like it, although it looks like it might be a military staff car."

"That's understandable since only 1,500 were manufactured for civilian use. It's a British 1938 Humber Super Snipe saloon with four doors and with six cylinders. According to the owner's manual the car has a top speed of 130 kilometers per hour on a goodly paved roadway. But, I've never had the opportunity to test that. Yes, the British army has a similar vehicle, which is reinforced."

"Very interesting. When I opened the bonnet to inspect the motor and shined my torch to check for any hidden items, I was surprised at the size of the motor. But, I'm curious as to how a priest or a religious order would own such a car, which must have cost a pretty penny."

Used to the innuendo, the priest replies, "Yes, you see, all these cars were marketed to upper-class managers, doctors, and lawyers. And a few made their way to South Africa and other Dominions of the British Commonwealth. The Church or my Order would never spend that kind of money on such frivolity. We were indeed fortunate that a very prominent Catholic doctor in Durban—God rest his soul—bequeathed the vehicle to my religious order, the Oblates of Mary Immaculate."

The taller policeman says, "How do you drive this car in the bush? It's not made for the kind of travel."

Father John replies, "I drive very, very slowly, since the ruts and the gullies can swallow the car and since the rocks can either flatten a tire or bust the oil pan. And, as you probably know, that's just in dry weather. I try and stay out of the bush during the rainy season, if you know what I mean, sir, since a sinkhole can swallow this car if it doesn't get washed away trying to ford a stream."

Smiling, the tall policeman says, "All right you can proceed. Drive safe and obey the law."

As they leave the checkpoint, Father John exhales, "Well, I got a little worried. We waited so long after they checked the car for contraband."

Mary says, "I didn't like those men. Did you see the other three policemen pull that young African man from the back of that lorry behind us? When he didn't have his pass book, they knocked him to the dirt and hit him with their rifle butts while he was down. Then, they took him to the back and put him behind that fence with the wire barbs. What will happen to that young man, Father?"

The priest sympathetically says, "No, I didn't see that since I was inside. But, it doesn't surprise me, Mary, since the law allows immediate detention and deportation to the Reserves if a Native doesn't produce the proper pass, and that's without any trial. It's very difficult for people living in the Reserves since the soil is poor and there's very little work. Nobody wants to be there. I suspect that the young man will try to sneak back but if he's caught, he'll go to prison. Sometimes, the prisoners are forced to work on someone's farm. It's called convict labor and it's legal under South African law. There are literally thousands of Blacks serving their sentences by working as forced labor for some White Afrikaner farmer. It's a very sad situation, Mary."

She shakes her head and says, "Yes, it's more than sad; it's terrible, just terrible!"

The priest adds, "You are right, Mary, but South Africa is not alone with this, because in the United States some southern States allow farmers to lease prisoners as convict labor. I think Louisiana is one. As I recall,

64

Alabama also forced vagrants unable to pay their fines to work as leased farm workers. And, according to a Miami newspaper, during the Great Depression, the city of Miami forced Black vagrants to work as garbage men."

Charles comments, "I didn't know that about America."

Father John continues, "Well, sad to say, but the ideas for many of the laws we are saddled with in South Africa originated in America against Blacks. There, they call them 'Jim Crow Laws.' I'll just give you a couple of examples."

"Yes."

"One is the law prohibiting Blacks from living in certain White areas or owning real estate in White areas. Racial zoning they call it in the city of New Orleans and the city of Baltimore."

"That's like the Pegging law."

"Another is the law prohibiting Blacks from sitting in the front of buses, or sitting at lunch counters, or using the same entrance or seating at movie theaters, or using the same washrooms or toilets, or even from drinking from the same public water fountains as Whites."

Charles says, "Is that so? Just like here?"

"Yes and I remember seeing a newspaper from somewhere in California where the town had posted a sign that said 'Nigger, don't let the sun set on you.' The newspaper called these places 'Sundown towns.' They are lots of these Jim Crow laws in America."

Mary says, "That's terrible, Father! And, South Africa got those terrible ideas from America?"

"Yes, and it is terrible. Let's see if I can recall another one about keeping Blacks away."

The priest says, "Yes, one said 'Whites only within the City Limits after Dark.' Scary, right?"

"Right."

"Of course, in America, their highest court declared these laws as unconstitutional and unenforceable, but in many places in the South, discrimination prevails through these local 'Jim Crow' laws."

Mary and Charles exchange a puzzled look, as they wait for the priest to explain how this discrimination still exists if these laws are illegal as declared by the highest court in America,. But instead, Father John continues.

"Right now, our Pass Book laws don't apply to Colored men. They just apply to Black men, eighteen years and up. So, you, Charles, are in the clear. But there's no guarantee that the law will stay the same. It may soon also apply to Colored men. If the law changes and since your eighteenth birthday is just around the corner, you could be required to always carry a Pass Book. You'll have to be fingerprinted."

Mary's eyes question.

"Right now, Mary, the law doesn't apply to either Native women or Colored women. But, that could also change. There's no telling what this government will do. So, watch the newspapers and the official notices."

Mary says, "In these stops I didn't see any Africans as policemen, Father. Not one."

"Well, in this part of the country where many Afrikaners live, they have obtained a lot of these positions. From what my friends tell me, Africans in the police departments, whether the Special Branch, Security Police, or just the regular police, are a minority and receive a heavy dose of discrimination from the Whites, no matter where their duties take them."

"Oh," Mary says.

"Many Africans as police are stationed with the Natives in various areas of the country. In the big cities, there are lots of Natives who are policemen since there can be a lot of unrest. But, in the rural areas as here, not many Natives serve as policemen."

"Really?"

"Lately, I haven't been to Pretoria or Johannesburg, so I don't have current knowledge but in the bigger towns, there also will be lots of White policemen. When you get to Cape Town, Mary, as I've said before, you will find that Cape Town is much more liberal than the rest of the entire country."

Accepting his explanation, Mary asks, "Do we have any more stops before we get to Pretoria, Father? These policemen don't seem very nice."

"Maybe, since we have three more towns. Thank the Good Lord. And let's hope that we won't have to stop at any of them."

Charles wonders, "Father, how much farther after that last town to Pretoria?'

"My guess is about 50 kilometers. Who knows how far that is in miles?"

Mary answers, "That's easy. Multiply the kilometers by point 6 and the answer is 30 miles. We learned that in school, Father."

The priest says, "Excellent, Mary. Once we get to Pretoria, we drive to Church Square and locate the Old Reserve Bank Building, number 40 if I remember correctly. That's the current office for the Minister of

Finance, since they are doing some repair work at the beautiful Union Building on the hill just north of town."

Charles says, "Father, if Mr. Hofmeyr is the acting Prime Minister, why do we need to locate the building for the Minister of Finance? Why not just go to the Union Building where the Prime Minister offices? I mean according to what I learned in school."

"That's an excellent question, Charles! You see, Jan Hofmeyr is a very brilliant man and the most able of Jan Smuts' Cabinet Members. He has been entrusted with two Cabinet Offices besides being the Deputy Prime Minister. He is also the Minister of Finance and the Minister of Education. So, today, according to the invitation, he is in the Minister of Finance's temporary office."

"That's very impressive, Father."

"And, unlike many in the Smuts Cabinet, Jan is a true friend of the African people, but he's not perfect since I know, from our private discussions, Jan still holds some beliefs about separation of the races. Yet, when he was a Member of Parliament, Jan made a speech that he would remove every color bar from the South African Constitution. I was very proud then to call Jan Hofmeyr as my friend. I still am."

They stop at the Security Checkpoint but were practically waved through. Father John says, "I guess they called ahead about us and didn't want to waste time since there's a long line behind us."

As they enter the city of Pretoria, Mary's eyes widen. She says, "I've never seen buildings so tall. In Nelspruit, there's only one that's four stories. I've never seen so many cars and buses. And look at all these people! I can't even guess at how many.

"I see lots of Natives standing on the verge and also walking along the side of the road. And, Charles, look over there; you can see Whites and Blacks walking together! And, look at that beautiful park!"

Her excitement eases Father John's concern over her anxiety.

As they near their destination, Father John announces "Well, we are almost there. I am stopping here, so you each may use the water closet since I suspect your entry into the government building might be a problem. I'll wait while you use the public facilities. Be sure to use the one for Non-Europeans."

When they return, Father John observes. "See those Jacaranda trees? In the spring, there will be a burst of lilac or light purple color. It's magical!"

The priest continues driving and turns onto Church Street toward their destination.

Father John spies a parking space in front of the Old Reserve Bank Building and expertly glides the Humber between a Model A Ford sedan and a highly polished black Rolls-Royce.

As he exits the Humber, he compliments the White uniformed chauffeur, "Nice car, sir."

Seeing the wooden guardhouse besides the building entrance, Father John stops and looks back inside the Humber and says, "Please wait in the car. Since we're parked in front of a government building just a smidgen from that guardhouse, you may get hassled if you get out of the car."

Charles face raises a question.

"Keep the windows rolled up. And, don't open the car for anyone unless a uniformed policeman requests.

Then show your identity documents and explain you are waiting for me while I visit with Mr. Hofmeyr. But, keep your windows rolled up and the car locked."

Mary asks, "Why is that, Father?"

"My dear, remember that we are in Pretoria, the seat of the Executive Branch of the country. In case you didn't know, there has been some unrest, some riots by Natives, and some strikes or work stoppages by miners. There are a lot of vigilantes, manly Afrikaners, who get suspicious when they see a car like this parked in front of this government building and strangers inside. So, I don't want you to take any chances."

"We understand, Father," Charles replies, knowing the priest has termed them as strangers instead of a Black woman and a Colored man.

"I don't think my meeting will last longer than an hour," the priest says, hearing the doors lock and seeing the windows close.

He walks away from the Humber automobile to the guardhouse.

***

After presenting his invitation and his identity card at the guardhouse, a tall uniformed guard with a sidearm accompanies Father John into the building and signals another White guard at the stairway to escort the priest upstairs to the reception desk outside the office of the Finance Minister of the Union of South Africa, Jan Hendrik Hofmeyr.

The priest notes the presence of White guards in military dress with carbines posted outside several doors, including two outside the office of Minister Hofmeyr.

70

Again, Father John presents his credentials and after examination, the priest enters another office, where again he presents his credentials to a White male secretary. The priest undergoes a short wait until a male aide of Dutch or Afrikaner descent greets him and cordially invites him into a private office with gorgeous furnishings and some outstanding artwork. The priest admires the artwork as he waits.

"Hello, Father O'Malley, I'm Daniel Reitz, Minister Hofmeyr's head assistant. I must apologize that Mr. Hofmeyr is unable to keep his long scheduled appointment with you and he sends his deepest apologies and regrets. The Minister has been called away to deal at this very moment with the Council of Non-European Trade Unions. Please sit down and make yourself comfortable. May I take your coat, sir? Would you care for something to drink, sir?"

"Oh, I see. No, I'll just hang it over the back of the chair. Yes, well, just some water would be fine, Mr. Reitz. By the way, sir, are you related to Colonel Denez Reitz, who was the Minister of Native Affairs, I think, and wrote a treatise on Guerilla Warfare, though I'm not in favor of that?"

"Yes, Denez is my uncle, Father O'Malley."

With that answer, Father John gets the picture as to how this man ended up as a top assistant for his liberal-leaning friend, Jan Hofmeyr. He says, "Yes, please correct me if I'm mistaken, but didn't Prime Minister Smuts remove your uncle from the Cabinet because he eased the application of the Pass Laws?"

"That's right. The Colonel in 1942 could see that the administration of those laws and the cost of that legislation as too burdensome, especially during the War. Even though my uncle still believed strongly in the separation of the races, Prime Minister Smuts fired him."

Giving his head an understanding shake, Father John is silent but thinks, "Politics does indeed make strange bedfellows."

The assistant buzzes and requests water as the priest inserts his right forefinger between his neck and Roman collar, giving it a slight yank.

"Minister Hofmeyr tells me that you were one of his best students and that now you are doing missionary work with the Zulus and other Natives in the Mpumalanga region. No doubt that must be challenging, very exciting, and, at sometimes, a little frightening since rumor has it that the Zulus still plot revenge for their many devastating defeats by both the Dutch and the British. I suppose that could be the reason. Do you still enjoy working with those Natives, Father O'Malley?

"Yes, I find the work quite rewarding and stimulating."

Changing the subject, Mr. Reitz explains, "As you may know from the newspapers, the Non-European Council of Trade Unions, that is the 119 unions, now has almost 160,000 Native members in commerce and in manufacturing. These Africans are behind these boycotts and work stoppages, although I prefer to call them labor strikes prohibited by law."

Father O'Malley just listens as Mr. Reitz continues

"It's disgraceful and unpatriotic, if you ask me, especially during the War. I sometimes wonder whether the Communist Party has joined hands with some of the Natives' political organizations, especially the African National Congress. These African political groups and the unions have become a real sore in the body politic. I hate to say it, but that sore could turn to cancer. And we certainly don't need the Reds creating up more strife in our country."

The priest just smiles.

"Anyhow, Minister Hofmeyr will settle those matters expediently, I am certain."

"Yes, I've seen the newspaper accounts," Father John says, not raising an eyebrow at the mention of any tacit joinder between the African National Congress and the Communist Party of South Africa.

"Father O'Malley, sometimes the newspapers don't get all the facts. The government is afraid that the African Mine Workers Union will strike over issues involving minimum wage, family housing, paid leave, and better food. It looks like the situation will get worse before it gets better."

The priest nods.

"I suspect that some of those leaders are Communists. Since Prime Minister Smuts is abroad working on the United Nations Charter, my boss has his hands full. My boss is doing triple duty, as you can see."

To get him off of his soap box and talking about the Communist Party, the priest asks, "Mr. Reitz, have you been with Minister Hofmeyr very long and do you enjoy your work?"

"Thanks for asking, Father. I've been with the Minister since he rejoined the Smuts government at the start of the War and it's been a high privilege to work with such a man dedicated to South Africa. Although I sometimes find myself disagreeing with some of Minister Hofmeyr's proposals, I'm a good soldier and follow along. And, yes, as you can tell, I enjoy my job to the fullest."

"Wonderful," the priest says.

"Once again, Father O'Malley, please accept the Minister's deepest apologies. I am instructed to give you any assistance I can and, if you are staying in Pretoria, to make you stay most enjoyable."

"I do understand, Mr. Reitz, and thank you, but I have a place to bed down before my return travel in several days to beautiful Pietermaritzburg. However, I do need a favor."

"Anything, Father O'Malley! Your wish, Father O'Malley, is my command."

"Fine. I have a young couple with me and they need to travel to Cape Town but do not have travel documents," the priest says.

"That's an easy fix. Give me the information and I'll get the travel authorizations for your people to travel to Cape Town. Of course, you are carrying their identity cards, correct?"

"Their identity cards are with them in the car. Is that a problem?"

"Not really. You can give me the information and then you can write in their id numbers on the travel documents, Father. Will they be traveling by auto or by train?"

"They'll be traveling by bus to Johannesburg and then to Cape Town by coach."

"Oh? Yes."

When Father John reveals that Mary Washington is an eighteen-year-old Zulu from the Natal Province and that Charles Washington is a seventeen-year-old Colored from Durban and that the newly married couple will be living permanently in Cape Town, he notices a wince in Mr. Reitz's face and a wrinkle in his forehead. But, Hofmeyr's assistant says with a fake but cordial smile, "Just give me ten minutes and I'll have the travel authorizations for both. Please make yourself comfortable, Father O'Malley."

He quickly excuses himself and exits his office.

Of course, Father O'Malley remembers that during the early years of World War II, Prime Minister Smuts had requested the Minister of Native Affairs to find a solution to the costly and difficult administration of the Pass Laws since the War had presented increased job opportunities for Blacks to escape the terrible poverty in the rural "Reserves" and emigrate to the urban areas.

Thanks to the intercession of Jan Hofmeyr, Prime Minister Smuts reversed his thinking, after firing Colonel Reitz, so that during the War, the Pass Laws were very lightly enforced. Father John knew that many local governments continued enforcement since the filtered word was that after the War, strict enforcement of the Pass Laws by the Smuts government would return.

Father John figures that Mr. Reitz abhors having more Non-Europeans such as Charles and Mary pour into the urban area of Cape Town.

Accepting from Mr. Reitz the travel authorizations to Cape Town for Mary and Charles Washington, Father John retrieves his coat and places the envelope with the documents into the inside pocket of his coat.

"Thank you so much, Mr. Reitz. You've been very professional. And please convey my best wishes to Minister Hofmeyr."

Father O'Malley shakes hands and takes his leave.

Before exiting the government building, the priest obtains directions to the men's washroom, enters, and relieves his bladder. After washing his hands with perfumed soap, Father John carefully dries his hands with a white towel. Before tossing the towel in the laundry basket of woven reed, Father John thinks, "Probably handcrafted by some Native," then wipes his face and, lacking a comb, brushes his slightly graying hair in place with the cloth.

"My, that was soft. I bet it is Egyptian cotton," Father John whispers and opens the washroom door.

Chapter 6

As the priest exits the building, he hears a commotion and sees two policemen and several men surrounding his car. He notices that the Rolls-Royce is gone.

Quickly approaching, Father O'Malley shouts first in Afrikaans and then in English to the crowd, "What's going on here? Get back, please! Get back, please!"

Noticing the Roman collar, one of the policemen responds in English, "Father, the Native lady and the Colored man inside the car were being accosted by several men who wanted them out of the car. We came because of all the noise and shouting and that some of the onlookers were rocking the car."

Sizing up the situation as he sees the crowd of Afrikaners step back in obedience to the policemen, Father O'Malley explains to the satisfaction of the two policemen. He produces all the necessary travel documents, his own identity card, and after receiving Mary and Charles' identity cards, also gives them to the two policemen. After examination of the documents, the two policemen shoo away the Afrikaners.

Receiving permission to leave, the priest keys the ignition and departs from the temporary office building of the Minister of Finance.

As they drive to the bus terminal in Pretoria, Mary and Charles express their fear of the threats from the gathering mob of Afrikaners around the car before the priest returned.

The priest does his best to calm them as he carefully drives to the bus terminal.

"Well, here we are at the bus terminal. Great, there's a handy parking space. Come with me so we can get your tickets to Johannesburg on this local bus which will drop you at the Johannesburg coach terminal so you can get a nice coach all the way to Cape Town."

As they walk toward the entry in the red-bricked building, Charles and Mary see the black sign with white lettering first in English, *BLACKS, COLOREDS, & ASIANS*, and just below in Afrikaans, *ANTSUNDU, KLEURLINGE, EN ASIERS.*

Inside the door, a Black policeman looks the other way as Father John enters with Charles and Mary. Although he has obviously seen the White priest, the Black policeman remains immobile.

Father John is not deterred, walking up to the ticket window, but he can't help thinking what would happen to Charles and Mary if they had accompanied him to the building for Whites Only. Charles and Mary would receive a rough escort by a White policeman from the Whites-Only building and they could have been arrested and fined on the spot and if unable to pay the fine, jailed, without any trial.

As the three wait their turn at the ticket window, a Black woman with two small White children is in front. Father John wonders if she is a nanny, or if the children are hers, or a friend's, or a relative's. The Black woman with the two small White children is getting change so she can pay the bus driver on a local bus from Pretoria to a nearby town.

At the ticket window Father John steps in front of Charles and announces, "Mary and Charles, as my small wedding gift to you, I'm buying your tickets to Johannesburg and to Cape Town."

"But, Father John . . . ," Charles says.

"It's the least I can do. A thank-you is not necessary."

The Black man at the ticket window says, "Give me their passes or documents."

"Charles and Mary, show the man your travel documents and identity cards. This bus will carry you to a coach terminal in Johannesburg where you will then board a coach for Cape Town. When you board this bus today and when you board the coach in Johannesburg, you must again show your travel documents. And, if there is a stop at any security checkpoint, then you must show them each time. Remember to be courteous and smile."

Charles says, "Thank you again, Father John. I notice that some people pay the bus driver when they board."

"Yes, that's the way it works for very local buses, but since you are traveling farther, you don't pay the driver. Just give him your tickets when you board either the bus or the coach."

"Yes, Father John."

The priest addresses the ticket seller, "Excuse me sir, but what kind of a bus is going to Johannesburg and what kind of coach will go to Cape Town?'

He replies, "To both Johannesburg and to Cape Town will be an Albion Valkyrie single decker."

Father John says, "Wait a minute. I thought for long distance the Daimler CDG 6 diesel double decker was used. I've ridden in that with the Weyman's coach work, very nice and comfortable, and it holds quite a few passengers."

The ticket seller replies, "Yes, it seats 56. But that luxury coach is used for only Europeans, sir. Your friends will be riding in the Albion bus to Cape Town, although it makes several stops. That bus will be leaving Johannesburg tomorrow morning at six o'clock."

"Oh, I see," the priest says, as he turns to Charles and Mary, "Well, I have arranged for you to spend the night at a friend's house in Johannesburg. Here is a note with their name and directions to their house. You must take a taxi from the bus terminal. Josie and Albert Simpson are old friends of mine and will feed you and put you up for the night, free of charge."

Mary and Charles thank Father John as he announces, "Well, we're in luck since the posted time for your bus to Johannesburg is just thirty minutes away."

Receiving their tickets, the three head to the waiting area with the posted signs in English and Afrikaans proclaiming that the room is for only Non-Europeans, but Father John again pays no attention and enters with Mary and Charles. He seems to be the only White person in the room.

Looking around, Father John sees that the dirty room has an insufficient number of chairs or benches, that women are lined up outside the toilet door for what must be a single toilet, and that for the men's toilet, several men wait outside one door for what must also be a single toilet. He blanches at the stink emitting from the toilet area.

When Mary gets in line for the toilet, the priest asks Charles, "Care for anything to eat?" He points to the snack or rest area. At first declining the priest's offer to bring him something, Charles selects two sandwiches wrapped in paper and containing what might be chicken or dried fish or jerky. As Charles and the priest return with the sandwiches, Father John notices a swarm of flies.

When Mary finally returns, she says, "This place smells and is filthy. There's no soap to wash your hands and no towels to dry your hands. It's worse than the public places in Nelspruit. In my village, we have more sanitary places then this."

She doesn't confess to the priest or her husband that, for the lack of any tissue, she had to wipe herself with the hem of her skirt.

Father John wishes he could wave a magic wand to banish forever these separate facilities for Blacks and Coloreds, but he understands that even with his friend Jan Hofmeyr in the Smuts Cabinet there is no chance for that to happen. His face reveals empathy and understanding, but no words emit from his mouth. He knows there is no authoritative person in the building or nearby either to accept his complaint or to remedy the injustice.

Somehow, Mary and Charles eat their sandwiches. As Charles and Mary head for the drinking fountain, Charles notices a sign above, written in Afrikaans, Non-Europeans Only. Pressing the button with his thumb produces just a trickle of water. Mary wrinkles her nose at the taste.

Father John agrees to wait with them for the arrival of their bus. But now, more than an hour has passed and he says, "Looks like your bus is late."

Overhearing, a tall Black man frowns and talks a blue streak,

"Father, these buses are never on time, unlike the buses for the Whites. And, they're run down and they break down a lot. They're dirty and overcrowded so many times we've got to stand up forever. It's a crying shame! There's talk that the bus company again wants to raise the price. Last year, they raised the price from four pence to five pence in Alexander Township and there was a huge boycott by Blacks. You know, people walked 15 to 20 kilometers each way to work when some White didn't give them a ride. If they raise the price here, there'll be a boycott. That'll force me to walk if I can't hitch a ride. Fat chance, since very few Natives have cars. If I can't ride the bus, it's almost twenty five kilometers each way from my house to my job in the factory. I don't know what we can do."

Father John knows the man speaks the truth and nods affirmatively. He says, "Well, you know the ANC helped organize that boycott in 1944 in Alexander Township and it had a lot of support throughout the country. And, sir, it worked because the bus company backed off. I bet they back off again, too."

"Well, I sure hope so. Nice talking to you, Father, but here's my bus."

Father John smiles, "And may God be with you, my friend."

As he ponders the situation, Father John wonders if he should have had the couple take a train, but quickly realizes he didn't have the funds to buy their tickets.

He can feel the sadness swell up in this throat over what's happening to his country. Maybe, with enough protests and resistance led by the ANC and other groups, the government will come to its sense of morality and change its course. A silent prayer rises from his lips.

Looking around the area, reality returns and the priest says to Charles and Mary, "Keep a close eye on your belongings since many deprived people in the big cities take the property of others, sometimes through force.

When you arrive at the terminal in Johannesburg to catch the coach to Cape Town, be aware of who is standing close to you since there are thieves and robbers, your fellow Africans, I'm afraid. Watch your wallet and hold tight to your purse. There are many desperate people hanging around the bus stations and the coach terminals. Be careful who you trust, too, because some people will scam you. And, be wary of the shanty towns since they contain lots of desperate people."

"All right, Father John, we'll be careful," Charles replies.

"And I recommend you sit as close as you can to the driver," Father John warns as he sees Mary's worried face.

"Charles, here is a letter I've written to a priest at St. Mary's Cathedral in Cape Town. The church is located on Roeland Street in downtown Cape Town. Father Vincent will help you and Mary get settled if you need any help. You don't have to see Father Vincent, but should you need any assistance, Father Vincent will be there to help."

Mary pockets the letter and the envelope in her straw bag of a purse as both Mary and Charles gush thanks to Father John.

"Father John, here is a letter to my mother, which I hope you will get to her. I've told her I am now married. I hope she will forgive me for abandoning the priesthood. And, I've told her that we are moving to Cape Town."

"Charles, your mother loves you and I'm sure she will be happy with your choice. I'll see that she gets your letter right away."

Just at that moment, before Father John can say more, the bus to Johannesburg arrives. Father John shakes hands with Charles, hugs him, and hugs Mary, saying goodbye, wishing them well, and telling them to write. He blesses them, watches them board with a crowd, and, as the bus pulls away from the terminal, Father John waves a farewell.

As the bus itself disappears from his sight, he can still smell the dark cloud of exhaust fumes from their bus.

**

Just a few blocks from the bus terminal, Mary looks out of the window and sees two bus ranks with a huge crowd of people at each stop waiting for a bus. One stop shows a large sign commanding in English and Afrikaans *Non-Europeans Only*, while the other stop commands in English and Afrikaans, *Europeans Only*. She sees both buses arrive and can easily tell which bus is for Whites and which bus is for Non-Whites.

As their bus leaves the city of Pretoria, Mary is seated directly behind the driver, while Charles is seated next to her but adjacent to the aisle. Across the aisle from Charles sits a heavy-set woman with a large leather purse with short straps. A young boy, maybe five or six years old, has the window seat and appears to be watching the crowds, the tall buildings, the houses, the stores, and the lights give way to open country, some twenty minutes into their journey. The woman points out to the boy things of interest.

Mary sees a big rip at the top of the back of the bus driver's seat and, looking at the floor, she sees a collection of trash and cigarette butts residing safely next to the side wall of the bus.

Suddenly, a bell chimes and the bus slows to release a passenger at an intersection with a narrow dirt road which is unlighted and appears deserted.

A slender Black youth, maybe sixteen years of age, appears from the rear of the bus and is standing between Charles and the heavy-set woman with the large leather purse with the short straps. He's waiting for the door to open when the bus stops.

As the bus door snaps open, the slender young man grabs the woman's leather purse and leaps down the steps and through the door. Crossing the narrow dirt road, the thief enters a path devoured by the dense brush and soon has vanished into the darkness.

Too late the woman screams, "Stop! He has my purse! Stop him! He has my purse with all my money! Help! Stop him! He stole my purse!"

But before either Charles or the bus driver can react, the young man has disappeared into the overgrowth.

The bus driver says, "There's no catching him now."

The bus driver, Mary, Charles, and a few other passengers offer sympathetic words to the lady, now a tearful wreck. The driver says to the still sobbing woman, "When we stop at the Security checkpoint, I will tell the police about the theft and give them a description of the man." But, the poor woman continues to sob and she knows she'll never see her purse or the thief again.

Mary can tell the poor woman understands her money is gone forever and the young man will never pay for his crime. But, from where she is seated, Mary cannot give the poor woman a comforting hug.

Mary carefully moves her straw bag of a purse so that it's next to the sidewall of the bus. Tightly, she grips the bag.

Just outside Johannesburg, along with a long line of vehicles the bus pulls into a checkpoint area so that the Security Police can board the bus to check Pass Books or travel documents and do a random search of any passenger's luggage. Thirty minutes later, the bus is again on its way to the bus terminal in Johannesburg. Mary is surprised to see three of the four Security Policemen are Black.

***

Finally, they arrive in Johannesburg where, to Mary's amazement, the buildings are even taller, and with lighted windows as high as one can see. Pulling into the terminal for long-haul coaches, the driver tells Mary and Charles, "Well, you get off here. Tomorrow, come and look at the chalk board for your bus number going to Cape Town. It's on your ticket. And that's your bus. Now, gather all your things as you leave the bus and, outside, pick up your luggage. Take care of your tickets. One more thing, be careful of thieves, pickpockets, and purse snatchers inside the terminal. Good luck! And have a pleasant journey."

Immediately, Charles locates the chalk board for departing buses and coaches, and, finding the number for their bus tomorrow morning, sees its departing location and its departure time. It still has a six o'clock departure time.

Mary and Charles head for the taxi stands for Black people and hail a taxi to head for the home of Josie and Albert Simpson. Mary declines the taxi driver's offer to store their two suitcases in the boot. Instead, in the back seat, she keeps a right hand-hold on her suitcase and her straw bag of a purse. Quietly, she moves her husband's hand from her hand to the handle on his suitcase.

After receiving the address from Charles, the Black taxi driver hesitates when his fare wants to go into a White neighborhood, but eventually calms himself and sets forth. He is desperate for the fare. He tells them about his last visit to this part of Johannesburg.

When he discharged his fare the last time in this neighborhood, a bunch of White hooligans pelted with rocks his taxi with the lighted sign, "Non-Europeans."

He says, "They shouted something in Afrikaans and then in English:

THIS LAND IS FOR WHITES ONLY! NO BLACKS ALLOWED! GET YOUR BLACK ASS OUT! NEXT TIME, YOU WON'T SEE THE SUN RISE!

As soon as the taxi nears their destination, the driver declares the amount of the fare, receives the money from Charles, then brakes hard in front of the red brick house, and directs his passengers to exit quickly so he can make his getaway.

Charles and Mary smell the rubber from the pavement as the taxi speeds into the night.

Knocking on the door, Charles and Mary greet Josie and Albert Simpson, who invite them in, take their suitcases, introduce them to their two boys, show them to their room, and suggest they wash up since supper is almost ready.

Neither Charles nor Mary has ever been inside a home housing a White family, but they hide their surprise and amazement at its warmth and cleanliness. Josie and Albert are treating them as if they are family and invite them to join the family at the dining room table.

Josie says, "Well, I've prepared some fried chicken, some mealy pap of grits, creamy spinach and onions along with spicy *chakalaka* but I've omitted the green chilies from the beans and grated carrots, since Albert doesn't like it that hot. Now, for dessert, we've fruit cocktail over vanilla ice cream. You've a choice of tea or fruit punch."

After a full supper, Charles and Albert retire to his office while Mary helps Josie clean up the dishes. The two boys are sent to their room to get ready for bed.

Charles learns that Father John and Albert were students at Witwatersrand University; that Albert uses a cane because of a knee injury in paratrooper training before the War; and that Albert served as a Member of Parliament until last year when he resigned.

Since Charles' face contains a question, Albert reveals, "So, what happened is that Prime Minister Smuts as leader of the United Party was talking overseas about 'human rights' but with the Prime Minister's knowledge, the United Party simultaneously was considering several pieces of more onerous legislation to advance segregation. It was just too hypocritical and I just couldn't join them, Charles."

"Well, Mr. Simpson, are there a lot of White people like that, I mean like you?"

"Yes, especially in the churches, except in the Dutch Reformed Church. Many Anglican and Catholic priests, like Father John O'Malley, and ministers of the gospel have decried the immorality of segregation. In the universities, especially Witwatersrand and the University of Cape Town, most professors and many students have spoken against what is happening in South Africa."

Charles is amazed.

"These and other Whites are working with many Black unions and other organizations to raise the moral consciousness of Whites about what is happening in our country."

Charles is paying close attention.

"Unfortunately, others, especially the livid Afrikaners, are working for more and more segregation by the government. It has already disenfranchised in the real elections all the Natives in the ordinary elections. If the situation worsens, I fear there will be riots which will ultimately lead to civil war. It doesn't look good."

Charles considers Mr. Simpson's opinions, but before he can comment, he hears Mr. Simpson, "Well, I didn't mean to sound off on my soap box. I know you've had a long day and a long journey ahead of you. So, I'll say good night now since I see the ladies have finished the supper dishes. And, my job is to read a few stories to my sons before they'll agree to close their eyes. I'll see you in the morning. Don't worry about getting a taxi, because I'll drive you to the coach terminal."

He smiles at Mr. Simpson, understanding that the man's simple revelations are a belated but heartfelt apology for the sins of the White controlled government, of which he used to be a part.

Albert Simpson remains closed mouth that tomorrow he and Father John O'Malley will meet secretly to plot strategy with some of the leaders of the African National Congress, unions, and some other groups in downtown Johannesburg.

The two couples exchange Good Night pleasantries.

In the morning, after a restful night but without any sex, Mary and Charles are awakened at four o'clock, dress quickly, breakfast, and gather their belongings. Josie has prepared some food for them and has packed it in a brown paper sack.

Mary is wearing a one-piece multicolored skirt, tied at the waist, similar to yesterday's brown one, together with a high-necked white blouse and brown scarf, while Charles is wearing the same khaki pants, a different long-sleeved white shirt, a light brown tie, a brownish sweater, and a brown sport coat.

Seeing their attire, Josie offers, "The radio says we will be getting heavy winter rains this June or July. Do you have slickers?"

Hearing their negative reply, Josie says, "Just a minute. I've got slickers for each of you. We've got extra ones."

Initially declining but finally accepting the raincoats, Mary and Charles thank Josie and walk with Albert to his car parked in the driveway. Mary stashes the two raincoats in the bottom of her straw bag of a purse.

As they near the coach terminal, Albert says, "A pleasure to be of assistance to you, Charles and Mary. I have a close friend in Cape Town. Frederick Kruger. We used to serve together in the Parliament. If you need help, just tell Fredrick that Josie and Albert Simpson sent you. Here, I've written his name and address and a little note on your behalf. God bless you and may you have a safe trip."

He hands the paper to Mary who places it inside Father John's envelope in her straw bag of a purse. Later she expects to read the note. It's just common courtesy to wait, she remembers from the Benedictine monk, her English teacher.

Thanking Albert at the curb side for the hospitality they received, Mary and Charles quickly enter the coach terminal. Locating the spot for boarding their coach to Cape Town, the couple stands outside ready for boarding in just twenty minutes. Since they are near the front of the line of passengers, they hope to sit near the bus driver in comfortable seats.

Chapter 7

Charles and Mary watch their two suitcases get loaded in the lower compartment beneath the seating. After boarding, they squeeze into the first vacant seats three rows behind the Black driver. Just as they are getting comfortable, a huge Black policeman approaches.

With a bulldog voice he demands, "Hey, get out of my seats! I take this bus three times a week and I always sit there. Now, get out or I'll punch you out!"

Mary sees the man with the visor cap in the brown police uniform carries no gun, but he does have a bully stick attached to his belt. She sees his twisting facial muscles and his wrinkling forehead. She knows intense anger when she sees it.

Protesting and not moving, Charles says, "But, sir, there are no reserved seats on this bus. It's all open seating. It is first come, first served. You can ask the bus driver."

"I don't need to ask the bus driver, little man! Now, move!"

When the big man reaches with a large right hand in the area of Charles' necktie and with his left on Charles' shoulder, Mary says before he grabs tightly on Charles' shirt or neck, "All right, sir! Just calm down! We'll move. You can have these seats. Now, let go of my husband and move back so we can move to other seats. I would appreciate it, sir."

Mary notes that the bus driver hasn't moved an inch although the commotion was loud enough for him to hear, just three rows away. She sees him looking out the window.

And the big man complies, withdrawing his fistful of anger. Mary and Charles move toward the very back of the bus. When Mary looks toward the front of the bus, she sees the Black policeman's body has covered two seats.

As the bus fills almost to capacity, with just three seats vacant, the bus driver shuts the door and announces, "The final destination is Cape Town. We will make intermittent stops and I will announce those stops ahead of time. The first stop will be Soweto, just to let off passengers. We don't pick up any people there. The second stop will be at Orange Farm, just to let off passengers. Then, in about three hours from now, we will stop in Kroonstadt, where you can also get a snack and use the toilet. When you re-board the bus, you must show your ticket. Now, relax and enjoy the ride."

The bus leaves the terminal and heads out of Johannesburg.

In the window seat with her straw bag of a purse on her lap, Mary watches the buildings and the houses sail by. She sees small groups of White men and women waiting at bus stops marked with signs for *NET BLANKES* and along with hordes of Black men and women waiting at the other segregated bus stops. She assumes all these people either don't have a car, or have no ride in a car, or have no money for a taxi. She suspects they are on their way to work somewhere in the metropolis of Johannesburg.

She would like to imagine visions of ambience and pleasantness in their homes and in their jobs, but she senses a foreboding of painful snares because of government interference in their everyday lives. To relieve herself of these paranoid visions of sadness, she rests her head on Charles' shoulder and closes her eyes.

Mary is awakened as the bus stops in Soweto to disgorge seven or eight passengers, including the Black policeman. Mary is glad to see him leave as the bus slowly makes headway through the narrow streets by dodging the throngs walking in its way.

Both Mary and Charles stare at the few red brick houses with lines of wind-blown laundry on clotheslines everywhere. Most of the red brick houses contain two rooms, although a few have unfinished additions with completion months away.

But instead of red brick homes, most residences appear as cheap clapboard structures with tin roofs or with army tarps draped over four uplifting poles as shelter from wind and rain. Very few of the shanties have electric wires and the few who do, the electric wires are strung haphazardly.

They see the heads of Black women carrying baskets containing bundles of sticks for the cooking fires aside the narrow and rutted dirt streets.

Dogs, in search of a meal, wander through what should be landscaped yards.

Where there is an open field, they see a few boys have strung together tin cans for wickets for a game of cricket.

Once or twice coming into view outside an unfinished house is a women working magic on a sewing machine as well as another woman scrubbing clothes on a wooden washboard.

All over, they see many small Black children playing in the side streets—some with mud holes the size of a lorry and some impassable for any vehicle.

The very few clunkers adorning front yards or on the unpaved streets have busted fenders or bumpers and mismatched painted parts.

Scattered among the houses and shanties are a few enterprising fruit or food stands painted vibrant colors.

Looking to the rear of many of the makeshift homes, they see a weed-filled ditch and the emitting smell tells them it contains raw sewage, especially when they notice a few people are dumping what must be buckets of shit.

Mary notices that the 'Whites Only' signs are absent in Soweto. She comments, "Charles, I bet very few Whites come here after dark."

Across the aisle, a muscular Black man interrupts, "Not just Whites because the government which set aside land for this ghetto allows just Blacks in Soweto although some Coloreds do live here. It has total control, too, with just two ways to enter or to leave. The government in these townships maintains forced control of the people."

Mary and Charles are listening.

"I don't think I could ever live in that squalor. It's just terrible. Many of these souls have returned from the Reserves and are living ten or twelve person to a room. It is downright disgraceful. I hate to make this trip because the bus always makes this stop."

Charles questions, "Have you been inside Soweto?"

"Yes, once the bus broke down and all the passengers had to get off and wait hours for another one. There are no stores and no public facilities. People sell groceries and tires and food and stuff from their front stoops or garage driveway, even though hardly anyone has a car or a garage. They have only outside toilets shared by several houses with only old newspaper to wipe oneself. You cannot imagine the numbers of flies or the stink. It's a terrible place!"

95

Shaking his head yes, Charles remembers that Father John alerted him about the law of the jungle operating in these camps by desperate and suffering people.

The man continues, "And, many of the people are living on scraps of meat, which they call sawdust because they mix it with wood chips or whatever. I've even seen people take bones away from dogs."

Charles and Mary momentarily remain silent, waiting for the bus to escape the pain of Soweto, and glad the man has stopped talking about it.

Finally, hoping for a friendly encounter, Charles asks the muscular Black man, "How far do you go on the bus, sir? My wife and I are going to Cape Town."

"About 50 kilometers to Orange Farm, where I'm the labor boss on a huge orchard farm. When the farm truck is busy, as it was yesterday, then I use the bus to the city to hire farm laborers. I am allowed to drive the family car but the family won't allow Natives to ride in their car," he answers.

"Mind if I ask you a question?" Charles ponders as the man's face signals a yes.

"Since we left Johannesburg, I didn't see any police checkpoints on our side of the road. They're all on the other side. And, why…"

Before Charles can actually ask the question, the man laughs, "That's because the police don't care if Blacks are leaving the cities. They just don't want us in the cities, unless we are working for the Man. And they're afraid we might be bringing in explosives or bombs into the cities. But, don't worry, because there will be a big stop for this bus and all the passengers in Kroonstadt. It's on your side of the road. But they still stop vehicles going both ways since they know some Blacks are moving from city to city."

Everyone is quiet as the bus reaches the fringes of the hamlet of Orange Farm and the driver announces the oncoming stop in 5 minutes. To Charles and Mary, the farm labor boss waves a goodbye and is quickly off the bus.

On its way again, the bus stops at the Security checkpoint, just outside the town limits of Kroonstadt. This time, everything goes well, with just a twenty-minute delay.

They finally reach the far side of Kroonstadt. The driver says, "Everyone, please take all your belongings with you because we will be taking a different bus on the next leg of our travel to Bloemfontein, about a four-hour trip. Your luggage will be loaded on the new bus. Be sure you get a snack and use the toilet because we won't be stopping anywhere on the way."

The driver declines to tell the passengers that he fears stopping at any unauthorized stop because of robbers masquerading as police.

With carry-on bags in hand, each passenger exits in Kroonstadt to a big café hosting a sign over the front door. In English and Afrikaans, the sign reads 'Europeans Only.' An arrow under a sign in both languages reads, 'Non-Europeans,' and points to the rear of the building. Over the rear door, entry is granted in both languages to 'Non-Europeans.'

As they enter, the hands on the wall clock point to ten past one o'clock. Mary asks, "How far have we traveled, Charles? It seems like forever. I'm getting tired riding."

"My guess is about five or six hundred kilometers since we left at about six. Are you hungry? Let's eat the packed lunches the Simpson's gave us."

Boarding the new bus, Charles and Mary sit two rows in seats directly behind the driver.

After everyone has boarded, the driver announces in a loud voice, "We'll have a quick stop in Venterburg and Winburg before we reach Bloemfontein, which is about three hours away. We'll be stopped in Bloemfontein for a little over one hour to take on additional passengers. So, there you can get a snack or use the toilet. So, relax and enjoy the scenery."

Charles and Mary settle in for the long ride.

Chapter 8

As Charles and Mary continue on the way to Cape Town and close the distance to Bloemfontein, Father John has parked his Humber in a downtown Johannesburg parking lot with a security guard, and, after ascertaining nobody is tailing him, begins his walk toward a non-descript storefront on a deserted side street.

Dressed in his usual Roman Catholic attire, the priest looks both ways and discovers just a few Blacks on the street. Father Hurley's warning to be careful has stuck with him, even though Father John isn't doing anything illegal. He knows that full freedom of assembly exists for Whites, but several friends, all White critics of the government, have been brought before the South African police for interrogation. Father John recognizes he faces powerful forces.

The priest hopes that this June 17th meeting will energize various and diverse groups to seek change in the government's racial segregation policies.

He knocks and sings the African hymn in a Native language, *Nkosi sikelel iAfrika,* and then, sings in English, "God bless Africa," and the door opens by a large Black man who greets the priest, "Good day, Father O'Malley, and welcome."

Inside, Father John feels the approach of Zulu Chief Alfred Luthuli, who exclaims, "Is it true that my good friend, Denis Hurley, is going to be the Catholic Bishop in Durban?"

Getting an affirmation, the chief exclaims, "Praise be to God!"

Father John O'Malley says, "Amen."

Chief Luthuli grabs the priest's shoulder, steers him to the side of the room, and says, "I want you to meet an outstanding young man who has recently joined the African National Congress, and that's Nelson Mandela. He owns an interesting story, Father John. While away at school, I think at Forte Hare in the Eastern Cape, his father, a chief in the *Thembu* tribe, arranged a marriage, but Nelson declined to be the groom, left home, and moved to Johannesburg. There he worked as a night watchman and took a correspondence course at the University of South Africa.

"But that didn't stop him and now, after getting his degree, Nelson is studying law at the University of Witwatersrand. He's the only native African student at the law school at Witwatersrand.

"Come with me to meet my amazing young Xhosa friend."

After the formal introductions, Father John comments, "Chief Luthuli has told me a little about you and attending Witwatersrand. Well, it's about time that Witwatersrand law school had a Black student. That's at least a little progress at the university since the time I attended the undergrad school. How did that happen, if I may ask?"

Nelson answers, "Fortunately, I began work as articles clerk for the law firm of Witkin, Sidelsky, Eidelman and had passed my BA exams from the University of South Africa. Then, with some recommendations, especially from my White friends, I was admitted to the University of Witwatersrand to study the law and work toward my Bachelor of Laws degree. Right now, I'm working as an articles clerk, as the law requires, toward becoming an apprentice in the law profession."

"Nelson, tell me, after you complete your apprenticeship, you are eligible for law exams, even before you complete your L.LB. degree, is that right?'

"If you get enough school credits, two years I think, and then you can take the exams. Then, Father, if you pass the law exams, you don't need a degree. Then, I will be a full -fledged lawyer, because I intend to pass the exams. I do confess I'm finding myself spread too thin and my law school studies are suffering. But, I will pass the law exams."

"Well, Nelson, welcome to our group and my sincerest congratulations on your successes. I'm sure more will come your way," the priest says, obviously impressed by the young man.

Chief Luthuli adds, "Yes, we are glad to have Nelson along with several other young members. Nelson Mandela has organized a mass youth conference in Johannesburg and is a rising star in the youth arm of the ANC.

"And, Father John, joining us is Walter Sisulu, very instrumental in getting Nelson to join the ANC. He also helped him get employment with Lazer Sidelsky."

"Yes."

"And here is also Oliver Tambo, one of Nelson's friends from his student days at Fort Hare, our own wonderful Native University. Both Walter and Oliver are also very active in the ANC Youth Arm. We are fortunate to have such talent."

Shaking hands, Father John says, "Welcome, Walter and Oliver. I look forward to working with you and Nelson. Well, Chief Luthuli, congratulations on being elected to the ANC Executive Committee in the Natal division."

The five men again shake hands, but before the priest can move, Chief Luthuli says, "Wait, Father, because I want to introduce you to my Anglican friend, Father Trevor Huddleston who has been ministering to towns around Johannesburg and is a strong believer in equal rights for all people."

After a brief conversation the Catholic priest and the Anglican priest meld and exchange contact information. Father John says, "Let me know if I can help you in working with my Catholic brothers and sisters. We are all opposed to the Smuts government."

Father Trevor Huddleston agrees.

Father John moves around the room and recognizes several Black physicians, one or two Black lawyers, and several Black university professors of the defunct All-African Convention which once had been the go-to organized opposition to the government's racial segregation.

He pays his respects to each of them, and, spying nine White university professors he recognizes, along with several students—all opposed to the Smuts administration's policies, he greets them and obtains what's happening at each university.

Circulating the room, Father John shakes hands with a few members of the once powerful Industrial and Commercial Workers Union, and trades a joke with them.

Moving toward him are four known members of the Communist Party, Joe Slovo, Ruth First, Bram Fischer, and Hilda Bernstein who was recently elected as Johannesburg's City Councilor. Ms. Bernstein says, "Hello again, Father O'Malley. I'm glad you could make our meeting to consolidate our opposition to these discriminatory pieces of legislation against the laboring class. Hopefully, we can all work together to end this oppression against the laboring class."

 All four Communists offer their hands to the priest who complies with a grin and handshakes.

The priest, not wanting to be too chummy with known Communists, smilingly replies, "Ah, yes! Perhaps with the Good Lord's Help, we can be successful to end this oppression toward everyone."

He makes sure to emphasize the 'Good Lord's Help' and then says, "Excuse me, while I say hello to my old friend, Albert Simpson who I'm sure will give us an update on where the Smuts administration is heading with new legislation."

Before he can reach Albert Simpson, the priest sees that his friend is conferring with someone else, rather intensely. He abides his time and glances around the room, now almost filled.

Father John sees several Protestant ministers, especially his Anglican friends, Father Michael Scott and Father David Russell who receive Father John's friendly wave. Father John appreciates these two Anglican priests, staunch allies in their common fight against racial segregation. He remembers that Father Scott has been working with the *Herero* tribe in South West Africa which is governed by South Africa and that Father Russell has been active among the universities in South Africa. He thanks God for their assistance in the struggle.

The priest sees that noticeably absent are any ministers or clerics of the Dutch Reformed Church still in favor of racial segregation because of the influence of D.F. Malam, the official Leader of the Opposition in Parliament and a former cleric in the Dutch Reformed

Church. Malan is grooming the National Party for the 1948 elections for the House of Assembly in Parliament.

Suddenly, two unknown Black men approach the priest. One says, "Hello, Father O'Malley, I'm Peter Abrahams with the ANC and the Non-European Council of Unions. My companion is Dan Kuzwayo also with the Non-European Council. We heard you had a meeting with Daniel Reitz, Hofmeyr's assistant and after today's meeting, we'd like to pick your brain about what the Smuts government is going to do about our striking mineworkers."

"Certainly, gentlemen, I'll be glad to meet with you later, if you like. Right now, I see a very old friend and I'd like to say hello before the meeting starts. I will tell you this, though, I don't have much to report except that Mr. Hofmeyr is trying to avert a miners' strike. But, I suspect you already knew that. How he's going to do that, I'm not privy to because Mr. Reitz wasn't forthcoming with any information."

From their reaction, Father John knows they will not waste time meeting him later.

Before the priest can reach Albert Simpson, someone taps Father John's shoulder and, turning, the priest greets an old friend from Durban.

"Doctor Naicker! Hello! So good to see you! I hear you and the South African Indian Congress are working in the Natal Province into forming a very effective Anti-Segregation Council, correct?"

"Yes, Father John, and we are making a lot of progress. We are organized against all this terrible anti-Indian legislation. Especially, I'm happy to say, against the

104

'Pegging Law,' an abomination. Our membership is increasing day by day."

Before any more small talk occurs between the two, a bell rings and Alfred B. Xuma, as President of the ANC, opens the meeting. "Welcome, everyone! Let's begin after our African prayer." They all sing: *Nkosi Sikelel iAfrica* in unison.

After the usual long discussions about the difficulties Blacks, Coloreds, Indians are facing from the Smuts government, the first focus is on the recently enacted *Natives (Urban Areas) Consolidation Act No. 25.*

Everyone agrees that the Smuts government has trashed its word to lighten up on the 'Pass Laws' and has not only drastically restricted Blacks' ability to stay in urban areas but also allowed the government to deport Blacks leading an idle or dissolute life, or not working, or guilty of certain offenses, under new legislation.

Of course, many calls for disobedience come from some attendees, especially the Communists. The unionists shout words of agreement.

From the back of the room, Walter Sisulu shouts, "I think now we should hold an organized burning of the Pass Books."

After some discussion, eventually more level heads prevail and that talk of burning Pass Books fails. The room fills with silence until President Xuma introduces Albert Simpson to report on possible actions from the Smuts-controlled Parliament.

After limited applause, Albert Simpson stands behind the podium after setting aside his cane.

"Hello! Let me give you a quick update about what my friends tell me that some Members of Parliament and the Smuts administration may be planning."

He sees that he has the attention of his audience.

"First, for my Indian friends, there has been much discussion about restraining Indians in South Africa. While, as yet, no legislation after the 'Pegging Law' has been introduced, many meetings among proponents have occurred."

He hears the groans, but continues, "The gist of this kind of legislation would create definite hardships for Indians in South Africa. In essence, these proposed laws would place all Asians in ghetto areas near the cities, terminate economic and business opportunities for Indians, and prohibit Asian ownership or occupation of property without a government permit. Should these proposals ever become the law in South Africa, then I would expect a mass uprising from all Asians, especially the Indians in the Natal Province. And in Durban, where Indians may outnumber Whites, there could be riots."

The shouting drowns Albert Simpson's continuance for several minutes until President Xuma quiets the audience, many of whom stand with arms flaying.

Albert Simpson says, "I understand your anger, but there's more. As you may know, the Smuts administration is bending over backwards to appease the Afrikaners who outwardly worked against South Africa's support for Britain and the Allies against Nazi Germany. As you know, Smuts and his United Party won control of the House of Assembly in 1943 because of the votes from returning war veterans and from the active duty military. And, Smuts won because of the non-voter-registration of many Afrikaners and because of the disunity of the Afrikaners' organizations. And, my friends, that win for Smuts came in spite of the fact that the Afrikaners comprise almost fifty-five percent of the electorate!"

To agreeable exclamations from the audience, Albert Simpson holds up his hand.

"Now, you know the Smuts administration has enacted war pensions, old age pensions, and disability pensions but the amount payable to non-White pensioners is drastically less than the amount paid to White pensioners. You've heard, no doubt, that Malan and his party opposed the enactment of this pension legislation because payment to Black pensioners would undermine White farmers to get work from these, and I quote, these naturally lazy Natives, end quotes. Malan wants to stir up Afrikaner dislike of Jan Smuts as a prelude to the 1948 election."

Several shouts of disgruntlement reach Albert Simpson, who again gives the stop sign with his hand and then continues.

"But don't think for a minute that the Smuts administration isn't sitting down for the next election. They are currying favor with the Whites. Notice that there's no talk favoring Blacks, Coloreds, or Indians. They know who butters their bread."

Someone shouts, "Shameful when the current numbers show more than a thousand Blacks, all volunteers, died for their country against the Axis powers."

Another voice declares, "I read in the newspapers that the leader of the Reunited National Party during the war protested in Parliament the use by Non-Europeans as gunners during the war."

Albert Simpson responds, "Yes, that's right. So, for the upcoming election in 1948, we must instill religious fervor into every White voter since our Black and Indian friends, and most Coloreds, have been effectively disenfranchised. There's more talk that the *Ossewa Brandwag* will be using every election trick known to humanity to sway the Afrikaners to vote for favorable candidates for Parliament. How would you like to see Daniel F. Malan as the next Prime Minister after the 1948 elections?"

The partisan crowd shouts, "NO WAY! NO WAY!"

Albert Simpson points with his right hand to the audience, 'Remember, my friends, Malan's party won every seat in Parliament that Smut's party didn't win in 1943. If we don't act, the handwriting is on the wall, and I don't like what I see. Well, then, we need to inspire our White friends under our compulsory voter registration law to go to the voting booth and to vote right! If we don't . . ."

Before Albert Simpson can finish, from the back of the room, someone hollers, "Yes, but we also need to stop this oppression! We need to shut down this government. We need work stoppages and strikes. And, yes boycotts! And, demonstrations, too! And if necessary, we should be ready to go to prison!"

Someone joins in, "So far, we've obtained no progress in getting Smuts and his cronies to lighten up by cooperating with them. I think more drastic action is what we need! If we put the fear of God into them, we'll get some results! Filing petitions and petitions and petitions will not get us anywhere! We just get more of the same! They'll never invite us to sit with them at the table! We need action!"

Another loud voice says, "Isn't it time we quit writing petitions and quit parading outside government offices with handwritten signs? No matter the size of the crowd, even with a few White faces, we've gotten

108

nowhere with the Smuts government. These demonstrations have not been effective and, in my opinion, just anger Whites by blocking traffic and access to government offices. Don't you think it's time that we convey a message to the government that a revolution is coming? That's what we need: a Revolution!"

Father John identifies the three voices as coming from Nelson Mandela, Walter Sisulu, and Oliver Tambo who are sitting next to the three Communists, who are clapping encouraging hands. Ruth First actually pats a seated Oliver Tambo on his shoulder and then loudly claps her hands. He notices that Father Huddleston is seated with the Communists.

Oliver Tambo, rising from his chair, shouts, "We've achieved nothing by telling our children to speak softly, dress well, and mind your manners. Be dignified around Whites. Avoid saying anything offensive to Whites or doing anything that will make Whites look down on Black people. That talk has gotten us nowhere! That kind of talk makes racial discrimination acceptable. It's time we stand up for our rights!"

Father John cannot determine who is and who isn't agreeing among the shouting Black attendees, but he calculates plenty of agreeing voices.

But, President Xuma eventually quiets the crowd and calls on several older members of the ANC to speak in opposition.

The elder members of the ANC argue that the country doesn't need a civil war. They point out that Gandhi backed down the government's attack on Indians by using non-violent resistance.

Cooling tempers ends any talk of violence.

Father John raises his hand to speak and getting an affirmative nod from President Xuma, he stands and says, "Yes, we do need more positive action but not violent action. In 1919, the ANC sent a delegation to London to meet with the Prime Minister about South Africa's segregation policy and, in spite of a sympathetic reception, were told this was a problem to be solved by South Africa."

Someone shouts, "Yes and where did that get us? Not anywhere!"

Father John replies, "Yes, that's true. But, times have changed. Right now, Prime Minister Smuts is attending the opening session of the United Nations General Assembly, who will vote on approval of fundamental rights for all people. I have it on good authority that several countries, especially India, may seek censure against South Africa because of the discrimination against Indians in South Africa."

There is a cheer in the back.

"We need a champion to tell about South Africa's racial segregation as a contradiction to human rights. I think we should send President Xuma to America to argue our case. In case you didn't know, President Xuma is well known both in America, where he received a degree from the University of Minnesota and well known in Britain, where he received a medical degree in Scotland.

"With pressure from the rest of the world, the Smuts government will have to curtail its segregationist policies."

To sustained applause, the group decides to study the situation and, when the time is ripe, to ask the ANC to send President Xuma to America to speak at the United

Nations meeting against South Africa's racial segregation policy.

The group, by majority vote, agrees to reason with the government and to sway Whites that segregation is morally corrupt. They agree to get out the White vote for the oncoming election in 1948. Nonetheless, the younger members want more positive action, such as boycotts, strikes, work stoppages, and perhaps sabotage, but—for the moment—will accede to the will of the majority.

At the close, the group promises to meet again for more strategy sessions. They again sing the African hymn.

As Father John waits for Albert Simpson to work his way through the crowd, he finds himself standing next to Chief Albert Luthuli and he sees Nelson Mandela, Oliver Tambo, and Walter Sisulu engaging the three Communists.

"Chief, I worry that your three young friends may be buying into Communism," Father John says.

"Oh, Father John, don't worry about Nelson because, like me, he is a strong believer in God and in Christianity and has a Methodist upbringing. Those atheists will never touch Nelson. Besides, he's told me that we are in a racial struggle, not a class struggle with the South African government. He may associate with the Communists, but he will not become one of them. Nelson will get the Communists to do things his way. He will actually convince them, not the other way around. He will use them to meet his goals.

"About Walter and Oliver, I don't know. These two are very independent. I can't predict what they'll do."

Father John smiles and takes his leave. Finding Albert Simpson, the priest heads for the door.

He says, "Albert, the fact that these diverse groups have actually met and have organized raise my great hope that racial segregation's curtailment and its ultimate end is dead center in the spotlight."

Using his cane to walk, Albert agrees, "Praise the Lord, if that comes to pass."

Father John adds, "Albert, look how much progress this country has made since the British Empire in 1834 abolished slavery. The country survived the Great Trek when the majority of Dutch farmers pulled up stakes in the Cape Colony and moved inland, taking with them their belief that Blacks equaled cheap labor. Progress did come to the Cape Colony. Now, if we can just convince the consciences of Whites how immoral segregation is, then maybe, just maybe we can get a new Parliament to overturn the inequality in the law."

Albert Simpson replies, "Father, people usually vote their pocketbooks. We have to show them that the government's policy of segregation hurts Whites just as much as Blacks. That'll be a hard sell to the Afrikaners when their church supports segregation and when Smuts is bending over backwards to comply with their wishes."

Father John says, "I understand what you're saying. I guess I'm just dreaming, just hoping. But, here it is, June of 1945, I think we can convince enough people before the 1948 elections, don't you, Albert?"

"Yes, Father. But even if we defeat Malan, we will still have the Smuts' government in place. I don't see Smuts changing his views."

As Father John and Albert travel in separate vehicles to the Simpson home, the priest says a silent prayer that soon racial segregation will yield to racial equality,

Then, he adds silently, "And, please, Dear God, help us defeat Daniel F. Malan, who surely will worsen our plight, should his party win control of Parliament in 1948."

Chapter 9

Charles and Mary awaken as the bus pulls into a Security Checkpoint just outside of the town of Bloemfontein, headquarters of the South African judiciary. Since the police examination for Pass Books and travel documents devours little time, the bus travels easily to the Bloemfontein bus terminal.

Mary exclaims, "Charles, this is a beautiful town! I wish we could get off and walk around, even go into the countryside."

Overhearing, the man across from Charles comments with a toothy smile, "Well, yes, it is a beautiful town, but going out into the countryside could be dangerous since the area is full of cheetahs. You know, cheetahs are one of the fastest running animals in South Africa. You can run, but you can't out run a cheetah."

Mary smiles a thank you.

Immediately before the bus stops, the driver announces, "You may leave your carry on things in the bus since we'll be stopped for about one hour. I advise you to eat something here and use the toilet. This bus will make very limited stops for passengers to depart before we arrive at Beaufort West where you can get a room for the night. You will re-board in Bloemfontein before any new passengers. Please keep your tickets with you so you can re-board. Thank you."

As they exit the bus, Charles notices a huge sign over the front entrance: *Vir Gebruik Deur Blankes* and other words in Afrikaans. Below in English hangs another huge sign; Charles reads what must be the translation from the big sign:

"For the Exclusive use of White Persons: These Public Premises and the Amenities thereof have been reserved for the Exclusive Use of White Persons.

By Order: Provincial Secretary"

Charles sees another sign in English, "For Black Persons" and motions for Mary to follow an arrow pointing to the entrance in the rear of the building, near the garbage containers.

Having agreed to conserve their limited funds, they each order fruit juice, chips, and a baloney sandwich served on coarse brown bread. Charles remembers that white bread is still scarce during the War because of government rationing and those policies are still in effect. Raised mostly on white bread, he still doesn't like eating the coarse brown bread.

Downing their supper, they line up for the toilets.

Charles has a good laugh when he sees Mary holding her nose as she exits the women's toilet.

They wait for the boarding time and then Mary and Charles follow the bus driver to the bus and take their seats.

Re-seated, they welcome four new passengers, two young women with two small children, both well behaved.

As they leave the outskirts of Bloemfontein, Mary and Charles converse about what their new life will be in Cape Town. Mary suggests they meet the priest, Father Vincent, recommended by Father John. Agreed, they settle in for the long ride.

The towns of Edenburg, Springfontein, Coleburg, Richmond, and Three Sisters eventually come into and out of their view as Charles and Mary doze. As the bus approaches Beaufort West, the driver pulls off the high road into a Security Checkpoint.

After two Security Policemen, one White and one Black are satisfied that every one of the passengers has a legal Pass Book or travel documents with matching identify cards, the bus enters the city limits of Beaufort West, but on an obviously poorer side of town.

As the bus stops in front of a run-down hotel, the driver says, "Well, folks, it's twenty minutes after midnight. At this hotel, the bus company has arranged for you to receive a discount on a room. You cannot sleep on the bus. It isn't safe to sleep outside. Please take all of your luggage and belongings since they may not be safe on the bus, even though I will lock the door. The bus will leave tomorrow morning at eight o'clock. I will need to see your tickets before you board. Have a good night."

Charles and Mary secure a room for the night. Although they are bone-tired from sitting on the bus, they make love, their second time.

Arising and at Mary's suggestion, they skimp on breakfast, each having some fruit, strong coffee, toast and jam. Charles learns from another passenger that Cape Town is about 500 kilometers from Beaufort West.

The man says, "I ride this bus often. It'll take about eight to nine hours because we have to stop at two or three checkpoints before we even get there. The authorities are cracking down on too many Natives moving to Cape Town."

Charles asks, "Are there plenty of jobs in Cape Town, sir? Do they pay well? What about housing for me and my wife?"

The man says, "Housing is scarce and a lot of people live in the shanty towns where you can just find a space and set up a shelter. But, if you're willing to work, the jobs are there. Some pay very good and some don't. If you need a job, see my friend, Tabo Jabavu, who is the labor boss at a construction company. Mention my name, Robert Sobukwe. Here is his name and address."

Charles replies, "Thank you very much, Mr. Sobukwe," and hands the note to Mary for safekeeping in her straw bag of a purse.

As Mary places the note in her purse, she realizes that she has forgotten to read Albert Simpson's note to Frederick Kruger. She unfolds the paper and sees that Mr. Simpson has mentioned that she and Charles are friends of Father John O'Malley and to help them relocate. She hands the note to Charles, who, after reading, returns the note to Mary for safekeeping.

Taking the same seats two rows behind the driver, they settle in for the long ride as the thunder claps overhead and the rain starts falling.

First, the bus stops outside of Lainsburg for a Security Police check. One passenger is removed from the bus since the policeman claims his Pass Book has been altered.

Driving into Lainsburg, the bus driver announces, "Friends, it is lunch time. We'll be stopped her for an hour so you can use the toilet or purchase a snack. Our next stop will be in Paarl, about four or five hours away. Maybe six since we may run into more rain. Looks like a break from the rain, right now. You can leave your things on the bus. Don't worry, the door will be locked."

Charles and Mary are surprised that most of the passengers disembarking in the town of Lainsburg won't continue onward. They bid a farewell to Tabo Jabavu and thank him again for his help. Now, besides themselves, only an elderly woman and a young teenage girl remain on the bus. Explaining, the driver says, "All those people live in the town."

After hours of difficult driving in the rain, the bus reaches the Security Checkpoint just outside of Paarl, pulls into a covered area in front of a small house, and waits until three Security Policemen enter. Review of Pass Books and travel documents is completed in less than ten minutes and the bus is headed for the terminal inside Paarl.

The bus driver advises the few remaining passengers, "I suggest that you use the toilet and get a snack before we reach Cape Town, just about 65 kilometers away. Yes, it's not too far but the rain will slow us down. We will have to ford some streams, you see, and that will slow us down. Or, we may just have to stop because of the rain."

When the bus pulls into the terminal, the rain also has momentarily stopped, but still, everyone runs for the covering over the entry for Non-Europeans. Fortunately, Charles and Mary have the raincoats from the Simpsons.

When the bus is ready for re-boarding, four young Black men join Mary and Charles along with the elderly woman and the young girl, maybe 15 or 16 years old. Mary surmises that the young girl is probably the elderly woman's granddaughter.

The four young Black men are carrying duffel bags.

Nobody carries an umbrella and, besides Charles and Mary, only the bus driver has a rain coat. But, fortunately, there is a break in the rain.

Charles and Mary sit two rows behind the bus driver while the elderly woman and the young girl sit on the opposite side, six rows from the front.

Charles notices that three of the men have scruffy beards and are wearing army fatigues. The other man, apparently the group's leader, wears a brown suitcoat and trousers, and a black tie over his white long-sleeved shirt. His face reflects a clean, recent shave.

Two of the men sit across from Charles, in the front of the bus, while one trudges midway and sits in a huff behind the elderly woman and the young girl.

Turning around and looking toward the back, Mary sees what she thinks is a leer in the man's eyes as he leans forward and places his face close behind the young girl's neck. A little worry crosses Mary's face as she notices only one of the Black men is clean shaven.

The man in the suit walks to the rear of the bus as if he owns it.

As the bus gets underway, thunder booms and the rain begins with its drops increasing in size and sound.

Mary watches the rain splatter the windows.

About 5 minutes pass as the driver nears a big highway intersection a few miles on the other side of Paarl.

Although the windows are fogged, Mary sees a highway sign showing Cape Town is straight ahead and that Stellenbosch is to the left.

Suddenly, one of the young men across from Charles stands and moves toward the driver. He pulls a pistol from his duffel bag and shouts, "Take the road to Stellenbosch, NOW!"

The other man stands and points his pistol at Charles and directs, "Keep your seat! And don't try anything! Understand?"

Eyeing the pointed gun, the driver instantly obeys and turns onto the road to Stellenbosch.

Charles and Mary dare not move but see that the third man behind the elderly woman and the young girl has a knife pointed at the young girl's neck and that he has grasped a handful of her hair. A leer of lust enfolds his face.

Looking to the rear of the bus, Charles and Mary see that the man in the suit is moving to the front of the bus and acts in command.

The man in the suit stops and says, "Listen carefully and nobody will get hurt. Take out your wallets and your purses and hand them to me as I pass by."

He says to the bus driver, "I'll get yours when we stop. Now everyone, just keep your seats and keep quiet. Do that and nobody gets hurt."

Trying to maintain her composure, Mary retrieves her small purse from inside the big bag, but not the loose coins or the notes. Quickly, she scoots the straw bag underneath the seat. She hands the small purse to the man in the suit.

Charles gives the man his wallet.

The man in the suit, after collecting Charles' wallet and the women's purses, grabs the bills and tosses the wallet and the purses to their owners. He says, "Thanks. Now just relax, look out the window, and nobody gets hurt!"

Mary then peers out the window spattered with raindrops, but can see only a little vegetation along the roadway, but not any lights.

Eventually, she sees a road sign showing a "Y" and an arrow pointing to the left and the town of Wemmershock and an arrow pointing to the right and the town of Stellenbosch.

The man in the suit, now sitting behind the driver and directly in front of Charles and Mary, directs "Follow the road to Stellenbosch. Continue on this road passed the towns of Pniel and Lanquedoc. You stay on this road until I tell you where to turn off. You got that?"

As the driver complies, Mary sees a few lights from houses or businesses on either side of the road, but as the bus passes the town of Lanquedoc, the last of the scarce lights disappear. Mary tightly grips Charles hand.

A few minutes pass before the command comes that the bus must slow so the driver can turn to the right onto an unmarked road, more like a path than a road.

When the bus has followed the now muddy road around a bend so as to be hidden from the paved road, the man in the suit says, "All right, Mister Bus Driver, hand me your wallet. And pull off the road into that open area beneath the big tree. The rest of you, get your bags down from the rack and open them so we can see if you have anything of value."

The four men find nothing worth keeping in their search for anything of value, but they overlook Mary's straw bag on the floor.

One thug says to the driver and to Charles, "Pick up those bags and get off the bus with them! Hey, wait!

Get all those carry-on items, too. Take all of it off the bus!"

Mary hands Charles her straw bag, while the elderly woman hands the driver a small suitcase and a paper bag half full of what appears to be clothing. The young girl gives the driver a small carry-on case.

One of the thugs takes the driver's seat. The other two follow the exit of the driver and Charles and all the bags and carry-ons.

Luckily, the rain has halted as Charles, the driver, and the two thugs stand outside.

All carry-on bags are set aside and one thug examines the contents, but overlooks Mary's straw bag when he hears the other thug.

The other thug says to the driver, "Open the baggage compartment."

As he complies, the thug asks, "Whose is that?"

Charles says, "That's mine and my wife's."

"Open it!" the thug commands, and as Charles obeys, the thug searches finding nothing of value.

"Whose are those bags?' he asks.

"That lady and the girl" the driver replies, "but it might be locked."

"It doesn't matter. If locked, rip it open!"

But, neither suitcase is locked. Rummaging through each bag, the thug discovers some jewelry and, not realizing it is costume jewelry, hurriedly tosses it a sack.

Motioning to the other thug, He says, "Get those other parcels and packages inside the baggage bay and put those inside the bus. There are always some valuables in those parcels. And get the ropes from my duffel bag."

The thug guarding Charles and the driver points his pistol and says, "Don't get any ideas, boys, because my gun has bullets with your names on them! Just sit tight and keep quiet. And, I promise, you won't get hurt. We try not to kill anyone. So, keep your mouths shut and don't try nothing."

One of the thugs brings the ropes.

The two thugs quickly tie the driver's and Charles' hands behind in the back so tightly that both men cry out, especially when forced to sit. Next, the robbers bind each man's feet.

"Now, just sit and keep quiet. If you don't, I'll stuff this rag in your mouth!" one thug threatens as he stands guard.

The other thug re-boards the bus.

Of course, Mary and the elderly woman cannot see that the driver and Charles are hog-tied and incapable of returning to the bus. The teenaged girl is still in the clutches of the thug with a knife pointed at her neck.

The man in the suit says to Mary and the elderly woman, "The men are outside, tied up, and cannot help you. I want you to pull up your dresses and pull down your panties. Obey us and you won't get hurt and neither will the men tied up outside. Just relax and enjoy it!"

The thug holding the young girl says, "I want the young girl. I need some tight pussy this time. You get the old lady this time," he shouts to the thug who re-boarded the bus. "You can stick it in her butt hole if you want it tight," he laughs

At first, Mary's ready to defend herself, but when the man in the suit produces a six-inch switch-blade from his pocket, she realizes she will be raped no matter what. She worries that her husband will be harmed if she fights her attacker. But those rational thoughts do not prevent her from crying as the man in the suit penetrates her vagina and, almost in minutes, his sperms shoots inside.

Mary hears the anguish cry from the young girl from the first assault and then her repeated screams from the second. She knows she will never forget the pleas of the elderly woman trying to save her granddaughter from violation, even though the elderly woman offers to sacrifice herself, even by giving oral sex to the two thugs.

Mary wishes that she did not memorize the man in the suit's voice, his smell, his touch, and the pleasure in his smile on his face. She understands that no matter how hard she tries, those horrible qualities will stick with her memory whenever any sign or symptom, accidental or intentional, clues her brain electrodes to ignite the memory.

Within ten or fifteen minutes, the four rapists have finished their assaults. The man in the suit ushers Mary, the elderly woman, and the teenaged girl off the bus.

As she exits the bus, the elderly woman exclaims, "You can't leave us out here! There are wild animals out here! We don't have any weapons to defend ourselves! Have you no mercy? Please, don't leave us out here!"

The man in the suit says, "Quit that crying, lady! Just take the dirt road and walk back to the main road. It's about five kilometers to the town."

Her continued pleas fall indifferently as the bus door closes with the four men inside. The motor starts and the bus leaves, stranding the five people in the dark.

With some difficulty, the women manage to untie the driver and Charles.

Immediately, Charles hugs and kisses Mary amid his words. "Mary, I'm so sorry I couldn't help you. I'm so sorry. When we get to the police station, we will tell them about these robbers and bring them to justice. I have made a mental picture of each one. We will catch them and make them pay. I'm so sorry, Mary!"

Mary responds, "I know, Charles. I know you couldn't help. But, I do not want to report this rape to the police. We can report the robbery, but not the rape. I don't want there to be a record because I'll have to live this shame in public. I don't want that. I could never live it down! It will be bad enough to have the memory!"

She turns to the elderly woman, "Do you want that for yourself and for your granddaughter?"

As the elderly woman shakes her head negatively, she explains, "No, we don't. In reality, the police will do nothing. Absolutely nothing will happen to help us. Instead we will be shamed forever. It will be another rape by the Natives and on the Natives. They'll say, 'Well, that's the way these Africans live.' It's better to let this live just between ourselves. Just tell the police about the robbery. We will all be better off, if we just forget about the rape."

At first, the driver and Charles protest, but eventually each man swears to keep the rapes of the women and the horror of the rapes to themselves, never to be revealed without the consent of the woman raped.

Then, Mary calmly says, "Good, and I thank each of you for your silence. I'm Mary and this is my husband Charles."

The bus driver responds, "You're right, Mary. I'm William Noah." He reaches for Charles' hand and pats the elderly woman on her shoulder and smiles at the young girl.

"Yes, I'm Ruthie and this is my granddaughter, Maggie. We are pleased to meet you."

Mary suggests, "Let's walk toward that glow in the low sky, which must be the town of Stellenbosch."

She hears no opposition and picks up her suit case and her straw bag. The others follow suit carrying their luggage, while Charles and William Noah assist Ruthie and Maggie with their things.

As the five people head for what they believe is the town of Stellenbosch, they hear a roar from some wild animal.

Ruthie, the elderly lady, exclaims, "That sounds like a lion! Lordy, I don't want to be eaten by a lion! What can we do?"

William, the bus driver, says, "Now, ma'am, I don't think it's a lion because the Dutch and the English have hunted the Cape lions into extinction. So, it'll be all right. You women get behind Charles and I'll bring up the rear. I'll be looking around to see if anything is following us. It'll be all right."

Taking the lead with Mary directly behind him, Charles hears Mary whisper, "If it's a lion, Charles, it'll be a lioness first because she's the scout for the whole pride. We'd better hurry!"

William says, "Now, everyone, please calm down. It's probably a cheetah."

The roar comes again from the bush.

William shouts, "Charles, don't stay on the side of the road. Get in the middle of the road so we all can see better! If anything comes, hit it with the suitcase!"

Ruthie declares, "Those evil men didn't even leave us with any kind of weapon to protect ourselves. May they rot in Hell!"

Her granddaughter is holding tightly to Ruthie's skirt.

Their pace quickens as they complete the first kilometer and round a bend in the two-lane road, the surface still glowing wet with rain.

Suddenly, the bush rustles with movement.

Chapter 10

Returning from an inspection of his vineyards near Stellenbosch, Frederick Kruger slows his Ford truck to cross water flowing over the charcoaled crown of the paved roadway. Fortunately, the sheets of rain have dribbled to a stop and he has a reasonably clear view with no fog, as his high beams illuminate the tarmac roadway.

As soon as he rounds the bend, he sees in the middle of the road five figures with all arms waving. He counts two Black men and two Black women, one of whom appears to have a pronounced limp, and a young Black girl. The lady with the limp appears to be elderly.

Frederick slows as the people hurry to the side of the road as if they will be getting a ride. He sees them all waving their arms and through the closed windows hears them shouting something.

But he doesn't stop his truck because he remembers the reports of good Samaritans relieved of their wallets and pocketbooks after stopping to help strangers in deserted areas. As he drives passed the startled people, Frederick looks sideways to see where he suspects any main force of bandits might be hiding.

However, when he discovers no hidden robbers and obeying his conscience and moral upbringing, he slows his truck. The five people hurry toward his truck.

Frederick rolls down his window, shouting, "Please stand in front of the truck so I can see you!"

They comply.

The bus driver shouts, "Sir, we've been robbed and four men stole my bus! We need to get to town. To notify the police! And, we just heard some roaring from the bush, over there! Please help us!"

"Come on," Frederick waves toward the group. He has heard the stories about White police forcing a Black bus to use back roads if bribes aren't paid.

He has heard stories about Blacks masquerading as police who demand 'travel fees' from each Black passenger, the price based on the Black passenger's rich appearance. A refusal or a failure to pay means the Black passenger will be yanked from the bus, relieved of his wallet, pummeled before being allowed to slip away into the bush.

He's heard stories about Black women taken from the bus, by both White policemen and by the fake Black policemen, robbed, and violated.

"Come on," Frederick repeats, scanning the bush for any roaming wild animals. He sees movement but no animals.

He expects the two Black women and the young girl to ride inside the cab and the others to climb in the bed of the truck. But, instinctively, the Black driver and the elderly Black woman and the young Black girl head to the truck bed, while the young couple opens the passenger door to ride inside the cab with the White man.

He sees that the woman is Black and the man is Colored.

Inside the truck, Frederick welcomes Charles and Mary, hears their story of the robbery, and proceeds to drive to the Stellenbosch police station.

He says, "Well, at least they didn't harm you and we can thank the Good Lord for that. There are some very horrible stories about these robbers. By the way, I'm Frederick Kruger and you are …"

Wide-eyed, Charles and Mary stare at the man and, finally tongue-tied, Mary and Charles introduce themselves.

Mary tentatively says, "Sir, Mr. Kruger, I have a letter, or I mean, a note from Albert Simpson about my husband and me," as she reaches for the envelope inside the straw bag.

She hands him the note, but he says, "I'll look at when we stop at the police station. I see we're just about two blocks away. But how do you know Albert Simpson?"

Interrupting each other, Mary and Charles explain.

Frederick Kruger says, "Very interesting. Well, let's go inside so the police can make a record of what happened."

After receiving a warm greeting from the policeman on duty, who gathers the five people for his report, the policeman asks Mr. Kruger, "Now, is the date June the sixteenth or the seventeenth?"

Before Frederick can replay, Mary quickly answers, "Sir, it is June seventeenth since we just got married two days ago on the fifteenth."

As the policeman writes his report, Mr. Kruger reads Albert Simpsons' handwritten note:

"Frederick: Charles and Mary Washington, recently married, are friends of Father John and need employment in Cape Town. Both are hardworking, honest, and decent people. Charles is educated and has experience as a gardener. Both speak excellent English. They are good people. Help them if you can."

Frederick Kruger carefully reviews what appears to be the signature of his friend, Albert Simpson.

Over the police radio in the station, they all hear a patrolling policeman report that he has found the stolen bus on the other side of town.

"It's empty," the radio voice crackles.

Mr. Kruger surmises, "Well, I suppose the robbers had a getaway car parked where they dumped the bus. Can the driver retrieve the bus, officer?"

William, the bus driver, responds, "If the police don't want it, I sure will, tonight," and looking at his passengers, "Don't worry! You can all go with me and get another bus to Cape Town in the morning. Plus, I'll get the bus company to put you up for the night without charge."

The on-duty policeman, knowing that they won't take any fingerprints or look for any other clues, says, "We don't need the bus. So, yes you can take it tonight. Mr. Kruger, would you mind driving them to the bus since we are a little short tonight on personnel. It's just a two or three minute drive from here."

Frederick Kruger says, "Yes, certainly, just give me the exact location. That's fine, but Charles and Mary will be coming with me since I've a job for them."

Naturally, surprise rests on everyone's face, but the faces of Mary and Charles bear the most surprise.

With William, Ruth, and Maggie in the truck bed with all the luggage and with Mary and Charles inside the cab with Mr. Kruger on their way to the site of the stolen bus, Mary and Charles listen as Mr. Kruger explains that his gardener has recently quit, along with his wife and they also need some household help, particularly since his wife is expecting their second child.

"The man and his brother are opening a *shebeen* in the Northern Cape," Frederick explains to Mary's and Charles' questioning eyes for the man's reason for leaving.

Innocently, Charles asks, "What's a *shebeen*?"

Before Frederick responds, Mary smirks, "It's a low class bar with music and dancing and prostitutes for Natives! I don't want to ever see you in one, Charles!"

Seeing the surprise on Charles' face, Frederick correctly guesses Charles has never been in one. He also ignores Mary's remark because he's well aware that many Black men treat Black women as passive adults with the privileges of children in the traditional Native social order. He does recognize that the Zulu women are reputed to be faithful and obedient while the Xhosa women bear a promiscuous reputation. As a Member of Parliament, he knows the State treats all Black women as cheap labor units. He understands why Mary must feel that way about the *shebeens*.

But, Frederick also knows that many *shebeens* serve as meeting places for activists against racial segregation since Blacks are prohibited from drinking in bars and pubs. Many also serve as community meeting places in rural areas. As a matter of fact, he met some people at one *shebeen* last week when connecting with some opponents of racial segregation. But, he also knows that many serve as houses of prostitution.

He continues talking about the employment of Mary and Charles.

"That is, of course, if you are interested. We live very near downtown Cape Town and have a small furnished house not too far away in an area known as District Six. And, all utilities are included with the house. The house just vacated. I will pay you both a living wage equal to if not better than what others pay for similar employment. But, Mary, you must work to help my wife with the house work and our son and Charles you must attend to the gardens and perhaps a little carpenter work. Well, what do you say?"

Neither Charles nor Mary hesitates to accept, as they all exchange handshakes to seal the deal.

***

After signaling to the two armed guards outside the huge stone wall and iron fence, Frederick drives through the big wrought iron gate and enters the Kruger homestead very near the biological gardens of Cape Town.

Charles says, "Excuse me, but Father John told us that everything is wonderful in Cape Town and people get along fine with each other. Why do you need guards and walls around you home?"

"Yes, it's true that people do get along here in Cape Town, but unfortunately, many poor people are moving here, just as they are to all the cities. Some of them steal so it is necessary to have protection. These two guards, one White and one Black, work for the protection service we hire."

"That's understandable," Charles says.

Frederick drives to the house. His pregnant wife, Henrietta, and his nine-year-old son, Hans, meet his truck just outside the front door.

After introductions, Frederick says, "Darling, Charles has agreed to work as our gardener and Mary will help you around the house. They will stay in the District Six house, but they'll spend the night with us and we'll show them the house tomorrow."

Seeing Henrietta's curiosity, he explains, "Albert and Josie Simpson and Father John O'Malley recommended them. They just got married by the magistrate in Nelspruit and were on a bus to Cape Town when some men took control of the bus, took the bus toward Stellenbosch, and robbed the passengers. After all that, I happened to be returning from the vineyards and came upon them walking on the roadway."

Understanding, Henrietta quickly offers her hand to Charles and Mary. "Yes, of course, and you will stay for supper. Frederick, while I finish in the kitchen, please show them to the guest bedroom so they can wash up and store their things."

When Charles and Mary return, Henrietta invites Mary into the kitchen to finish the supper preparations, while Frederick steers Charles to the living room so he can chat with Charles about some of the chores a gardener performs. He points to the windows which show some of the flower beds and the vegetable gardens.

In the kitchen, Henrietta works to make Mary comfortable and Mary reveals the circumstances of their marriage. "So, you and Charles are newly-weds, married just two days ago, after eloping. Congratulations, Mary!"

But, in looking around the spacious kitchen, Mary volunteers that she is not familiar with many of the household things. She explains, "Before my marriage to Charles, I lived in a Zulu tribal compound and many of these things I do not know in our village. We are strangers to each other, these gadgets and me. Forgive me for my ignorance."

Henrietta declares, "My dear, don't worry. I also had to learn about some of these gadgets, as you call them. You will catch on quickly. You will be a fast learner. So, Mary, just listen and watch me. It will be fine. So, don't worry."

"Yes, Ms. Kruger."

"Now, Mary; my name is Henrietta. Not Ms. Kruger. Both Frederick and I prefer you call us by our first names. Understood?

"Yes, Ms. Kruger, I mean, Henrietta."

"Fine. I'm adding two plates to the table in the dining room. Now, do me a favor and have the husbands come to the table for supper."

Henrietta tells nine-year-old Hans to take his usual seat.

During the supper meal, Frederick says, "Since you are new to the Cape Province, let me tell you both that racial segregation is kept to a very minimum here, unlike in the rest of the Provinces. District Six is very close and you can walk from here to there. You will find in District Six, a wonderful intermingling of people—Blacks, Coloreds, Asians, and Whites. District Six is not far from the center of Cape Town and consists mainly of artists, craftsmen, musicians, small shopkeepers with a wonderful example of harmony and cooperation by, of, and among all races. It's a very good community."

Henrietta adds, "Tomorrow, we'll take some household things to the District Six house. It is furnished, but you will need some knives and forks, bed things and towels, and kitchen stuff to get you started. I'll bring those. You can get your groceries at the local store.

"And, you won't have any trouble making new friends."

**

After supper, Charles and Mary retire to the guest room and get ready for bed. They are both pleased to have arrived at the Kruger homestead and have employment.

But, eventually, the return in their memories of what happened on the bus impacts their faces, and with eye glances, each waits for the other person to open the conversation.

But, down deep, neither Mary nor Charles wants to discuss Mary's violation.

Finally, Mary takes Charles' hand and gently kisses his forehead. "Charles, my dear, I don't think I'm ready for any love-making for a while. I hope you understand, my dear."

Kissing her check, Charles says ever so softly, "My dear, dear Mary, yes, I understand. You just tell me when you are ready. I understand completely." He embraces her and holds her protectively.

"Thank you, Charles. I love you," as she tenderly kisses his lips.

"And, I love you. Mary, we'll get through this. Yes, we will, with the Good Lord's Help."

Chapter 11

In the next several weeks, Charles and Mary have tried their best to bury thoughts of what happened on the bus and are focusing on their new life working for Frederick and Henrietta Kruger.

This morning, after the early walk from District Six, Mary and Charles have been invited to breakfast with Henrietta and Frederick. Later, Charles will be working in the vegetable garden while Mary will be helping Henrietta with housework, doing the heavy stuff because of Henrietta's pregnancy. She is due in December, just before Christmas.

When Mary stops her dusting as if she will faint, Henrietta asks, "Mary, are you all right? I notice you seem a little tired this morning. Is something the matter?"

"No, I'm just fine, maybe a little tired."

"Well, I did notice when we cooked the pancakes and fried the eggs for breakfast, you looked a bit ill. I can tell you, I identify with that feeling," she laughs.

Mary looks away.

"And, for just a moment, Mary, I was afraid you might throw up. And, now that I think of it—yesterday, you also looked a little pale."

"No, Henrietta, I'm just a little tired today, that's all."

Suspicious, she asks, "Mary, do you mind if I ask you some questions to see if I can figure out what's causing this?"

Getting no response, Henrietta probes, "Mary, are your breasts tender to your touch? Are they swollen? Are you peeing more than normal? Is your back sore?"

"Yes, that's the case." The words dribble from Mary's mouth.

Almost gleefully, Henrietta asks, "My dear Mary, have you missed a period? When was your last one?"

"Henrietta, that was before we got married, over a month ago."

"Well, in my best medical opinion, these signs tell me that you are pregnant! Congratulations, Mary! I'm so happy for you and Charles!"

Henrietta doesn't understand why Mary's tears aren't tears of joy and why Mary looks like her world is falling apart. Trying to console Mary, she asks, "What is it? What's wrong, Mary?"

When Mary reveals the story of the rape on the bus by the man in the suit, she explains that before she married Charles, she was a virgin and that she and Charles had sex only twice before the assault.

"Just on our wedding night on June 15th and then two days later. So, I don't know if the baby's father is Charles or that horrible man's. Since that night, Charles and I have not had any love-making. That horrible man is still with me. I just couldn't bear to have the man's child! I just couldn't!"

"Mary, does Charles know you are pregnant?"

"No, I'm afraid to tell him."

"Why is that?"

"Because Charles once studied to be a priest and his very strong opinions about …"

"Oh, you mean he wouldn't want you to get an abortion, is that it?"

"Yes, and I don't know what to do."

"I see. Well, I think the first thing is to tell Charles."

Henrietta reaches for Mary and hugs her. "I will help you if you need me. Now, you just take it easy. But, Mary, tonight I suggest you tell your husband."

That late afternoon, with work finished, as Mary and Charles return to their house, Mary avoids what is troubling her and chatters endlessly about nothing important. But she has a plan.

**

Mary's supper that night serves Charles his favorite meal and when he has finished, she says, "Charles, please sit down, because I have something to tell you."

Hearing the news, Charles exclaims, "Mary, that's wonderful! Will it be a boy or a girl? My goodness, I don't care. I just hope the baby will be healthy! That's wonderful! And, thank God for bringing us this joy!"

Jumping from his chair, he reaches for Mary for a hug and a kiss, but she recoils.

"What is it? You don't seem happy. Is there something wrong with the baby? Or is your own health in danger if you carry the baby till birth? What is it?"

From her mouth come the words she has been unable to form with her tongue, "The baby may not be yours, Charles."

Before he can absorb the blow, Mary adds, "Charles, the baby might be that man's who …"

"What? Can't the doctor tell?"

"'Yes, after the baby is born there may be some signs. But, not now, I don't think medicine has that ability in this day and age. And not before the baby is born can anyone be certain."

"Oh! Well, then what's the problem, Mary?"

"The problem is that I don't want that man's baby. I just don't! And, I don't want to take a chance that it's his. I cannot have that baby! I don't want to be reminded with every breathe I take of that violation by that man! I don't want to take the risk and find out! So, I don't want to have that baby!"

"Mary, are you saying what I think you are? No, Mary, I won't agree to that! Plain and simple, that would be murder, against God's Law! No, I won't allow it! I have been taught that life begins at conception. Abortion is a mortal sin, Mary! What would Father John say to us about killing a baby? No, I won't agree to murdering a baby, which might even be my own flesh and blood. I won't allow it!"

Pounding his fist on the table and glaring at his wife, Charles stands, but before he can say another word, Mary calmly says, "Charles, I understand your beliefs but I cannot have that baby. I don't want to take the chance that the baby might be his and not yours. I just can't do it. Do you understand? And, Charles, it's not yet a baby. I hope you understand."

Flustered, Charles hesitates but finally responds, "Yes, I understand and I'm sympathetic to your concerns, because I certainly wouldn't want to raise that man's baby, either. But, I cannot agree that we kill a baby. That's murder. But, I think I have solution to the problem, if you will listen."

Reluctantly, Mary's eyes widen and she bites her lip, waiting to hear his solution.

"What if we have the baby and discover it's not mine? We then put the baby up for adoption. Think about that, Mary. Can you agree to that, my dear?"

She's silent for a moment but hears Charles profess his undying and eternal love and devotion to her. He holds her tightly and smothers her face with tender kisses, finally landing one on her waiting lips.

Smiling, Mary shakes her head affirmatively.

Charles says, "Good. Good. Thanks for agreeing with me."

He is desperate for the subject to change to some other topic.

Finally, his words creep out, "Do you still want to have dinner with our neighbors, Harold and Susan? They seem like fine people and hardworking in their tailor shop."

Noticing how Charles has changed the subject, Mary nevertheless plays along.

"Yes, that would be fine with me. And, yes, that's right and they do a great business with many people from downtown, Whites, Coloreds, Blacks, Asians, and Indians. And, Susan and Harold Langho are very nice people. So, yes, we'll have dinner with them tomorrow. Excuse me, while I go next door and invite them."

**

The next day on Saturday afternoon, with the Kruger's permission, Mary and Charles have the rest of the day off because Mary will be cooking an early supper for their neighbors, Susan and Harold, both Coloreds.

After supper, Harold asks Mary and Charles, "Well, since you don't get out a lot, would you like to see the old Victorian buildings along the waterfront? It's really something special and it's an easy walk from your house. We can stop and have some juice or soda or something and look at all the boats. And the weather is

141

just right, tonight—not too cold and not too hot, even though it's still winter in late July."

Charles comments, "Harold, as I look around District Six, I don't see all those signs forbidding use or entry by Non-Europeans like you do in most of the rest of the country. Is that also true downtown here in Cape Town?"

"Yes. We don't have many of those signs here in District Six or in Cape Town. Here in District Six, people live where they want to. People here live according to their class, not their race. It's a very multi-racial community, with its true name as *Kanaladorp'* translated as 'help one another.' We are lucky to be here," Harold says.

Susan says, "Are you ready for a look around the waterfront?"

Agreeing, the two couples arrive at the waterfront and, a little short of breath but thirsty, stop at one of the waterfront bars located outside the building. After ordering sodas at the outside bar, with Charles paying the tab, they find some seats on the wooden deck. Awaiting their drinks, the two women and Harold sit at one of the wooden tables, while Charles returns to the bar to bring their drinks.

As Charles retrieves the drinks, one of two drunken Afrikaners bumps him and knocks one of the drinks to the wooden deck.

Before Charles can speak, expecting an apology and an offer to pay for the spilled soda, the Afrikaner hollers in English, "You dumb ass, watch where you're going! I think you spilled that shit on one of my boots! I just had those boots shined! Fork over a shilling, you dumb ass! And you Black people shouldn't even be here where liquor is served! It's against the Law! Or, you stupid ass-hole, didn't know that! Pay up or else!"

Charles shouts, "Or what? You should pay for bumping me and for spilling the soda!"

The other Afrikaner grabs Charles from behind and pins Charles arms to his side as the loudmouth socks Charles below his belt.

Harold rises but before he can reach Charles, two White policemen approach, as Charles doubles over onto the wooden deck.

After fault and responsibility are sorted out, Charles and Harold, handcuffed, are placed in a paddy-wagon and taken to the local Cape Town jail, which is really a holding cell so that a magistrate can determine whether the accused should be immediately transported to Pollsmoor Prison in a Cape Town suburb.

Since Susan Langho knows that Pollsmoor Prison owns a notorious reputation as South Africa's most feared and hated place of detention, Susan hurriedly looks for a public phone to call Frederick Kruger before the two men are transferred.

Fortunately, she quickly reaches him and explains the situation.

Frederick says, "Don't worry! I'll phone the magistrate and have the men held until I arrive. I'll have both men released into my custody. Take the bus or a taxi and meet me at the local jail. And, don't worry, Susan. Convey my thoughts to Mary, please."

At the local jail, when the men are offered coffee, a sur-prised Charles says, "I don't believe this! It's not what I expected from the police, even in Cape Town. I expected to be roughed up and thrown in some drunk tank."

Harold replies, "That's because they know Mr. Kruger is our lawyer. Otherwise, we'd be stuck in some piss-smelling tank after a shell of a hearing by the judge and on our way to Pollsmoor Prison, Charles. That we don't want."

When Frederick Kruger arrives, Harold and Charles talk at once about what happened and dispute the 'official' report of the incident.

Frederick Kruger says, "Enough, Harold and Charles! Quit arguing about the damn report, because you won't change a thing. We'll pay a small fine and it'll be over and done with. So let's get out of here and meet Susan and Mary who are in the waiting room."

Charles says, "But, neither of us is guilty. The Afrikaners were dead drunk and started the whole thing! I don't like pleading guilty when I'm not. It's just not right to do that! We should exercise our rights, Mr. Kruger!"

"Listen up, Charles! And don't call me Mr. Kruger. Yes, in a perfect world, I agree with you. But, this is South Africa and the Magistrate is a government appointee and he alone must decide who and what to believe."

"If I may say so, Frederick, we have the four of us as witnesses against the two drunks," Charles argues.

"Yes, that's true. And, if this was a perfect world I would be glad to try your case before the Magistrate. But Charles! Let's look at the real situation.

"You, Harold, Susan, and Mary will tell your version. The two Afrikaners will differ. The bartender, who is White, will side with them, regular customers, no doubt. And the two waitresses will say what? The two Afrikaners will have friends at that bar who will testify for them. Since the two policemen didn't arrest the two Afrikaners, who you claim were drunk, but instead arrested you and Harold, the Magistrate is going to decide against you.

"Since you want a trial, the Magistrate will make sure you get one since you are wasting his time. He will throw the book at you, meaning you'll get the maximum sentence which will include time in prison."

"Oh?" Charles frowns. "But, there were also English-speaking Whites who witnessed what happened."

Mr. Kruger responds, "Yes, they may help you and they may not. We can't chance it and put you in Pollsmoor."

Harold responds, "No, Charles, we don't want any time in Pollsmoor or any other South African detention center. Those prisons are a hole in hell! People are reputed to catch a disease like pneumonia or tuberculosis and never recover. I certainly don't want to catch tuberculosis from one of the other prisoners. I don't want to be in there. A man could die in those prisons."

Mr. Kruger adds, "Charles, what's important is that I believe your story one thousand percent. We will pay a small fine and we will forget this ever happened. So, while you kiss your wives, I'll pay the agreed fine. And, don't worry; you don't have to pay me back."

But, in Charles' mind, the incident is not easily forgotten, and it means he now has a police record. He's smart enough to know that blight could harm him in the future. But, he'll do his best to follow Frederick Kruger's advice.

During the ride to District Six, Charles has remained silent even though Mary has tried to bring him into the conversation. He's trying hard to come to grips with reality in South Africa in 1945. Working for Frederick and Henrietta Kruger, he and Mary have avoided the brunt of racial segregation.

Finally, Frederick deposits the two couples in front of the rent house. They all gush exclamations of gratitude to him. Susan and Harold walk to their house.

Frederick says, "Charles, put this out of your mind. Just think about your wife and plan to live your life day by day. You need not worry so much about this. Just live your life, day by day. You're a good man and I'll see you tomorrow."

As soon as Charles is inside, Mary passionately kisses her husband to his surprise.

She says, "My darling, the very thought of you in that Pollsmoor prison made me remember how much love I have for you. I think we can work out our problem. I'm ready for some loving on this beautiful July night."

Chapter 12

As World War II in Europe is winding down, South African Prime Minister Jan Smuts is in San Francisco to serve as the President of the Commission on the General Assembly of the United Nations. He has been there since April, 1945 and expects to return to South Africa in late June of 1945.

Smuts is polishing his thoughts about 'human rights,' words that he has written in the Preamble to the Charter of the United Nations. He first introduced the idea of 'human rights' in the fall of 1944 when Smuts had attended the Dumbarton Oaks Conference in Washington, D.C. His old fashioned idea that rights and duty go hand-in-hand, meaning rights must be earned, is getting a good work out. He still isn't quite sure of the extent of 'human rights.'

Of course, most people equate 'human rights' with the fundamental rights of all humans, similar to those rights enshrined in the United States Constitution, namely the right to life, liberty, and the pursuit of happiness and the right to be free from oppression. Smuts doesn't think the term includes the right to vote or the right to be free from racial discrimination, especially in South Africa where, in his view, South Africa has a sacred trust for the more advanced people to look after the backward, by whom he means the Natives, so that each can live side by side in a sort of 'trusteeship,' an attempt to dignify differential classes of citizenship. His idea of 'human rights' pertains to basic human needs, such as having food, water, and shelter.

Suddenly, Smuts' thoughts are interrupted by one of his aides, who announces, "Prime Minister, please allow me to read what one of the San Francisco newspapers is saying. It's good news, sir! I'm sure you'll be most pleased!"

Looking up from his desk, he nods approval as the aide reads in a voice of approval:

"STATESMAN OF THE WORLD"

"South Africa's Prime Minister, Jan Smuts, is the acclaimed author of the phrase, 'human rights,' to be enshrined in the Preamble of the Charter of the United Nations.

"During the War, Prime Minister Smuts earned the British rank of Field Marshall and advised Winston Churchill on strategic decisions in the North Africa Campaign against the Desert Fox, Nazi General Erwin Rommel. As a member of the Imperial War Cabinet, Smuts was responsible for bringing together British proposals for a peace settlement with the Axis Powers and often attended the British Commonwealth Prime Ministers' Conferences.

"Prime Minister Smuts was no stranger to military maneuvers because during World War I, Smuts—then, General Smuts—led South African forces to capture South West Africa from Germany and thereafter help govern the once-German Protectorate under South Africa's mandate from the League of Nations. And, today, under Smut's leadership, South Africa still governs the former German Protectorate under the laws of South Africa.

"Many British politicians, such as Lloyd George and Winston Churchill, are singing his praises as 'an extraordinary man from the outer reaches of Empire.' Even Churchill's private secretary has publically suggested during the World War that should Churchill die, Smut should become wartime Prime Minister of Britain.

"South African Prime Minister Smuts has been an early supporter of the creation of the League of Nations and, now, of guaranteeing 'human rights' to every person by positively inserting that phrase in the Preamble of the United Nations Charter. He understands perfectly well the horrors of oppression inflicted on people by the Nazis in their quest to dominate the world.

"Rightly so, many government leaders seek advice from Prime Minister Jan Smuts who isn't afraid to leave his country in the hands of a deputy prime minister as he devotes his talents to making the world a better place. The civilized world is indeed fortunate to have Prime Minister Jan Smuts working for the good of all humanity throughout the world.

"Jan Smuts deserves his international reputation as a Statesman of the World."

Smiling, Jan Smuts says, "Well, that certainly makes my day! But, I am getting frustrated with how slow our progress is in this international political theater. It seems that politicians are everywhere and just can't get enough space to hear their own words and talk. And, talk and talk, and talk. I'd hoped we left that bickering back in Cape Town. Everything here in San Francisco is going at a snail's pace."

"Yes, it is, Mr. Prime Minister."

"While we are in California, perhaps I can use the time to visit the giant sequoia trees in Yosemite. And, I'd like to take a look at America's Wild West. I need some time to find some spiritual sustenance and rationalize what the idea of 'human rights' might play at home. Just having some time off will clear the cobwebs."

His aide replies, "Yes, sir, that is important to clear away the cobwebs. But, remember, we need to work on the idea of our plan for South Africa and for UN approval of South West Africa as our country's fifth Province. After all, we've been the caretaker of South West Africa since World War I."

"You are one hundred percent right about that. But, let's not be too overly pushy because, my young friend, I think, after hearing that newspaper piece, I've got the world in my pocket."

"Right you are, sir!"

"Now, let's plan on a trip to Yosemite, tomorrow. I've seen the pictures and can hardly wait to be there in person. It'll be good to smell some country air and view Yosemite and another part of some of the American Wild West."

"Yes sir. It's supposed to be quite stunning."

Dismissing his aide, Jan Smuts thinks about his venture into what he's read about America's Wild West, its frontier and the lonely days of the Cowboy, braving the local savages, the forbidden terrain, and the ferocious weather.

To the image in his mirror, he confides, "Yes, much like South Africa, where we had to take responsibility for ourselves and not depend on someone to save us. The American Cowboy was isolated and relied on himself alone and didn't wait for someone else to bail him out of any trouble. We Boers were like that, yes indeed, and still are, yes indeed."

While Smuts' thinking seems to suggest no necessity exists for 'human rights' for the less fortunate, he suddenly realizes that even the American Cowboy needed governmental help in allowing homesteading the land, clearing away the native Indians with government troops, crisscrossing the territories with the iron horses, getting the mail across open country, and damming the rivers into bountiful lakes for irrigation. As he readies himself for bed, Jan Smuts begins reconsidering the idea of 'human rights' and what that will mean in South Africa.

The next day, before leaving on his jaunt to Yosemite, Smuts writes Jan Hofmeyr, the deputy prime minister, that the idea of universal human rights will bring embarrassing proposals to South Africa, but he admits he cannot disavow the words, 'human rights.' He also writes that he remains highly skeptical of the new catchwords, such as 'democracy' and 'freedom,' being tossed around by diplomates of several countries, especially by his fellows in the British Commonwealth.

Smuts insists that his idea of a 'trusteeship' for South Africa will preserve his own country's separation of the races, since the idea of a 'trusteeship' worked and was approved under the League of Nations for South Africa's control over South West Africa. He remains a true optimist.

***

Jan Hofmeyr isn't so sure about that optimistic outlook, even though not much UN news has filtered down to South Africa. Hofmeyr hopes to keep it that way. He has a standard reply to any nosey reporter's question about what he hears from the Prime Minister and his idea of 'human rights.'

"Sorry, my good man, I haven't heard anything about it, but when I do, you, my friend, will be the first to know."

Nonetheless, the *Manchester Guardian* on May 8, 1945 reports that "General Smuts' preamble to the new world charter—his declaration of human rights—has been accepted as a basis for future discussion."

The newspaper piece wonders what this will mean for South Africa.

Jan Hofmeyr senses something isn't politically correct with this declaration of human rights as he previews the South African newspapers after the *Guardian's* revelation. He knows something needs to be done and quickly, before this talk of 'human rights' gets out of hand.

He thinks that a governmental campaign for helping the less fortunate, for the rise of social reform, and for a more just society will turn the tide. Back in 1942, the Smuts' administration had launched the Social and Economic Planning Commission with post-war plans for construction of public works and parks, with plans for training young Natives for productive jobs, with plans to teach Afrikaner farmers about soil erosion, and even with plans to turn Zulu villages into tourist's sites. But, so far, none of those plans have been fully implemented. Hofmeyr knows that he must await the return of the Prime Minister for actual instigation.

He remembers that in May of 1944, over 12,000 marchers protested in downtown Johannesburg that Natives were not getting a true education. The teachers had urged the African National Congress to take 'direct action' to improve education of the Natives. But, Smuts ignored the protests, in spite of Hofmeyr's advice.

In some of the urban tent towns now peopled with more Black women than Black men, the Black women have become more vocal with a pervasive insurgency. Hofmeyr understands the meaning of the wearing by women of red and black scarves, which they call *doeks.*

"Those red and black scarves symbolize the blood of Blacks," he says.

He knows something must be done, and quickly.

***

When Smuts returns to South Africa in late June of 1945, he discovers his enhanced reputation as an international statesman has done nothing to endear him either to the British workers and socialists or to the Afrikaners.

Because of his 'human rights' proposals at the United Nations, Afrikaners tag Smuts as a 'handyman of the Imperial British Empire', while those English-speakers favoring socialism tar him as a 'lackey of the capitalist class' and many other English-speakers tag him as a 'destroyer of the South African social fabric.'

Smuts assumes his international reputation in leading efforts to make the world a better place would not only protect South Africa from criticism of its racial policies but also enhance his own standing in home politics.

But, nonetheless, Jan Smuts is no fool, either.

He recognizes his political party must demonstrate fervent loyalty to the cause of racial segregation. He will end the relaxation of enforcement of the Pass Laws and will propose more onerous legislation to keep South Africa lily White.

153

In meeting with his advisers, Smuts hears their agreed suggestions. "Sir, the general consensus is that we focus on the Indian problem. That will definitely gladden the hearts of both the British and the Afrikaners. We can't go wrong there. And, the Blacks and Coloreds will probably be happy someone else is now in the bottom of the barrel."

"All right, but should we hold back enacting more legislation on racial segregation? After all, I have taken a slightly different tact at the United Nations."

"Not at all, sir. We must keep our eye on the upcoming elections in 1948. We must appease the Afrikaners as well as the British Whites by offering each voting bloc enough to pacify them and keep the loyal opposition led by D. F. Malan from winning the election."

While Smuts agrees with his advisers, his ears appear to be plugged because he is missing the wagging tongues in South Africa about 'human rights' enshrined in Smuts' Preamble in the United Nations Charter. Some South Africans have substituted 'equal' rights for 'human' rights—most definitely not a favorable interpretation for Jan Smuts.

To satisfy his White supporters, in January of 1946, Jan Smuts announces that the *Pegging Act* will be replaced by more onerous anti-Asians legislation: *The Asiatic Land Tenure and Indian Representation Act.*

This more restrictive law will prohibit Indians from land purchases from non-Indians except in limited areas and will prevent Indians from occupying property in the excluded areas. Additionally, Indians' voting rights for special White Parliament Members will be even more curtailed.

Needless to say, the opposition party of D.F. Malan and his followers show surprising enthusiasm for the proposal and urge its passage. They praise God in the Dutch Reformed Church and declare the proposed new law as, 'a gift from heaven.'

Naturally, replacement for the Pegging Act is not well received either by Indians in South Africa or by Indians in India.

Chapter 13

It's early November in 1945 and, to use the old saying, spring is busting out all over South Africa. Charles has been busy in the flower and vegetable gardens of the Kruger homestead.

Today, pregnant Mary is tidying the kitchen while pregnant Henrietta is supervising a temporary helper to prepare the supper meal when Frederick returns from checking all of his vineyards in the Stellenbosch area.

Henrietta asks, "Mary, how are you feeling today?"

"Fine, though I am a little tired. How are you feeling today?"

"Also tired, but I'm just about a month away from delivery. So, pretty good."

"Mary, I think I need to remind you that you are now in your 18th or 19th week. Doctors say that before the 22nd week is about the last safe time for an abortion. If we count from June 15th or the 17th, then I think November 26th would be it. After that, my dear, from what I've been reading, the doctors say it's too dangerous after number twenty-two."

Mary is silent.

"If you don't mind me talking about it, I think you should have the abortion. That is, if you are still considering it. Are you still thinking about it, Mary?"

More silence from Mary, although stress lines appear on her face. She fidgets with the nails on her right hand.

Henrietta continues, "If you want it, I can make arrangement with a good doctor. And don't worry about the cost because Frederick and I will cover it."

"I just don't know. I just don't know. I'm just scared, you know."

"Mary, I know, but the longer you wait after 22 weeks, the more you run the risk that you must give birth because the closer it gets, the risks of abortion are very severe and a greater danger to you. Worse, if you wait too long, then the fetus will become a baby and then an abortion will be k …"

Mary finishes the sentence, "I know, killing the baby."

"Well, whatever you decide. Please know that I will be there for you. I will help you with Charles, too."

Mary says, "If I have the abortion, Charles will have a fit."

"I know, but I will support you all the way."

**

Over supper, Henrietta decides to tell Frederick about Mary's predicament, unsure of his reaction to her ultimate request to help her obtain an abortion

Frederick replies, "Well, I must say that is very strange. When I picked them up outside Stellenbosch, nobody— not Mary, not Charles, not the bus driver, not the elderly lady, not her daughter or granddaughter—said anything about any rape or rapes. Just about a robbery! And not a single word about any rape!"

"My dear, that's because none of the women want to be branded with the shame of rape. And the women got the men to go along. You know that in our South African society and culture, Black women are not expected to be chaste, but to be obedient and to silently suffer the consequences. You know that."

"Yes, I guess so," Frederick sighs.

"If Mary decides she wants an abortion, I think we should help her, don't you?"

"Well, yes, I suppose so," he answers slowly.

Henrietta says, "I read in the Afrikaner paper, *Weekblad,* a story about a doctor in Johannesburg by the name of Gerhardus Buchner operates an abortion mill on Eloff Street. As I recall, it's called 'Castle Mansions' or something like that."

"Yes, I'm aware of Doctor Gerhardus Buchner."

"You are; how so?"

"My Committee in Parliament has been investigating these things."

"Oh! Well, anyway, I was very impressed with Dr. Buchner who said many Black women and very poor White women insert liquids, such as soapy water or disinfectants, or even lye into the vagina. That doctor also said that these women also will insert objects, like coat hangers or knitting needles to abort."

Frederick doesn't want more information but Henrietta continues.

"He said that some Black women will squat for hours over a pot of boiling onions or various plants in following a Witch Doctor's suggestion. The doctor said that soap or a disinfectant injection kills one in two hundred women because of gangrenous of the uterus."

"Unbelievable! And that is so gruesome, Henrietta!"

"The newspaper article reported that Doctor Buchner inserts a soft rubber catheter sealed off with a sterile cotton wool dipped in a disinfectant and that he shaves all pubic hair to lessen any chance of infection," Henrietta adds.

"You really kept a lot of that article inside your head, Henrietta. I know you graduated from law school, but I didn't realize you attended medical school as well," he laughs.

"Very funny, dear. Well, in case you've forgotten, I am pregnant and I keep up with these things. Anyhow, there's more in the newspaper article."

"Go on."

"Afterwards, the doctor performs a dilation and curettage to clean away any tissue. He opines that the D & C will help the woman if she later wants another pregnancy. Frederick, you said you are aware of Doctor Buchner. What do you know of this Doctor Buchner?"

"Yes. I do. Doctor Buchner graduated from the University of Cape Town Medical School. Because of that newspaper article, his abortion clinic has the full attention of Parliament. Probably, Parliament will curtail his activities, I think, by getting the police and authorities to watch him."

"Oh."

"More investigation reveals that the doctor is paid 75 pounds in advance and that he does free work for the girl friends of certain members of the South African police force."

Henrietta says, "That's an outrageous amount in these days and times for such a simple procedure. And he does abortions for girl friends of the police? I don't want this man working on Mary. Is there anyone here in Cape Town you might know?"

"Well, yes. Young Doctor Derk Crichton, two or three years out of Medical School might be the ticket. You may remember he's the son of Doctor E. C. Crichton, head of the Department of Obstetrics & Gynecology at the University of Cape Town Medical School. The elder was our dinner guest a few years ago. Young Derk is extremely self-confident and, I am told, that he has written a paper on abortion."

"Well, that's promising."

"Henrietta, I must say you are well versed on abortion."

"Yes, thank you, and Frederick, you are not very shoddy about it, either, my dear."

"That's because I am on the investigating committee to look into Doctor Buchner. And you think we should help Mary?"

"Yes, Frederick, I do. Of course, if she wants it. By the way, let me ask you since are investigating abortion—is it still legal in South Africa? I remember from law school that under the South African combination of English, Roman, and Dutch Common Law, abortion is acceptable only to save the life of the mother. Is that still good?"

Henrietta smiles to allow her husband to expound on the subject with his knowledge, even though she knows the answer. But, she knows how important it is to baby her husband's tendency to expound.

"Well, yes and no. Let me explain. South African Law by itself considers the fetus as a part of the mother until the fetus is viable, that is, capable of living apart from the mother. And that is usually seven months from the time of conception."

"Oh," she exclaims as if she didn't know these facts and the South African Law.

"So, you see, there is a problem with the clash of these different legal concepts. But under South African Law, the mother has the absolute right to control her own body—the same as if she were amputating a finger. The State doesn't have the right to forbid her choice to protect herself. Under South African Law, she has the right to choose. She should have the right to choose if she wants to amputate a part of her."

"Ouch! That's an odd way of putting it!"

"Yes, it is."

"Why don't we hear more about abortion gone wrong by a doctor?"

"That's easy, Henrietta, because of studies done for Parliament. Unless a White woman dies because of an abortion by a doctor, the South African police and authorities just look the other way. Nobody is ever prosecuted because of a botched abortion on a Black or Colored woman. So, I hope that answers your question."

"Yes, I guess."

"You let me know if Mary decides and I'll contact young Doctor Crichton."

"Frederick, will you help us with Charles?"

"Certainly, but from what you say, I take it Charles is not on board."

Henrietta just smiles.

***

A few days later, Frederick, Henrietta, Charles, and Mary engage in a lengthy discussion about abortion. Henrietta informs Charles that under South African Law, a woman has the right to control her own body before the baby becomes viable as Henrietta posits, "Charles, I understand the Catholic Church teaches that human life begins at the moment of conception. But,

161

what I don't understand is that the Catholic Church doesn't have priests say a funeral Mass for the fetus when a woman suffers a miscarriage even after a few weeks when the pregnancy is showing. To me, that's such an unbelievable contradiction—no funeral, no burial, no cremation, no requiem ceremony for the miscarriage material, namely the unborn fetus."

Charles is wide-eyed as Henrietta continues.

"To me, that means the Catholic Church opposes contraception efforts and opposes abortions, even in the case of rape, incest, or to save the mother's life, to increase the procreation of more and more little Catholics. To insure that this goal is reached, the Church makes any effort to prevent conception to be a mortal sin, which will send a person to everlasting damnation, unless the Church doesn't work the magic of redemption through the priestly administrating by the Sacrament of Confession."

Charles is stunned at what Henrietta is preaching.

"And I say this even though I am a practicing Catholic."

But Charles is definitely paying attention.

"I don't want to appear as too harsh, but for me, I cannot accept the Catholic doctrine that human life begins at the moment of conception. My intellect tells me that when the fetus is viable, able to live apart from the mother, is when human life begins. Think about it."

Mary sees from Charles' eyes that Henrietta's words are making a difference.

"And, Charles, here's another thought. Have you ever heard of any Catholic priest giving the miscarriage material the Sacrament of Extreme Unction? You know, the Last Rites?"

Charles shakes his head negatively.

"I certainly haven't heard how the blot of Original Sin we are all taught we have and that Jesus died on the cross for our redemption is wiped away. If life begins at the moment of conception, then the fetus or miscarriage material has the blot of Original Sin and cannot enter Heaven without its removal. That is, of course, if the fetus or miscarriage material has a soul and is a human."

Charles' face signifies acceptance of Henrietta's arguments.

She says, "I have also never heard of any Catholic baptizing any fetus or miscarriage material to wipe away the blot of Original Sin."

Charles is pondering.

"Think about it, Charles. At the very least, if not convinced, you will have doubts that what you've and what I've been taught makes any good and common sense."

After a momentary pause, Charles puts aside his Catholic training that life begins at conception as conflicting with South African law that a woman has the right to choose an abortion until the baby is viable.

And, Charles is convinced that viability has not yet happened. He agrees that it is Mary's body and she should have the right to choose. He understands that if he had to lose and arm or a leg, he would have the right to decide. And that concept seems fair for women, too.

***

Even though young Doctor Crichton is White and Mary is Black, the doctor performs the abortion in his office without any problems.

Later, Charles and Mary view the skin color of the fetus with Doctor Crichton, who positively attributes the color to two Black parents, not just one. The doctor says, "Look at the baby's hair and you can see it is very kinky, not a bit straight. Charles, those two signs mean positively you are not the father. This is a Black baby."

The doctor knows that at this time, medical science in South Africa has no positive scientific way to determine the exact identity of the fetus' human creators.

His words soothe Charles' doubts about the morality of aborting the fetus partially created by the man in the suit on the bus.

The doctor also convinces Charles that Mary's body is ready for another pregnancy and that they should get to work.

***

In December of 1945, Henrietta Kruger gives birth to a baby girl, Robin, to join her big brother, Hans, almost ten. Both Mary and Charles join in the celebration.

***

Remembering young Doctor Crichton's advice, Charles and Mary finally produce nine months later a new baby, born a year later on October 30, 1946.

According to their agreement, Charles selects the child's name for his son, John, after Father John O'Malley. He has promised Mary that she can select the name for their next baby.

"Welcome to the world, John Washington," Charles smiles.

Chapter 14

Much to the dismay of Charles' father, Sol Washington, and all of the Indians living in South Africa, the Smuts government is proposing in 1946 to replace the *Pegging Act of 1943* (which will expire in March of 1946) with more onerous legislation against Indians.

The scuttlebutt for Smut's reasoning is that this legislation will play well not only with Whites, but even with Blacks and Coloreds since all three groups must compete with the Indians for bites of the diminishing economic pie.

Sol is aware of the passive resistance to these anti-Indian laws, although he remains silent, on the sidelines to safeguard his economic interests, most importantly his job.

After the Pegging Act became law, the Indian Community in April of 1943 massed in protest at the Avalon Theater in Durban, except Sol excused himself since his job as a dockworker on the Durban wharf would have been jeopardized if he participated. Sol understands from where his bread received its butter.

But, massed protests don't stop the Smuts administration in its attempts to root out Indians from White areas. In fact, as the official documents report, hundreds and hundreds of Indians in 763 residences are relocated. But, Sol, Alice, and young Charles weren't included in the removal under the Pegging Act in 1943, and, of course, Sol is thankful for that.

When the new legislation is officially introduced to Parliament in 1946, the Indian Community promptly labels the new law as 'The Ghetto Bill.'

On February 20, 1946, Sol joins in the organized 'Day of Prayer' which closes all Indian business from one to five o'clock in protest of enactment of the proposed 'Ghetto Bill.' The Smuts government is unmoved.

Sol is so agitated that he joins over 6,000 others as they march, four to five deep, arms linked, on West Street in downtown Durban in protest of the proposed legislation. To his astonishment, Alice joins him; he sees many other Blacks and even Coloreds and Whites in the parade.

In spite of the organized protests from the Indian Community and its allies, the new law is signed and is effective on June 6, 1946.

As a result, the Indians in South Africa put aside their petty differences and fully organize against the law. Many uninvolved Indian onlookers now are ready to join their activist fellows opposing the Smuts government.

Sol Washington has had enough and is joining the South African Indian Congress to protest 'The Ghetto Act.'

Tonight, Sol is meeting with the Natal branch of the South African Indian Congress to organize a 'Resistance Day,' as proposed by the local chapter President, Doctor G.M. "Monty" Naicker, a friend of Father John O'Malley. Tomorrow, June 11, is named 'Hartal Day,' a day of a massive strike and of passive resistance.

Nonetheless, the authorities continue with enforcement of The Ghetto Act.

On June 15, 1946, over 15,000 people mass in Red Square in Durban, with the result that several dozen protesters pitch tents on vacant municipal lands in defiance of The Ghetto Act.

Sol and Alice stand across the street and watch some of the protestors putting up tents.

Sol announces, "Alice, I'm going to the park and join the protesters tomorrow. The South African government can't tell us where we can live. That isn't right! It's an insult to basic human dignity. I have to do something."

"Sol, don't you think that is very dangerous to go and be with the protesters on the city property? Don't you think the police will put a stop to staying on city property in violation of the law? Didn't you see the faces of some of those Whites looking at the protestors? There are a lot of angry Whites, especially the Afrikaners. I don't think you should go. It isn't safe, Sol!"

"Oh, I know, but I cannot sit here and do nothing about this injustice. It's just not right. Besides, what would Gandhi do? What would your sweet and holy Jesus do?"

Alice ignores the dig. "It isn't safe, Sol. Let's go home before some trouble starts. Come on, Sol."

"Okay," he agrees, knowing that when they get home, he will leave her and return to the protest. He will not wait for tomorrow. Tonight is the time to act.

At home, against his wife's wishes, Sol grabs a few blankets to join those camping on the municipal lands in clear violation of the Law.

He kisses her goodbye, saying, "Alice, don't worry. The Hindi gods and the Christian one with the two heads and the dove will protect me since our cause is just and right. Just say a prayer for me, my dear, with your Jesus."

Before Alice can say another word, Sol is out the door, blankets in hand.

He quickly finds a vacant spot on the grass to put down his blankets. He greets a few of his fellow protestors. He is glad to see some of the leaders of the local Natal Indian Congress and shakes hands with Doctor Naicker, the local president.

Sol sees the Anglican priest, Father Michael Scott, moving among the protestors of all races. That sends Sol's hopes and spirits sky high.

Initially, nothing happens and there is joviality and camaraderie among the large number of Indians, the few Whites, the few Blacks, and the few Coloreds throughout the resistance campsites.

The South African police patrol but make no threats and make no arrests.

But when the next fall of night arrives at the campsites, so do several hundred White hooligans with clubs, picks, crowbars, sledgehammers, and shovels. They attack the resistance camps by tearing down tents and swinging clubs.

Many of the young Whites, especially Afrikaners, have knuckle dusters or brass knuckles to beat any stray Indian anywhere near the city property.

Morning light reveals several Indian bodies—mostly female—in a deadly state of repose lying in the weed-filled drainage ditches near the municipal lands.

The South African police observed the melee but took no action to halt the violence, or to remove the protestors, or to make any arrests.

One of the dead is Sol Washington, with his skull exposing brain matter. Over his body a hand-scrawled sign in

Afrikaans reads, **"A good Indian is a dead Indian!"** No doubt, the sign is a copycat from the American West.

As the protests continue into the next few days, the South African Police finally arrest protestors and cart them away in police vans. Charged with trespassing, many are fined and released. Yet, some more prominent protestors, like G. M. Daidoo, a leader in the Natal Indian Congress, are imprisoned for 6 months. The radical Anglican priest, Father Michael Scott, is jailed for a while, until Father John O'Malley makes his bail.

Die Transvaaler, an Afrikaner paper, editorializes on June 28, 1946 that South Africa should boycott India and all Indians.

***

Alice accedes to Sol's wishes and cremates his remains in accord with his Hindu beliefs. She writes her son, Charles, and tells him that his father died for freedom and for justice for the oppressed. She tells her son that the Indian community honored his father with a plaque in the temple.

***

Protests and resistance over The Ghetto Law continue throughout the country, with many Whites joining the resistance. But the Smuts government ignores the protests.

Unknown to Prime Minister Smuts and to the South African Government, the Indian government, in response to The Ghetto Act and the protests, has decided on June 22, 1946 to seek inclusion of South Africa's treatment of Indians on the agenda for the Second Part of the First Session of the General Assembly of the United Nations in the autumn of 1946.

When Smuts finds out, he will be pissed.

Chapter 15

Prime Minister Jan Smuts is readying himself for his role at the Second Part of the First Session of the General Assembly of the United Nations. He will be leaving South Africa in October of 1946. He knows that his reputation as 'A Statesman of the World,' reported in the San Francisco newspaper, is on the line.

After receiving some stinging criticism in August from non-White organizations, Jan Smuts establishes the Fagan Commission to investigate the country's laws relating to economic backwardness, to the Black Pass Laws, and to the socio-economic circumstances of migrant workers. But, he's not a bit worried about the gripes from the Indian community in South Africa.

Smuts wholeheartedly accepts the Fagan Commission's findings that Whites and other races should exist side by side and account for their differences. But Smuts refuses to accept the Commission's recommendation that the Natives should be separated to live in their own *kraals,* as favored by D. F. Malan and his National Party.

But, Smuts still strongly believes in racial segregation and the superiority of the White race. He's not backing down.

Discussing the turmoil he views on the home horizon, Jan Smuts suggests to Deputy Prime Minister Hofmeyr, "Jan, we must make rapid progress with practical social policy away from politics. We need to turn the eyes of the people to social improvement and away from racial segregation. We must improve people's economic well-being."

171

Hofmeyr knows, without being told, that the 'people's well-being' refers to Whites, especially Afrikaners, and not the well-being of the Natives or of the Asians.

But, before any progress can be accomplished, the Smuts government is faced with a massive union organized work stoppage from Blacks in the gold mines. The union stoppage eventually becomes a strike two months before Smuts plans to leave for the United Nations meeting.

He is in no mood to even listen to the miners' demands which have been going on for months before a strike is actually called by the union's president in August of 1946.

Over 74,000 African Union Mineworkers strike the gold mines in the Witwatersrand for higher wages. The union president, J.B. Marks, is also a member of the South African Communist Party and, he and his Party are perpetually accused by the Smuts government of stirring up unrest. Smuts promises, "There'll be hell to pay, Marks!"

Not only does the miners' strike impose a downturn on the South African economy, but it also puts into the hearts of White South Africans the fear of immense civil unrest, especially because of the immergence of huge squatter camps of Blacks outside the larger cities. Over 90,000 Blacks live in Soweto, a slum just outside Johannesburg. No matter the government's efforts to control the influx of Blacks into urban areas, the squatters are like crows in a cornfield and just fly away to another spot for residence when threatened by the police.

Jan Smuts cares nothing for the demands of the miners and openly supports the owners of the mines.

Thirteen thousand more mineworkers strike on August 12th while another four thousand march on the Johannesburg city hall but are pushed back to West Spring by government forces.

The army and police use batons, bayonets, and guns to drive striking miners back into the underground mines and force many to continue working.

A few days later, when miners outside the mines peacefully march from the East Rand to Johannesburg, then at Smuts' command, the police and the army crush the strikers, leaving at least twelve dead and hundreds injured.

One left-leaning South African newspaper on page one prints;

> "We have not forgotten that Prime Minister Smuts as General Smuts had brutally and callously put down strikes of mine workers in 1917 and again in 1922, with scant concern of the due process of law and with little regard for the loss of life. Now, he's done it again, this time by having the police and the army fire on a peaceful procession of unarmed people. This day is now called Bloody Tuesday."

The Natives Representative Council, an informal discussion group between African leaders and the Smuts government (and specially created by the Smuts government for race relations) condemns the police and the army's action in ending the miners' strike. In effect, that's also a condemnation of Jan Smuts.

Of course, Smuts ignores the newspaper's and the Natives Representative Council's condemnations.

The next day, in the Natives Representative Council's final action of the day, the Council demands the abolition of all racially discrimination legislation as contrary to the letter and spirit of the Atlantic Charter of the United Nations.

Smuts recognizes the put down and declares, "That's the last straw!" and disbands the Natives Representative Council.

During the next week, several workers of the African National Congress, the Communist Party of South Africa, the South African Indian Congress, and the Colored People's Congress are arrested. Some are imprisoned, like J. B. Marks, the Communist president of the Miners Union, and some are deported.

Smuts doesn't hold back spiteful retaliation.

Not only does Jan Smuts ignore the Natives Representatives Council's demands, but in the next two months before his departure from the country, he also ignores more bad press about his extreme method in the termination of the miners' strike.

***

In October, Smuts departs for New York, via Paris, for the Second Part of the First Session of the General Assembly of the United Nations.

Prime Minister Smuts expects success in convincing the United Nations General Assembly to grant approval of South Africa's annexation of South West Africa long governed by South Africa under an old League of Nations mandate. After all, South Africa has been treating South West Africa as its fifth Province since its invasion and capture from Germany in World War I.

Jan Smuts prides himself in bringing back to South West Africa the indigenous *Herero* tribe—almost completely annihilated by the Germans before World War I. Some people classified the Germans' attack on the outgunned *Herero* people as genocide.

Jan Smuts also prides himself, in creating a voting system, just as he did for the Blacks in South Africa, so that these Native pastoral cattle-raisers in South West Africa could vote for selected White representatives in the South African Parliament. Smuts crows, "Both Natives in all our Provinces now have equal rights!"

He will feature these two accomplishments in his United Nations' presentations.

Smuts thinks he owns sufficient political capital at the United Nations to achieve this easy goal to annex South West Africa into his country and he is more than willing to spend a little of his political capital to get what he wants.

He will first lobby the diplomats from the rest of the British Commonwealth countries and then, with those assurances in his pocket, he will work on the other Western nations, especially the United States. He thinks it's a done deal.

When he will return triumphantly to South Africa, Jan Smuts firmly believes his country will give him a well-earned hero's welcome and when the country votes again in 1948, another election victory.

In fact, Prime Minister Smuts believes it is God's Will.

Chapter 16

In late October of 1946, Frederick Kruger, a member of the South African Parliament, has invited for lunch his old friend, Jan Hendrik Hofmeyr, the acting Prime Minister of the Union of South Africa while Prime Minister Jan Smuts is attending the Second Part of the First Session of the General Assembly of the United Nations in New York.

Just the two men, political allies of Jan Smuts, are meeting at the Kruger homestead and will be kicking around strategy toward keeping control of the South African Parliament in the upcoming election of 1948, even though the vote is almost a year and a half in the future.

Henrietta Kruger, a very pregnant Mary Washington, and a temporary worker have prepared lunch for the two men as well as their attendants, while Charles has worked tirelessly to glorify the garden.

As a Bentley and a Rolls Royce, both black and highly polished, with special license plates, stop in front of the main house, Charles—now dressed in a coat and tie borrowed from Frederick—approaches to open the door of the acting Prime Minister's limo, but before he can act, an aide from the other car steps in front of Charles to complete the task. The White aide gives a big, friendly smile to Charles and offers his hand, taken hesitatingly by Charles.

Immediately, Henrietta and Frederick appear from inside to welcome their old friend to their home. Following, Mary and Charles stand beside the front door and the temporary maid, Ophelia, joins them.

To the acting Prime Minister's protection detail, Henrietta points toward a huge umbrella sheltering from the glorious sunshine ten chairs seated around a long table, appropriately covered with a red table cloth and a huge vase of multicolored flowers. She offers, "Gentleman, please make yourself comfortable over here, where we've set up a hot buffet for your pleasure. There's red and white wine from our very own vineyards, iced and warm beer, tea, and filtered water. Please help yourself, enjoy, and thanks for visiting our home. My assistant will serve you gentlemen. If you need anything, just ask Ophelia."

The men bow their heads slightly.

After the exchange of kisses on the check between Henrietta and the acting Prime Minister, Henrietta says, "So wonderful to see you again, Jan! I know you are pressed and want to meet with Frederick so I won't bother with small talk. But, I do want to introduce you to Mary Washington and her husband Charles, two of our long time employees, and to Ophelia Jones, who is helping out today."

Wearing one of Henrietta's pregnancy dresses and her accessories, Mary smiles, gives a slight curtesy, and, per the instructions from Henrietta, offers Jan Hofmeyr her hand as he appears near the front door. Ophelia bows.

Turning toward Ophelia, Mary, and Charles, Jan Hofmeyr extends his hand and politely says, "So very good to meet you, Mr. and Ms. Washington and Ms. Jones. Frederick and Henrietta, very dear friends of mine, are very lucky to have such loyal and honest people as their employees. And thank you for helping to make my short stay here a very pleasant experience."

Then to Mary, the acting Prime Minister says, "And, Ms. Washington, it looks like your baby is almost ready to pop out. When is your expected due date? Are you hoping for a boy or girl?"

Without hesitation, Mary answers, "A boy, sir. It's just a week away, on October 30th."

"Wonderful, and good luck to you and your husband, and may God bless you and your new baby," Mr. Hofmeyr adds.

With that, Jan and Frederick retire to an ante-room for their private lunch. Mary fills the two men's plates for Henrietta and Ophelia to carry and place the meal on the table. There, Ophelia waits after filling their glasses with the chosen beverage. Henrietta returns to the kitchen.

Mary waits in the kitchen to rest and lunch with Henrietta and Charles. As the three seat themselves, Charles says, "Those are some beautiful automobiles out there."

**

Jan compliments Frederick on the bouquet wafting from the Chardonnay produced in the Kruger's vineyards. He adds, "I suppose by now, you are one of the country's largest wine producers. Are you exporting much to other countries?"

"As a matter of fact, Jan, we are. As you know, none of our vineyards had any tank tracks or demolition from bombs or artillery shells as existed in France and Italy during the War. So, we've caught up with both the French and Italians in shipping wine, especially to Brazil and to the United States. One of our biggest shipments—almost a whole boat load— leaves tomorrow for Houston and New Orleans. We are making quite a splash in those markets."

"Well, how are your reds doing?"

"Excellent, both the Pinotage and the Cabernet, I must say. I'll have Charles get you a case of one of the reds, if you like."

"Wonderful, just make it a half case of the Chardonnay and the Pinotage, Frederick, and that will be wonderful."

Frederick says, "I'll have Charles pack a case for you, Jan."

Behind the closed door both men dig into their salads, with Jan Hofmeyr beginning the frank political discussion.

"First, I've got a question for you about Jan Smuts. When you took a leave of absence from Parliament you served in the Army with him before you were wounded. Did the Prime Minister ever talk in front of the men about human rights?"

"Jan, the first I ever heard of human rights emitting from Smuts was reading about it in the newspapers. And, I confess that was very surprising."

In a serious tone, Jan says, "Frederick, I'm afraid than the Prime Minister doesn't see the contradiction he's placed himself at the United Nations. He's basically telling the world that all people should have 'human rights' and that idea has grown to be fundamental rights or equal rights, including the right to vote. While, here in South Africa, the Natives are denied the right to truly vote, the right to freely assemble, to just name a few. When the local newspapers play that card of 'human rights,' the Natives get excited. And the Afrikaners and their party keep spitting angry venom that the Prime Minister is selling out his White countrymen. What are your suggestions?"

"Jan, no doubt it's a huge problem. I hear that the National Party, assisted by a plethora of local branches of Afrikaner organizations, are gathering the rural and the urban classes of Afrikaners, and are appealing not only to their economic desires but also to their racial and ethnic attitudes. It's fearmongering at its worst and I'm feeling I'm reliving Hitler's rants."

"Frederick, you said the National Party; don't you mean the Reunited National Party?'

"Jan, it's the same thing now. Malan fears that using the word 'reunited' will confuse his constituents with us, the United Party. So, now he's calling it the National Party. You remember he quit calling it the *Herenigde* National Party and the *Herenigde* Re-United Party to invite the British voter to vote their ticket."

"Well, yes, Frederick, I see. Well, Malan and his stogies are attacking the British link involving the two World Wars and, worse, the National Party figures that Smuts will not be successful in getting the United Nations to allow us to incorporate South West Africa into our country."

"Yes, Jan, that's all true."

Jan comments, "The bastards are hollering to high heaven that our party hasn't been able to stop the flow of the Natives into the towns and hasn't been able to halt the outburst of African industrial strikes. You know the mine workers in '45 gave me a lot of trouble, but I did avert a strike. It's too bad about the latest strike in August by the miners and the sad, sad brutal outcome. However, from what has been reported in the Afrikaner press, Smuts' brutal handing of the strike certainly doesn't hurt Smuts and our Party. Those Afrikaners seem to enjoy physical punishment on Blacks."

"Right you are, Jan."

"How do you see the coming campaign, Frederick?"

"The way I see it is that these Afrikaners are worried that the State should maintain White supremacy and assure the purity of the White race. The damn Afrikaner business people want unimpeded access to Black labor along with stringent government controls over its allocation and discipline. Then they want all the regulations changed."

"Yes, that's true."

"Then, the Afrikaner workers expect greater protection from competition from the Natives. Naturally, the so-called Afrikaner intellectuals insist upon a political segregation of South African society. The whole Afrikaner community is organizing against us."

Frederick stops to wipe his mouth.

Frederick adds, "Damn it! The Afrikaner press and the Reformed Dutch Church are publicizing the idea of absolute racial segregation. I just read an article in that Afrikaner rag, *Die Afrikananse Patriot,* talking about the Afrikaners as the chosen people for their country, meaning South Africa, of course."

"I've heard that. If we're not careful, we could lose this election. God knows what that would bring to poor South Africa."

"Jan, I know at heart you are a liberal and can tolerate less segregation. And, while I hate to say it, but, with Smuts out of the country, Jan, you've got to step up and put up a strong face, perhaps even adopting some of the National Party's crap. I don't like to say that, but ..."

Of course, you are right. Frederick. You know, I hate to admit it but, just between you and me, the rest of

Smuts' Cabinet is inefficient and complacent. But, you didn't hear me say that about my fellow Ministers."

Frederick smiles.

"As you know, Smuts is pushing eighty years. I wonder if he still has the fire in his belly to preserver through another campaign."

"Well, Jan. What are we going to do in the next year or so?"

Jan announces, "Next month, I'll be speaking to the Natives Representative Council and hopefully will be able to calm these hot heads, some of whom dislike our handling of the Witwatersrand mining strikers. Yes, I know some miners were shot by the police. I know these Natives in the Council have gobbled Smuts' words in the Preamble of the United Nations Charter."

"Jan, wait a minute. Didn't Smuts disband the Natives Council?"

"Frederick, that's right, but I've suggested we have an unofficial meeting. I think it's important to keep open the communication lines. Some of them are reasonable men and are willing to hear me."

"Jan, what will you say to the disbanded Natives Representative Council?"

"Simply this: The government's trying to increase social welfare and will move toward more conciliatory practices on the racial front. How's that, Frederick?"

"Well, that will help although the Blacks can't vote. Of course, there's very little danger that any of the few eligible Colored voters in Cape Town will support Malan's candidates.

"It's the White voters we must convince, especially the Afrikaners. When you speak to any of the Afrikaners' groups, what will you say?"

"That's easy, Frederick. The government's removal of discriminatory laws will not be in the interests of the Natives since our experience clearly demonstrates that the average Native has not reached a stage in his development where he can retain ownership of land under conditions of free competition."

"Yes, you're right about the Afrikaners loving that line, Jan. In my hands, is a pamphlet entitled, *Raase en Rasvermenging*, about the evils of mixing the races. Let me, if you will, read just a bit:

> 'The preservation of the pure race tradition of the *Boerevolk* must be protected at all costs in all possible ways as a holy pledge entrusted to us by our ancestors as part of God's plan with our People. Any movement, school, or individual who sins against this must be dealt with as a racial criminal by the effective authorities. The mixing of the races, no matter the color, whether white, black, yellow, or brown is a grave sin against God.'

Frederick continues. "If you want, you can have this copy. In my opinion, we own a heavy burden, especially since the rural vote favors the National Party and the Afrikaners as far as the allocation of seats in Parliament. When Smuts returns, we must, absolutely must, do everything possible to combat the Afrikaners. Though, I confess neither my heart, nor my soul, nor my intellect believes in continued and total racial segregation in our country."

The Deputy Prime Minister is listening.

"And, yet, I know if the National Party won the election in 1948, my God, things will surely worsen, Jan. It means to keep the bad guys out, we must spread their garbage. Otherwise, we will lose this election. Jan, I hate it! We've got to reach some of these Afrikaners who just react to slogans without evaluating the real political issues."

Jan comments, "Yes, if one can print a message in a hundred or so characters, even if false, some people will buy it. I know how you feel about racial segregation, my friend. Well, hopefully the Prime Minister will return from New York with the United Nations' approval of the annexation of South West Africa into our country. Do you think that will ease some of these concerns? I hope so."

Frederick answers with a slight laugh, "Yes, I do. That should please everyone except the Black people in South West Africa and their brothers and sisters, mothers and fathers, sons and daughters, aunts and uncles, nieces and nephews, and all their cousins here in South Africa."

The men agree to put forth all efforts to get out the White vote opposing the Afrikaners. Clinking their wine glasses, Frederick says, "Jan, here's to getting out the White vote and to bringing our country together and to halting these divisionary attacks."

They will mobilize those few Cape Province Colored eligible voters who can still vote in the ordinary Parliamentary elections. They both sigh that their most favorable voting block and the majority of the South African population has been disenfranchised by a lily White Parliament.

Frederick says, "Well, Jan, it is very sad to admit that long ago in the spirit of political compromise we voted to deny the vote to all Blacks in the ordinary Parliamentary elections and to the Coloreds outside of the Cape Province. That might be our undoing."

Jan replies, "Yes, and creating more seats in the Assembly for voters in rural districts, with a lesser number of required voters than are required in in urban districts. But, that's history and it's too late now to do anything about it."

"Right you are."

"Well, thanks for your input, Frederick. Now, I've got to get back to governing the country until Prime Minister Smuts returns."

***

Ready to leave, Jan Hofmeyr thanks Frederick and Henrietta and gives her a hug. But, he avoids hugging a pregnant Mary, instead giving her and Ophelia a bow and a tip of his hat. He shakes hands with Charles, steps outside, and before entering his limo, waves a goodbye to the group.

Frederick reveals to Henrietta, "Jan's leaving with six bottles of the Kruger Pinotage and six bottles of the Kruger Chardonnay. Charles already placed it inside the limo."

She says, "I am very proud of that and proud that we are shipping so many cases to Brazil and to America. And, my dear Frederick, I am proud of you."

Chapter 17

Today is October 23, 1946, precisely a Wednesday, and it's one of those beautiful autumn days in New York City.

But, Jan Smuts is paying little attention to the perfect crispness of the air or the brilliant sunshine reflecting off of the multi-colored array of the autumn leaves or off of the many skyscrapers' windows in New York. Other things are clouding his mind.

Jan Smuts cannot believe that India has successfully included South Africa's treatment of Indians in South Africa as an item for discussion at the Second Part of the First Session of the General Assembly of the United Nations. Of course, he knew the Indian delegation had requested from the Secretary-General that this item be placed on the provisional agenda, but he never believed that would actually happen. He assumed his political capital and reputation would prevent that. After all, he is a 'statesman of the world.'

Now, he can't believe that the Secretary-General Trygve Lie, as a Norwegian, is sympathetic to those Asians, including Indians. "If the man was an Asian," he says to himself, "I would expect him to take care of their own, those Asians. But, the man is a Norwegian! What a travesty!"

Prime Minister Smuts doesn't want to deal with this Indian problem, hoping to secure acceptance by the UN of South Africa's annexation of South West Africa. That Indian problem just sidetracks his engine.

But now he'll have to deal with the Indian problem.

Immediately, he requests the General Committee to remove India's motion from the agenda since, he argues, the matter is essentially within the exclusive domestic jurisdiction of South Africa, not within the jurisdiction of the United Nations.

But, he is unsuccessful and on Friday, October 25, 1946, the General Committee will consider India's complaint against South Africa's treatment of Indians.

Before the General Committee meets on Friday, Smuts is rounding up the opposition from friendly diplomats, with personal meetings. He will be spending Thursday night on the telephone.

Hearing that some woman diplomat from India will be presenting India's case against South Africa, he instructs his aides to find everything about her. As an old army general, he's not above playing dirty if it's necessary to win any war. "It's kill or be killed," Smuts remembers, "and, all's fair in love and especially in war."

Reporting a few hours later, an aide says, "Vijaya Pandit is a forty-six-year-old widow, one of the most beautiful women in India, they say, and a seasoned political operative, with high connections. Her brother is the Prime Minister of India, Jawaharial Nehru. Ms. Pandit is currently a Minister of Public Health. Also, she has been re-elected several times to the Legislature. From what I understand, she has spent some time here in the United States."

Smuts is paying close attention.

"She is very smart, Mr. Prime Minister, and an accomplished public speaker and loves a good argument. Some say she has a sharp tongue. One of her opponents called her a 'nasty woman.' Another opposing party member accused her of corruption and demanded that she be locked up and jailed. But, by and large, Mr. Prime Minister, the woman has an excellent reputation for long-standing service to her country. That's all I could learn about her in such a short time."

"Fine. Thank you for your report," he says, as he fingers his white beard and pushes his glasses toward the bridge of his long, narrow nose. Smut understands that he has his work cut out for him.

Before retiring, Jan Smuts prepares his rebuttal for what he supposes the lady from India will say on Friday. He will be ready for her.

Although he receives daily reports from South Africa, the Prime Minister's mind is not focused on what Deputy Prime Minister Hofmeyr is dealing with in South Africa.

***

Back in Durban, South Africa, on the night of October 23, 1946, a massive demonstration is occurring at Red Square and speakers from the Natal Branch of the South African Indian Congress are celebrating the opening session of the United Nations. The crowd contains Whites, Blacks, Coloreds, Asians, and especially Indians.

One speaker receives roaring approval when he shouts, "Now, General Smuts is in the dock! South Africa is on trial! And the complaint from India is a test for the future of the UN! Justice will finally come to us! And, now, my friends, let's give a moment of silence in honor of the Indians who died in their protest for justice and equality on this very spot—what I consider as hallowed ground!"

Reading the list of names of protestors killed during the uprising, he fervently begins, "Sol Washington ..."

When the demonstration has subsided, over 350 people have defied "The Ghetto Act" and camped on the same municipal land. The protesters dare arrests, hollering at the African State police as well as the police from the provincial and local authorities.

But Deputy Prime Minister Jan Hofmeyr is no fool and a stand down order from the national government is in place for all police. No one is arrested. And, after a standoff, the crowd disperses peacefully. Hofmeyr bubbles with satisfaction.

* * *

As the United Nations' General Assembly begins its meeting on October 25, 1946, Jan Smuts will forever remember this day. He sits with the South African delegation awaiting the presentation from the Indian delegate.

Walking on her way to the speaker's podium, Vijaya Pandit looks directly at Prime Minister Jan Smuts and the South African delegation. She makes no attempt to hide the smile on her face as she carries a thin brown briefcase.

Greeted with a handshake and a hug at the speaker's podium, Ms. Pandit adjusts her sari and removes a few papers from her briefcase, but she quickly tosses them aside to the floor. Ms. Pandit has no need for any prompts and can freely speak her mind, even without notes.

When the applause has stopped and her brief introduction has ceased, Ms. Pandit begins with a few preliminary remarks, to warm up her audience. Then, sensing the mood and watching the eyes of her audience—especially those of Jan Smuts, Ms. Pandit thrusts forth her main presentation in measured, level tones:

189

"We seek no dominion over others; we claim no privilege position over other peoples. But we do claim equal and favorable treatment for our peoples wherever they may go, and we cannot accept any discrimination against them.

"We have brought before the Assembly the treatment of Indians in South Africa. The way this Assembly treats and disposes of this issue is open to the gaze not only of those who are gathered here, but to the millions of the whole world—progressive peoples in all countries, more particularly, non-European peoples, who are the overwhelming section of the human race.

"Bitter memories of racial doctrines are still fresh in the minds of all of us. Their evil and tragic consequences are part of the problems with which we are called on to deal. India firmly believes that imperialism, political, economic or social, in whatever part of the world it may exist and by whomsoever it may be established and perpetuated, is totally inconsistent with the objects and purposes of the United Nations and its Charter.

"The sufferings, frustrations and violation of human dignity, and the challenge to world peace, freedom and security that the Empire represents, must be one of the prime concerns of the parliament of the world's people. Millions look to us to resist and end imperialism in all its forms, even as they rely on us to crush the last vestiges of Fascism and Nazism."

Then, with a finger pointing toward the South African delegation, Ms. Pandit raises her voice and continues:

"We express our regret that not all the mandatory powers have offered to place the territories for which they hold Mandates under United Nations trusteeship. We are gravely concerned that South Africa proposes

190

that South West Africa should be incorporated into South Africa."

Hearing Ms. Pandit's last sentence, Smuts swears, "Damn those Indians! They're out to block our annexation of South West Africa! Well, we'll see about that! We're out of here!"

The entire South African delegation rises from their seats, packs up papers, and noisily trudges out of the Assembly. They ignore the stares and shouts of several other delegations as the call for "Order, please! Order, please!" comes from the Chair.

Not in the least upset and waiting until the roar has quieted, Ms. Pandit finishes her speech:

"We move, in spite of difficulties, towards closer cooperation and the building of a world commonwealth. Let us do this with more deliberation and speed. To this end, let us direct our energies and remind ourselves that in our unity of purpose and action lies the hope of the world. Thank you for your attention."

Prime Minister Smuts and the entire South African delegation can feel the thunderous applause as they exit the hall.

They miss the view of Ms. Pandit returning to her seat amid the applause as she wipes the tears of joy from her eyes with her sari.

Outside, Smuts says, "Just Peachy! Now we've India's opposition against our annexation of South West Africa and when this issue comes up before the Trusteeship Committee, we will have to be ready to attack. I want all the dirt you can find about India and its treatment of its so called untouchables! Get going, while I've some phone calls to make."

Much to the chagrin of Jan Smuts, on October 26, 1946, the General Assembly includes on its agenda an item entitled "Treatment of Indians in South Africa" as an issue not within the domestic jurisdiction of South Africa but an issue within the jurisdiction of the United Nations. Then, on October 31, the General Assembly decides that India's complaint will be heard jointly by the First and Sixth Committees over the next several weeks.

Prime Minister Smuts feels he can win this issue with India if he can stall long enough to appear to be willing to compromise, not that he will, however. In the meantime, he's going forward with South Africa's plan to annex South West Africa and make the territory its official fifth Province. His plan includes a few private lunches and dinners for selected representatives. He and his delegation will lobby people on the telephone. If he and his delegation are invited to any meetings, no matter who is the sponsor, they will attend.

**

During the month of November one of the leading New York daily newspapers is throwing one of many press parties for many of the diplomats and dignitaries attending the Second Part of the First Session of the General Assembly of the United Nations. Naturally, the newspaper hopes to secure some tidbit of information or some downright gossip from some loose-lipped diplomats.

Jan Smuts and his aides plan on using these social functions to lobby some of the representatives of other attending nations to vote favorably for South Africa's plan to annex South West Africa and make the territory its official fifth Province, and, of course, to defeat

192

India's attempt to sanction South Africa for its treatment of Indians.

He's especially working on his fellows from the Commonwealth countries, except those fellows from India.

"After all," Smuts argues to a Canadian diplomat, "South Africa has been governing the territory as its unofficial fifth Province for years—in fact since the 1920s. Why, all the inhabitants are governed equally under our country's laws, whether civil or criminal, and have exactly the same rights as do the people in the other four Provinces of South Africa. Our Constitution is very similar to yours in Canada and to the rest of the Commonwealth."

Suddenly, Jan Smuts cannot believe his eyes as he sees two Black men and a Black woman entering the room. Instantly, he recognizes that they are walking straight for him and the leader is carrying a huge smile with his white teeth showing. Jan is certain he knows the smiling one; he stops talking, looks for an escape, but realizes he's trapped as the three Blacks box him in.

"Hello, Mr. Prime Minister! Yes, it is I. Indeed, Alfred B. Xuma, President of the African National Congress. What a pleasure, sir, to at last meet with you face to face! Please, sir, allow me to introduce my wife, Maddie Hall, an American social worker, and to my friend, Paul Robeson, a leader here in America for equality for all African Americans."

Jan Smuts is befuddled, but manages to offer his hand and say, "Yes, good to see you, Mr. Xuma, and pleased to meet you, Ms. Hall and Mr. Robeson. What in the world, Mr. Xuma, are you doing in New York?"

Ignoring Smuts' direct question, Alfred Xuma replies, "Well, Mr. Prime Minister, you may recall that a while ago that I sent you a copy of the ANC's policy document, 'Africa Claims' explicitly modeled on the Atlantic Charter. I wanted to discuss this document with you. It was about granting full citizenship rights for the African people of South Africa. As my memory serves me, your office refused me an interview. In fact, the reply I received from your office was that no useful purpose would be served by such a meeting by discussing such propaganda."

"Well, no doubt at the time, I was very busy, Mr. Xuma, and I don't remember that. No doubt, one of my aides was mistaken to say that. My apologies to you, Mr. Xuma."

"I understand perfectly, Mr. Prime Minister, and that's why I'm here in New York, having had to fly more than 10,000 miles to meet you, my Prime Minister. I find it strange that here in New York you talk about us but you won't talk to us in South Africa. Perhaps, now we can sit down and discuss your idea of 'human rights' and the plight of the African people. And, perhaps, we can even discuss as reasonable people some other of our common interests, say, about South West Africa, for example?"

"Yes, of course, Mr. Xuma, please ring my office tomorrow and we'll set up an appointment to do just that, but"—looking at his watch—"we are just leaving for another appointment," Jan Smuts offers, knowing he will avoid ever meeting with Alfred B. Xuma and his African American friends as if they carried some transferrable dreaded disease.

Ever the crafty politician, nonetheless, Smuts directs an aide to give Mr. Xuma his private phone number.

"Wonderful, Mr. Prime Minister! I certainly will and look forward to visiting with you throughout the meetings of the General Assembly. I will be here the whole time. Thank you, sir," Alfred B. Xuma bows and cheerfully responds, as he duly records the phone numbers, rightly suspecting that the gifted private phone number is incorrect.

To Smuts astonishment, Alfred B. Xuma, his wife and Paul Robeson after leaving him, circulate among the diplomats, obviously lobbying them about some issue. Nervously, Jan Smuts directs his aides to exit.

But, as they leave the November press party, Jan Smuts and the entire South African delegation miss seeing Mr. Xuma greet Dr. Y.M. Daidoo and Dr. G.M. Naicker, two representatives from the South African Indian Congress. Worse, Smuts and the entire South African delegation miss the arrival to the press party of Father John O'Malley, an activist Catholic priest, and of Father Michael Scott, a radical Anglican priest once imprisoned for joining Indian protesters against 'The Ghetto Act.'

Alfred Xuma warmly greets the four men and says, "Welcome, gentlemen. You just missed Prime Minister Smuts and his aides. Please join me in having a bite to eat and something to drink. Tomorrow morning, let's meet at my hotel room to discuss our strategy over the next several days of these meetings. Let me introduce you to my American friend, Paul Robeson, and, of course, my wife, Maddie Hall."

They all exchange warm handshakes.

**

Jan Smuts decides the most important issue for South Africa is that obtaining the United Nations' approval of the annexation of South West Africa by South Africa. He immediately schedules this issue on the agenda of

195

the Trusteeship Committee and when the day arrives for the discussion, the Prime Minister is ready.

He begins his speech to the Trusteeship Committee, first making reference to India's complaint against South Africa:

"One does not like to refer to painful matters, but at least the Indians should be the last persons to throw stones and also make charges of class distinction and discrimination.

"I speak not in anger but in pain, sorrow, and deep sympathy with India's suffering millions, the untouchables, but no less in solicitude to the people of South Africa. My country is still a peaceful, well-behaved, and well-ordered country, free from these violent internal antagonisms. And it is the policy of my Government to keep it so.

"It is to prevent such conditions of social clash in South Africa where so many races, cultures, and colors come together that the Union is doing its best on fair, decent, and wise lines to keep the different elements as much as is convenient and possible, part and away from unnecessary, inter-mixture and so to prevent bloody affrays like those in India or such as we read in other countries— even here in America.

"We are honestly trying to find a human way of life for a racially, socially, and culturally mixed community where the different sections may dwell alongside one another in peace and goodwill.

"I should, however, not pass by in silence, the allegations made by the Indian Delegate against the Union in its internal Native Policy. The Indian Delegate speaks as a witness but presents an entirely prejudicial, one-sided and distorted picture of the situation in the

Union. This, perhaps, is based on ignorance as well as prejudice.

"The Indian Delegate has forgotten to mention that the Natives in the Union have their own elected representatives in the Union Parliament. The Union is spending more money on Native education than all the territories of Africa south of the Sahara.

"This charge of India comes with ill grace. Is there another country in the world where there is more social discrimination between communities and classes than in Indian society? Has the Indian Delegate forgotten the fifty million, so called 'untouchables, of the depressed classes with all the social stigma and humiliation they have to endure—a phenomenon unknown in South Africa and in the rest of the world? "

Hardly a sound is heard as Jan Smuts concludes his plea for South Africa's annexation of South West Africa since the territory has been governed competently and fairly since the 1920s under a mandate to South Africa from the old League of Nations.

After polite applause for Prime Minister Smuts' presentation ceases, the Chair of the Trusteeship Committee calls for any interested parties to make any rebuttals.

Much to the distaste of Jan Smuts, Alfred Xuma of the African National Congress, two representatives from the Natal Indian Congress, Father John O'Malley, and Father Michael Scott—at the invitation from the Indian Delegate—all five oppose South Africa's annexation of South West Africa.

When the Anglican priest finishes, he says, "Now, with the permission of the Chair, let me introduce you to a chief of the *Herero* people actually undergoing the daily hell of South African oppression in South West Africa." The tall man arises, bows, but says nothing.

After Father Michael Scott's short speech, the Trusteeship Committee ends the discussion and retires to make its decision and recommendation to the General Assembly.

***

In the next few weeks, after more discussion among the subcommittees of the First and Sixth Committees about India's charge of South Africa's discrimination against Indians living in South Africa, a decision and December recommendation is made to the General Assembly.

***

The December story featured in one of New York's daily newspapers is carried throughout the world and especially to South Africa:

> "The most controversial issue before this session of the United Nations General Assembly was decided last night, December 8, in an atmosphere of considerable excitement. The long bitter and vigorous debate on the South African-Indian dispute came to a close as the hands of the clock in the big assembly hall crept toward midnight. It ended with a complete victory for India, a victory which the Indian delegation had not expected.
>
> "The General Assembly adopted Resolution 44 (1), which held that the treatment of Indians in South Africa should be in conformity with the international obligations under the agreements

concluded between the two nations and the relevant provisions of the United Nations Charter.

"In her final plea to the General Assembly, Ms. Vijaya Pandit as the leader of the Indian delegation, in part declared: 'I ask for the verdict of this Assembly on a proved violation of the Charter; on an issue which has led to an acute dispute between two member States; on an issue which is not confined to India or South Africa; and on which must make or mar the loyalty and the confidence which the common people of the world have placed on us. Mine is an appeal to the conscience of the world.' The applause was deafening.

"Although the General Assembly voted to have Indians in South Africa treated in conformity with the two government's obligations under the relevant provisions of the Charter, subsequently a compromise suggested by Britain to send the dispute to the International Court of Justice moved the dispute to be heard by the Joint Legal and Political Committee.

"And that Committee voted to recommend that the General Assembly defer its decision pending the decision of the International Court of Justice.

"While Prime Minister Smuts of South Africa reluctantly acceded to that recommendation, he consistently argued that the real issue was whether India's complaint even came within the jurisdiction of the United Nations.

"Ms. Vijaya Pandit, head of the Indian delegation, totally disagreed with sending the dispute to the International Court of Justice, but signaled that she was satisfied that the United Nations had fulfilled its responsibilities to the provisions of its Charter.

"On the issue of South Africa's attempt to annex South West Africa, the United Nations' Trusteeship Committee voted overwhelming to deny South Africa's request. Prime Minister Smuts commented, 'This issue may also end up before the International Court of Justice since South Africa has been governing the territory for over twenty years and we're not ready to cease governing the territory. And, we don't even think the United Nations has any jurisdiction over the question."

***

The headlines in many of the South African newspapers, especially the Afrikaner ones, reveal that Prime Minister Smuts suffered a serious loss at the United Nations.

Those newspapers favoring the government carry the story as one of victory for Prime Minister Smuts, "who refused to back down from his principles and kowtow to some do-gooder organization trying to change the world and treating South Africa as some backwater nation or banana republic."

The newspapers favoring the government also receive a planted news item to endear the Smuts administration with both English and Afrikaner White voter. These newspapers prominently display in the afternoon editions that the Smuts Administration has set aside more than 30 times the funding per capita for the education of White Children than for the education of others.

And that evening, the piece leads the South African radio newscasts favoring the Smuts administration.

Chapter 18

Before Alfred B. Xuma leaves the United Nations General Assembly in December of 1947, he meets an old friend, Roy Wilkins, Assistant Secretary of the National Association for the Advancement of Colored People, to plot strategy to end racial discrimination in the United States and especially in South Africa.

They spend several days together, with Mr. Wilkins promising to include in the NAACP's campaign opposing racial segregation in the United States a like campaign in the United States opposing the racial segregation in South Africa. Mr. Wilkins tells his friend that progress is coming to America, though slowly, since the United States Supreme Court in 1944 outlawed the Whites Only primary in Texas.

Enthused with their successes at the United Nations, Dr. Y.M. Daidoo and Dr. G. M. Naicker of the South African Indian Congress also fly from New York to Paris and then to Cape Town. They have many ideas against inequality.

Father John O'Malley and the radical Anglican priest Father Michael Scott and his charge, the chief of the *Herero* people, have booked passage on a steamship for a long journey home, but at a much less cost. The two priests are developing strategic ways to convince Whites of the immorality of racial segregation.

When Alfred B. Xuma arrives in South Africa, he leads the African National Congress to quickly endorse the United Nations Atlantic Charter as ending South African racial discrimination. Mr. Xuma in his address to the ANC declares the endorsement as a Christmas gift to South Africa. He says "We will make Mr. Smuts pay attention to us, even though Mr. Smuts has banned the Natives Representatives Council! I promise you, my friends, we will be heard! The Smuts government hasn't heard the end of our protests!"

***

After Prime Minister Jan Smuts and the South African delegation return in mid-December, Smuts schedules an early meeting in January of 1947 with his Cabinet and valued political advisors to devise a coherent strategy to defeat D. F. Malan and his National Party in the upcoming 1948 election for seats in Parliament. That's the number one concern on his mind.

The Prime Minister wants his ducks in a row before Parliament officially opens on January 16, 1947. He calls first on Jan Hofmeyr, his trusted and most able Cabinet Minister, to begin the discussion.

Mr. Hofmeyr reports, "Mr. Prime Minister and Gentlemen, even though the election is over a year from now, already the National Party has taken to the radio airwaves, the newspapers, highway billboards, and paper handbills or flyers to rally White voters against Blacks and Coloreds. As you drive around the towns and cities, you will discover plenty of light poles plastered with their garbage. They've even purchased a few billboards."

He approves of the nodding heads.

Continuing, Jan Hofmeyr says, "Mr. Prime Minister and Gentlemen, here is just a sample of their attempts to stir up White fear of the Natives. Look at these pamphlets printed in English and in Afrikaans at your leisure but pay attention to the one in English which I'll read aloud."

One of the aides hands out several flyers to the group. Halting until everyone has received a handful, Hofmeyr reads in a loud English voice from one printed in very bold black ink.

"Dear South African Voter:

"DO YOU WANT TO ALLOW BLACKS TO VOTE?

"WILL SOUTH AFRICA BE RULED BY A BLACK MAJORITY?

"That's what the United Party hopes for our beloved country. We know that:

"The Blacks, by and large, are NOT patriotic and have No Love for our Country.

"The Blacks are free-loaders looking for their next handout.

"The Blacks are inclined to crime and to organized criminal gangs.

"The Blacks do NOT respect Law and Order.

"The Blacks hate the South African Police who protect us.

"The Blacks steal jobs from poor Whites.

"The Blacks threaten White women with rape and robbery.

"The Blacks are multiplying like flies and will soon overtake our towns.

"The Blacks are lazy and shiftless and expect taxpayers to give them a free ride.

"The Black women are welfare queens sucking our country dry.

"The Blacks want to open the borders to let in more of their relatives.

"The Blacks demand more free education so they can take the good-paying jobs.

"The Blacks use and deal with dope, including heroin and cocaine.

"The Blacks want to live off the backs of hard-working South Africans.

"The Blacks want to elect their own Black leaders.

"The Blacks want to make the 10 plus Bantu languages official languages.

"The Blacks want the right to vote for Blacks in Parliament.

"Is this what you want for South Africa?

"**VOTE FOR THE <u>NATIONAL PARTY</u> TO KEEP SOUTH AFRICA WHITE!"**

"Well, there you have it. This pamphlet is also published in Afrikaans. Here are a few more for you in Afrikaans with slogans as headlines. I'll just read the headlines in both languages:

"Swart Gevaar or Black Peril; Die kaffer op sy plek or The Kaffir in his place; Rooi Gevaar or Red Peril.

"You can see what we are up against with every White voter, especially the Afrikaners. As you know, as Minister of Education, I gave out some information to the press in December that we are increasing funding for White schoolchildren twenty-fold per capita over government funding to the Natives. That should help, I think, with White parents."

The Prime Minister says, "Yes, Jan, that's a good move. But, before we move on, who was the author of the first flyer you read?"

"Sir, I believe it was Henning Klopper, the founder of the *Broederbond,* but I'm not certain."

"That wouldn't surprise me. Now, Jan, how did you discover those awful flyers?"

"Sir, a friend of mine, Father John O'Malley, a Catholic priest, mailed all of them to me. He'd come across them in one of his missionary trips."

"Ah, yes, that Father O'Malley. I remember him, Jan. I met him and that ANC guy, Xuma, in New York. They were also at the United Nations meeting and worked with those Indians against us. Isn't he also a protégé of Bishop Hurley in Durban? The Bishop preaches against the government almost every Sunday I'm told. And, Jan, you say he's a friend of yours?"

"I didn't know he went to the United Nations; that is a surprise. Father O'Malley was one of my college students, Mr. Prime Minister, and I've kept in contact with him through the years, sir."

"I see. Well, I don't understand why he would be trying to help us in the oncoming election. But, nonetheless, we'll take all the help we can get. Yes, we will need it, I fear."

Jan Hofmeyr knows that his priestly friend will support the Smuts government as the lesser of two evils. Father O'Malley could never support a government led by D. F. Malan and the National Party or by one of the splinter political parties. Of course, he understands that the Prime Minister wouldn't like that explanation—that he and the United Party are the lesser of two evils.

From the back of the room, one of Minister Hofmeyr's aides says, "If I may, Mr. Prime Minister, you may remember that a proposal was made in November while you were at the United Nations about having a national discussion to come up with a national policy of solving racial problems, even if we have a country-wide separation."

But before the aide can even ask his question, Prime Minister Smuts interrupts, "Young man, yes that is something we must consider at some time in the distant future. As I've indicated, we have taken a practical approach toward a racially integrated approach and very, very gradually reforming the political system to benefit the Natives. But we must be definitely vague about such a sensitive topic. But this is not the time to talk about any such approach. Not at this time can we do that."

After a lengthy discussion about proposed tactics during the remainder of 1947, Prime Minister Smuts says, "All right, gentlemen, thank you for the very frank discussion. Now, we must get to work immediately, even though the election is over a year away. Next week on January the sixteenth, we have the opening session of Parliament. So be on your toes. Be on your toes, even though the election is a year away."

After almost everyone has vacated the room, one of the Prime Minister's aides pulls him aside and suggests that the government should seize the passports of several known troublemakers who are planning trips to India.

When Smuts hears the names of the travelers, namely, Dr. Y.M. Daidoo and Dr. G.M. Naicker of the South African Indian Congress, who were in New York and spoke at the United Nations against South Africa, his face reddens and he commands, "Do it immediately!"

A smile crosses his face as he mutters, "Those bastards! They'll think twice before they cross me again."

But Smuts acts too late and both travel to India to meet Gandhi and Prime Minister Nehru.

Chapter 19

It is the opening day of Parliament, January 16, 1947, a pleasant day in Cape Town, with bunches of flowers setting on tables and credenzas throughout the Parliament building.

And inside the building before business begins, pleasantries are generally exchanged among and between the different Members and their staffs. Frederick Kruger, returning as a Member of Parliament, is amazed at the show of the apparent camaraderie.

As the opening session begins, the traditional song, 'God Save the King,' rings out and is followed by the Afrikaner, *Die Stemva suid Afrika, w*hich is translated by English interpreters for the audience as 'The Voice of South Africa.'

Ordinarily, the leader of the opposite party, now D. F. Malan—head of the National Party—would rise to deliver a fiery speech for non-confirmation of the Smuts government and his United Party, including their entire legislative agenda. But, not today will Malan fall in line with tradition.

Instead, Mr. Malan ends his presentation with a motion to terminate any and all voting rights of Natives, Coloreds, or Indians for even a White Member in the House of Assembly as a representative for any of these groups. He then follows that stunner with a motion to permanently abolish the Natives Representative Council, which he berates as a treasonous mob ready to harm South Africa.

Frederick Kruger expresses surprise to his bench-mate that Malan's motion is so narrowly defeated.

Next, when Jan Hofmeyr is nominated to be the Deputy Prime Minister, Frederick is shocked that Hofmeyr's confirmation is opposed so viciously by Malan and his National Party and is barely defeated.

Frederick wonders if some threatening cracks are showing in the Smuts' governing foundation because of these shoestring victories.

Naturally, during the rest of the month of January and even into February and March, the National Party does everything possible to demonstrate Smuts' United Party is ruining the country. They've also become expert obstructionists.

In the Prime Minister's office, Jan Hofmeyr is listening to his boss lament as he dictates a letter to an old friend.

"These years of post-war peace have been in many ways a heavier burden for me than the war years themselves. War is a great stimulus and an effective answer to our opponents. Now, we are back in the old pulls and divided counsels and the world of small things. Life is much more of a burden than ever before. I confess that my outlook is now much more pessimistic."

Hofmeyr offers, "I certainly understand you feelings, Sir."

Continuing with his dictation after an appreciative nod, the Prime Minister adds, "Nonetheless, I must confess that my heart is not in this business and sometimes I'm wasting what time I have left on this earth with mere trifles. The day's march for this old soldier is all uphill most of the time."

Hofmeyr's face raises a question and, as if reading his mind, the Prime Minister immediately answers, "I view the world with America and Russia growing stronger, becoming the two powers in the world. I fear Russia's domination of Eastern Europe. I fear for the safety of the world about Communism. There will be much dissent."

"Hofmeyr says, "Yes, we may be getting ready for another World War, this time between Communism and Democracy. Where will England be?"

"I see the British decline as an end to European dominance, all of European nations being booted out of Africa and Asia and the Far East. I feel a great sadness about the state of the world and of South Africa," Smuts responds.

To ease the Prime Minister's mind, Hofmeyr reminds the Prime Minister of the announcement that the British Royal Family will visit South Africa next week.

He says, "All that adversity in Parliament will take a back seat. Not only will King George VI and Queen Elizabeth be visiting the country, but so too will the two princesses, Elizabeth and Margaret. Things will definitely quiet down while the British royalty are here."

***

But, opposition to the Smuts government is coming not only from the National Party headed by D. F. Malan, but also from the African National Congress and from the South African Indian Congress. ANC President Alfred B. Xuma signs a pact with Dr. Y. Daidoo and Dr. M. Naicker of the South African Indian Congress to have the two organizations join forces in opposition to all unjust laws. The two groups will pressure the Smuts government on its racial segregation policies.

Father John O'Malley pats himself on the back for his small part in the formation of this alliance.

***

On March 21, 1947 the Royal Family arrives in Cape Town, where they will celebrate Princess Elizabeth's twenty-first birthday. Naturally, Prime Minister Smuts, Deputy Prime Minister Hofmeyr, and all the Cabinet Members as well as many Members of Parliament hover around the Royal Family. But, notably absent is D. F. Malan, the leader of the opposing National Party and all his cronies in Parliament.

Traveling on a special train, painted white, the Royal Family visits St. George's Park in Port Elizabeth, as well as the Drakensberg Mountains, and other places in South Africa. Princess Elizabeth even befriends some Native girls and joins them in a celebration dance.

After witnessing Princess Elizabeth's warmth to the Natives, Jan Hofmeyr remarks, "I think Princess Elisabeth will someday make a great queen and be loved by her people."

Naturally, Prime Minister Smuts accompanies them on their journey, and, at one point invites the Royal Family to tea at his homestead with his wife, Ouma.

At one of the state dinners, King George compliments the owner of the Kaazicht Estate for the wonderful Chenin Blanc and raves over the smoothness of the Pinotage from Frederick Kruger's Stellenbosch Vineyards. The King raises his glass in salute.

Naturally, Frederick is elated. He and Henrietta stand and bow to accept the compliment.

All in all, the Royal Family's visit lightens the intrigue in the House of Assembly, with little legislation accomplished.

When the Royal Family has departed, Jan Smuts meets with Jan Hofmeyr and begins their continuing discussion about the election in 1948.

"You know, Jan, in May, Ouma and I will celebrate our golden wedding anniversary, but I must confess that I'm getting tired of politics and all the small potatoes we have to deal with to save our Union. I confess that sometimes, I'm just tired of the whole mess."

Hofmeyr responds, "Yes, Mr. Prime Minister, but we've come through a lot, getting mostly passed wartime shortages of food and coal and petrol. I don't think of our fights in the Assembly as small potatoes and I'm not pessimistic about our chances in 1948. I understand that you are tired, especially from the fight in the United Nations. Surely, that took a toll. But, that is behind us. We will campaign that you stood up to the powers that be. We will show that you fought for South Africa and that the fight is not over."

Smuts says, "Well, Jan, thank you for that. You are right that I'm tired and I'm thinking that after the 1948 election is won, I will consider stepping down and pushing you as the new Prime Minister. No, don't say anything. That's my hope for you."

"Thank you, sir. I will do my best to earn your confidence."

**

Eventually, the time passes with the South African legislature accomplishing little during the ensuing months.

"Mr. Prime Minister," Jan Hofmeyr says, "Today, August 15, 1947, the British have given independence to India and Pakistan. They both are now independent nations and are republics."

"I can't believe it. I am disillusioned by that. Well, we need to increase our own emigration numbers. I want 50,000 immigrants from Britain into South Africa in the next two or three years," Smuts posits.

"Begging your pardon, sir, but Malan and his party will strongly oppose that as an attempt to pack the voter rolls. He'll rile up the Afrikaners. We should hold up on that because already, in years past, numerous British immigrants have ended up with homes and jobs formerly held by White South African citizens, namely the Afrikaners. They're not happy campers, sir."

"Is that right?" he says, but thinks, "Well, too bad!"

"Yes, the Afrikaners fear that unloading British immigrants will eventually be felt at the polls, because even with their higher birth rates, the Afrikaners cannot keep up with the influx of massive British immigrants. Already, they fear the immigration numbers and adding 50,000 more will simply intensify their anger. And that's true even though none of those admitted could vote for at least two years after the 1948 election. It's not worth it going forward. So, my advice, Mister Prime Minister is to hold up on that."

But, Smuts ignores Hofmeyr's advice.

**

In November of 1947, Prime Minister Smuts takes a break from the campaign to attend the Royal Wedding of Princess Elizabeth and Phillip in England. While there, the Prime Minister sees that much of Eastern Europe is under Russian dominance. He learns that while he once admired Josef Stalin in the world's fight against Nazi Germany, Stalin has created a new organ for international Communism, totally controlled from Russia with plans to dominate the world.

Smuts is happy that the United States is countering with the 'Truman Doctrine' to assist Greece and Turkey toward economic recovery and is countering with the 'Marshall Plan' to economically help Western Europe, especially Germany and Italy, both bombed to smithereens by Allied warplanes and artillery.

Prime Minister Smuts characterizes the eventual conflict between Russia and the United States as the 'Cold War.' In spite of his admiration of Stalin during the War, Smuts is an avid anti-communist and now understands Stalin is a dictator and pledges President Truman that South Africa will stand with the United States.

On his return from England, he hears during the rest of 1947 that people are still complaining about wartime shortages of petrol and food and the cost of living.

Even though government statistics demonstrate that the per person median income of Whites is ten times that of Blacks, six times that of Asians, and five times that of Coloreds, Whites are complaining the loudest.

Smuts understands the importance of this issue and will not allow the government to raise the price of wheat or maize, worsening the cost of living.

After reviewing the crime statistics for just the Witwatersrand, showing in 1947 that there were 110 assaults by Non-Europeans on European women; 338 murders by Non-Europeans of Europeans; and 12,204 burglaries and thefts by Non-Europeans, Prime Minister Smuts orders a crackdown against Non-Europeans.

"That is totally unacceptable. We cannot tolerate a lack of law and order. I want action! These Natives must respect the Law! And we need to put a stop to these unlawful strikes and work stoppages," he tells his Minister of Justice.

Smuts feels that taking a definite and strong stand for law and order will endear him with all White voters. He also believes White voters will appreciate his strong stand against Black unions and their demands for decent wages and living conditions.

When in December a delegation from the South African Trades and Labor Council seeks a meeting about prices and shortages, Smuts refuses.

Instead he crows, "Contact me after we win the election!"

Chapter 20

Today, October 30, 1947, Mary and Charles along with Frederick and Henrietta are celebrating little John's first birthday.

New friends of Charles and Mary have filled every room in the house provided by Frederick and Henrietta in District Six. A few White friends of the Kruger's are also present.

Father John telegraphed that he would be unable to attend his namesake's birthday because he was doing 'missionary' work in Mpumalanga at the behest of Bishop Dennis Hurley. The priest noted he had said a special Mass for both the Washington family and for the Kruger family.

Jim Wright sent a congratulatory package of baby toys, some handmade by the Zulus in Mary's old village.

Henrietta brought her record player and some American records to liven up the crowd. Many of the guests, Black, White, Colored and even a Chinese couple, are jiving and singing the English lyrics with the music.

When Henrietta puts on the turntable the Glenn Miller hit of 'That Old Black Magic,' several more people push aside some chairs to enlarge the dance area.

Watching the dancers, Charles says, "I'm not familiar with those singers."

Henrietta replies, "That's Skip Nelson and his group. It was the number one hit in America. We'll play the other side when this finishes. That's called 'A Pink Cocktail for a Blue Lady.' Later, I've got some Frank Sinatra, some with the Dorsey Orchestra and some when he went solo. You will love them."

"Yes, I've heard him on Frederick's radio, even during the War. Wasn't he nicknamed the Voice?"

Henrietta laughs, "That's right."

Overhearing, Frederick says, "Charles, I wondered how you learned to hum and even whistle some of those tunes. Well, I think everyone is having a good time and nobody has to talk about politics. It's a relief to take a break, Charles."

"Well, when I listen to those songs on the radio, I do hear subtle messages which I take as support of the United Party."

"Yes, we need that because it will be a close election, Charles."

"Frederick, explain to me about the voting rights of the Non-Europeans, because that is very complicated to me."

"Yes, it is complicated. Let's see. Well, in 1910 when the Union of South Africa was created, Non-Whites who were over 21, met literacy and property ownership requirements could vote in the Cape Province and this law could only be overturned by a two-thirds vote in both Houses of Parliament. But, in 1936, the Parliament voted to no longer allow Blacks to vote in the ordinary Parliamentary elections, effectively disenfranchising Blacks, although Blacks could vote in special elections for three White Assembly Members, selected by Whites."

Charles asks, "What about women and Coloreds and Asians?"

"Only White women are franchised. Coloreds in only the Cape Province who meet the age, literacy, and property ownership are still eligible to vote in the ordinary Parliamentary elections. Colored men will have the right until two-thirds of both Houses of Parliament changes the law. As for Asians' voting rights, that's a little complicated."

"So, Frederick, the long and short of it is that no Black man or Black woman in the entire country can vote in the ordinary Parliamentary elections and only Colored men in the Cape Province who are over 21, can read and write, and own real estate can vote in those ordinary Parliament elections."

"That's it in a nutshell, Charles. Plus, I forgot to add, that White men over 21 now in both the Natal and Cape Provinces can vote without meeting any property ownership or literacy requirements."

"I don't mean to be pushy, but how do the number of Whites relate to the total population of South Africa, Frederick?"

"That is a very good question. Whites are about one-quarter of the total population. Let me say that if I were in charge, Blacks and Coloreds and Asians throughout the entire country could vote for a person of any race."

"Well, Frederick, if I were eligible as a Colored man to vote, I would be voting for the White candidates of the United Party for the Parliament. But, I don't own any property."

"Yes, I know, but you can urge your eligible Colored friends to vote for the United Party candidates."

Charles replies, "That, I will do. If you want, I will be glad to distribute some flyers and put up some posters here in the neighborhood. And, if it would be helpful, I can go outside of District Six and put some in store windows. I know you have quite a stash of flyers and posters at the homestead. I can do it on a few Sunday afternoons."

"Yes, that would be truly helpful. I'll get you some tomorrow when you return to work. But you don't need to hurry since the election-day won't arrive until next May. We've got plenty of time, Charles."

"Frederick, by the way, thanks for bringing us some of your wine and getting the beer and soft drinks for the party since we can't legally get alcoholic drinks."

Frederick replies, "You are more than welcome, Charles. It's the least I can do to repay you and Mary for all your hard work. And thank you and Mary for the wonderful food. That was quite a feast!"

Frederick sees Henrietta walking to the record player she had brought from home. She puts on the turntable Frank Sinatra's rendition of 'Night and Day.'

She watches more couples arise to dance to the music as she hears her husband continue talking with Charles.

"I'm sorry Father John couldn't make it. I would love to have seen my old college classmate."

"Yes, that was sad news that he couldn't make it. I owe Father John a lot, Frederick. I miss him."

Henrietta exclaims to Frederick and Charles, "Would you look at that?"

She's pointing out the window at the Kruger's children who are playing in the yard with some of the kids living in District Six. Nobody is fighting. Instead they are all laughing as they play some children's game.

Henrietta observes, "Now, that's the way it should be—with every color of the rainbow enjoying the festivities. That's the way the whole country should be—like District Six—with everyone getting along with everyone else."

Along with Henrietta, the two men smile as they watch the kids having a great time. She says, "Well, Charles, in a couple of years, your son will be out there playing with the other kids."

Frederick remarks, "You know, Charles, little John looks just like you."

A broad smile hurries across Charles' face.

He enthusiastically says, "Yes, Frederick, my baby's hair, just like mine, isn't kinky. A comb won't remain in place on his little head, now or never. And the little guy's bronze skin color matches my own. Our noses are alike. I' m a happy man and our life is good. We enjoy living in District Six and enjoy our friends and neighbors. And, I thank you and Henrietta for that."

Frederick says, "No need to mention it. You and Mary deserve it. And I thank you and Mary for your hard work. Well, I think we'll leave a bit early because in the next month or two, I'll have a lot of work getting ready for the next election. I'll have those flyers and posters ready for you. But do be careful if you are traveling outside of District Six."

As the party winds down and after the mutual hand-shakes and the hugs, Frederick and Henrietta leave and are driving the short distance to their home when Henrietta comments, "Looking around the room, I couldn't help but notice that the mixing of the races is a direct threat to racial segregation. It's exactly what the Smuts government doesn't want. Worse, Frederick, it's exactly what Malan and his thugs don't want. The mixing of the races is a direct threat to racial segregation."

"You are one hundred percent correct, my dear about Malan. However, Smuts and Hofmeyr will tolerate the

Coloreds and have done so. They understand that any correction must be a gradual one to avoid violence. I agree that the very fact that we classify some people as Colored means the races are mixing. I call it biracial harmony because it brings us together."

"Frederick, that's a good name for it, biracial harmony."

"My dear, Judge Henry Fagan chaired the Native Laws Commission which declared that total segregation is impossible although there was no recommendation for social or political integration. I see that as a gradual beginning for biracial harmony."

Henrietta says, "Yes, but the Paul Sauer Report argues the contrary position that only total segregation will prevent equality and control by Blacks. That's exactly what Malan argues for Blacks. I know there are other parties to vote for, but none of them has a chance at getting control of Parliament. I know our real choice is just between Smuts and Malan."

He says, "Yes. Nonetheless, we will all be better off with the return of the Smuts government than with one run by Malan. At least, we know that with the Smuts government, there is hope for racial progress. It might be slow, but I feel it will be coming, especially if Jan Hofmeyr is the new Prime Minister. That's why we must re-elect the United Party's candidates to the Assembly. But, I am worried about the election in some of the rural districts."

At home, Frederick retires to his office and begins to play with his travel schedule to help some of his fellow party members in their Districts where the winning margin is slim. He understands that because of these rural Districts with fewer voters, the United Party could lose enough seats to throw the Parliament to Malan and his

National Party. He'll campaign hard for these United Party candidates in these voting Districts containing fewer voters.

***

With the start of 1948, the newspapers highlight the continued shortages of food, coal, and petrol. They report: "The worst thing facing South Africans is the cost of living. Constant demand for government action seems to fall on deaf ears."

The National Party of D. F. Malan seizes on the general dissatisfaction and in speeches in Parliament demands government assistance. The election campaign, though about 5 months away, has begun in earnest.

Prime Minister Smuts thinks he has an issue to distract people from the cost of living. Having thought about Russian efforts to dominate Eastern Europe as well as the Balkans, and Poland through godless Communism, Smuts schedules a nationwide radio speech to warn the country of the 'Red Menace of Communism.'

He even describes Communism by using the Afrikaner words, *'ROOI GEVAAR,'* as a warning. He figures that the men and women of his country will rally around him to fight the 'Red Peril.'

He remarks to an aide, "That should make Malan shut up about wartime shortages."

But Malan is no fool and he actually applauds the Prime Minister's speech. But Malan twists the issue as he exclaims in perfect English, "Communism is a threat to Christianity and to White civilization. We cannot let the Communists and their friends govern our Union of South Africa. Our White civilization is at risk with Communism. We can have no truck with Communists. Yes, we must fight the 'Red Peril' with every ounce of strength in our beings."

In March, when the Prime Minister seeks support of certain groups, Malan quickly in a radio broadcast tars—sometimes incorrectly—these groups and their members as friends of Russia and as affiliated with the Communist Party of South Africa. Malan calls these Smut supporters and friends as 'fellow travelers of the Communists' and even names one left wing newspaper as a 'Communist rag' run by militant Communist sympathizers, the 'Springbok Legion.'

Malan hollers, "Just go to the last page of this Communist mouth organ and read the last page in the 'What's On' column and you can discover where and when these Communists are meeting."

In that March radio broadcast, Malan pounces on Smuts,

> "The Prime Minister has always been cozy with Russia and I've heard him say during the War he was an admirer of Stalin and developed a good working relation with Stalin. You don't believe me? Well, listen to the actual words coming from the Prime Minister's hypocritical mouth."

First, a little screeching as a recording begins with a voice sounding like Smuts' voice proclaims in complimentary language, "I doff my hat to Stalin."

After the recording, D. F. Malan continues his attack,

> "Smuts' support from these Communist front organizations proves he is a Red Lover. Smuts will give the country to the Natives and the Communists.

224

"As you know, godless Communist Russia has invaded Czechoslovakia and now has total control over the country. News reports say the godless Communists are ridding Czechoslovakia of Catholic priests.

"Now, my friends, we must be wary of both a 'Black Peril' and also of a 'Red Peril' in this election. We cannot afford to take these kinds of risks. Security of our country is foremost in my mind. We must protect South Africa at all costs."

Smuts can hardly believe his cars about the repetitious lies and fake news spinning from Malan's mouth. The more he denies the untruthful allegations, the more Malan repeats them. And the more of repetition there is, the more it seems to prove that repetitive use can ultimately become the truth.

***

On March 26, Jan Hofmeyr informs the Prime Minister, "The Election Day is now scheduled for Wednesday, May 26th. I understand that Malan will be outlining his new policy of 'Apartheid' in an upcoming gathering in Paarl. We will have some people in the audience to get information, sir."

Smuts replies, "Wonderful!"

The day after Malan's March 29th talk to his constituents, Hofmeyr hands a summary of Malan's new government policy.

The Prime Minister reads:

"A new registration system for Whites and Non-Whites will be introduced to deal with the ever increasing influx of Natives and Indians in European areas.

"We will improve development in the Natives' Reserves for the African population. Permitted Black workers in White urban areas would live in segregated areas when not in the Reserves.

"Indians and Coloreds would also live in segregated areas.

"No Blacks would have any political rights except for representation by Whites in the Senate, the same as Coloreds.

"We will end the marriages between people of different races."

The summary of Malan's speech causes Smuts to reconvene the political advisers of the United Party and his Cabinet Ministers for ways to appeal to the voters.

"Gentlemen, we need to ingratiate our Party to every voter. Initially, we need to combat that kind of talk, but, in my opinion, we must stay away from the Natives question and deal with the issue most people are concerned, namely about the cost of everything."

Getting an almost unanimous affirmative head nodding, Smuts asks, "What can we do?"

Smuts looks directly at the Minister of Agriculture in charge of agricultural production and gives a go ahead signal to speak.

"Mr. Prime Minister, as you know we've had a big problem during the war with the issue of white bread. You may recall that we required the weight of white bread be reduced by ten percent. Because of the wartime shortages, we replaced white bread with the standard wartime loaf, made courser and darker. We put biscuits and cakes on the no-bake list."

Stuttering, the Minister of Agriculture continues, "To guarantee reduced shortages, we declared that bread could not be served on Wednesday afternoons. We prohibited all hotels from serving toast. All of this was done under the auspices of the National Wheat Board for the war effort. It was patriotism at its best, sir."

"A fine speech, but what do you suggest?"

"Mr. Prime Minister, as you are aware, we've had a drought in the southern and eastern grazing areas. The wheat crop and maize crop will be ruined if rain doesn't come soon. All those farmers want either a subsidy from the government or a government-inflicted price increase now, before the election."

Stoking his beard, the Prime Minister says, "Granting either suggestion will not play well with the rest of the country, sir. Your suggestion will benefit only farmers, millers, grain storage operators, and bakers. It will do nothing to help the general public."

"If you'll forgive me, sir, the Afrikaners in the north rely on cheap Black labor to make their profits grow. They are joined by the big farms and big banks and big businesses all of whom think the National Party will help grow the economy in the north of the country. I strongly suggest you re-think this issue, sir."

Before anyone can speak, Jan Hofmeyr says, "Well, Mr. Prime Minister, after you read this, you might want to re-consider."

He circulates a flyer and says, "Our opposition has a new slogan in English and in Afrikaans. Before you ask, sir, yes, the flyer comes from my friend and former student, Father John O'Malley. Here take a look at this."

As expected, the flyer causes a stir among the group.

"WHITE Bread for a WHITE South Africa!"

Prime Minister Smuts releases a groan and a sigh, "My God, will the election be won or lost over white bread?"

Recovering, he says, "I don't like it, but helping the farmers and their ilk will hurt us with the rest of the country when prices rise. We just cannot raise those prices. What are we doing about the housing shortage?"

"Sir, we are a little behind schedule, but we are making good progress," the Minister of Public Health declares.

But, Jan Hofmeyr, as the Deputy Prime Minister, knows better—out of the 24,000 planed housing units, less than 3,000 have actually been built—but he remains silent as he hears another report about hospital beds.

The Health Minister says, "I'm pleased to report that we've increased the number of hospital beds, especially in hospitals for White persons at the expense of hospitals serving Non-Europeans."

"That's wonderful, sir. Now what have we done to please all the business people, whether British or Afrikaner, who object to those controls and to wartime rationing?"

That report pleases Prime Minister Smuts, but the use of 'wartime rationing' reminds him that the rationing of meat during the war produced 'Meatloaf Wednesdays.' Maybe, he chuckles, Malan will come up with some slogan about Meatloaf.

Before the strategy sessions ends, Smuts recognizes an upheld hand from one of the lower ranking aides. "Yes, sir, go ahead young man."

"Excuse me, sir, but I picked up this 'Bastard Poster' written in Afrikaans which demonstrates the evils of mixed marriages."

He stands, hands the poster to the Minister of Agriculture, and the poster is passed forward to the Prime Minister.

The young aide says, "As you can see, the poster shows a very pretty young White woman in a revealing dress with downcast eyes and she is sitting on the knee of a well-dressed Black stud in a slum shanty with two ragged, barefooted Colored children playing outside in the dirt. The Black buck has a huge grin on his face and a leer in his dark eyes. It's disgusting."

Fortunately, today the Colored representative in charge of getting out the Colored vote in the Cape Province is absent from the room. The remaining men—all White—understand the ramifications of the poster.

The young aide says, "Sir, if you will forgive me, our campaign should also address the Colored issue. We should end the practice of having more and more Colored babies in our country. It is a dilution of the White race, sir."

Jan Hofmeyr responds for the Prime Minister, "I understand your concern, young man, but remember eligible Coloreds can vote in the Cape Province for any White candidates, and we will need their votes. So, I suggest we put that issue on the back burner."

The Prime Minister says, "Yes. We need every vote. Alright, gentlemen, let's get to work."

When the Prime Minister stumbles over the date of the election, Jan Hofmeyr realizes that Smuts has momentarily forgotten the date of the election. He says nicely, "Yes, Mr. Prime Minister, the election is set for May 26, six weeks away."

Chapter 21

On April 16th, when Parliament is dissolved, the United Party holds 89 seats while the National Party holds 48, with the minority parties holding the remaining 13 seats. Now, with the election scheduled for May 26th, the political campaigning has intensified with the nomination of candidates.

That morning, Charles and Mary push little John in his baby carriage to the Kruger household and start their chores—Mary inside the house and Charles in the garden.

When their work has finished that evening, Charles gathers more political flyers and posters for distribution in District Six. He's been at it on Sundays, but now he plans on working each evening.

After supper, Charles says, "My dear, I have promised myself and Frederick that I will visit every Colored man who is an eligible voter and give the prospective voter positive information on the necessity to vote for the United Party candidate. So, Mary, again I'll be gone for a while this evening."

"Yes, that's good, dear, but be careful and don't stay, too late."

However, even after several days and nights in his previous campaigning, Charles has discovered that hardly any Colored man living or working in District Six meets the voting eligibility requirements. In fact, in his several weeks of canvassing Charles has discovered only three Coloreds who can vote in the ordinary election. Naturally, all three men promise that they will go with the United Party White candidate, a pleasing outcome for Charles.

He has deposited posters with District Six shopkeepers to place in their windows, although several refused, citing possible vandalism from supporters of the opposite political party.

He remembers one Colored man's typical response, "Sorry, I'd like to accommodate you, but we do have Afrikaners come in to the area and I can't afford the loss of any business when times are hard in making ends meet. I don't want my store windows broken or smeared with nasty slogans. And, my friend, you'd better be careful because not everybody around here likes the United Party and Mr. Smuts."

"What? Why is that?" He asks the man.

"The Smuts government has no love for Blacks, or Coloreds for that matter, or even Indians. Perhaps, somebody new will give us a better shot. Otherwise, we just get the same old same old. If I could vote, I be willing to let the other guys run the show. Maybe they can do better. I hope you understand," the man warns.

"Yes, sir, I do understand but have you thought of the alternative? That guy Malan and his cronies? In my humble opinion, sir, Malan and his National Party will make all of our lives worse than you can ever imagine. I hope you will think about it. And thanks for your time," Charles engages before moving on to his next prospect, who, he remembers, also declines accepting any political material.

But now, days later, he feels a surge of fear thump in his chest as he thinks about the man's warning about Afrikaners. In a few store windows, he has seen a few posters in the Afrikaner language, such as *Die kaffer op sy plek!* and *Die koelies uit die land!* Charles knows enough of the language that one poster wants to keep Blacks in their place and the other wants coolies, meaning Indians and Asians, deported. Yes, he must be careful, even in District Six.

But, this evening, after he has practically covered the remaining area of District Six, Charles decides to work his way downtown, since the central business district abuts District Six. He understands he'll have trouble convincing some Whites to accept the posters. But, he'll try nevertheless. He puts the man's warning to bed because he has a foolproof plan.

When he sees Blacks or Coloreds working inside a business, he will inquire. Charles figures that when he sees Black or Colored workers, that will be a good sign.

But, to his dismay, he's not having much luck after a few tries.

As he talks with a Black clerk in a furniture store, the White owner interrupts, "We don't need that kind of trash here. Take your garbage and get out! You people and Smuts and his ilk are ruining our country."

Holding Charles' shoulder, he ushers Charles out the front door, shouting "If I see you here again, I'll call the police to arrest you for trespassing and vagrancy! Go back to where you came from!"

The front door closes and Charles hears the White man chastise his Black employee, "Don't even think about that garbage or you won't have a job here! Maybe you'd like living in the Reserves! Now, get back to work!"

As Charles retreats from the furniture store, he stops in front of a café. A sign reads that the cafe caters to Non-Europeans. Entering, Charles seats himself at the counter and orders a cup of coffee from the Black waitress. He hears a radio loudly broadcasting a speech in English from D. F. Malan, head of the National Party.

Charles listens as the speaker pauses to let each thought sink into the listener's brain:

"You ask, what is 'Apartheid'? The answer is simple, my friends, because God tells us so. The Good Lord Himself tells us so.

"Apartheid means no marriages between Whites and Non-Whites.

"Apartheid means no Natives' Representative Council.

"Apartheid means no African representatives in our government.

"Apartheid means the Natives' Reserves become their 'Homelands' as a separate nation.

"Apartheid means no influx of Natives into urban areas.

"Apartheid means no African Trade Unions.

"Apartheid means protection of European workers against Non-European workers.

"Apartheid means maximum segregation.

"Apartheid means preservation of the good life for the real South Africans.

"Apartheid means no votes FOR Non-Europeans.

"Apartheid means no votes BY Non-Europeans.

"So, my Friends, please cast your votes on May 26 for candidates of the National Party! You won't regret it, believe me.

"And, may God Bless you and may God Bless the Union of South Africa!"

Suddenly, the radio begins playing German marching music and as it fades, an announcer begins playing some jazz music.

Returning with his cup of coffee, the Black waitress whispers, "Can you believe that? No wonder we Blacks cannot vote! We would never vote for them."

Charles asks, "Why do you listen to that kind of talk?"

"Because we want to know what their plan is; that's why," she says in a lowered voice.

Charles says, "Yes, I understand. I'm here for the United Party. For your window can I leave a poster favoring the United Party candidates?"

"Sir, my husband and I don't own this shop. If we did put up the poster, we'd get in trouble with the owner and with other businesses. Plus, some people might trash the place. Not everyone around the center of this city likes Blacks or Coloreds. So, I'm sorry, but we can't risk it. I hope you understand."

Charles nods, drinks his coffee, smiles a goodbye, and drops a few coins on the counter before he leaves for another opportunity to place a poster in a Cape Town window for Frederick Kruger's United Party.

Passing several stores, Charles notices the many windows display Afrikaner slogans. The most prominent say *"Die wit man moet altyd baas wees!"* which Charles roughly translates as "The White man must always be the boss." Certainly, no opportunity exists there for a United Party poster.

Rounding the corner, he spies a brightly-colored banner hanging overhead between two buildings of the Dutch Reformed Church—*Eie volk, eie taal, eie land!* Charles translates this as meaning, "our folk, our language, our land." He knows from his Catholic schooling that the Dutch Reformed Church considers Africa as the Promised Land for White people, a gift from God, who indubitably must also be White.

Charles feels anxiety creeping upwards from his esophagus and is almost ready to call it a day since he is near St. Mary's Cathedral.

He starts to turn back, but across the street he spies a promising opportunity—a Black woman entering a self-service laundry. Peering in the window, he sees several Blacks and Coloreds.

But, as he nears the front door, he realizes he's made a serious mistake because four doors down and near the street corner, he spies a gang of White men speaking in Afrikaans.

As he turns to walk away, one of the Afrikaners catches him and says in English, "Oh, yes, I see you are the guy giving out those damned flyers of the United Party. Give me all that shit!"

After grabbing a poster from Charles he shouts in Afrikaans," Hey, guys! Come over here and look at this shit! He's got a whole bag full of shit!"

Before Charles can escape, the men grab him, pin his arms behind his back, and—one by one—pummel him with their fists until Charles falls in the street with some of his posters and flyers spilling from his bag.

One man is trying to stomp on Charles' head. He misses because Charles rolls away, the bag still around his shoulder.

Somehow, Charles manages to crawl to the curb and right himself with the near empty bag of political material over his shoulder. He runs for his life because the men are chasing him.

Rounding the corner, he spies St. Mary's Cathedral and, breathing heavily, sees his escape. He runs for the entrance door, squeezing inside before the men can catch him.

Inside and running toward a side altar, Charles bumps a strolling priest, almost knocking the man to the floor.

"Oh, sorry, Father Vincent, but some men are after me because I had some political stuff for the ..." he stops in mid-sentence, afraid to reveal he's a volunteer for the United Party.

Eyeing his bag of United Party material, the priest says, "Whoa, my friend. Slow down! You're safe here. Charles, come with me to my office."

Looking toward the door, Charles sees that the men have not entered the church. He readily follows the priest.

The priest says, "Good to see you again, Charles! What happened to you? Here, have some water and let's put some band aids on those cuts, fortunately not too serious. I'll drive you home. You can tell me the rest of your story."

Catching his breath, Charles tells the priest what happened.

"Say, have you heard anything from Father O'Malley?"

Charles tells Father Vincent that he hasn't heard from Father O'Malley in a while.

Charles knows he'll have some tall explaining to Mary about the cuts on his face. Tomorrow, he'll tell Frederick it's too dangerous for him to deliver any more flyers or posters in Cape Town.

But, he is now energized against Apartheid, even though working for Frederick and Henrietta has safeguarded him and his family from most of the evils of Apartheid.

He will obtain more information about joining the African National Congress.

Chapter 22

The next morning, Frederick graciously accepts Charles' apology about not placing the posters and the flyers. He says, "Charles, there's no need to apologize. I'm so very sorry you had that terrible experience. Don't worry, because we will do fine in this election. I'm leaving this afternoon on another trip to visit some of the rural districts to campaign for our candidates. I'll see you when I return."

***

A few days later on April 26th, Frederick returns. In his office, he picks up a stack of old newspapers which usually favor the opposition. He is hoping to gauge the spirit of the campaign since the election is just one month away.

A headline in the April 18th edition of *The Cape Town News* smacks Jan Hofmeyr with an attack on Smuts:

"A VOTE FOR SMUTS IS A VOTE FOR HOFMEYR."

Curious, Frederick reads the article.

> "According to certain sources, Prime Minister Smuts, age 78, has already promised Jan Hofmeyr, age 54, to be Smuts' successor as the Prime Minister. Although Hofmeyr has issued disavowals, not a single Member of the Smuts cabinet believes Hofmeyr. And this newspaper doesn't believe that either."

Frederick doesn't stop reading in spite of the misstatements about his old professor and fellow Party member. He flips the page.

"Jan Hofmeyr is on record as favoring both marriage and adoption by persons of any race. He has stated in Parliament that 'there should be no discrimination in marriage or in adoption' in spite of how that increases the dilution of the White race."

Tossing the issue of *The Cape Town News* aside, Frederick reads the headline in the April 21st edition of *The Cape Overview*:

"VOTE AGAINST HOFMEYR AND THE UNITED PARTY AND SAVE SOUTH AFRICA FROM RUIN."

Frederick finishes leafing through *The Cape Overview* and then picks up the issue of the usually reliable throw-away weekly. He begins reading, thinking, "Hopefully, these guys will have some real, honest-to-goodness news and not be all one-sided."

"An unconfirmed rumor circulated in the trenches is that the Afrikaner Party and the National Party will join forces to assure the United Party is soundly defeated.

"Of course, the Labor Party will side, as always, with the United Party.

"The Afrikaner Party has received pledges, unnamed sources report, that the National Party will soften its stand toward Nationalism, separation from the British Commonwealth, and for a Republic of South Africa.

"H. V. Havenga, the head of the Afrikaner Party said, 'That will be quite an alliance, very strong to defeat Smuts and his gang of soft-hearted and soft-headed liberals, believe me!'

"Although many moderate Afrikaners, especially the English speakers who sided with Britain during the War, disdained any thought of leaving the Commonwealth, now that the National Party has softened the idea of a Republic and of leaving the Commonwealth, our surveys reveal that many moderate Afrikaners are switching from the United Party to the National Party. That could tip the scales in this election in favor of the National Party.

"As might be expected, both the Afrikaner Party and the National Party have attacked the Smuts administration for incompetence over rationing, nationwide shortages of meat and bread, especially in Johannesburg and Pretoria."

Frederick stops, "Damn it, that is partly true, but, couldn't they at least give us credit for improving the situation!" He keeps reading.

"Previous undisclosed discoveries now reveal that the Smuts administration exported building materials to other countries, although housing in South Africa is miserable, with many people living in garages.

"Nobody disputes the fact that during the end of the War, the Smuts administration gave millions of gold to the British government instead of purchasing goods to help South Africans when South Africans were suffering from shortages in everything.

"Both the National Party and the Afrikaner Party decry the Smuts' immigration policies taking away needed jobs among White South Africans, especially the plan to allow more than 50,000 new immigrants from Britain. As Mr. Malan said, 'It's an evil scheme to pack the voting rolls to assure future victories for the United Party.'

"Although comment was sought several times from the Smuts campaign, this newspaper received nothing."

Frederick tosses the weekly paper to the floor and says, "Okay, let's have a look at the *Rand Daily Mail* to see if they have anything nice to say about us."

He glares at the headline but instead of reading the paper, tosses it in a pile with the others.

Reaching for the left-wing mouthpiece of organized labor, *The Guardian of Cape Town* always critical of the Smuts as an anti-unionist in a column entitled "Parliamentary-Merry-Go-Round," Frederick sees that the newspaper has called the National Party and Malan as fascists. But he doesn't read it.

He walks to the liquor cabinet, but decides he'd rather have a glass of his wine than any hard liquor. He seats himself in his favorite leather chair, lets the Pinotage bouquet waft in his nostrils, swishes the contents in a deep red whirl, again breathes in the aroma, and then a sip. "Ah, that's the ticket," he says.

In walks Henrietta.

She says, "Well, Frederick, just a month to go. What do you think?"

"I'm very confident I'll be re-elected, but I'm not so sure Prime Minister Smuts will win his own seat in Standerton. Wentzel du Plessis, his opponent, is running a strong campaign against him. The Prime Minister has made repeated trips there for several different political rallies. He has posters showing Malan as a cartoon character applauding a Hitler cartoon character, which to me means the Prime Minister is running a bit frightened."

"What? Why Smuts has won that seat in Standerton forever, right?"

"Smuts has been here for twenty-four years, Henrietta."

"Well, how will we do in those rural districts?"

"Henrietta, it's hard to say about the rural districts. I see some very close contests there. We'll just have to wait and see. But I'm optimistic."

"Well, I guess, overall, that's good. Now, let's talk about some more important issues. You must talk with Hans about arguing with me. I've informed him that when Daddy gets home, you will explain why that's not acceptable conduct. You need to do this because—my God, our most precious son has our lawyer genes in him—he just wants to argue with me. And, Frederick, he's damn good at it. I dare say he'll grow up to be a lawyer!"

"Okay, Henrietta, I will lay down the law," he laughs. "And, yes, I need to get back to what's important to us, our family. Besides, we've got a month to go. And I do feel good about our chances!"

***

Like Frederick and Henrietta, Charles and Mary worry about who will control the new Parliament, but not in the same vein.

Mary does not expect their lives to change because she figures that working for the Kruger family and living in District Six has insulated them from most of the horrors of racial discrimination.

In Cape Town, by and large, people tolerate each other and Coloreds and Blacks are free to move about. Yes, once in a while, some Afrikaners are trouble makers, but that news is scarce. On the home front, little John is healthy and is a joy. For Mary, the marriage and their lives are good.

Investigating the African National Congress and becoming more in tune with the political news, Charles feels a calling to be more involved. He recognizes the evil in Apartheid and understands he must take a stand. Yet, he too understands that he and his family, living in District Six and under the Kruger's protection, are in a zone of safety.

***

Finally, the election is two days away.

Henrietta and Mary are listening to the radio in the kitchen when the music is interrupted by a news flash that Prime Minister Smuts has recognized Israel as an independent nation.

The announcer then says,

> "Before we return you to our regularly sched-
> uled program, we bring this paid political an-
> nouncement from J.G. Strijdom and the
> National Party:

"Hello, my friends. This is J. G. Strijdom, sometimes called the Lion of the North.

"As you know, I am a strong believer in South Africa. But, I am very worried that our country under the command of General Smuts is marching down the wrong road.

"Under the so-called leadership of General Smuts, I fear that soon, the Africans will cease to be barbarians and, instead, they will obtain the vote because the United Party will gradually extend political rights to those of darker skin.

"We can only remain a White nation in South Africa if we retain the right to govern.

"Remember, the Natives outnumber us four to one. If we lose our position as masters, we will surely disappear from South Africa.

"The Natives are encouraged by the United Party to believe they will become masters of the Union.

"I am, and the National Party is also, vehemently opposed to any advancement of the Natives.

"Please vote on May 26th for all candidates of the National Party.

"May Our Lord, Jesus Christ, bless you and the Union of South Africa?

"Thanks for listening. This is J. G. Strijdom, Lion of the North."

The announcer says, "This has been a paid political broadcast. And, now we return you to our regular scheduled program." The music begins.

Henrietta says, "Mary, that was the most disgusting and awful fearmongering I've heard. I hope that Strijdom and his like crawl back into their holes. It makes me ashamed that a White South African would even think thoughts of oppressive segregation let alone actually broadcast those thoughts over the public radio waves. I know you must be offended and I'm so sorry we have people like that in our government."

Mary replies, "Yes, I know. But, it's not your fault. We will continue to survive as we have done for many years. We Natives are tough. We have endured much hardship and oppression for many years. We will survive! We have the spirit!"

Henrietta says, "Yes, you do. Let's us pray that the United Party controls Parliament and that our country begins moving away from racial discrimination."

***

Two days before the election, Prime Minister Smuts is talking with Jan Hofmeyr as they review dispatches of prognosticated results.

"Jan, a spirit of change is sweeping the entire world and South Africa is not immune. Many other governments have fallen in this post-war time. Why shouldn't ours fall? It's true that people get tired or you. Perhaps, it's time. But, old friend, I'm optimistic."

"Mr. Prime Minister, I am also optimistic, although we may lose some of the rural districts because of that crap about how we favor an immediate end to racial segregation. Yes, it's true that we recognize the need for a practical approach."

"Well, Jan, the danger is that our practical approach appears to be a Pro-Native approach. Many White people cannot understand it and are running over with resentment. It could mean that we lose the election and hand the Natives over to the other extreme—Malan."

Hofmeyr shakes his head as the Prime Minister continues.

"And Malan and his Party naturally rejoice over my troubles at the United Nations. Here, he shouts about me that I am the author of human rights in the Preamble in the United Nations Charter now exposed as a hypocrite and a double-faced-time-server."

"Excuse me, sir, but most people understand that you stood up for South Africa against the world powers and demonstrated that all of the people of South Africa live and work in a well-ordered and civilized society, which equates with the meaning of human rights."

"That's fine, Jan. Yet, I certainly recognize the contradiction, because on the one hand, I am a humanist and author of the United Nation's Preamble about human rights, while on the other hand, I am a South African European, proud of our heritage and proud of the clean European society we have built in South Africa and which I am still determined not to see lost forever in a Black pool."

"I understand, sir."

"Well, Jan, the United Party's policy is clear. We stand for good treatment of the Non-Whites and we stand for the continued White leadership in South Africa, just as in the past. No doubt if White leadership is lost, then Whites will indeed lose South Africa."

"That's for sure."

"But Apartheid or separate development and Natives returning to the Reserves is not good.'

"Mr. Prime Minister, I feel confident that all sections of the population will agree with our policy and return our Party to another five years to govern the country."

"And, Jan, I hope you are correct and I pray that the Good Lord will make it happen."

Chapter 23

The night of the election, Frederick and Henrietta join Frederick's supporters at his campaign headquarters to await the returns.

Their two children, Hans and Robin, are spending the night with Charles and Mary and John in the District Six home.

Several spotters are phoning in the results from various voting stations in Frederick's district. So far, Frederick is slightly behind as shown from the early returns. But, he points out that no returns from his stronghold precincts have yet been counted. Nonetheless, he covers any concern with a smile.

Naturally, plenty of food, wine, beer, and alcoholic drinks are being consumed as the crowd rehashes the strategies of the different parties and are prognosticating the outcomes of various races.

Listening to the radio, the group learns that the initial reports indicate that out of 1,337,534 registered voters, over a million votes have been cast.

Henrietta says, "That is amazing! I guess tomorrow we'll find out the exact number, which will probably be higher. I wonder how many of those votes were cast by eligible Colored voters."

Frederick responds, "Well, they don't keep that statistic by race. But, most probably the overwhelmingly number of votes were Whites. We'll get the total number of valid votes in a day or two. But, based on past experience, a few thousand votes won't be counted because of some invalidity or because they were left blank.

"And, then sad to say, there will be many, many thousands who stayed home and didn't vote. That's always a very sad day for any democracy. Sometimes, those registered voters by voting could have changed the outcome of any election. I've seen it happen here, in Britain, and even in the United States of America."

A supporter shouts, "Sir, it looks like you've closed the gap. Congratulations!"

Immediately, the crowd surrounds Frederick, some people patting him on his shoulders and back and some reaching for a handshake. Henrietta embraces him and warmly kisses him. But, Frederick knows that the election isn't over till it's over.

As the sound and intensity of the celebration increases, someone shouts, "Quiet! Quiet! We've got an announcement over the radio! Quiet, I said! Listen up!"

With a little static, the news quiets the crowd.

Henrietta exclaims, "Oh, no, not Prime Minister Smuts! I can't believe it!"

The radio voice repeats the news,

> "Prime Minister Smuts has been defeated by Wentzel du Plessis of the National Party in his Standerton district after 24 years as a Member of Parliament. We have no word on the outcome of the number of seats actually won or lost because of the clear difficulty in counting the many paper ballots. Our election central says we may not have a final tally until tomorrow or even the next day."

The news dampens the air as tongues churn out different explanations for the Prime Minister's defeat.

Suddenly, the radio voice says,

> "This just in to our news room in this late hour. The Minister of Native Affairs, Major P. V. G. van der Byl, has been defeated by the National Party candidate in what was considered a very safe seat, especially since Major van de Byl previously won that seat by more than a thousand votes. That certainly is not good news for the United Party when a sure winner loses his seat. The control of Parliament hangs in the balance. More, as we receive the news. Now, we take a commercial break."

That news of a possible defeat by the United Party and loss of control of Parliament definitely push even the very thought of more celebration out of the room.

Frederick quickly stands atop a chair and says, "All right, everyone, let's be calm and await more results from our spotters about my race. Right now, we just need the returns from the last two precincts. And, it's a long night. There are lots of returns to come in about other races. So, chins up, please!"

As he sits, the radio delivers more news that the United Party candidates appear to be winning in all of the urban districts but that the rural districts are slow in reporting any results. The radio voice declares,

> "Based on information from election officials, we may not have a final determination until tomorrow or the next day. But, as we receive the news, rest assured that we'll bring it to you as soon as we receive it. Now, we take a commercial break."

That news uplifts the crowd.

As the night drones on, Frederick worries because he has a lead of just over seventy nine votes and, for some unknown reason, the last precinct containing voters around the Kruger vineyards has still not been announced. He keeps a straight, unconcerned face, but after hearing the defeats of Smuts and van der Byl, sure winners in his book, Frederick wonders if his days in Parliament are about to cease.

***

The next day, Frederick still has not heard whether he won or lost. He's preparing a speech to congratulate his opponent and to thank all of his supporters, and suffocating the tears about to bubble up as he practices giving his concession speech.

Finally, at four o'clock in the afternoon of May 28th, Frederick learns that he has won and will retain his seat in Parliament but just by forty nine votes. He breathes relief.

But which Party controls Parliament is still up in the air as the returns trickle in to the radio station

Although all urban districts have reported with the United Party in the lead for Parliament seats, the returns from the rural districts are lagging.

***

In the very late afternoon of May 28, Charles and Mary have completed the day's chores at the Kruger homestead and are readying John for the trip to their District Six home. Suddenly, bursting into the room, Henrietta says, "Well, Frederick will keep his seat in the Parliament."

"Wow! That is good news," both Charles and Mary exclaim.

"But, I am sorry to say, the United Party will not be in control of the Parliament, even though the United Party received more votes that the National Party did."

"Wait a minute. How could that happen if the United Party received more votes?" Charles asks.

"That's because the National Party won more seats than the United Party. Remember why Frederick was making all those trips to the rural districts to help the United Party candidates. Those rural districts for a seat in Parliament have fewer voters than do the urban districts."

Mary still has questions on her face

"Here, take a look at *The Cape Town News* which has the facts," she says as she hands Charles and Mary the newspaper.

Henrietta continues, "This news has sent shock waves throughout South Africa and throughout the entire world."

Charles and Mary begin reading the newspaper.

"Hooray, at long last the final outcome has arrived and we have the final election returns.

"According to the official voting information, 1,065,971 valid votes were cast for the candidates, with the United Party receiving 524,230 votes, with the National Party receiving 401,834 votes, with the Labor Party receiving 27,360 votes, with minority parties receiving 70,662 votes, and with remaining votes to splinter parties.

"Most splinter party candidates, included the Communists, forfeit their deposits.

"Clearly, candidates of the United Party won the popular vote throughout the country.

"But, the United Party will not control the Parliament since the powerful combination of the National Party candidates and of the Afrikaner Party candidates won more seats in Parliament than did the United Party candidates and its allied Labor Party candidates.

"Since the National Party and the Afrikaner Party are working together, South Africa will have a new government, under the leadership of D.F Malan, head of the National Party. Mr. Malan is expected to become the Prime Minister.

"Here is the final tally of the 153 Parliament seats:

National Party 70 Seats; United Party 65 Seats; Afrikaner Party 9 Seats; Labor Party 6 Seats; Independents 3 Seats*

"Of course, these three seats* were uncontested and held by the White Representatives of the Natives.

"The voters completely eliminated several splinter parties.

"Quite a change this has been from the 1943 election when the United Party held 89 seats to the National Party's 43.

"Prices on the South African Stock Exchange sharply declined today with losses up to fifteen percent after the news was announced.

"Today, Prime Minister Jan Smuts tendered his resignation to the British Governor-General in Pretoria, but Smuts will remain in office until the new government is formed.

"The Governor-General summoned D. F. Malan as leader of the National Party to discuss the formation of a new government, which should occur on June 4th."

Charles asks politely, "Henrietta, how will this proposed legislation play on you and Frederick?"

Before answering, she knows that as a White family and with her husband in Parliament, none of the legislation will be directed at them. They will retain their same privileged status as Whites, just like the rest of the White race. Though she and Frederick are liberal in their beliefs and in their actions, she recognizes that the Whiteness of South Africa will survive and prosper under the Malan government's Apartheid. And they will also. And for that, she is simultaneously gladdened and ashamed. She steers Charles' question toward their vineyards, since she thinks Charles' real concern is Mary's and his continued employment.

"Probably very little, although we might have some trouble with export permits for our wine. But, truly, I don't expect even that since Frederick is in Parliament and we have access to the courts. We are still a county operating under the Rule of Law. But, you need not worry, because you are safe with us. You are part of our family and we will always take care of you."

Setting aside the newspaper, Mary asks, "Henrietta, with Mr. Malan as the head of a new government, what is that going to mean for Charles as a Colored and for me as a Black? Some of his proposals are downright frightening!"

"I don't know for sure. But based on what has been said during the campaign about making South Africa a White republic, I don't think it will be very good for Non-Europeans. But, you need not worry, because you are safe with us, Mary and Charles."

Henrietta decides to withhold her real concerns, especially the threat of even more stringent racial discrimination and removal of more Natives to the Reserves by the use of the newly enacted laws. She remembers reading that the National Party considered Africans as mere part-timers temporarily living in urban areas and that Africans could be transported against their will to help rural Afrikaner farmers.

She recognizes that the stated philosophy of Malan and his Party means to convince the poorest and least educated White that under Apartheid the White is better off than the richest and better educated Black. It's the way to perpetuate White hatred for Blacks.

"My God," she silently thinks, "They want to deport as many Africans as possible. They want to outlaw Black trade unions, even outlaw any Non-European voting rights. And only God knows what else!"

A knock on the door interrupts Henrietta. Mary answers the door and retrieves from the postman several envelopes addressed to Frederick and one addressed to Charles.

Henrietta hands Charles the envelope addressed to him.

As Charles begins reading the letter, tears well up. He says, "My mother is dead. This is a letter from Father John who was away on a trip when she died and he just found out. He says she's buried in the Church's cemetery."

Mary runs to hug her husband.

"After my father was killed, she wrote that she lost the house because the government under 'The Ghetto Act' eventually forced all Indian owners out of the area. My mother wasn't Indian but the house was listed under my father's name."

Henrietta gasps because under Malan that can happen to any Black or Colored person.

"After that, she worked at the Church and they provided her with a place to live. Father John says she was a faithful servant of God and is enjoying her heavenly reward. Father John again apologizes for the late news since he's been away a long time."

He hands the letter to Mary and Charles looks away, the tears washing his cheeks.

After Mary finishes reading, she gives Charles the letter. Carefully, he folds the letter and receives sympathy and more hugs from Mary and Henrietta.

Then, he sits down and unashamedly bawls as Mary cradles his head with a bundle of kisses. Helpless, Henrietta stands nearby.

**

In Johannesburg, young Nelson Mandela and Oliver Tambo discover from the *Rand Daily Mail* that the National Party has won and will control Parliament.

Nelson cannot hide his dismay at the unbelievable result. "Who could have predicted that? It's not good for South Africa!"

But, Oliver is overjoyed, because he is turning lemon juice into lemon aid.

He says, "Nelson, not to worry, because now we can clearly identify our enemy and what he believes. Look, even Smuts says that Apartheid is a crazy concept, born of the worst prejudice and of the most awful fear.

"I'm certain all Africans will turn against Malan's Apartheid and unite to fight against the coming oppression. Yes, indeed! Believe me, Nelson it will help us in our struggle. We now have a true, real common enemy!"

Chapter 24

As his train pulls into Pretoria station on June 1, 1948, D. F. Malan rouses the large greeting crowd.

"In the past, we felt like strangers in our own country, but today South Africa belongs to us once more. For the first time since Union, South Africa is our own. May God grant that South Africa always will remain our own!"

During the next two days, Malan fills cabinet positions with like-minded people dedicated to the success of Apartheid. He's not interested in appearing fair-minded or inclusive, eliminating any thought of anyone of the opposition in the cabinet.

In the meantime, he and his aides are studying historical articles and newspapers from the United States and from other countries about Blacks and other immigrants.

He is looking for evidence that other countries, especially America, have already accepted many of his ideas for the control of Blacks in South Africa. That evidence will make his ideas of Apartheid much easier for White liberals to stomach in South Africa.

The Prime Minster freely shares with his aides what he discovers from how Blacks have been treated in America and in the British Commonwealth. He will show South Africans and the entire world that his policies are not so radical, but have been true tested.

"Look at this 1860 piece from the *New York Herald* about Negros in Canada. The article declares Negros as highly prone to criminality and immune to rehabilitation and control is mandatory," Malan directs.

One aide responds, "Look, here's an article that in the 19th century, the United States barred immigrants from a certain banned Asiatic zone."

Mr. Malan continues, "And, here's one from a 1886 *New York Medical Journal* concluding that Society must defend itself against and I quote, 'the crime-stained blackness of the negro' (quotes closed) and something besides the law of civilized men is needed to protect Whites. I couldn't have said it more honestly than that."

Another aide says, "In 1924, the US skewered quotas in favor of Western Europeans and excluded Eastern Europeans and almost all Asians and Africans. And in 1901, Australia enacted the *Immigration Restriction Act* to halt Asians entering Australia."

The Prime Minister smiles without reserve.

Another aide reports, "The United States in 1882 passed *The Chinese Exclusion Act* restricting U.S. citizenship and immigration to maintain White racial purity even though these Asians built the American railroads and worked in the gold mines."

Then, he adds, "And here is a transcript of a 1930 radio broadcast by a Catholic priest, Father Charles Coughlan in his America First campaign against Jews. These are very good examples, sir."

The first aide remarks, "Most definitely, Whites need control of the Blacks. I see, Mr. Prime Minister, that in 1904, the Governor of Mississippi refused any state funding for Black education because crime statistics demonstrated that over two-thirds of all murderers were Black."

Another aide says, "The U.S. federal government in 1914 enacted the *Harrison Narcotic Tax Act* in order to suppress cocaine-crazed Negros as the direct incentive for crime. And, according to statistics kept by the US federal government, between 1871 and 1909 in the Southern States, 90% of incarcerated prisoners were Black. That's a very scary statistic, sir."

The first aide adds, "In 1919, there was the *Final Report on Negro Subversion* prepared by the American FBI and this document warned that the revolution in Russia would inspire American Negros to become Communists. The FBI wanted controls on all Negros because they could become Communists. We could have the same problem in South Africa."

"Good, we'll use that as we crack down on Communists in our Union."

"And, Mr. Prime Minister, in the State of Virginia, they had a miscegenation statute entitled *Racial Integrity Act of 1924 Act* which prohibited race mixing between Whites and Coloreds, meaning Blacks. And, that law was patterned after one in Alabama that the U.S. Supreme Court decided in 1883 was constitutional."

"Is that so? That gives me an idea," Malan says.

The first aide says, "Look at this picture showing a little Black boy and a little White girl headlined in a circle through a gun scope. With an 'X' mark across the circle, the caption says, 'NO RACE MIXING.' That's really something!"

Prime Minister Malan says, "Yes, it is. I see also where many cities and towns in America declared certain areas as racially zoned for Negros. In other words, they were not allowed to live in areas zoned or set aside for Whites. And, the Ku Klux Klan dressed in white sheets made sure that the Negros obeyed the law by burning crosses in front of their shacks, whipping lawbreakers, and even lynching them."

As if they didn't know, the aides exclaim, "Wow!"

"Well, I've got a meeting with some Party folks. So, please excuse me. And keep looking for more evidence to prove that we must control Blacks in South Africa. It helps us when the stronger nations do so, like America. Then, we can cite these countries as the leading and best proponents and the ones setting the example for a White South Africa."

"Yes sir," the aides reply in unison.

"And, better yet, it makes the Black lovers go nuts when America, the world's leading democracy, has already done it to Blacks!"

He laughs loudly at his last vocal.

Then, meeting privately with just his National Party advisors, Malan laughs, "Gentlemen, in an odd way, we owe part of our victory to General Smuts because he is mainly responsible for the Constitutional provision creating rural electoral divisions for Parliamentary seats with fewer voters in the rural areas than voters in the urban electoral divisions. Without that, as you see from the popular vote, we would have lost Parliamentary control."

One of his advisors joins in the fun, "And, don't forget good old Jan Hofmeyr for all those liberal speeches which would bastardize South Africa. He pilloried himself by failing to recognize how much the voters wanted purity of the White race."

Another advisor says, "I'd say that he shot himself in his White ass with that liberal talk!"

They enjoy a good laugh as Prime Minister Malan gets serious.

"Gentlemen, our uppermost priorities are first to solve the racial problem; second, to control these work stoppages, strikes, and boycotts by Blacks; third, to change the citizenship laws relating to British immigrants; and forth, to work for a Republic of South Africa and independence from Britain."

The advisors nod approvingly.

"Now, of course, we don't want to advertise our hope for a Republic for fear of alienating our new friends in the Afrikaner Party who are still in love with the British Crown. We will need them if we ever are to have a referendum on this issue."

One advisor forcefully says, "And, we will need the Afrikaner Party to maintain control of Parliament. Remember, with them we have 79 votes. But if we were to lose their nine votes, we could lose control!"

To shouts of agreement, Malan directs, "So, gentlemen, let's get to work on some proposed legislation and keep the opposition in the dark. We'll play our hand in due time."

On June 4, the National Party, with D. F. Malan as Prime Minister, is in control of the government of South Africa and the wheels of governmental legislative proposals are turning, soon to be introduced in Parliament.

In the world of South Africa, racial segregation will only increase for Blacks and Coloreds who vastly outnumber Whites.

**

But, elsewhere in the world, racial segregation is receiving the notoriety of morality.

On July 19, 1948, the United States Democratic Party is holding its Presidential Convention. Hubert Humphrey, the mayor of Minneapolis and a U.S. Senatorial candidate, is pushing a platform plank against racial segregation.

When the plank is adopted by a narrow margin, Senator Strom Thurmond and other Dixiecrats of the South walk out of the Democratic convention.

The Dixiecrats form the States Rights Party with Thurmond as their presidential nominee.

Senator Thurmond crows defiantly, "There's not enough troops in the US Army to force the Southern people to break down segregation and admit the Negro race into our theaters, into our swimming pools, into our homes, and into our churches."

On July 26, 1948, U.S. President Harry Truman by Executive Order Number 9981 desegregates the U. S. Military. The President has already boosted the Civil Rights division in the Department of Justice, appointing the first Black federal judge, and inserting Blacks in high ranking positions in the Truman administration.

The Black vote helps elect Harry S. Truman as President in 1948 to a full four-year-term.

The United States Supreme Court in 1948 declares racial restrictive real estate covenants as unconstitutional; and declares that prohibitions against interracial marriages as unconstitutional.

In the previous year, Britain has granted independence to its former colonies, India and Pakistan.

In February of 1948, Britain gave another of its colonies, Ceylon, its independence.

Britain, France, the Netherlands, and other countries are slowly releasing their grip on colonies in Africa, all of whom yearn for independence, especially from White rule.

* * *

But in South Africa, Malan begins to push various Apartheid legislative proposals through Parliament.

One of the first enacted Apartheid Bills in 1948 is the *Asiatic Law Amendment Act* which eliminates the voting rights of Indian living in the Provinces of Transvaal and Natal, while allowing Coloreds in the Cape Province to retain their voting rights in Parliamentary elections.

After enactment, Malan crows, "That takes care of one of our campaign promises, to disenfranchise those Indians. We'll get the Coloreds later."

* * *

On December 4, 1948, Jan Hofmeyr, overburdened by his duties entrusted to him by Jan Smuts during the election campaign, suddenly dies in Johannesburg.

His funeral procession two days later covers over two miles in length and is witnessed by street crowds estimated at over ten thousand.

Before the funeral, Jan Smuts in a nationwide radio address pays tribute to his fifty-four-year-old friend.

"Jan Hofmeyr was a wonder of South Africa, with a record with which South Africa has no parallel, who from his youngest years beat all records, whose achievement in a comparatively brief life shows no

265

parallel in this land, whose star at the end was still rising.

"He has passed on, but his service and high spirit in which he sought to serve his country and his fellow men of all races remain our abiding possessions. This is a better and richer country for his services, and his message will not be forgotten.

"I will miss my dear friend."

Naturally, his funeral service at the Dutch Reformed Church and graveside service contains many government officials, friends, constituents, former students, and some opponents. Few dry eyes surface during the eulogies.

Frederick and Henrietta Kruger and Father John O'Malley especially cannot hold back their tears.

After the graveside service, Father John O'Malley and certain other attendees with the priest's clandestine group will meet at the same Johannesburg building designated as a "safe house" to plot strategy against the Malan government and Apartheid.

Chapter 25

After parking his car, Father O'Malley carefully surveys the area and begins a circuitous route to his meeting place. Assuring himself he has not been followed, he knocks on the door and sings, *Nkosi Sikelel iAfrika!*

Suddenly, the door opens. A huge Black man says, "Welcome, Father O'Malley. Good to see you again."

The priest responds, "Thank you and God Bless Africa and you, too."

Looking around the room, Father John recognizes many of the people. He immediately greets African National Congress President Alfred B. Xuma. Father John says, "I read that your American friend, Mr. Roy Wilkens, is making progress about civil rights. I wish we had him here."

"Ah, yes, I do, too. Father, meet some of my friends from the universities."

The priest makes the rounds, with small talk with students and professors, glad to see that there is organized resistance against the Malan government, especially among the White students and professors.

Then he heads to meet Dr. Monty Naicker, who is now the president of the South African Indian Congress.

"Hello, Monty, I hear that you and Dr. Daidoo are having great success with the Indian passive resistance campaign."

At that moment, Dr. Y. M. Daidoo appears and Father John turns to shake hands. The priest says, "Well, I hope you're surviving the character assignation on being a Communist, Doctor."

To his surprise, the priest hears Dr. Daidoo, "Father, it's no assignation of my character because I am proud to be a Communist. I've devoted my life to the principles of Socialism and of eventually ending the rotten system of capitalism bringing untold misery to millions. But don't worry, I'm not going to even try to convert you since I already know you are, at heart, a socialist and are a brother in our cause against this unjust government."

Father John wisely makes no reply other than giving an affirmative head shake and a smile.

Fortunately, his old friend, Albert Simpson, grabs his arm and saves him from getting into an argument about godless Communism. Certainly, Father John understands that among the many people attending, different viewpoints exist in spite of unified direction against a common enemy.

After a short conversation with Albert Simpson, Father O'Malley spies Peter Abrahams and Dan Kuzwago who still represent the Non-European Council of Unions and he is about to greet them. They are talking with a group he recognizes as Protestant Church ministers, although he notices no representative of the Dutch Reformed Church, which is still in goose-step with Malan's Apartheid.

But, before he can reach them, the priest is interrupted by Zulu Chief Alfred Luthuli.

"Hello, Father O'Malley. It's so good of you to come, because we will need all of our people to take on this Apartheid. It's absolutely amazing that we have brought together so many differing ideas. You remember my young friends, Nelson Mandela, Walter Sisulu, and Oliver Tambo?"

Agreeing, Father John replies, offering his hand to each. "Yes, of course. I hear great things about your activities with the ANC Youth League, gentlemen."

As another young man joins them, Alfred Luthuli says "And, Father, I want you to meet Peter Mda, the current president of the ANC Youth League."

"Yes, pleased to meet you and thanks for doing a great job, Mr. Mda."

Before he can continue, the priest is interrupted by Ruth First. "Hello, Father John. It's good to see you again. You remember my colleagues Bram Fischer and Hilda Bernstein, and, of course J. B. Marks, once president of the Miners union?"

The priest nods and shakes hands with all four people, all openly as Communists. He asks, "Well, Mr. Marks, do you think Malan will carry through his threat to ban the Communist Party?"

"Father, that wouldn't surprise me. But, no matter, because we will work against this oppression whether we are an organization or whether we work as a group of individuals."

The priest says, "Good for you, because we must all stand together. We will be stronger together."

Mr. Marks is pulled away by Ruth First to join some new arrivals, unknown to Father John. Because of the enthusiasm displayed on these new arrivals by J. B. Marks and Ruth First, the priest suspects these new arrivals are also Communist Party members.

After discovering that Doctor Y. M. Daidoo is an active Communist and counting others attending today's meeting, Father John wonders about the connection between the Communist Party and the African National Congress, but accepts it as a fact.

Just as Father John is about to greet his old friends, the Anglican priests, Father Michal Scott and Father David Russell, Dr. James Moroka interrupts.

"Hello, Father O'Malley, in case you didn't know, I'm Doctor James Moroka. I'm glad you have joined us today. How is my friend, Bishop Hurley? Hopefully, he's still pounding away at the government, although I myself am in more of a combative mode. I think we need more aggressive action. What do you think?"

Father O'Malley recognizes the man who barely disguises his ambition to become president of the ANC and who constantly talks up aggression rather than boycotts and petitions.

The priest muses, "If I'm any judge of character, there's something strange about this guy openly suggesting aggressive action, which I'm unsure what that really means. I wonder whether he will stick out his own neck before he sticks out the necks of others. If violence ever comes, I suppose we'll find out."

However, before the priest can say a word, President Xuma blows a whistle and says, "Will everyone take a seat so we can get started?"

Smiling at Dr. Moroka, Father O'Malley surveys the room. He estimates between two and three hundred people, all ready to battle Apartheid. He grabs a seat a few rows away from Dr. Moroka and the group surrounding Ruth First and her Communist friends.

After very short introductions, President Xuma says, "We are under siege with this Apartheid, my friends. Just this past November, after the Johannesburg City Council raised the fares on trams, we participated in a boycott and marched to the city center only to be met

270

by armed police. We can expect more of this from this Malan government."

The people are listening to the president.

"We know they are planning very onerous legislation according to their blueprint. Let me read their two priorities. First, they want to solve the racial problem; second, they want to control work stoppages, boycotts, and strikes by Blacks."

Someone laughs and says jokingly, "What racial problem?"

"You notice they don't say how either will happen. But we know that the Malan scheme of Apartheid means more and worse segregation, even banning, confinement to a residence, prison or jail, and even deportation"

Shouts of agreement pound the walls of the building.

"Malan thinks we people are only temporary dwellers in the cities and should be forced to return to the countryside. Malan wants to ban Black trade unions and to force Blacks to the Reserves, where, he says, our true fatherland lies. None of us will have any representation in the South African Parliament, in effect destroying our citizenship in our own country."

Someone hollers, "Terrible, just terrible!"

"Malan will segregate us all—Blacks, Coloreds, and Asians—without any rights, not even human rights.

"It is time that we put aside our petty differences and organize our opposition to any segregation laws. I know and understand that many of us have different ideas, different ways to overcome Apartheid. When we leave here today, we will have a workable and unified strategy to deal with Apartheid."

"Excuse me, Mr. Xuma," shouts Oliver Tambo, "I have a few things to get off my chest."

Standing, he continues.

"While I appreciate the work of the South African Indian Congress in our struggle, I am dismayed that right after the election, they sent a congratulatory cable to Mr. Malan. Yes, I know Dr. Daidoo and Dr. Naicker later called this a 'stupid blunder.'

"Even worse, I find it highly offensive to learn that right after Malan took office that one of our members, the Reverend J. A. Calata, spoke at the Cape Provincial Congress of the ANC that we should accept the Malan government and cooperate with it, as demonstrated in a speech pledging loyalty to Malan by three of our prominent members in the Eastern Cape. Yes, I also know that the ANC later passed a resolution opposing Apartheid and demanding African representation on all governing boards."

President Xuma wants Oliver Tambo to stop, but he continues.

"I'm critical because I want all of us to be on the same page against Malan and Apartheid. Without question, Malan and his Apartheid policy wants to split our nation along racial lines, eliminate Africans from economic well-being, and never extend any political rights to Africans."

A shout of agreement comes from the back of the room.

"Some of us have already suffered personally in jail and to just name a few as I look around the room, Dr. Dadoo, Dr. Naicker, and Father Michael Scott, and ..."

President Xuma interrupts, "A very good speech, Mr. Tambo and what are your thoughts as to what we should do?"

"Mr. Xuma, we in the Youth League don't think our strategy should be boycotts and work stoppages and demonstrations! Instead, sir, we should be challenging the Malan government with more aggressive actions. We in the Youth League are tired of seeing little, if any, success in appeasement. This government must understand that it cannot stamp on the basic rights of our people."

"Yes, go on Mr. Tambo."

"I have spent countless hours and days with our young people, giving them a sense of community, teaching them and encouraging them to join us in working to overthrow this dictatorship. I can tell you the young understand and are ready. They're not afraid. We must overthrow this government! And, we will not be able to do that with votes in an election box, because we have no vote."

Before Oliver Tambo can proceed with his thoughts, President Xuma blows his whistle and shouts, "Thank you, Mr. Tambo, but we are not ready to overthrow this government with violent action. We were successful to a degree with the Smuts government and were making significant progress until this horrible election."

Oliver sits as Mr. Xuma continues.

"We will work together to stop and turn back some of this legislation through economic boycotts and strikes and work stoppages. Hitting people in the pocketbook and, in their wallets will make them pay attention. That has worked with the Smuts government and it will work with the Malan government. The business people and the farmers, Whites and Afrikaners, will pressure the government to avoid economic slow-downs and economic losses. Even the White workers don't want boycotts and civil disobedience when that hurts their wallets, because they don't get paid when they don't work."

Startled, Oliver Tambo says, "Okay, I'm willing to see if that works. I will wait and see, Mr. Xuma. I am a reasonable man. I will give it time."

President Xuma says, "Yes you are, Mr. Tambo, a very reasonable man. I appreciate your views and I thank you for working for the cause and with me. We will win this battle, my friends, one way or another. We have great plans, as you will hear in just a moment."

After the plans have been discussed, President Xuma says, "We will meet again periodically. Next year, we will have our annual conference in Bloemfontein. In the meantime, we will see what works and what doesn't. Until then, please join us in our hopeful prayer, *Nkosi Sikelel iAfrika!*

**

A little over a year later in December, 1949, the African National Congress meets in Bloemfontein.

The Youth Leagues new president, A. F. Mda, leads a slashing attack against the ANC leadership as dilly-dallying, opportunistic, and half-hearted in its opposition to Apartheid.

With the support of the Youth League, including Nelson Mandela, President Xuma loses his office to Dr. James Moroka. Walter Sisulu is elected as Secretary to the ANC. Oliver Tambo is seated also on the Executive Committee as is an absent Nelson Mandela.

To explain Mandela's absence, Oliver Tambo explains. "Because of his active involvement, Nelson Mandela has failed his final law school exams for the third time and has dropped out of Witwatersrand University.

Although he is still able to work as an articles clerk, his new employer, while a liberal law firm, refuses his absence to attend the ANC annual conference."

"What a shame," comes the reply from Walter Siisulu.

"In short, my friends, Nelson can't afford to attend the ANC meeting, but he is with us in spirit," Oliver says.

After much discussion, the conference passes a resolution entitled 'A Program of Action.' The resolution declares the ANC will fight all forms of "White dominance" and will demand "direct representation for all Africans in all governing bodies of the country."

The ANC votes to educate people to implement the abolition of all differential political institutions and to employ the "weapons of the boycott, the strike, civil disobedience, non-cooperation, and such other means as may bring about the realization of our aspirations."

Unified plans include a national stoppage-of- work-day to protest the Malan government's policy of Apartheid.

But much dissatisfaction reins within the African National Congress at that meeting, especially between some of the lower-ranking Indians and some of the lower-ranking Blacks.

A few days after the conference, riots between Blacks and Indians break out in Durban with extensive property damage leaving over 40,000 homeless, with 123 people killed, and over a thousand injured. Fortunately, leaders of the ANC and the South African Indian Congress are able to heal the wounds and convince both sides that the best hope in fighting Apartheid is unity among all groups.

The new leadership team of the ANC in December of 1949 is ready for less collaboration and for more aggressive action against the Malan government, even as Apartheid legislation is being introduced in Parliament.

But the ANC leadership team is not ready for a revolution, but instead still hopes for reform without violence.

Chapter 26

Of course, the new South African Parliament must deal with many other bills in 1948 and 1949 not directly connected with Apartheid, such as dealing with finance and conservation, by way of limited example.

Prime Minister Malan meets with his legislation managers, "Gentlemen, I confess that I am very worried about the United Nations. I am concerned over Smuts' failure to secure the United Nations approval to allow South Africa to annex South West Africa as the fifth Provence of our country. They think we are treating the people there very unfairly. What ideas do any of you have to nip in the bud any UN trouble?"

One aide suggests, "That's easy, sir. Let's give the people in South West Africa voting rights in Parliament, six Members of the Assembly and four senators. Not only will that satisfy any UN disgruntlement, but that will increase the National Party's voting strength in Parliament."

"Why do you say that?"

"Because most voting residents of South West Africa are of German descent or Afrikaner descent and will vote our way. We'll have a built-in guarantee of victory in future elections. We will pack the electorate with our voters."

"Excellent," the Prime Minister responds.

Soon, Parliament enacts the *South West Africa Affairs Amendment Act,* a show piece to prove to the world that South Africa believes in equality. Malan crows, "Yes, now the people in South West Africa have the same representation in Parliament as do people in the Provinces of South Africa."

Of course, by 'people,' he means in both places, the Europeans have those rights, not the Non-Europeans.

The Apartheid agenda begins to grow with the enactment of the *Unemployed Insurance Amendment Act,* a bill offered in Parliament in early 1949. Frederick Kruger, re-elected as a Member of Parliament, speaks out against the law because it excludes most Blacks from receiving the bulk of the new benefits, but his words matter little as the bill passes, on a party-line vote.

***

In April of 1949, Prime Minister Malan and his delegation attend the British Commonwealth Prime Minister's Conference in London. There, India has requested continuing membership in the British Commonwealth in spite of its independence as a Republic. India wants to retain its British connection. All of the British Commonwealth Prime Ministers, except Prime Minister Malan, give strong acceptance to the proposal, with approval of India's request expected within the year.

Malan argues for independence from the British Commonwealth, but, of course, he doesn't want that known in South Africa, especially by his new ally, the pro-British Afrikaner Party. But, he'll cover his tracks.

Returning to South Africa, Prime Minister Malan in a nationwide address announces.

> "What this means, my friends, is that if South Africa ever votes to become a Republic nation, then South Africa will not have to sever its ties with Britain and the British Commonwealth. And for your information, my friends, besides India wanting this status, the new Republics of Pakistan and Ceylon have also applied for

British Commonwealth status. Of course, we must wait and see if London will approve, although I'm told, that appears to be a certainty. We are certainly in favor of the proposals.

"And, my friends, that is very good news for South Africa. When the time is ripe, with Parliament's consent, we will then consider a referendum for our citizens to vote on the question. But, not to worry, my friends, for we are pro-British."

After his speech, Malan reflects, "When and if we become a republic and remain in the British Commonwealth, we will pass legislation dropping the word, British, from the Commonwealth name as used in South Africa. Make no bones about it."

The Prime Minister's speech fires up talk in Parliament, with the National Party members urging pro-republican status and remaining in the British Commonwealth. The United Party members argue against South Africa becoming a republic.

Plotting its strategy for possible legislative success of its priorities, the Malan government realizes its best chance for an enactment of a Republican South Africa, independent from Britain, centers first on closing immigration loopholes favoring the British.

"Gentlemen, what suggestions do you have for me? You know that under the Smuts' government, we South Africans were considered as subjects of the British Crown and not citizens of South Africa, though we Europeans were born and raised here. What are your ideas?" Prime Minister Malan asks.

The ideas come fast and furious. One aide say, "Look, under present law, a British immigrant becomes a South

African with just two years residency. That immigrant is now a citizen, the same as you or me, life-long residents, born and raised here. Let's add a few more requirements and stretch the time to five years before a British immigrant becomes an eligible citizen of South Africa."

Another aide says, "That's a great idea! Let's add that the British immigrant must also register as a foreign alien while waiting the five years for citizenship."

The Prime Minister says, "Done."

Cleverly, the National Party names their legislation *The South African Citizenship Act,* and dares the United Party to oppose it.

***

Frederick Kruger, one of the few who takes their challenge, receives plenty of hate mail since most letter writers consider themselves as citizens of South Africa and not subjects of the British Crown. Nonetheless, he recognizes that the true purpose of the legislation is to assure an Afrikaner majority and pave the way for a successful referendum to declare South Africa as an independent Republic.

He knows that the National Party promised the Afrikaner Party in order to get its support in the 1948 election that ties with Britain would be maintained. He sees where Malan is heading, but if—somehow—the Afrikaner Party would see through Malan's scheme to cut, if not severely limit, its ties with Britain, the Afrikaner Party might shift its support to the United Party.

Frederick almost drools as the thought arrives.

He thinks, "The Nationals have 70 votes, 79 with the Afrikaner Party. If the Afrikaner Party didn't join the National Party, we'd be in control. We have 65 votes, the Labor Party has 6 votes, and they're with us. Together, we would have 71, a majority. Yes, we must drive a wedge between the National Party and the Afrikaner Party!"

Frederick waits for the next opportunity. He thinks he has a chance to prevent enactment of the *Natives Laws Amendment Act,* which will create local labor bureaus to match workers to jobs and to further limit illegal Black entry into urban areas. He argues that it's really discrimination against poor Afrikaner farmers. But the bill passes with the support of the Afrikaner Party. Frederick's hope results in disappointment, but he still has hope.

***

That night, Frederick discusses with Henrietta some of the legislative agenda of the National Party.

"Henrietta, you won't believe this! Malan thinks that the enforcement of racial segregation on the railways is lax. I agree that in spite of signs prohibiting use or rides by Non-Europeans, sometimes authorities look the other way, but that's just in the Cape Province. That's not the way it is in the rest of the country. That last time I was in Pretoria or in Johannesburg, there were signs everywhere, some in English and some in Afrikaner, in the train stations and on every public facility."

"Don't we already have enough signs?"

"Of course, but he has proposed legislation to increase enforcement on trains. The bill is entitled the *Railway and Harbors Amendment Act* Sadly, the bill will become law, I sad to say."

She shakes her head, agreeing with his predicament.

"Henrietta, our only chance to stop these horrible bills is to get the Afrikaner Party to vote with us. Without them, we can delay, we can tie up these bills in hearings; we can use points of order, but we cannot stop these horrible bills from becoming law."

Henrietta asks, "Is N. C. Havenga still the leader of the Afrikaner Party? You and Mr. Havenga used to be good friends. We even had him at our house once for dinner. As I remember N. C., as the man likes to be called, is very pro-British and wants our country's ties to remain close to England's. Do you think talking with him will help?"

"I wish. I wish. But since Malan appointed him as Finance Minister, I doubt it, especially after Malan's speech. Havenga has bought hook, line, and sinker Malan's malarkey that Malan's administration has become pro-British. Plus rumors say that when Malan retires, he's picked Havenga as his successor."

"Oh."

"However, there are some in the Afrikaner Party who don't trust Malan, especially since he's always been so against Britain. Hopefully, they'll remember his campaign words. I'll see what I can do."

"Isn't there any possibility of compromise on some of their proposals, Frederick?"

"The National Party is against any compromise because they don't recognize the opposition and are not about to agree with us for any of what the country needs. To parrot that old adage, 'It's my way or the highway.' They plan on ruling our country and maintaining order by authoritarian measures. In other words, Henrietta, the

National Party doesn't believe in compromise, at least not now."

"Well, what's the next expected blockbuster from the Nationals?"

"You'll love this, my dear. Malan proposes to prohibit all marriages between Whites and Blacks or, as in government-speak, between Europeans and Non-Europeans. Malan claims the law will simply protect the purity of the White race and that it is not at all related to the separation of the races. Can you believe that?"

Henrietta laughs.

"Frederick, we've always had racial segregation in South Africa, but this Apartheid differs so much. This Apartheid is segregation systemically enacted into Law."

"You are 100% correct, my dear."

"Although I recognize this dictatorial mixed marriage law also affects men, I feel this mixed marriage prohibition is directed primarily at women. It seems to me that every totalitarian country or every religion and religious society throughout history asserts or seeks to assert control over women by a number of repressive measures."

Frederick asks, "How?"

"These authoritarian regimes assert control in several ways or methods. First, they try to prevent birth control by forbidding the use of contraceptives. Or they try to prevent unwanted pregnancies or unwanted births. An example of those two, I'm sad to say, is our own dear Catholic Church. Or they demand more and more births to increase the population of a certain religion such as in Muslim or Hindu countries."

Frederick says, "I agree."

"Or," Henrietta continues, "They force women to bear children for adoption by the well-off, and I think that is the case in Russia. Or they limit the number of births or celebrate babies of the male sex, as in China. Or, they order babies must be conceived from parents of a certain race, as under Nazi Germany."

"I see your point, Henrietta."

"So, now the Malan government under Apartheid is following the Nazi racial theory by controlling who can marry who, to eliminate Coloreds. Women aren't just demoted as second class citizens; instead they lose their citizenship through repression."

"Yes, you are correct, Henrietta."

She says, "It looks like under Apartheid, we're heading toward more repression of women's rights. It looks like Apartheid is becoming more and more authoritarian."

Frederick agrees, "No question about it."

Henrietta says, "To change the subject, I've had several discussions with Mary and Charles, but mostly with Mary, about the possible effects Malan's Apartheid may have, particularly with them. They both listen to the radio and read the newspapers and those stories about bus stoppages and the violent responses of the police scare them. I've stressed that they are safe here with us and that we consider them as family."

Frederick nods.

"But, I think if you would speak especially with Charles and give him some assurance that they will be safe with us, no matter what evil scheme Malan creates, that would ease his anxiety and especially Mary's."

"Yes, Henrietta, I don't foresee anything terrible right now directed against them specifically, but that could change. But I'll talk with Charles, although I too am worried about the police reaction to the bus boycotts and stoppages."

"Yes."

"I notice that Malan has expressed his appreciation to the Smuts government for leaving Malan with a very strong and well-armed police force and military to suppress riots, strikes, work stoppages, boycotts, and insurrections."

***

In late June, Frederick is listening in the House of Assembly to the argument against the *Prohibition of Mixed Marriages Act* which is ready for enactment. Many of the United Party members oppose to the Bill, but none is speaking out, apparently afraid to be classified as favoring marriages between Blacks and Whites.

But, one of the Natives' White House of Assembly Representatives, Sam Kahn who is also a member of the Communist Party, is speaking with fervor. He's not afraid.

"Fellow Members of Parliament, this bill is the immoral offspring of an illicit union between racial superstition and biological ignorance!"

That wakes up a few Members.

"At this time in 1949, this Bill is a solution in search of a problem! That's right—a solution searching for a problem to solve! Why? Because in the last three years in the whole country, there have been just 75 recorded mixed marriages as opposed to over 28,000 pure White marriages. You heard me correctly—just 75 mixed marriages in the whole of South Africa in the last three years! There is no problem."

Shouts of agreement from his Party members fill the chamber.

"The true reason behind this legislation is fear—fear that too many poor, working-class White women are marrying Black or Colored men. This bill disgraces White women by implying White women want to marry Blacks or Coloreds. This bill should not be enacted!"

Another United Party member signals that he wants the floor, but Mr. Kahn refuses to yield.

He argues, "As you have heard from the overwhelming number of Ministers of the Gospel and Priests—Anglican and Catholic, marriage is between God and the bride and the groom, not the State."

A few of the National Party Members recognize the logic in where he is going with his argument.

"Moreover, for Churches which don't approve of or accept divorce, this bill means that in the eyes of the State, people are divorced while in the eyes of the Church, the people are still married, not divorced. It's an abomination! Moreover, the State is permanently making children of these prohibited marriages as bastards. Can you believe it—bastardizing innocent babies?"

His attack that the children of mixed marriages will be considered forever and ever as illegitimate hits home.

With an amendment legitimatizing any children from a mixed marriage entered in reasonable good faith but annulling the marriage itself, the *Prohibition of Mixed Marriages Act* passes on June 29th and becomes law on July 7.

Although every previous South African administration had signage separating Whites from Blacks or Europeans from Non-Europeans, the Prime Minister demands that signage increase. He wants more signs boldly proclaiming use and admission is for **Whites Only** in Afrikaans and in English. But first he wants Blacks removed from train coaches reserved for Whites.

To Paul Sauer, his Minister of Transportation, Prime Minister Malan says, "Paul, your campaign to keep Blacks and Coloreds out of the first class suburban coaches doesn't appear to be working."

The Minister of Transportation can tell what's coming.

"A good friend of mine recently road a suburban train outside of Cape Town and saw several Blacks and Coloreds sitting in the White coach. He reports that not a single South African Railways staff asked them to move," the Prime Minister says.

"Sir, we have been working very hard…"

"Yes, I understand that the laws are being enforced with vigor outside of the Cape Province, but not in the Cape. So, in addition to more signage, I want the laws on the books to be rigorously enforced."

"Excuse me, Mr. Prime Minister, but over this, we've already experienced boycotts and downright violations, organized by protesters. In one, over fifty Blacks crowded in on two White coaches and refused to leave. They claimed that they had always ridden in these coaches without any difficulty."

"What's that, you say?"

"Additionally, Mr. Prime Minister, the press has labeled our campaign as 'undemocratic' and 'a shameful outrage,' to name just a few. And, now, the Bishop and Archdeacon of Cape Town have spoken against the law. I suspect that more and more people are complaining, especially from the Universities. But, sir, I will do my very best to make sure the Blacks obey the law. If they don't, we will arrest every last one of them, take them before the Magistrate and inflict fines and jail time"

To avoid a verbal browbeating, Mr. Sauer wisely fails to report that Fred Carneson, the local secretary of the Communist Party of South Africa, and another Communist Member of Parliament, Sam Kahn, have been some of the leaders in the boycotts and organized sit-ins on White trains.

"Listen, Mr. Sauer, I don't give a hoot if the Blacks and the Coloreds don't like the law, but they shall obey it. And, the Churchmen should close their mouths and stay out of politics. Protests and boycotts, you say! Jail them; fine them if they don't comply! The Smuts administration left us with a strong Army and a strong police force. So use them!"

***

As Apartheid gets underway, the Malan government increases signs segregating use or admission not only on trains, trams and buses, but also on taxis, ambulances, hearses, boats, ferries, airplanes, and even on elevators.

And more signs impose segregation at lavatories, water fountains, toilets, parks, benches, beaches, swimming pools, church halls, town halls, cinemas, theaters, cafes, restaurants, hotels, schools, and universities as well as even in cemeteries.

The government especially increases signage in the Cape Province.

Interestingly, the Malan government has installed some new and alarming signs for Whites, wherever Blacks gather, as if they are wild animals or poisonous snakes:

"CAUTION!!! BEWARE OF NATIVES!"

Chapter 27

As Mary and Charles push little John in the baby carriage from the Kruger homestead toward their home in District Six, Charles says, "Frederick told me today that no matter what the Malan government does, we'll always have a home and that they will take care of us. He says that we can expect more onerous legislation, but he didn't specify what might be coming."

Mary says, "Well, I see that in 'The Sun' there is a crackdown on Blacks and Coloreds ridding in coaches marked for Whites Only and that there are big protests and threats of boycotts of the trains in the Cape."

"Yes."

"I see that the Communists want civil disobedience while the Teachers League favors boycotts. What is the ANC going to do? These groups don't seem well-organized; at least that's what the paper reports."

"Well, Mary, we'll have to wait and see. I myself tend to side with the ANC. But, you know, we don't ride any of those trains. Thank goodness that we live close to the Kruger's homestead and the stores here in District Six, we have everything we need. We walk almost everywhere we go. Frederick stressed that we are safe here and they would help us."

"Charles, that's what Henrietta has said on several occasions. She said we should just live our lives, period."

"Well?"

"But, I am worried because the radios and the newspapers report that over 18 people were killed by the police because of the stoppages of trains and trams. I read in the Kruger's newspapers that commuters boycotted buses in the town of Evaton because transit operators would only use tarmac roads and go only to the edge of the townships. That forced commuters with a long walk to a bus rank. I know we don't ride the buses unless we go to the seaside, but this scares me."

"Yes, Mary, I understand. But, I think Frederick and Henrietta will take care of us."

"You know what else I'm worried about? I'm worried for our friends here in District Six, because they do ride the trains and the buses, especially Harold and Susan Langho."

"Yes, that's true, Mary."

"Do you think we'll have any boycotts or the like here in Cape Town?"

"Maybe, but in District Six, I doubt it, but who knows for sure. Well, I do we have some very good news, my dear."

"What's that? I am definitely ready for some good news!"

"Frederick also said that when John is old enough for school, that they would pay his tuition for Catholic school if we wanted that. He told me that our son would get a better education there than in the public schools, since the government is cutting funding even more, especially under Mr. Malan. I told Frederick immediately that we would send him to Catholic School to get the same education as I did."

"That is wonderful news, Charles! We are blessed to be with Frederick and Henrietta."

"Yes, and as I'm a Colored and you are a Black, we still live below the lines, sort of out of the limelight. Let's hope it stays that way. Mary."

In the meantime, the Malan government churns out more Apartheid legislation.

Frederick hands his wife a copy of the *Immorality Amendment Act, 1950* and Henrietta begins reading, "BE IT ENACTED by the King's Most Excellent Majesty, the Senate and the House of Assembly of the Union of South Africa, as follows," but she skims over the six sections in the legislation.

She says, "Frederick, this law prohibits illicit carnal intercourse between Europeans and Non-Europeans, unless the two people of different races are married. Unless, of course, the charged person has reasonable belief that the partner was not a prohibited person, then there is no offense."

"Keep reading."

"And, get this, the Act defines a European as a person who appears to be European, or by general appearance or repute, is European. So the definition is based not on biology but upon a person's social perception and the accused's association. That means the crime is in the eye of the beholder. I will know it when I see it, in other words."

"Amazing, don't you think?"

"How in the world can this law ever be enforced?"

"I know, my dear. It means that good citizens will have to report suspected violations by their neighbors. It means that the police will have to have suspicion and break into mixed couples' bedrooms, cars, or whatever. They will break down doors and invade homes. Even if the police don't actually witness the sexual act, they will use the people's underwear and their bed sheets as positive evidence of a violation. I know, it's unbelievable, but we in Parliament cannot stop the enactment of these ridiculous laws."

"Oh, it's too bad we didn't win!"

"You can see that Malan is creating legal impediments between the races by making a marriage illegal between a European and a Non-European and now by making sex illegal between Europeans and Non-Europeans."

Henrietta comments, "Malan's Apartheid and his hatred for Non-Europeans remind me of the 19th century Prussian Nobles. They had such hatred of other races that they attempted to force their race and culture throughout the continent and perhaps worldwide."

"It's part of Malan's grand plan of Apartheid to separate the races, Henrietta."

"What's next on the Malan government's agenda of horrors?"

"Henrietta, Malan's new legislation will be worse than you can ever imagine, much worse. Malan's new proposal is the *Population Registration Act,* which will become effective on July 7, 1950. As I read his law, eventually it will require identification and registration now and from birth as a member of the White race, the Colored race, the Bantu/Black/African race. Each person's identification number will reflect his/her race when the implemental documents are issued."

"I hope you are kidding around, Frederick! I know what a jester you are."

"No, Henrietta, I'm not. Every person in South Africa will be required to obtain an identification document which will also reflect the person's race. Even you and I, as well as Hans and Robin, Charles, Mary, and little John, will get the new documents, which will have all our personal information as well as a new photograph.

Of course, we'll have to carry the new identification card."

"Frederick, you can't be serious!"

"The national registry will have a copy and a copy will be maintained in the Magistrate's office in each person's residential district. We will all be marked so there's no escape."

"That's unbelievable!"

"Wait, there's more. The definitions are a joke. Whatever is the impression of the beholder viewing the suspect will be the rule of the day. Let me read from the Act the definitions of a White person, a Native person—meaning a Black person, and a Colored person:

"White person means one who in appearance obviously is, or who is generally accepted as a white person, but does not include a person who, although in appearance obviously is a white person, is generally accepted as a colored person.

"Native means a person who is in fact or is generally accepted as a member of any aboriginal race of a tribe of Africa.

"Colored means a person who is not a White person or a Native."

"There is another proposal of the law which says that children are considered White if both parents are White. But, then another part says that no person shall be classified as a White person if one of his natural parents has been classified as a Colored person or as a Black person. So, even if a child looks White and is generally accepted as a White person, the child is not White."

"That's unbelievable! That just contradicts the definition."

"I know. I know. As you can see, the Law is very, very imprecise and will lead to confusion as well as wrongfully declaring people of the wrong color or race."

Henrietta says, "Why the government didn't research the laws in the United States where blood tests determine a person's race? As I remember, the State of Texas used these hypodescent laws, where one drop of African blood rendered a person of Black ancestry."

"And, as the Act stands now, Indians and other Asians—like the Chinese, Koreans, and the Japanese—are by definition: Colored. I expect an amendment to correct that problem since these people might now qualify as 'voters' as Coloreds in the Cape Province."

"So, if the law is not amended, some of our Asians owning property and living in the Cape Province will be considered Colored and able to vote. I don't think Malan had that in mind."

"No, he didn't. It is another part of Malan's Apartheid scheme to have each race have its own culture and to assure the superiority of the White race has absolute control of the country."

"Tell me, Frederick, what test will differentiate the races. We know some Coloreds who have skin as white as ours. Why, they even have blue, hazel, or green eyes. We know Blacks with tan skin. Some even have blond or red hair. We know Indians with skin almost black. All our Asian friends have yellow skin. Is there some real and honest racial test in the law or in the regulations the Director will propound to enforce this law?"

"Henrietta, that's a good question."

"Yes, Frederick, I know the country's custom can change a person's race, such as when a White man marries a Non-White woman and he is classified as now a person of her race; or when a White woman marries a Non-White man and now she loses her White race and takes that of her Non-White husband. But, that's just a tradition, a custom, and not the Law. What will be the legal test to determine one's race?"

"Although all of the regulations have yet to be written, I suspect the regulations will be grounded on appearance, social acceptance, and descent. But, some of them you can guess their race. For example, if a person's skin color is white, the person is White, I guess. If the person's skin color is black, the person is Black. If a person's skin color is black, but the person's hair is not kinky but straight, then the person is Colored and not Black. But if the person's skin color is tan or bronze or brown and the person's hair is kinky, then we run into trouble. Is the person Colored or Black?"

"This is just crazy!"

"Henrietta, no matter what the regulations say, by using sight and appearance to determine a person's race will cause many problems, even with a Classification Board making the final decision over any contests."

"Frederick, that is correct. I can picture some family members being classified as White while one or more of their children might be classified as Colored. That could happen not just to British Whites but also to Afrikaner Whites. Misclassification could break up families."

"You are right."

Henrietta says, "Although I'm certain Mary and Charles may have seen something in the newspapers, I know they will be worried when the law is effective. I must explain to Mary and Charles that they need not worry about it, other than to register and get classified"

"That's the extent of it. And, of course, you and I will also have to register and get our classification," Frederick says.

"Oh, my God, I just had a terrible thought! What if the Classification Board determined both Mary and Charles are Black and little John is Colored? No, that couldn't happen! Tell me I'm mistaken."

"That's not going to happen. But, sorry, my dear, there is more bad news. The worst is yet to come!"

"What could be worse than what you've already told me?"

"It's called *The Group Areas Act of 1950*, a so-called improvement on older laws setting aside prohibited zones for certain races. You remember the Indian riots in Durban during the war because of 'The Pegging Act?'

"The new law of 1950 forces actual physical separation of the races by creating special residential areas for different races and requiring removal of people living in prohibited areas. It is also effective on July 7th."

"No way!"

"To hear Malan tell it, this law will curb the movements of Non-Whites, especially Blacks, into the big cities and into Whites-Only areas. Mr. Malan wants to create semi-urban townships for Blacks, Coloreds, and Indians so as to curb any uprisings, riots, or threats against Whites and, he thinks, this is the way to control them. People will be forced from their homes and businesses by this law, just like the old Ghetto Act on Indians."

Henrietta shouts, "This law simply transgresses against people's property rights! Does Malan think that people are just going to blindly and meekly accept this bullying? There is going to be lots and lots of resistance by all of the races!"

Frederick comments, "Yes, that's true. Right now, we must think of Charles and Mary, because the government will, in my opinion, eventually use this law to make District Six a forbidden area for Coloreds. I've heard Malan scream obscenities about how District Six is a blot on his plan to demonstrate the races cannot work together."

"I don't know if I take any more of this!"

"In my opinion, Henrietta, District Six will contain eventually only Whites, because all other races will be forced out."

"That is terrible! Some people will be totally uprooted and moved miles and miles away to a place absolutely foreign and strange to them, where perhaps they have no family or no friends and, of course, no employment.

"Yes, that's what will happen, I'm sad to say."

"Doesn't this former cleric of the Dutch Reformed Church remember what Jesus stood for and how He cared about the poor and the disadvantaged? I cannot believe Malan is a Christian!"

Henrietta can feel her anger firing up to a higher degree.

Frederick says, "I've heard Prime Minister Malan rail how he hates District Six and all areas where there is racial harmony. District Six has been and is a monument for racial togetherness, harmony, and peace."

Henrietta says, "So, my dear, you think Malan and his stooges will put District Six on the list?

"Well, when and if that happens, we will move Charles and Mary to our little guest house."

"Yes, of course."

Henrietta says, "Wait a minute! We've lots of workers, White, Black, and Colored, in the vineyards and at the winery in the Stellenbosch area. Will this law force the Black and Colored workers to move to some other area?"

"Perhaps, but…"

She interrupts, "We've provided our regular workers with good housing on our property or helped them find satisfactory housing nearby. The seasonal ones, I don't know where they live."

"Don't worry, Henrietta, because the law makes exceptions for Black and Colored workers needed in White areas, especially if the workers are farm laborers. So, none of our workers will be forced to move. I'll get the necessary permits. It'll be all right."

Chapter 28

Without a doubt, both Henrietta and Frederick Kruger own anxiety in 1950 over the already-enacted and the impending legislation of Apartheid, but, of course, not in the same degree as do the members of the African National Congress or as do the members of the South African Indian Congress.

But the most fear because of the Apartheid legislation lay in the laps of the Communist Party of South Africa.

Immediately after the election of the Malan government, the new Minister of Justice began a departmental inquiry about Communist activity in South Africa. In his report in February, 1949 to Parliament, the Minister of Justice declares, "Vigorous action is required to combat the dangerous subversion of our national life, democratic institutions, and outlook by the Communist Party and its various front organizations."

Already thoroughly investigated by the Courts from 1946 to 1948 in a sedition case which was abandoned for lack of evidence of subversive activity, the Communist Party of South Africa defends itself against these current attacks by showing that its aims listed in its constitution are freely available to the public.

But that doesn't stop the hatred which Malan's Government directs at Communists. South Africa will side with the Western Democracies, especially the United States and Britain in their continuing battle against godless Communism sponsored by Russia and its Soviet bloc.

Prime Minister Malan fears Russian Premier Josef Stalin and his evil desire to dominate the world.

The Minister of Justice begins its attacks on the Communist Party of South Africa by using the old *Riotous Assembly Acts* of the 1930's which empowers the Executive to confine dissidents to particular areas without judicial authorization. The Minister of Justice, if satisfied that such person "is promoting feelings of hostility between European inhabitants and of any other section of inhabitants," can confine the person without any hearing or appeal.

Using the 1930's law, the Malan government bans speeches by known Communists, including Parliament Member Sam Kahn and Dr. Y. M. Daidoo of the South African Indian Congress. It denies passports to other Indian representatives and to Indian students seeking overseas study.

And in the official *Government Gazette*, a list of forbidden imported publications appears—a prognostication for eventual all-embracing censorship of any material criticizing the government.

Under siege, the Communist Party of South Africa allies with the African National Congress and the South African Indian Congress to oppose the Malan government with boycotts, work stoppages, strikes, stay-at-home days, civil disobedience, and other forms of non-cooperation.

The Communist Party of South Africa issues a statement published in friendly newspapers through the country.

> "South Africa is entering a period of bitter national conflict. An intensive racial oppression, an aggressive and virulent Afrikaner nationalism are provoking an exclusive national consciousness among the

Indians, Africans, Coloreds, and even among the English-speaking Whites, whose former unchallenged preeminence is now being threatened. On all sides the national and racial divisions are being emphasized, and the realities of the class divisions are being obscured. All but a small minority of class-conscious South Africans view the clash of interests, not as one between workers and employers, but view it as a clash between White and Black, or as between English and Afrikaner."

***

Meeting with his advisors, Prime Minister Malan demands, "Gentlemen, we must have more extensive legislation than those old laws. We need something that we can use against all dissenters who wish to overthrow our democracy. Underhanded forces are at work. We need something that will truly punish these rabble-rousers. Get to work on it at once."

As the legislative work progresses, the African National Congress, the South African Indian Congress, and the Communist Party of South Africa react after two of their supporters are banned under the old law. They call for a nationwide stay-at-home-day on May 1.

Although successful, the May 1st event leaves 18 dead and scores injured in violent classes with the police.

***

The Minister of Justice is speaking to the House of Assembly about the Communist Party of South Africa.

"These Communists are making plans for a coup and have already placed in key positions many Blacks for the new government.

"They are planning to sabotage the country's electric power stations and to dump poisonous materials in our reservoirs and water supplies.

"We cannot dilly-dally to let this Red Peril take over our beloved Union of South Africa. I urge all Members of Parliament of every Party to support this important legislation."

After Prime Minister Malan announces in a nationwide address that *The Suppression of Communism Act* has been introduced in Parliament, the Communist Party of South Africa can read the handwriting on the wall and votes to dissolve on June 20, 1950.

The same day, Communist Party member Sam Kahn reads aloud in the House of Assembly, as a Member of Parliament, the surprising announcement.

"Recognizing that the day the Suppression of Communism Bill becomes law, every one of our members, merely by virtue of their membership, may be liable to be imprisoned without the option of a fine for a maximum period of ten years, the Central Committee of the Communist Party has decided to dissolve the party as of today.

"This decision has been forced upon us in the name of Democracy by a Government that received a minority of the votes in the General Election, a Government that represents at most 1,250,000 out of a total population of 11,000,000 people.

"We are confident that if the issue of our continued existence were submitted to a national referendum in which not just one section of the people, but all sections, were allowed to participate, an overwhelming majority would record their vote in favor of our party's right to exist.

"Adopting the technique of all Fascists, the Government destroys what it claims to defend.

"Such vestiges of Democratic rights as left in South Africa are being extinguished in the present Parliament by a clique in its efforts to impose a dictatorship, suppress all opposition, and remove every obstacle to a Fascists Republic."

Immediately after Kahn's speech without the blink of an eye, the Police Special Branch hurries to the Communist Party offices throughout the country, but they find the offices empty, with all files and papers removed, and furniture sold.

***

A copy of the proposed new law against Communism is rushed to the African National Congress executive office for review and President James Moroka huddles quickly with the Executive Committee members, including Nelson Mandela, Walter Sisulu, and Oliver Tambo.

Nelson Mandela, still an apprentice lawyer, quickly reads the law and says, "This law makes the Communist Party and the propagation of Communism unlawful. But, the law is not just directed against the Communist Party. No, there's more, but let Oliver talk since he's already taken his law exams and has a better understanding than I do."

"Thanks, Nelson. That's right. The law is directed against any group opposing the government, plain and simple."

President Moroka asks, "Are you saying that it isn't just against Communism? But the law is entitled *The Suppression of Communism.* Why do you say that, Oliver?"

"The law defines Communism extensively, by referring to any non-parliamentary political opposition to the government. That means, as I read it, a sanction by any group who does anything with intentions to cause political, economic, industrial, and social change through the promotion of disorder or disturbance, using unlawful acts or encouragement of feelings of hostility between the European and Non-European races in the country. And, we in the ANC are included because that is exactly what we do and should do. This law is directed against anyone in opposition, except in Parliament!"

Asked if he agrees, Nelson says, "Absolutely."

"What's the punishment, Oliver?" Mr. Moroka asks.

"The Minister of Justice has the power to ban or restrict any person, with confinement to a particular district, with preclusion from occupying any office in any trade union or political organization, and with prohibition from attending any political meetings, as well as imprisonment."

President Moroka directs, "Walter, please notify the South African Indian Congress and other friendly organizations that we must unite our opposition."

Walter Sisulu says, "Consider it done."

In a show of unity the African Nation Congress and the South African Indian Congress join ranks with others for a National Day of Protest to be held on June 26th, the day *The Suppression of Communism Act* is enacted.

Walter Sisulu, Oliver Tambo, and Nelson Mandela, and other ANC Executive Members, express delight that the country's first national political strike by Non-Europeans is successful, with Port Elizabeth, Durban and other ports shut down. In many towns, including Johannesburg, most people stayed home with almost all Non-European shops closed.

Nelson says, "These strikers are brave people who may not only lose their jobs but may lose their right to remain in the area of their residence. We owe each one our gratitude."

Oliver says, "That is certainly true. You know, as much as I detest Apartheid, I must confess that it is helping our membership increase and we are even having more Whites join in our struggle."

"I agree, and even better, with all their oppression, more and more people are focusing their anger and disagreement directly on the Malan government. As I travel around the country with my speeches, I find it astonishing how much hatred has grown with the enactment of every piece of the legislation of Apartheid." says Walter Sisulu.

Nelson makes no comment. His memory remains sad that Doctor A.B. Xuma, once President of the ANC, resigned in May from the organization because of disagreement with the Youth League's more aggressive tactics. While Nelson still remains committed to the Gandhi principle of aggressive protest without violence,

Xuma thought the Youth League was leaning toward sabotage. Xuma preached in his farewell message to the ANC that violence leads to more violence, especially from the Malan government. He reminds them that the South African Army and the South African Security police are well-armed against Blacks with few guns.

Nelson has considered Xuma's message but he isn't so sure that the ANC may have to ultimately resort to violence. But, he hopes not.

He has told many of his White friends, without lessening their White pride, that they will have a place in South Africa to soothe their fears of a militant Black takeover.

***

At the breakfast table, Henrietta is alarmed at the June 26, 1950 morning newspaper headline.

She says, "North Korea, supposedly backed by Russia and Mainland China, invaded South Korea. The United States is marshalling military action and is petitioning the United Nations Security Council to provide a military defense of South Korea.

"Won't Russia exercise its veto in the Security Council to stop that? Are we about to have another World War?"

Frederick responds, "Since Russia is boycotting the Security Council meetings because it thinks mainland China should have a place on the Security Council instead of Taiwan China, an absent Russia cannot exercise its veto to stop the UN action. No, it won't be World War III, but this will pit Communism under the Soviet bloc against the Western Democracies, including South Africa."

"Frederick, it seems like the world is being ripped apart between the Western Democracies and the Communists!"

"Although there are very few pieces of legislation I support from the Malan government, this 'Suppression of Communist' law is timely. Of course, the law is too overly broad and can be used against anyone or any organization disagreeing with the government."

"What will South Africa do?"

"I suspect the UN will ask many nations to provide troops and materials, including South Africa. Hopefully, South Africa will not have a major part. We have enough problems at home with Apartheid."

Henrietta comments, "We sure do. Buried on page two is news that the ANC is starting another shutdown today and is calling today as 'National Freedom Day.' The government won't like that."

"No, they won't. The way things are going, we could be heading into our own civil war. Forget about North and South Korea."

"That's for sure."

"The Malan government will respond with more arrests and that means more violent clashes between demonstrators and the police. Some protesters will be injured, maybe even killed. And that will produce a reaction from the ANC to avenge that. And soon, we may be on our way to a civil war."

"Let's hope not, Frederick. A civil war will destroy our country. It'll put Blacks, Coloreds, and Indians against Whites. And, worse, other countries like Russia and America will choose sides and may send in troops. It could be very, very bloody."

Chapter 29

It's the middle of a moonless August night in 1950 when Charles and Mary hear a repetitive banging on their front door and loud voices. "Open up! Police! Open up! Police! Police! Open up!" The shouts come first in English and then in Afrikaans.

Jumping from bed in his pajamas, Charles runs to the window and sees four or five men in the uniforms of the South African Security Police. In the street he sees a paddy wagon and several police vehicles with red lights whirling.

He quickly unlocks the chain and opens the door. He sees that all the policemen are White. None of them produces any identification, although he concludes from their uniforms and badges that they are all real policemen.

"Yes? May I help you?" Charles asks.

Paying no attention to his question, two of the policemen with bully clubs enter and one policeman commands, "Who lives here besides you?"

"My wife and son," Charles replies, as Mary in a night gown appears in the bedroom doorway after her assurance that John is still asleep in his bed.

"Show me your identification cards. Is this your house?" one policeman commands.

Charles retrieves his identification card from his wallet in a drawer in the buffet and says, "No, sir, it belongs to Frederick Kruger."

After Mary hands her identification card to Charles, he hands the policemen the identification cards.

Before the policeman can say anything as he looks at the two cards, Charles adds. "You know, Mr. Kruger's a Member of Parliament," hoping that adds a shield of protection.

"Okay," the policeman says with an understanding nod and a slight smile.

Brushing Mary aside, the other policeman enters the bedroom, first looks in the closet, under the bed, and sees a sleeping John in his bed in the next room. He says, "That's it! No White person here. Let' go. Hit the next one!"

There's no explanation or apology as the two policemen leave.

Charles sneaks a look out the front window between the curtains and discovers the police are conducting searches in every house in District Six, as far as he can see.

He tells Mary, "Ha, you won't believe it, but I bet they are looking for Whites violating the Mixed Marriages Law."

"What?"

"You remember that newspaper article with the picture of the White Dutch Reformed Church minister caught with his pants down in his garage with the naked Black maid. Someone told on him and the police came. The magistrate gave him probation and a light fine but heavily fined the Black woman and gave her jail time, too."

Mary says, "Well, I hope some of our neighbors down the street didn't get caught because I've seen a few White men have either Black or Colored girlfriends or wives."

Charles coughs a laugh and says, "Well, John slept right through it. Let's get back to bed. I've got a long day ahead of me."

***

The next day, both Mary and Charles inform Henrietta and Frederick about last night's intrusion by the police.

"No, nothing like that, just about our race," Charles answers to Frederick's question about any police order to pack up and move.

"They just barged right in after I opened the door."

At first, an angry Frederick says, "That's terrible! I'll call police headquarters and complain about the harassment!"

But, a few words from Henrietta calm him.

Finally, the lawyer inside Frederick's head says, "Well, I suppose the police under the new laws must search for violators, but they should at least have reasonable suspicion to enter someone's home."

Henrietta asks, "After seeing your identification cards, did they hassle you about your race?"

Charles says, "No, they could see that the cards were correct. They could tell that Mary is Black and that I'm not Black, but Colored. They just shot a glance at John."

"So, none of them stuck a pencil in anyone's hair for the test to determine race?"

Mary laughs, "No, Henrietta, but if they did, the pencil would stay in my hair and fall out of both Charles' and little John's, even if we all shook our heads. I know because I've already tested it. We are all classified correctly. You see, I read in the newspaper about the pencil test to distinguish Blacks from Coloreds. And then, there's the paper bag test to separate Coloreds from Whites."

"How does that work, Mary?" Henrietta asks.

"If a person's skin is darker than the color of a paper bag, then he or she cannot be White!"

Henrietta laughs along with Mary and says, "I didn't know about that one.

"Frederick, you weren't there when we went to be classified and people were commenting about the authorities carrying pencils to stick in people's hair. Along with our two children, I lined up in the one of Whites. Mary gets in the line for Blacks but hands John to Charles so he can get in the line for Coloreds. It was a mad-house, because some people had to change lines."

Frederick laughs.

"Plus, what was even funnier was in the Colored line, where the Chinese and other Asians had to line up with their yellow skin! The clerks didn't know what to do since by definition, a Colored is not a White or a Native!"

When the laughter dies, Charles asks, "Frederick, why did you ask about the police moving us out of the house?"

He patiently explains what might happen under the new law, *The Group Areas Act, No. 41*.

"I'm not saying this will happen in the next few days or weeks or even months or even years, but the Malan government is definitely working to separate people. We'll be seeing more of this type of onerous legislation."

Charles asks, "What else is coming?"

Frederick replies, "Sorry to tell you, but, according to a good friend in the National Party, the legislation doesn't yet have an official name but it will establish

312

what will be called 'Bantustans' or 'Homelands' for Blacks based on a person's tribal group. It looks like Malan wants to move people to the Reserves and create separate little countries and terminate South African citizenship for Blacks."

Mary utters a cry almost a howl.

"That hasn't happened yet, Mary, but my National Party friend says this will be on the agenda for next year. He says the 1951 legislation will solidify Malan's scheme."

Frederick can see her forehead wrinkle.

"Now, don't worry, because this kind of legislation always has exceptions to keep safe any Black servants and workers of Whites. Otherwise, Whites would revolt."

Mary asks, "Why do you say that?"

Henrietta answers for her husband, "Most Whites depend on Black and Colored workers since uneducated and poor Whites won't take those kinds of jobs because of the low pay and the low status and the poor housing if any is offered."

Frederick adds, "Unfortunately, many Whites don't treat their employees as the Good Book requires. They have forgotten the Golden Rule to treat others as each of us would like to be treated."

Seeing the anxiety of Mary's face, Frederick says, "Mary, don't worry because any government action to move people from District Six is probably years away. You and Charles are safe with us. You are family, Mary!"

"When and if ever it happens, we'll gather all your things, Charles and Mary. You'll move in to our guest house. That will be your new home and you'll be safe there," Henrietta says.

Smiling with a flash of light, Henrietta hugs them.

Frederick says, "It's probably a long way off. In the meantime, just go about your business. Be certain to carry your Pass Books and if stopped, always cooperate with the police. I'll make sure you have any other necessary papers needed when you travel to the house from District Six."

***

In early December of 1950, Frederick, reading the newspaper, says, "Henrietta, did you see this item buried on the back pages of the 'London Guardian' that the United Nations General Assembly has passed a Resolution which declares that South Africa's 'policy of racial segregation, also known as Apartheid, is necessarily based on doctrines of racial discrimination'?"

"No, I didn't see that. That's certainly not in any of the South African newspapers. What happened?"

"Yes, it appears that at a United Nations suggestion, the Indian question was to be discussed in Cape Town with South Africa's agreed participation with India and Pakistan. But, after South Africa enacted the *Group Areas Act of 1950,* India backed out of the conference. The UN General Assembly realized that with the passage of the *Group Areas Act of 1950* the Malan government's Apartheid policy was racial discrimination."

"Wow!"

"I expect the UN in the next years to come down even harder on South Africa."

"Frederick, if the UN acts, that may save our country from civil war. Malan has his sights set on even worse racial separation. I think the opposition to the government is gearing up for more than boycotts, work stoppages, strikes, civil disobedience, and more. Let's hope the UN acts quickly."

Chapter 30

Nelson Mandela is no dummy and easily recognizes that the Malan government by enacting the *Bantu Self-Government Act of 1950* has created separate areas, "Bantustans" or "Homelands," for Blacks based on their tribal and ethnic groupings.

He suspects that this law is the forerunner of legislation to not only separate Blacks from the rest of the races in South Africa but also to permanently drive Blacks from all urban areas and to permanently settle Blacks in these special areas labeled "Homelands."

Nelson wishes he had more time to fight the government but he understands that he has conflicting demands from his family, from the African National Congress, and from his desire to become a full-fledged lawyer, all requiring more financial support.

Completing his law articles while at Watkin, Sidelsky and Edelman as an apprentice lawyer, Nelson has taken a new job, paying more money, with a blue-chip firm in Johannesburg.

At lunch, Nelson often meets Oliver Tambo at the office of Oliver's employer, the law firm of Kovalsky and Tuch, where they often discuss ANC business and they plot responses to Apartheid and the Malan government.

In June of 1951, when the Malan government has introduced *The Bantu/Authorities Act No. 68* in Parliament, Nelson Mandela immediately meets with Oliver Tambo to plan strategy against this offensive legislation to take effect on July 17th.

Arriving at Oliver's law firm's offices, an angry Nelson first ignores the directions of the White receptionist and, instead, enters the Whites Only waiting room and

316

seats himself in a cushy chair labeled Whites Only. But, nobody asks him to vacate to the Black waiting room before Oliver greets him.

When Oliver steers them to his office, Nelson comments, "I know, I could get you in trouble with your firm and I'm sorry. But I just found out that my firm charges Black clients, criminal or civil, twice as much as they charge very wealthy White clients. It makes me sick. I can hardly wait until I get my law license. You know that I petitioned the Dean to allow me to retake those finals, but the faculty committee refused. With some help from my White friends, the Dean allowed me to return but I couldn't afford to pay the fees."

"I didn't know that."

"I would like to complete my studies to obtain my LLB degree at Wits, but if I don't, I'll work to get enough other credits to take the bar exam."

Oliver responds with a bright face, "That's the ticket! I know you'll succeed. I need your talents. Now, let's talk about this new law.

"This is a system of indirect rule through subservient, money grubbing Tribal Chiefs to enforce South African laws in the Reserves. Those Chiefs will have power to allocate land, to oversee welfare and pensions, and to absolutely rule over the people who are sent to the Reserves. Those Chiefs will be beholden to the Minister of Native Affairs and to the Malan government. You agree?"

"Yes, that's the story. Plus, Oliver, the proposed law abolishes the Natives Representatives Council, the last nationwide government sponsored organization for

Natives. That's the end of a national government approved voice by and for Natives."

"Nelson, we will necessarily have to become more aggressive and defiant. We need to work on Moroka. He talks a good game, but I don't know if he really believes it because as a very rich doctor, he has a lot to lose getting caught up in talk against the government."

"Yes, I'm also concerned."

"And we need to get other organizations to join us. I understand that the Communist Party is now going underground. We can use their help."

"Agreed, Oliver; yes, we do. But, we must be careful not to run afoul of the *Suppression of Communism Act.* We are going to be extra, extra busy helping our brothers and sisters because this July, the Malan government will put on the law books the *Prevention of Illegal Squatting Act* which will allow the forceful removal of squatters by landowners and government entities, including the demolishment of the houses of squatters."

"Nelson, yes, it is going to be a busy time for us. These two laws will keep us very busy. I think both of our law firms will give us these cases to handle. In my case, the partners won't want to touch these cases. Let's meet next Wednesday for lunch."

***

Frederick cannot believe what he is hearing from the National Party's representatives in Parliament, that the Malan government wants to disenfranchise all Coloreds, not just in the Cape Province. He tries to get recognized to speak against the proposed legislation.

When he finally is recognized to speak, he begins his address to Parliament.

"Fellow Members, this proposal, *Separate Representation of Voters Act, No. 46,* removes Coloreds from the common voter rolls and creates a separate voters roll allowing Coloreds to elect White representatives.

"While I strongly disagree with any so-called logic behind this proposed legislation, I brand this proposal with the fire of Injustice and Inequality. I also shout out to you that the proposal is clearly unconstitutional. It is a waste of our valuable time and work to pass this onerous piece of legislation. Why, you ask? Because the proposal will never receive the necessary two-thirds approval in both Houses of Parliament and the Courts will declare the legislation as void in violation of the Constitution. It won't even get the necessary two-thirds vote in this House of Assembly, gentlemen."

That brings a rumbling sound from the opposition.

Frederick says, "I predict without hesitation that the Courts will strike this law as in absolute violation of our beloved Constitution. It is an attack on our Colored citizens of South Africa who do not deserve this treatment. The vote of Coloreds is guaranteed in the Constitution of South Africa and cannot be changed without a two-thirds approval vote in both this House of Assembly and in the Senate."

However, after great difficulty, the Malan government by less than the two-thirds vote secures passage of the law disenfranchising Coloreds from the common voting rolls.

Immediately, several groups sue to declare the law void and in violation of the South African Constitution.

***

In late July of 1951, the ANC invites to Johannesburg the South African Indian Congress and several other organizations opposed to Apartheid. ANC President James Moroka is leading the discussion.

"Ladies and gentlemen, do I hear any dissent that we should pressure the Malan government to terminate these unjust and discriminatory laws? None, then we go forward with our ultimatum?"

A few voices argue, "Telling the government to stop and trying to stop its operation isn't going to work. There will be a very strong reaction and maybe even bloodshed."

Father John O'Malley says, "Yes, my friends, that is a definite possibility. Nonetheless, we must stand tall against the Apartheid regime and urge the people to resist in a peaceful way. Warning and executing our warning will make the government think twice before considering any more harmful legislation. I am in favor of the ultimatum."

The priest's words produce an overwhelming vote to begin The Defiance Campaign.

**

A joint planning ANC council drafts a letter giving Prime Minister Malan an ultimatum to reform these unjust laws. Nelson Mandela is designated to secure ANC President Moroka's signature, at his home near Bloemfontein.

Returning with Moroka's signature, Nelson reads the words:

"The Government must repeal all discriminatory laws on or before February 29, 1952. If the Malan Government fails to do so by that date, then a mass contravention of such legislation will be launched throughout the country."

It's a showdown that Nelson Mandela, Oliver Tambo, and Walter Sisulu have been working to achieve. If the Malan government doesn't act, the ANC will.

If the Malan government fails to act, then nationwide demonstrations will begin on April 6, the day White South Africans will be celebrating the 300th anniversary of the founding of South Africa. It is also the day that South Africans revile as the founding of 300 years of enslavement.

And then, the Defiance Campaign will begin in earnest on June 26, 1952.

Chapter 31

Walter Sisulu has some thoughts about the January 21, 1952 ANC ultimatum letter to Prime Minister Malan. Walter Sisulu says, "Get ready, Dr. Moroka because my sense tells me that the Prime Minister will explode when he reads this ultimatum. You and I will be on his shit list."

"Walter, I'm not afraid and will stand up for my rights in the courts. He can't push us around," President Moroka says.

Not responding, Walter thinks, "You talk a good game, but we'll see if you've got what it takes, my good Doctor Moroka. We'll find out if you are truly committed to our cause, or whether you are just here for the notoriety and the money you will surely make as the president. You have a lot to lose, my rich doctor, if they decide to go after you."

***

When an aide delivers the letter to Prime Minister Malan, he explodes, "Ultimatum? Who do these Natives think they are? Writing me directly when they should be addressing any complaint to the Minister of Native Affairs! They are so ignorant that they don't even understand the correct diplomatic protocol. I'm not even going to reply directly to that crap!"

He turns and says, "Mr. Camp, as my private secretary, I want you to reply and tell them that their ultimatum is totally rejected! You sign the letter and inform the ignoramus to send any future correspondence through the right channels."

To another aide, Malan commands, "Contact the Minister of Justice to watch the African National Congress

322

and all their known members and any friendly groups. Pay close attention to these two idiots, Moroka and Sisulu. And get me the names of the other leaders. We'll stop any attempt to shut down our government through civil disobedience!

"They're in for big surprises when Parliament gets going this year. Yes, indeed!"

***

Receiving T. L. Camp's letter on February 11th, instead of one directly from the Prime Minister, the ANC reacts with an arrogant reply from Walter Sisulu that their communication is not limited to the Minister of Native Affairs and that the February 29th ultimatum still stands if the Malan government fails to act.

Walter notices that this time, President Moroka isn't signing the response.

***

The Prime Minister laughs, "We'll see about that. I've got some real legislative surprises for these idiots."

Turning to an aide, he says, "Wherever this Walter Sisulu is, I want him harassed, even detained and anyone with him. I see that the ANC President omitted his name from the response. That tells me that he's weak and can be bought or scared into cooperation. Find out about this James Moroka."

"Yes, Sir."

"Have the Minister of Justice get those two Communists, Kahn and Carneson, out of Parliament. I'm tired of listening to their godless harangues against Apartheid."

***

Malan's orders receive prompt attention.

In April, Walter Sisulu and Doctor Y. M. Daidoo are detained temporarily for traveling into another area of the country without the necessary permits. Held for two days with no explanation, both men vow to continue their fight against Apartheid.

The Minister of Justice terminates Members of Parliament Sam Kahn and Fred Carneson as known Communists, silencing their official governmental dissent.

Much to the disappointment of the Malan government, the Appellate Division of the Supreme Court of South Africa declares that the *Separate Representation of Voters Act,* disenfranchising Coloreds in the Cape Province, is unconstitutional because the legislation lacks the necessary two-thirds approval of both Houses of Parliament.

When Frederick Kruger receives the news, he sends a telegram to Prime Minister Malan, "Told you so."

The Prime Minister rips Frederick's telegram into tiny bits as he threatens, "That smart ass Kruger better kept his mouth shut if he values his wine export license!" Then, he shouts for his aides to enter his office.

"I want new ideas to overturn the Court's decision giving the Coloreds in the Cape Province the right to vote in the ordinary elections."

Stuttering, finally one aide suggests, "Sir, why don't we make Parliament itself as the final word on what's constitutional. We'll just pass new legislation that Parliament becomes the new High Court as a replacement for the South African High Court."

Malan smiles, "Yes, and since we control Parliament we'll be the last word. Very good; now see to it."

Immediately, the *High Court of Parliament Act of 1952* is introduced.

***

Frederick Kruger rises in opposition, "Has the opposing Party lost its mind? Certainly, the Courts will not abdicate their judicial power in favor of Parliament in an absolute and complete violation of our Constitution. The proposed so-called law is also unconstitutional. It is a waste of this esteemed body's time to enact this junk."

But, to no avail because Parliament votes along Party lines substituting Parliament as the Court of Last Resort in South Africa.

Frederick thinks, "The way things are going, soon Malan will control every breath we take."

***

Even though more Apartheid legislation is working its way through Parliament for enactment, the African National Congress, the South African Indian Congress, and other groups are meeting in Port Elizabeth, finalizing the details of the Defiance Campaign to begin on April 6 and June 26th with mass rallies and stay-at-homes.

***

Father John O'Malley has sent Charles a letter imploring him to join the local chapter of the ANC in Cape Town.

"Charles," the priest writes, "You know Apartheid goes against every Christian teaching you learned in Catholic schools. You know your dear mother, that Zulu Princess, would not stomach this hateful and oppressive

325

racial segregation. Even your father died because of Apartheid. It is time for you to stand up. You cannot hide behind the secure walls of the Kruger's protection. You owe it to you son to fight Apartheid.

"I will be in Cape Town next Saturday evening for a meeting with the local chapter of the ANC and invite you to meet me at the rectory at St. Mary's Cathedral at six o'clock. We'll have a surprise speaker.

"Please do not tell Frederick of my presence because I don't want to endanger either him or others at our meeting, which I suspect will be under the ever roaming eye of the Security Police."

Sharing the priest's letter with Mary and getting her permission not to tell, Charles will attend his first meeting of the local chapter of the ANC with Father John.

***

Of course, Charles is no stranger to St. Mary's Cathedral since he usually walks John each day to and from the nearby Catholic School, where John is getting an education on the inequality of Apartheid. Charles is proud that his young son is readily expressing his feelings, but a little afraid that those feelings have turned hateful. He worries that John may grow up to be an activist and get into trouble.

Inside the rectory, Charles spies Father John O'Malley and quickly walks to him. After big mutual hugs, the priest says, "Let me introduce you to Walter Sisulu, who is on the Executive Committee of the ANC and who has traveled today in secret from Johannesburg. Walter has been traveling throughout the country and telling people about the evils of Apartheid. He is not a favorite of our government. And, Walter is our speaker this evening."

Shaking hands, Charles says, "A pleasure to meet you, sir. I notice that some of the newspapers write some unflattering things about ..."

Laughing, Walter fills in the blank space, "my Communist ideas."

Charles blinks.

"Yes, they do and I take it as praise from those government-loving newspapers for my fighting this dictatorial government. I am proud to have these Communistic beliefs, having traveled into many countries. As long as I am able to breathe, I will continue to speak out against Apartheid."

Charles is impressed.

"Well, if you will excuse me, I see they are calling me to the podium."

Father John quickly steers Charles to meet Oliver Tambo.

"Charles, please meet Oliver Tambo, who like Walter Sisulu is on the ANC Executive Committee. Oliver is also a lawyer in practice with Nelson Mandela, another Executive Committee Member. They are doing wonders in representing people in the courts. No doubt, you've seen Nelson Mandela's name in the newspapers."

Shaking hands, Charles bobs his head approvingly and asks, "What kinds of cases do you handle, Mr. Tambo?"

"No need to call me Mr. Tambo. Instead please call me Oliver. Well, actually Nelson handles the bulk of the courtroom work while I keep things running in the office. Well, I'll answer your question about our caseload. Our clients, mostly Black although we do have some Coloreds, are people charged with forgetting to carry their Pass Books; or people uprooted from where they have lived for generations and moved to scraggly land without a penny of recompense; or people charged with living in the wrong place; or people charged with walking through a Whites Only door or using a Whites Only drinking fountain; or people charged at being out at night past the curfew."

Charles is listening.

"I try to send each one as much empathy as possible and place myself in their situations of humiliation, just as thousands of Africans suffer each and every day."

Somewhat in awe, Charles says, "Oliver, thank you for that."

As Oliver smiles with a slight bow, the three men turn their attention to the podium where Walter Sisulu's introduction begins.

Charles hears Walter Sisulu's convincing speech and looks around at the uplifting faces in the crowd ready to take part in the Defiance Campaign. Many will march in downtown Cape Town without the necessary permit, carry protest signs and placards against Malan and Apartheid, and maybe skip work for a day.

Noticing the puzzling look on Charles' face, Father O'Malley says, "Charles, you need not join in any of the protests or openly participate in the Defiance Campaign. Why? Because I know that will implicate Frederick and we do not want to compromise Frederick in any way. He is very important where he is and what he is doing in Parliament."

Charles is glad to hear the priest's admonition because he doesn't want to sneak around behind Frederick's back.

The priest says, "I've cleared with the local officials that you can become a block captain. In this position, you will be given the names of one or two men. To these, you will relay instructions and notices to. They will do likewise to others. Your contacts will all be in District Six. At the same time, you will be under-cover. Come, let's meet your contact."

After getting his instructions, Charles thanks Father John who is leaving for another town meeting somewhere else in the Cape Province. Tomorrow, he'll tell Frederick that he's joined the ANC and hopes he approves. He thinks that he can protest without being one of the protesters.

***

Charles practices on Sunday what he'll tell Frederick on Monday.

Then, before Frederick leaves the house on Monday, Charles reveals his membership in the ANC, what he will be doing, and his meeting with Father John.

"You met with Father John? And, he didn't even contact us! Well, I'm not happy about that. I wonder why he didn't contact me. Well, I'll find out about that later. No, Charles, I don't have any objection to your joining the ANC. But, please be discreet since I am still in Parliament. I don't want what little influence I have to be compromised by charges of emotional bias not based on reasonableness. I hope you understand."

"I do."

"I'm glad you will be working out of the limelight, as a block captain and not taking part in any protests or demonstrations. Why? Because the Security Police photographs every public protest and identify each protester. I ask that you be a silent protester. That's what I do for obvious reasons. A time may come when we will all be protesting and demonstrating against Apartheid, Charles. That will happen, I promise you."

***

As the Defiance Campaign begins, in Durban, Port Elizabeth, and in most of the Natal Province a complete work stoppage occurs. While, in Johannesburg and in Cape Town, most Non-Europeans stay home, with many shops closed. The South African Security Police are making lists of the names of the operators of any closed shops.

But Charles is not one of the work stoppers.

More than 8,000 volunteers protest and risk arrest and imprisonment for violation of discriminatory laws and regulations.

But Charles is not one of them.

***

Frederick Kruger is again protesting in Parliament against the onerous Apartheid legislative proposals.

He reads that the first proposal, the *Natives Laws Amendment of 1952*, will limit the category of Blacks owning the right of permanent residence in certain towns.

Hardly able to contain his anger, he reviews a proposed law to change Pass Books.

Aloud, he says to his bench mate, "This law will require all Blacks—now including women—over the age of 16 to carry a detailed Pass Book.

"Besides identification, the Pass Book will include a photograph; list all details of one's birth place, employment record, tax payments, and police encounters; and contain the holder's fingerprints."

His bench mate adds, "And, Frederick, the Pass Book must also contain an employee's work performance record and behavioral record and the worker's qualifications to perform work in the urban area. Lastly, the Pass Book must show the government's permission to allow the worker into the urban area for work."

Behind him, someone says, "This isn't just a Pass Book; it's a reference book! Some will need a wheelbarrow to carry the damned thing."

Frederick says, "My God, the mere failure to produce a Pass Book for any police officer is a criminal offense, with the penalty of imprisonment! Misplacing it, having it stolen, or forgetting to carry the Pass Book is no defense."

Reading further, Frederick says, "Now, a Black worker will not be able to leave a rural area for an urban area with first obtaining a permit from the local rural authorities. When the poor man or woman arrives in the urban area to seek employment, the person must obtain an urban work permit within 72 hours."

Reading near the end of the proposed legislation, Frederick gasps, "If an employer writes anything derogatory in the worker's Pass Book, the worker's continued right to remain in the urban area is jeopardized. That worker can be expelled by government officials at any time and for any reason and without explanation."

"That's terrible," Henrietta says.

"Even worse, family members of an expelled worker also forfeit their right to remain in the urban area and can be sent to the Reserves, now called Homelands."

"I thought we did away with slavery years ago. But, apparently not! If that's not slavery, I don't know what is!" Henrietta exclaims.

His speeches and those of his fellow United Party Members of Parliament cannot convince the purveyors of Apartheid. The new Pass Book law is enacted and is effective July 11, 1952.

***

Arriving home late on a July night, Frederick carefully explains to Henrietta the ramifications the new Pass Book Law will have and its effect on their work force in the vineyards, the winery, any household workers, and especially on Charles and Mary.

"I think that with this Defiance Campaign underway, more and more people are going to hate the Pass Book law, Henrietta."

Henrietta says, "Yes. We need to be certain every worker obtains the right Pass Book documentation. I will talk with Mary and Charles. I don't trust the Security Police. So, I'll drive them and some of the other workers to get the new Pass Books."

***

Charles is reading a December, 1952 ANC-favored newspaper reporting that the Defiance Campaign led by the African National Congress is spreading across the country. He tells Mary, "One of the leaders is Nelson Mandela."

"Who is he?" she asks.

"He is on the ANC's Executive Committee, one of the few Black lawyers in South Africa, and a very impressive speaker against Apartheid. He left several White

332

law firms and opened his own law office in downtown Johannesburg."

"I see."

"This article says that Nelson Mandela spoke to over ten thousand people last June in Durban to initiate mass protests in the Defiance Campaign. When he returned to Johannesburg, he was quickly arrested and interred in Marshall Square prison but got out on bail. That didn't stop him and he is still preaching against Apartheid."

"Really?"

"The newspaper continues that the Malan authorities a month later arrested him, Walter Sisulu, and twenty others. After a speedy trial, all were convicted of violating the 'Suppression of Communism Act' and were sentenced to nine months hard labor but the sentence was suspended for two years. The article goes on to report that the President of the ANC, Dr. James Moroka, sought leniency, cooperated with the prosecution, and disowned equality principles. Now, he is out as ANC President, replaced by Alfred Luthuli, a Zulu chief."

Mary asks, "Wasn't that the Walter Sisulu you heard speak in Cape Town with Father John?"

"That's correct. But, Walter Sisulu is still traveling around the country. The newspaper goes on to say that Nelson Mandela received another ban, two years this time, from speaking to others. The newspaper suspects that he is secretly speaking to groups. I wouldn't be surprised about that. The newspaper goes on to say that Mandela is the new Deputy President and that he has a secret plan to fight Apartheid."

Mary says, "Well, that's certainly interesting, but I have something more important."

"Oh? What's more important than what's going on in the country?'

Laughing, Mary says, "What's more important is you are going to be a father again, my dear! And it's my turn to name the baby!"

Excited, Charles asks, "When is the baby due? Do you have names?"

"In July or in August of next year. I'm still thinking about a name."

Chapter 32

In 1953, the Malan government proceeds with new Apartheid legislation, beginning with two new laws which allow the government to declare stringent states of emergency and to increase penalties (such as public whippings) for the mere protesting against any law.

Malan says, "I am confident the National Party will maintain control of Parliament since the advertising campaign highlights the necessity for White security and the reasons for the enactment of the emergency powers under the two new laws. White people want the Union to be safe and secure from terrorists."

He preaches, "We cannot let the Blacks intimidate us and we will safeguard our country against this Black Peril. We must also be ever vigilant against the Red Peril sponsored by Communist Russia. These two laws are necessary for public safety."

Malan confides to his aides, "The news from Washington that the United States government has been infiltrated by Communists is very, very disheartening, gentlemen. That President Eisenhower and U.S. Senator Joseph McCarthy are worried about Communists is alarming. We must keep South Africa safe from Communism. I suspect we'll find these Communists in our country going underground."

"Yes, we must, Mr. Prime Minister."

"Please ring up the US Ambassador for me so I can get an update and soothe our American friends since I've heard a few disparaging remarks about our racial policies."

"Yes sir."

"Please, gentlemen, convey my concerns about the Communist threat to all responsible Ministers, to all appropriate Generals, and to the Police Commissioner."

"Mr. Prime Minister, I have US Ambassador Gallman on the phone."

"Yes, thank you.

"Waldemar, it's very good to hear your voice! Tell me, what's happening back home in your country with those Communists. I hear some strange things going on in America."

As the ambassador explains, he finishes, "Well, Mr. Prime Minister, please rest assured that the Eisenhower administration understands that peace in the uranium mines, peace in the homes, and peace in the streets of South Africa is essential to America's economic interests and, more importantly, essential to America's security. We understand and appreciate South Africa's fight against internal strife brought on by Communists and Communist sympathizers."

Malan listens but reveals nothing.

"Certainly, it would be helpful, to both our countries, if harmony can be achieved among different groups, Mr. Prime Minister."

Diplomatically, Malan replies, "Yes, of course. You know, Waldemar, America has a very good friend in South Africa and we are glad to keep the uranium mines working in South Africa to secure our mutual interests and security. You can rest assured, sir, that South Africa stands ever ready to help America safeguard the world against the Red Peril of Communism. We are America's strongest force against Communism and have outlawed the Communist Party in South Africa."

"Yes, Mr. Prime Minister, and we appreciate that. By the way, I have submitted your request for more arms and we should hear from the Secretary of Defense and the Secretary of State very soon. We don't want South Africa falling into the Communist bloc."

Naturally, Malan will not budge on Apartheid and he knows how much America needs uranium for its atomic bombs, and how much America needs anti-communist allies. Malan's no country bumpkin from some banana republic.

**

New ANC President Alfred Luthuli suspends the Defiance Campaign because of the two laws, even though some people continue opposing the government with acts of civil disobedience and even though an interracial group of ministers calls for a national day of prayer in support of the Defiance Campaign.

Luthuli recognizes that the Malan government intends to clamp down on any dissent, especially dissent from the ANC and the South African Indian Congress. Now, with the *Public Safety Act,* the government has the legal authority to do so.

He tells the Executive Committee, "Under the *Public Safety Act,* the government can declare a state of emergency and the Minister of Law and Order, the Commissioner of the South African Police, any Magistrate, or any Commissioned Officer can detain any person for dissent without any trial. I mean, a person doesn't even get a trial! We cannot subject our people to that!"

He calls for a halt, at least temporarily, in the Defiance Campaign.

**

The day after the April 15, 1953 Parliamentary election, Frederick Kruger is finishing reviewing the election returns showing that the National Party is still in control of the government of South Africa.

Frederick retains his seat and will oppose all proposed Apartheid legislation over the next few months. He is trying to maintain a positive outlook in spite of the overwhelming odds that he can accomplish anything short of delaying the enactment of any legislation.

Nonetheless, he is thankful that the Korean War has stopped in late July and the 800 plus South African troops, including his nephew, are returning home.

When China and Russia joined North Korea, Frederick feared an escalation but a stalemate resulted.

***

Later in that year, Charles and Mary are having breakfast with Frederick and Henrietta.

Frederick says, "Charles and Mary, I suppose you've read something about the new *Bantu Education Act of 1953,* just passed in October by Parliament but not effective until January 1, 1954. Do you have any questions about it?"

Charles says, "As I understand this new law, a Black Education Department has been established in the Department of Native Affairs. From what I read, Dr. Hendrik Verwoerd, the Minister of Native Affairs, wrote this law which will compile a complete study suited to the education of Black people. At first, that sounded like this law would help Black people, but, after thinking about it, I concluded that something is not right about that."

338

Henrietta chips in, "That is correct, because the real purpose of the new law is to prevent Africans from receiving an education to work in jobs reserved for Whites. Instead the law gives Blacks training for work in the Homelands or for work with a White employer. It's a terrible law."

Frederick says, "Yes, sadly. Verwoerd's law is to prevent Blacks from receiving an education so they could aspire to obtain jobs reserved for Whites. He's made fun of Blacks leaning mathematics, saying they don't need that study since they're never going to use it in digging holes or shoveling dirt."

Mary says, "That is horrible."

"Yes, it is. The law will also transfer funding from mission schools to the State because these 5,000 or so religious schools are producing students learning English and, in the words of the Apartheid leaders, 'producing dangerous liberal ideas about equality.' It's another horrible law designed to separate the races from one another. It's Apartheid," Frederick says.

"Even worse, the law requires primary grade students to be instructed in the Black child's mother language so as to increase the Black child's ethnic awareness," Henrietta adds.

Mary contributes, "From my experience in my village and around Mpumalanga, many Natives have abandoned their mother tongue and their children have been taught mostly in English or perhaps in Afrikaner. They won't be able to learn much when a teacher is talking to them in a foreign language, even if the language belongs to their grandparents."

Charles says, "Everyone knows that without the mission schools, Blacks would get a terrible education since the State underfunds the State schools. The State teachers are poor, the State buildings are in terrible shape, and the State schools are overcrowded. Mission schools provide the difference with money from the government. How will the mission schools continue to operate without money from the government?"

Frederick replies, "They won't, Charles. This law will force most of the 5,000 or more of the mission schools to close unless the Church itself can continue to financially support their own schools. Additionally, all mission schools have been ordered to quit teaching science, history, and social studies since the government wants all attempts to anglicize the Blacks to stop. The government wants the schools to teach only useful subjects, meaning, of course, labor skills."

"What happens if the mission schools refuse?"

"Charles, there's a provision in the new law that any remaining mission schools after four years must sell the schools to the government. But that's not going to apply to John's school, because it's not considered as a mission school. Many of the church funded schools are not considered as mission schools."

As Mary and Henrietta place the dishes in the sink, Henrietta comments, "Well, thank goodness, we've got John in the Catholic school. He'll get a sound education there and completely understand the evils of Apartheid. Don't worry, Mary and Charles, because we will continue with the tuition payments to the school for John's education."

Frederick nods his head, rubs his chin, and says, "Yes, of course we will. You know, I'm thinking that this law may be something that ultimately truly angers all Natives—Blacks and Coloreds. They are smart enough to see what is happening and, in due time, will strongly resist, I think."

"They will see that Verwoerd is not at all catering to their heritage, but actually is trying to isolate them."

Charles looks at Mary and they both affirmatively shake their heads in answer to Frederick's comment.

* * *

After opening his own law office, Nelson Mandela asks Oliver Tambo to join him in central Johannesburg by renting space from Indian owners in Chancellor House, just across the street from the marble statues affronting the Magistrate's Court. Their new name plate, 'Mandela & Tambo,' proudly hangs on the front door.

Oliver Tambo says, "Too bad, Walter isn't here to see this. We are the only all Black law firm in the entire country. Why, we've got people waiting on the stairs, in the halls, outside the water closet, and besides the front door since there's no more room in the reception area."

Nelson Mandela replies, "Yes, I owe Sisulu plenty. He is going to get a real and true education in his secret journey in those communist countries. I myself hope to visit some of them some day."

"Is it true, Nelson, that Walter forged a passport under a fake name to leave South Africa?'

"Correct. Now, let's get to work with these new clients."

Many face fines and/or jail time for not carrying their Pass Books or *dompas,* as their clients called the most hated symbol of Apartheid.

But in spite of the daily besiegement, Nelson and Oliver gladly spend compassionate time with each Black client. It's why Nelson and Oliver had become a lawyer in the first place.

Yet, both young lawyers continue working diligently with the African National Congress as part of the National Committee, except that Nelson again catches the eye of the Security Police, is arrested, and again is banned after giving a speech entitled, "No Easy Walk to Freedom."

***

Besides increasing the membership in the ANC, the new laws create the South African Colored People's Organization and create the Congress of Democrats, composed of White supporters of the ANC.

Nonetheless, after a court ruled public facilities for separate races must be equal, the Malan government enacts in October the *Reservation of Separate Amenities Act of 1953* which forces more signs prohibiting use and admission between Europeans and Non-Europeans in all public buildings, public transport, public amenities. The law allows inequality in all public facilities between the races, meaning especially any inequality for White facilities can lawfully be superior to Black ones.

Malan crows, "We are going to eliminate all contact between Whites and the other races, including such contact even in the Cape Province."

Chapter 33

In 1954, Parliament enacts the *Riotous Assemblies and Suppression of Communism Amendment Act* empowering the Minister of Justice to prevent any person from attending any gatherings or from membership in certain organizations as well as preventing any particular gathering in any public place

Prime Minister Malan instructs the South African Security Police to carefully root out all dissenters, targeting the African National Congress and the South African Indian Congress as well as any other friendly groups, new or old.

To his Minister of Justice and to the Commissioner of the Security Police, Prime Minister Malan commands, "I want the police to focus on the leaders of this Defiance Campaign, especially the leaders of the African National Congress. As I read the papers, that young Black Mandela and others are stirring up people by speaking against the government and aiding in these shutdowns and demonstrations."

"That is the case, sir."

"We cannot allow people to discover when and where these speeches are scheduled. Any and all weekly newspapers and any periodicals opposing the government must cease publication. Shut down those papers!"

"Yes sir!"

"I want Mandela arrested and the full impact of the law tying him up. And, I want every one of his co-conspirators rounded up and put away, especially that Walter Sisulu."

"Yes sir!"

"And, get all those leaders of any organization cooperating with them. We are going to put a quick end to this so-called 'defiance' business. See to it, at once!"

Sitting alone in his office, Prime Minister Malan confesses to himself, "This constant chaos is getting me down. I may think about retiring and letting someone else deal with this mess."

Unknown to the Prime Minister, the Minister of Justice and the Commissioner of the Security Police have already had Nelson Mandela photographed by undercover agents stationed in the crowds. Some of those agents are operatives from the Central Intelligence Agency from the United States.

Recently, Mandela's speech—over two hours before a huge crowd in Soweto about the Defiance Campaign—has also been recorded for use in a future trial as proof of his treasonous activity.

***

In spite of the government's activity against the ANC, President Luthuli instructs the Women's Branch and Youth's Branch of the ANC to oppose the 'Bantu Education Act' and to engage students and teachers in the opposition to the law. He hopes this opposition will halt Parliament's enacting any new legislation.

Undeterred, Parliament enacts *The Natives Resettlement Act No. 19 of 1954,* which allows the government to remove any person near certain areas near Johannesburg, meaning the areas from the towns of Sophiatown to Soweto. The government's resettlement and separation of Natives campaign is on its way.

***

In August of 1954, Charles welcomes Frederick and Henrietta to Mary's bedside in the District Six home to see their new son, Tyrone Washington.

Looking at a glowing Mary and a proud Charles, Henrietta says, "I love the baby's name, Mary and Charles. How did you pick that one?"

Charles glances at Mary, who says, "I wanted my son's name to be different and distinctive. I can't tell you how many girls named Mary I've come across. So, I thought about it for a long time. Then, I remembered the American movie, 'The Mark of Zorro' and the American movie star, Tyrone Power. That was it, because I've never heard anyone called Tyrone. Our baby's name is unique."

Seeing the questions on Frederick's face, Mary explains, "We Africans always pick non-African names, especially Christian names or biblical names, since most Europeans cannot pronounce African names."

Henrietta laughs, "That's the God's truth. Yes, Indeed! Well, I love it—Tyrone! Maybe he'll grow up to move to America and be a movie star!"

***

Prime Minister Malan is reading a newspaper article that the United States Supreme Court in 1954 has declared school segregation is unconstitutional. Already in poor health, D. F. Malan, after that distressing news from America, decides in November to retire.

He hopes N. C. Havenga, the one-time head of the Afrikaner Party and now one of his closest confidants will become his heir. He intensively lobbies the Party for him to be the Prime Minister.

But, J. G. Strijdom, once labeled as 'the Lion of the North,' outfoxes Havenga and, instead, becomes the leader of the National Party.

Now, Johannes Gerhardus Strijdom is the new Prime Minister and is forming a new government on December 4, 1954.

***

In January of 1955, Prime Minister Strijdom, "J. G." to his close friends, is having breakfast in the newly decorated office in Pretoria, with his Chief of Staff, when they are interrupted by an aide, clearly in a state of anxiety.

"Excuse me, gentlemen, but I have some dreadful news from Cape Town!"

The Prime Minister says, "Oh, what is it?"

"Sir, the United States Navy aircraft carrier, 'Midway,' has docked for shore leave and has refused our orders not to allow any Black sailors to leave the ship. The American Black sailors are flooding the streets of Cape Town and are ignoring the signs prohibiting entry or use by Non-Europeans. The local Cape Town police cannot stop them. And the merchants are glad to see the Americans, even the Blacks, with their dollars."

To another aide, the Prime Minister says, "Get me the Captain of the ship on the phone. We'll put a stop to that."

But, before the aide can comply, the Chief of Staff interrupts, "Begging your pardon, sir, but the entire waterfront of Cape Town depends on those hundreds, maybe thousands, of American sailors spending dollars. If we try and stop shore leave for the Black American sailors, the ship Captain may stop shore leave for all those sail-

346

ors, Black and White. We'd have hell to pay with the merchants of Cape Town."

While the Prime Minister mulls over the suggestion, the first aide says, "Well, sir, while the ship is docked in Cape Town, the ship Captain has invited any and all South Africans to come aboard and tour the aircraft carrier. If I may say so myself, sir, since this aircraft carrier is reputed to be the biggest ship in the entire world, everyone wants to view it. Already in the first day, over five thousand have accepted."

Eyebrows rising, the Prime Minister says, "You mean that there's no racial segregation? Are you telling me that there's no separation between the races—Whites and Blacks are intermingling on the ship? Doesn't the American ship Captain know we have Apartheid laws?"

"Pardon me, Mr. Prime Minister but the Americans said South African laws do not apply to an American warship. They said anyone wanting to tour may do so. We should not let any Blacks tour the ship, because the dock is South African territory."

Fuming, Prime Minister Strijdom says, "Get me the new American Ambassador, what's his name?"

"Yes, sir, Edward Wales is his name."

After a ten-minute phone conversation, the Prime Minister grunts to his Chief of Staff, "Well, Ambassador Wales says the Eisenhower administration is trying to avoid dealing with civil rights issues, even though there is no racial segregation in the U.S. Military."

The aide's eyebrows rise.

"He says adverse publicity about this will hurt both of our countries, politically and economically. He says if we prohibit Blacks from touring the ship, the Captain will end any more shore leave for the sailors, because

347

that would be bowing to a foreign jurisdiction. The Ambassador says that will create an international incident and get the attention of the United Nations, already looking at our domestic policies. We certainly don't need that. The Ambassador says he can't promise a recurrence won't happen if we want American dollars spent in South Africa. But Ambassador Wales says he'll suggest a different US policy in the future for their ships here on shore leave."

"That's good, sir."

"The man suggests we look the other way because the ship will depart in a day or two. So, we grin and bear it. But, the next time an American ship wants shore leave in Cape Town, we will demand the Americans comply with South African laws."

Nonetheless, the Prime Minister is resolved to move quickly with more Apartheid legislation.

***

At breakfast, Henrietta is reading her morning newspaper and comments, "Frederick, one of the first orders from Prime Minister Strijdom has directed that all Non-European women must now carry Pass Books."

"What?"

"According to the newspaper, thousands of Black women are protesting and confronting the police. My God, the police have indiscriminately killed at least three women and injured scores more through gunshots. It's no wonder that throughout the country, women of all colors are enraged. I certainly am!"

She hands him the newspaper.

Frederick says, "We are in for real civil unrest because Prime Minister Strijdom has just used the provisions of the *Group Areas Act* to force the removal of over 80,000 people near Johannesburg. You heard me correctly, over 80,000! The paper lists a few of the leaders, which include Father Trevor Huddleston and Nelson Mandela."

"Remove people from where?"

Frederick answers, "From Sophiatown, and now the town is now re-named 'Triumph' and will be a Whites Only town. The newspaper also reports that the Government is assuming control of the Bantu schools. I suppose that means the ANC will conduct a massive boycott by teachers and students against Bantu Education."

***

In June of 1955, Charles, sitting in his favorite chair at home, is reading a newspaper favorable to the ANC and tells Mary, "The ANC in Kliptown, a suburb of Soweto, met and will adopt a Freedom Charter."

"Oh?"

"The paper says that the police put up barricades to keep people away from the meeting, but to no avail. It says some people did get arrested, though."

"Yes."

"Besides the ANC, the South African Indian Congress, the Colored Peoples Organization, and even the White Congress of Democrats were there. They called for South Africa to be a non-racial society without any special rights or privileges for any group, for equal treatment under the law, and for a sharing of the country's wealth."

Mary replies, "I like that."

"The paper says that over 3,000 delegates met and that they also formed 'The Congress of the People' to engage in future demonstrations. I'm thinking that maybe I should join the Colored Peoples Organization. What do you think?"

Mary says, "Let's first see what they are going to do since you're already in the ANC. And, Charles, you'd better clear that with Frederick."

***

Prime Minister Strijdom, angry that the Courts have declared unconstitutional two prior Acts of Parliament disenfranchising Coloreds in the Cape Province, demands, "I want legislation to keep those Coloreds from voting in the ordinary elections. We don't need Indians, Coloreds, or Blacks trying to run our country. What are your ideas?'

An aide replies, "Sir, since the Constitution requires a two-thirds vote from both Houses to disenfranchise Coloreds in the Cape Province and we already have two-thirds in the House of Assembly, we simply increase the number of nominated senators in the Senate to reach the magical two-thirds."

Another aide adds, "Then, to make sure the High Court plays ball, we increase the number of High Court appellate judges from five to eleven. That gives us a majority vote."

"I see."

"Then, Mr. Prime Minister, when the case finally winds its way through the judicial maze in the next year or two, our own new appellate judges will be there to approve the legislation ending the rights of Cape Province Coloreds to vote with Whites in the ordinary election. We win, six to five, sir!"

"You two, thank you, because that is brilliant, full of cunning and legalese. See to it."

"Yes, sir, the legislation will be introduced tomorrow and passage is certain. It will be *The Senate Act of 1956*. And by the time any contested lawsuit reaches the appellate High Court, we'll have the votes in the new High Court to assure its constitutionality. You can say goodbye to any Colored votes in an ordinary election for Parliament!"

* * *

In the Kruger household the same day as Mary and Charles are having breakfast, Frederick and Henrietta are reading a newspaper not favorable to the African National Congress, obviously different from the one Mary and Charles are reading.

Henrietta exclaims, "Did you read this? The Security Police massed and surrounded the building where all those thousands were meeting in Soweto. They recorded the names and addresses of every single one of those delegates. Why, the government is even considering charges of treason, although none have yet been filed."

Frederick says, "Read a bit farther down and you'll see that Strijdom is ordering a search of every house of every leader opposing Apartheid. They are curtailing the right of free speech and free assembly."

"Yes, I will."

"And, I can tell you that Parliament will be cranking out more Apartheid legislation in 1956. One already in the pipe line is the *Natives Prohibitions of Interdicts* which will, when enacted, deny Blacks the right to use the courts for protection through an interdict or injunction against any of these draconian laws, such as

351

against forced removals or as against prohibition to use or enter a White facility."

Henrietta says, "That is terrible! Denying people court protection is itself draconian! No wonder there is more and more unrest throughout the country. It's getting worse, much worse. Black women are being arrested for burning their Pass Books. At several Pass Book delivery centers, women are throwing stones at the officials. And, there are more and more bus boycotts."

"Yes Henrietta, and Strijdom, if he had any scruples about Apartheid, which I doubt, has certainly thrown them in the toilet. He has become more and more livid."

"Amen to that."

"Now, the National Party is considering legislation to allow the government to slap Africans with banishment and exile to remote rural areas far from the person's usual residence. That will be in addition to the government's confinement of people to their own homes. He is using the South African Defense Force to counter any insurgency."

Henrietta says, "Strijdom is just terrible. I can hardly bear to hear any more. It's just terrible. Let me change the subject. Let me give you something that may brighten you day, Frederick. It'll take a load off your shoulders. It did mine."

"A good idea, Henrietta."

"A friend somehow got this smuggled copy of a 1953 *Ebony Magazine* which contains a very interesting article entitled, 'Some of My Best Friends Are Negros' about Eleanor Roosevelt's friendship with Pauli Murray, a leading woman anti-racist in America. You will enjoy it, my dear."

In early August of 1956, Mary smiles, "Charles, I have something to tell you. We are enlarging our family."

Thrilled, Charles rises from his favorite chair, kisses Mary, and says, "When is the wonderful event, my dear?"

"Probably in April of next year, I'd say."

"Wonderful! That makes me very happy! Now that we have two boys, would you like to have a girl, Mary?"

"Yes, because with John and Tyrone, I've already got my hands full. I think a girl will be a true blessing."

Chapter 34

It's Sunday, but Charles is reading the old newspaper of August 10, 1956.

He says, "It says here in the *'Rand Daily Mail'* that over 20,000 Black women marched in Pretoria to the Union Building in protest of the Pass Book law required of women. Many of them were arrested."

Mary's forehead wrinkles.

"According to the newspaper, both the ANC Women's League and a new group, the Federation of South African Women, organized the protest. The women presented a petition signed by over 10,000 people opposed to the Pass Laws."

"Ten Thousand?"

"Yes. The article says the government is not going to tolerate this kind of disobedience to the law and that any person, man or women, without an authentic Pass Book will be arrested and thrown in jail or removed to the Reserves. The newspaper goes on to say that the authorities are going to ask for a high amount of bail, no matter whether the violator is a man or a woman."

That scares Mary.

"And, the government may even remove a woman's family to the Reserves if the woman is guilty of repeated violations of the Pass Book law."

Mary is paying close attention.

"Prime Minister Strijdom remarked that nothing will ever deter the Nationalist government from implementing Apartheid," Charles reads.

Mary is still thinking about the Pass Book Law as Charles continues his reporting.

"The Prime Minister also said that since the new *Riotous Assemblies Act* allows the Minister of Justice to prohibit any open-air gathering and ban those in violation, he vows that further outside gatherings or demonstration will subject violators also to that Law. He warns everyone to obey the Law and carry their Pass Books or face the punishment.'

Mary is fidgeting with her nails.

"Remember what Frederick said about those Pass Books. There isn't any excuse for not having a Pass Book in your possession. Having one but leaving it at home is no excuse. So, be sure to carry yours, Mary, when you are out and about, even when traveling to and from the Kruger's. We don't need to be out in the front lines. We are secure and safe here."

Although Mary seems ready to speak about the Pass Book Law, but before she can, suddenly, a knuckle raps the front door. Holding her precious little Tyrone, she looks up.

Charles rises, sets aside the newspaper, and peaks outside, as John tails him to the window.

"Oh, it's all right—Frederick and Henrietta and Robin! Oh, come in. Come in. Welcome!" Charles says, with the door wide open.

Henrietta says, "Hi! We've brought some of Hans' clothes for John. Now that Hans is in the University he has way outgrown them. And, if you have a girl, we've got Robin's things for you, too. Sorry, but we don't have any of the baby clothes from the two kids."

Mary smiles a big thank *you* as she rocks Tyrone in her arms.

Charles offers Frederick a chair.

After words of gratitude and offers of something to drink, Henrietta says, "Just juice for Robin, but nothing for us, Mary. Now, Robin, after the juice—go outside in the yard and play a game with John."

John grabs his soccer ball and invites Robin outside into the small backyard, where at one end Charles has crafted a soccer goal, net and all.

As the two children leave, Henrietta turns to Mary, "Well, Mary, you don't even look pregnant, and are as beautiful as ever, carrying this second baby, probably barely a month old. How is little Tyrone?"

Mary smiles.

"Are you feeling all right? Are you getting all the food-stuffs you need? If you can't find anything at the local District Six market or stores, let me know and I will get it for you."

"Henrietta, I'm feeling great, not even any morning sickness, at least, not yet. And thanks for your offer, but right now, I've been getting everything I need. And, as you can see, little Tyrone, now two, is growing like a weed."

Sitting near the newspaper, Frederick says, "I see, Charles, you're reading about the latest protest, this time by scores of women objecting to the burden of carrying their Pass Books. Actually, I see that the government has coined a new term for the Pass Books. Now, they're calling them 'Reference Books,' and rightly so, since the things are truly a book, certainly not thin like my passport, and difficult to lug around."

Charles says, "Do you think the government has figured out that trying to force Black women to carry the Pass Books will be a losing battle?"

Whispering so the women can't hear, Frederick smiles, "Have you ever tried to force any woman to do anything she didn't want to do?"

But, he quickly says aloud, "I doubt the government knows anything about women."

Henrietta and Mary giggle. Finally, Mary answers, "Ha! This government is run by White men and they don't have a clue about trying to force Black women to do something now that they have never, ever been required to do since the day they were born. It's not at all surprising that Black women are resisting."

Henrietta says, "You are one hundred percent right about that!"

Mary doesn't offer that she is thinking about "forgetting" to carry her Pass Book when she walks the few kilometers from the District Six home to the Kruger homestead. She feels that in this way she can register opposition to the government and, of course, in her mind, of little risk in such a short distance. But, that will be her little secret.

After an hour and a half visit, Frederick and Henrietta and Robin leave.

***

Finishing a very early breakfast in his office this Thursday Frederick is getting ready for an early December trip to his Stellenbosch area vineyards. He will be gone before Mary and Charles arrive for work.

As he is collecting his breakfast dishes to transfer to the kitchen, Henrietta marches into his office and says, "Take a look as this special edition of the newspaper. You won't believe what you're reading, my dear!"

He begins reading and as his eyes grasp the story, he thinks that his wife is right; he can't believe what he is reading.

"On the morning of December 5, 1956, the Security Police swooped down on several opposition political leaders and, armed with warrants signed by the Johannesburg Magistrate, arrested 156 people and charged each with High Treason.

"The opposition political organizations include leaders and members from the African National Congress, the South African Indian Congress, the South African Colored People's Organization, the South African Congress of Democrats, the South African Congress of Trade Unions, and the outlawed Communist Party of South Africa now apparently operating in secret under a new name, as the South African Communist Party.

"The Government said this was the most dramatic single police action in the history of the Union, because this police action covered wide areas of the country and was directed against several organized political dissenting organizations.

"All those detained, in groups of twenty, appeared before the Magistrate, formally charged with High Treason, and placed in the custody of the prison officials at The Fort, Johannesburg's Central Prison.

"Unnamed sources say that the prosecution may not have a solid case against several of the detainees, even though the police have been seizing documents from many of the defendants' offices and have a large number of witnesses, especially policemen, to verify treasonous speeches.

"This newspaper will publish just a few of the names of those of public notoriety in order to safeguard the privacy of the lesser knowns.

"A few of the most prominent opposition leaders charged with High Treason are some of the leaders of the African National Congress, namely Alfred Luthuli, Walter Sisulu, Oliver Tambo, and Nelson Mandela.

"Mr. Mandala, a Johannesburg lawyer with a reputation of defending Blacks charged with crimes against Apartheid Laws and Regulations, has a history of opposing the Government.

"Previously, in 1952, Mr. Mandela was banned for 6 months by the Minister of Justice from attending any gathering in his Magisterial District or in living outside his Magisterial District.

"Thereafter, along with twenty others, Mandela was charged under the 'Suppression of Communism Act,' convicted, and received a suspended sentence because, in the words of the trial Judge Rumpff, 'the defendants had always asked their followers to pursue a peaceful course of action and to avoid violence.'

"Mandela is well known throughout the country as a dynamic public speaker and as one of the few Black lawyers taking cases for Blacks against the government.

"All defendants have requested a hearing for bail and—according to our unnamed source—a hearing should occur on or about December 19th.

"Already, Queen's Counsel Vernon Berrange, hired for and by the defendants, has released a pre-arraignment statement.

"He claims that 'the government's boot-jack arrests reminds me of how Hitler's Gestapo operated and how these charges are just like those trumped-up charges by Church authorities during the Inquisition or by the Nazis in Germany.'

"To the contrary says the prosecution, 'because these organizations, that is—the African National Congress, the South Africa an Indian Congress, the Congress of Democrats, and the South African Communist Party—and, as shown by speeches and writings of the accused and in this so-called 'Freedom Charter,' they also advocate violence and bloodshed set out in particularity the steps for the overthrow of the government and the creation of a Communist State to achieve this hideous goal.'

"In latter editions, this newspaper will update profiles of other accused."

Frederick puts the paper aside and says, "Henrietta, we are in for some trouble if these leaders are convicted. And that is especially true about Nelson Mandela, who has indeed, just as the paper indicates, become quite famous and especially revered by not only the Blacks, but also by the Coloreds, and by the Indians.

"If Mandela gets the death sentence, they will make him a martyr.

"Well, if those anonymous sources are correct that the government doesn't have a sure fire case, some of the accused will have their cases dismissed. That will be a real blow to the Strijdom government."

"Frederick, I think the Strijdom government will also be on trial by the entire world, no matter what." Henrietta comments.

"You are right about that, my dear, but that won't stop Strijdom from coming up with more Apartheid legislation.

"Well, I'm off to the vineyards. See you this evening. Drive safe in taking Robin to school. I love you."

Chapter 35

Since Mary and her neighbor Susan switch days in babysitting, today Susan is caring for her own and for little Tyrone, while pregnant Mary begins her morning walk to the Kruger homestead.

Charles has already left their District Six home to walk John to Catholic school in downtown Cape Town.

She and Charles used to walk together to John's school and then to the Kruger homestead. But, now, her pregnancy in early December demands she skip the school trip and just make the trip alone to the Kruger homestead. To and from the Kruger homestead, is plenty of walking.

She knows Charles will meet her at the Kruger's homestead.

Mary is taking her time, stopping and stretching every so often along the side of the roadway.

Suddenly a South African police vehicle pulls off the roadway and stops in front of her, with its rooftop lights flashing red.

Two uniformed Security Policemen quickly exit their vehicle. The younger policeman closest to Mary says in Afrikaans, "Stop right there and let me see your Pass Book!"

Mary's confused look tells the older policemen she doesn't speak Afrikaans. He says in English, after doffing his cap, "I'm Sergeant Vanderwaal and this is Officer Aarde from the Security Police and we want to see your Pass Book."

Frightened, Mary stammers as she looks in her purse, "Well, sir, it seems I've left my Pass Book in my other purse. I'm sorry about that, sir."

In Afrikaans, the Sergeant says, "Piet, new as you are in this job, you'll discover that's a very common trick used by the Natives to pull the wool over your eyes. Remember, it's a crime for not having a valid Pass Book in a person's possession, men and now, women, too."

"Right."

"Handcuff her and we'll take her to the Magistrate. Congratulations! This can be your first arrest, Piet."

As the young policeman reaches for his handcuffs attached to his leather belt, the Sergeant says in English, "No Pass Book in your possession is a crime. You are under arrest. Put out your hands."

Mary instinctively decides she must escape and begins to run toward the Kruger homestead, not very far away.

But, before getting very far, she trips and falls, landing awkwardly with her abdomen striking a large boulder.

As the young policemen reaches for her, she clutches her abdomen in pain and cries out, "My baby! My baby! Help me! I think my baby is coming!"

Reaching down to her panties, she feels liquid and brings her hand to her face. Seeing the blood, Mary cries, "Oh, no! I'm going to miscarry! I need to go to the hospital."

Mary doubles over and passes out.

Office Aarde asks, "What do we do with her? Is she dying?"

The Sergeant directs, "Help me get her into the car. Radio the dispatcher that we need to take her to the Natives' hospital. That we have an emergency."

The young policeman suggests, "But, there's a hospital closer than that."

The Sergeant replies, "No, they won't take a Non-European there. It's against the law. When we get to the hospital, we'll put a hold on her since she must appear before the Magistrate to see if she'll be fined, confined, or removed to the Reserves."

"Right."

"Look inside her purse for any identification," the Sergeant says as he guns the police vehicle.

Officer Aarde says, "Mary Washington, a domestic worker for Frederick and Henrietta Kruger; she lives in District Six with her husband Charles and a son."

The Sergeant replies, "Oh, shit! That's a Member of Parliament and they live just down the road! No, don't worry, because we'll just do our duty. I'll tell the officer in charge when we file our report. They'll take care of any negative feedback."

* * *

When Charles arrives at the Kruger homestead, he enters the kitchen to find a solitary Ophelia, brought in to help during Mary's pregnancy. "Where's Mary?"

"She hasn't arrived yet, Charles."

"What? She should've been here already."

In walks Henrietta after delivering Robin to school. She asks, "Where's Mary?"

Before anyone answers, the phone rings. Henrietta answers and discovers that Mary has miscarried and is in the Natives' hospital.

Telling the others the news, she tells Ophelia to get the bed in the guest room ready for Mary.

Asking about Tyrone, Charles tells Henrietta the boy is with a baby sitter.

Henrietta says, "Charles, come with me to the hospital."

* * *

At the Natives' hospital, Mary tearfully explains what happened. But she omits the truth that she purposefully left her Pass Book at home.

Perturbed, Charles' voice rises, "You left your Pass Book at home? In your other purse? After our talk? What were you thinking, Mary? That wasn't very smart!"

But he quickly realizes casting blame is not the way to handle the situation.

"Well, I guess we all forget things. It's all right, my dear. Don't worry. We talked with the doctor and he says you will be fine and that we can still have another baby. You just need to rest. Now, just relax, my dear. Henrietta will check to see if we can take you home. I love you."

Leaving the room, Henrietta learns from the nursing staff that the remains of the partially formed fetus have already been disposed of by the Natives' hospital staff. She isn't surprised that there will be no funeral preparations, but she'll keep this information to herself.

Rather than have Mary remain in the Natives' Hospital, understaffed and with poor medical equipment and perhaps with ill-trained Black nurses or nurses' aides, Henrietta wants to obtain the treating doctor's permission to transport Mary to the Kruger homestead.

Besides, the place doesn't look as if any sterile cleaning procedures have been followed.

The doctor certifies Mary will need about 2 or 3 weeks of bedrest. Henrietta has plenty of pads to soak up blood discharge and aspirin for the cramps.

The Black doctor says, "Sorry, but you won't be able to take her because she is under arrest and is awaiting a doctor's release for transfer to the Magistrate Court for a hearing and sentencing because of the Pass Book violation."

Henrietta realizes she must contact the Magistrate to solve that problem.

She explains the situation to Charles that a release must first be obtained from the authorities. She says, "I'll phone the Magistrate."

Although Henrietta doesn't practice law, as a lawyer she knows that, because of the country-wide Pass Book violations by Black women, the government is cracking down on women violators.

She remembers reading that recently, over a thousand Black women in Johannesburg stormed the central Pass Book office and chased away those women lining up for Pass Books and kicked the Pass Book clerks from their offices. Hundreds of women were arrested, packed in vans on their way to the Marshall Square police station. The next day brought a repetition but with over two thousand women joining. The prison at the Fort had too few toilets, too few blanket, too few mats or cots, and too little food. The Prime Minister was beside himself and asked the Magistrates to send some of the protesters to the Reserves.to teach the Black women a lesson.

If a Black woman ended up before a hardnosed Magistrate in favor of the government, Henrietta almost gulps at the thought.

Mary could be separated from her family and exiled to the Reserves.

Of course, she keeps this information to herself, not wanting to upset Mary and Charles.

She immediately telephones the Magistrate and, fortunately is able to plead her guilty in exchange for a fine if Henrietta will appear post haste. After explaining the situation to Charles, she drives to the Magistrate's office.

Since the Magistrate knows that Henrietta is a lawyer, at first he gives her a difficult time, but eventually after several bouts of negotiation in his office, the Magistrate agrees to a much lower fine.

He laughs, "My goodness, Madam Kruger, you are just too difficult to deal with. I must thank the Good Lord that you do not frequent my presence. Yes, indeed!"

Silently, she thanks God that Frederick is a Member of Parliament, that she is his wife, that she is a lawyer, and that she and Frederick are White. Henrietta is no fool to think her arguments alone won the day.

Henrietta pays the fine and secures a release of the hold on Mary.

As she drives to the Natives hospital, Henrietta realizes that Mary's identification record on file with the authorities and especially with the District Magistrate will now show a criminal violation. She will ask Frederick about the process for eradication or expunction from Mary's record since "a criminal record, no matter other how minor, can be grounds for removal to some forlorn place like the Reserves.

She remembers that Charles also has a criminal record because of his assault on the Afrikaner in Cape Town. Maybe Frederick can get that also expunged.

Since this government doesn't want 'criminals' in the country, the thought of losing Mary and Charles is disturbing. She remembers reading that the Minister of Justice labeled Blacks and Coloreds as dope dealers, rapists, and murderers and the Prime Minister himself broadcast that falsity.

She quickly returns to the Natives Hospital with the release paperwork and receives permission to remove Mary.

Mary, Charles, and Henrietta return to the Kruger homestead. Mary is bedded in the guest room. Henrietta makes sure Mary is comfortable.

"Charles, don't worry about picking up John from school because when I get Robin, I'll swing by the Cathedral School for John. Forget the rest of your work. You stay with Mary. You and the boys can stay here tonight in the guest house while Mary stays with us. I will personally watch over her."

Charles says, "Please also go to Susan's house next door and pick up Tyrone and some diapers and his bottles and the like."

Henrietta replies, "Yes, of course. See you in a bit."

After Henrietta has returned with John and Tyrone, the supplies, and Robin, she assures herself that Mary is sleeping. She says, "Charles, everything is under control. Ophelia and I will take care of Tyrone. John can play with Robin. So, you go finish your work in the garden and wrap it up."

Charles, trying hard to avoid a tear because of the loss of the baby and trying hard not to blame either Mary or the South African police for causing Mary's miscarriage, hesitates but then goes to busy himself in the vegetable garden.

But, this development and the news of the civil unrest sweeping the country and the passage of more and more restrictive legislation is unsettling even though Charles appreciates he and his family have been living in a sanctuary place.

Charles wonders what will happen to his family if their protection disappears. Worry lines appear on his face.

***

After Mary has satisfactorily recovered from her miscarriage, Charles says, "I've been wondering what we should be teaching John and Tyrone about White people. I guess they know that all Whites are not bad people, since we have Frederick and Henrietta as a fine example."

He looks at his wife, "What do you think, Mary?"

"John has grown up with Hans and Robin, who have always treated him with respect and dignity. They learned that from Henrietta and Frederick. Little Tyrone tells me how much he likes Robin, though she is older. They get along very well. Of course, he hasn't been around Hans very much since Hans is away at university."

Charles says, "That's true."

"But, of course, we know that not all White children, even at Catholic school, are like the Kruger children. I did get stares sometimes from White parents," Mary adds.

"I agree, but what are your thoughts as far as other Whites are concerned?"

Mary says, "As a Zulu, we were taught to be suspicious of Whites. My mother told me not to trust Whites. She discouraged me from being friends with any of the

Whites when I went to Catholic School. Of course, as I grew older, I found that not every White person was untrustworthy and that I didn't have to be so cautious in being friends."

"The same for me."

"Yet, now, Charles, the way this government is acting, I think we must tell John and Tyrone to be cautious in befriending very many Whites."

"Yes."

"My personal test as to whether or not I can trust a White is to see if they have ever participated in any protest against racial segregation. If a White openly opposed racial segregation with actions or even with words, then I feel that I can trust that person. That's what I think we should instill in both children."

"I agree, Mary."

"I am a little afraid that John appears to hating all Whites. That I don't like."

Charles says "Yes, no question that John is antagonistic to Whites. Sometimes he even lays into Frederick. I'll speak with him about that."

"Good."

"For me, when I was growing up in Durban the priests and nuns in school made sure every Black or Colored was treated with dignity and respect by White students. I must admit, however, that that was not the case in my neighborhood. The Whites around my house weren't very friendly. They also didn't like my father or any other Indians. I always kept my distance from them."

"That was smart."

"With Tyrone, I think your test is the way to go. To use the old adage, actions speak louder than words. But, even a few words of opposition are better than no words."

"Yes, I agree."

"Of course, I know that some Whites, though opposed to Apartheid, cannot afford to march as protesters and also cannot afford to speak out. I understand that's true with Blacks, too. I can identify with that."

"That sounds like us, Charles."

"If a White person has opposed racial segregation, like Frederick and Henrietta, then they are worthy of trust and friendship. But, we must look at each person individually. Agreed?"

"Yes. I agree, Charles."

Chapter 36

A worried Frederick Kruger sees in the January, 1958 newspapers that the treason trial of the 156 leaders of opposition groups will move forward.

Many South African policemen are testifying about documents seized from the offices of the ANC, the South African Indian Congress, the South African Colored Peoples' Organization, the South African Congress of Democrats, the South African Congress of Trade Unions, and the underground South African Communist Party.

Frederick remembers that the newspaper's suspicion of some dismissals has been justified because several people have been dismissed by the prosecution for lack of evidence. But the trial for the remainder is continuing.

He sees that both Albert Luthuli and Oliver Tambo are among the dismissed, but that Nelson Mandela is not.

Now, the newspapers report that daily overflowing crowds of Blacks in the spectator seats in the segregated second floor balcony at the courthouse are becoming more and more antagonistic, especially since Nelson Mandela is still on trial and that they are angrily shouting that his case should also be dismissed.

Frederick thinks again, "The government had better be careful about Mandela because the wrong decision will make him a martyr. He is too popular with all Non-Europeans."

Throughout the country, the African workers' unions are engaging in work stoppages, Black women are refusing to carry their Pass Books, all sorts of demonstrations are occurring, and the opposing political organizations are engaging in more acts of civil disobedience—all signs—Frederick thinks of what could lead to a possible civil war.

Although Frederick strongly believes in the Rule of Law, especially that everyone should obey the law, he understands that some Blacks, some Coloreds, and some Indians will disobey oppressive laws.

Some people will take the Law into their own hands. That could be the start of civil war, a race war.

Yet, personally he is torn between obeying an unjust law and the traditional rule of law. He wonders, "Who determines when a law is unjust?"

Under the leadership of Prime Minister Strijdom, the government pays no heed to the danger and more Apartheid laws are proposed. Frederick cannot stomach these unjust laws.

In Parliament, Frederick, and what remains of the United Party, appeals to basic common sense and reasonableness in hopes the National Party Members will halt their suicidal march to a civil war because of Apartheid.

But, he knows they won't.

When the *Immorality Act No. 23* prohibiting adultery or attempted adultery or related immoral sexual acts between Blacks and Whites is proposed, Frederick says, "This law is not needed since we already have laws to take care of any such problem. "This legislation will drive another stake in the relations between the races and will create more trouble for the police in trying to enforce this stupid law."

But Frederick's protests are in vain.

On April 16, 1958, the White voters, now the only eligible ones to vote in the ordinary elections, empower the

National Party candidates to continue its control over Parliament.

Evidently, the National Party has examined the pulse beating in the veins of White voters. As much as Frederick hates to admit, the majority of White voters have taken Apartheid to heart, having accepted the inferiority of all Blacks.

Frederick thinks the continued existence of the United Party is doomed because of the overwhelming loss of seats in Parliament in 1958.

Although Frederick retains his seat in Parliament, neither he nor his United Party own the votes to stop any of the Apartheid legislation, including a new law requiring all Black men, age 18 and up, to pay a higher annual tax than Whites.

After its enactment, Frederick comments to his bench mate, "Can you think of another way to piss off Blacks other than by increasing their taxes at a higher tax rate than that tax rate applied to Whites?"

***

Frederick, frustrated and disillusioned, is having breakfast with Henrietta. She is reading the August 25th edition of the *Rand Daily Mail.*

"Frederick, Prime Minister Strijdom died yesterday! The newspaper says that Doctor H.F. Verwoerd is expected to become the new Prime Minister and the leader of the National Party, although he has competition from Eben Donges and C. R. Swart!"

"Henrietta, with Verwoerd as the new Prime Minister, the divide over racial relations will become a chasm. I hope Donges or Swart gets the nod."

"Why/"

"Why, you ask? Verwoerd, elected to the Senate after Malan came to power, was then elevated by Malan as his Minister of Native Affairs, where he sits today."

"So?"

"As Minister of Native Affairs, Verwoerd has been a prime mover in enacting the bulk of these Apartheid laws. He will be no friend of Blacks if he becomes Prime Minister and will work his heart out to continue to make Apartheid more onerous."

Henrietta responds, "You are right, my dear. And, as I remember my history, Verwoerd studied Nazi eugenics in Germany, railed against South Africa admitting Jews to escape Nazi persecution before the War, and then publically opposed our country's siding with Britain against Germany."

Frederick says, "Wasn't Verwoerd one of your professors at Wits?"

"Yes, he was. At Wits, we were required to study some of his treatises on psychology and philosophy. As I remember, he was a big fan of the Nazi Socialist, Stefan Kuhl, who argued that Nazi's treating Jews in Germany the way Blacks were treated by Whites in America was morally correct. I must confess though, most of the university students thought of Verwoerd as a brilliant man."

"Henrietta, I whole heartedly agree that Verwoerd is well educated, but because of his intellect he is a dangerous man and will greatly antagonize Blacks, especially Black leaders like Nelson Mandela, as well as the leaders of every opposing organization. I fear if Verwoerd becomes Prime Minister the likelihood of civil war intensifies."

***

On September 3, 1958, H.F. Verwoerd takes the oath as Prime Minister and in nationwide radio address calms the country.

> "My friends, you have no need to worry about Apartheid, because Apartheid is simply a policy of good neighborliness.

> "With Apartheid, we will make South Africa an economic powerhouse and create thousands of job opportunities, not dependent on the British Crown. South Africa will come first!

> "I don't intend to slow down our progress. Instead, my fellow citizens, I intend to speed up our progress so that South Africa will be the brightest diamond in the world, an example of what Apartheid can bestow on our country.

> "Nothing will impede our growth. Nothing! We will not tolerate any acts of violence by these rebels who want to destroy the Union. We will not tolerate that! Heed my warning, your terrorists, because we will hunt you down like rats!"

To his aides, the new Prime Minister directs, "Gentlemen, I want some meaningful legislation to shape the further implementation of Apartheid policy. And, I want prohibiting signage to read not only in Afrikaner and English, but also in the local African tribal language, whether it is Zula, Xhosa, Swati, or whatever."

"Mr. Prime Minister, I suggest we prohibit Blacks from attending White universities and create tertiary institutions for the different races, not only along racial lines but also along ethnic lines," one aide says.

"Explain that," Prime Minister Verwoerd says.

"Yes, that means not only will Blacks, Coloreds, Indians have their own universities but it also means their own universities would be further segregated by language. For example, the University of Fort Hare would have just Black students who speak Xhosa. Other universities would just be for those who speak Zulu, Tsonga, and so on."

"Very good; I like that—more separation. Now see to it."

The aide leaves the room and begins writing the *Extension of University Act No.45 of 1959.*

Another aide suggests, "Sir, we should separate Blacks by classifying them according to their ethnic grouping, of which I believe there are eight ethnic groups, so as to allocate each to their respective Homelands."

"An excellent idea, and begin writing the proposed law, which I'm going to name as the *Promotion of Bantu Self Government Act of 1959.* Include in the new law that a Commissioner-General will be in charge to develop each Homeland until the Commissioner-General is satisfied that the particular ethnic group has proven itself capable of self-government without White intervention," the Prime Minister directs.

"Yes sir."

Verwoerd says, "Let's also shore up the laws against opposing political groups, especially the African National Congress, and for more days of detention by the Attorney General without any bail."

"Yes sir."

"In fact, I want the African National Congress and any of its fellow organizations declared as unlawful. We'll put a stop to this unrest and put some of them in jail."

After holding a bottle for Tyrone, Charles puts the baby in his crib and begins reading the newspaper in 1959. Mary is nearby working with thread and needle.

He discovers that the more liberal United Party members have become more dissatisfied with the leadership of the United Party because of lukewarm opposition to the new Apartheid legislative proposals.

They have split and formed the Progressive Federal Party, vowing continued opposition to Prime Minister Verwoerd, who considers himself as the Architect of Apartheid.

He is taken aback when he reads that a rumor says Frederick Kruger is thinking about joining the Progressive Federal Party or about resigning his seat in Parliament. Frederick has said nothing about leaving the United Party or about resigning from Parliament. He knows Frederick has expressed disillusions with his effectiveness in Parliament, out voted on every issue.

As he spies another piece in the newspaper that the African National Congress has also splintered, he reads it out loud to Mary.

"The ANC leadership forced out of the organization some people who challenged its policy of working with Whites.

"The piece goes on to say that the split occurred because the leaders in the African National Congress are relying too much on Whites and White ideas. The article says Robert Sobukwe is the head of the Pan Africanist Congress and wants a government of Africans by Africans for Africans."

Mary comments, "Didn't we meet that man on the bus to Cape Town?"

Charles answers, "I think so. The newspaper points out that Sobukwe fears that the ANC will be controlled by the Congress of Trade Unions, the South African Indian Congress, the South African Colored Peoples Organization, and the Congress of Democrats for Whites."

"And that's the same man?"

"I think so. The newspaper concludes that Sobukwe vows to have the new Pan Africanist Congress conduct positive action against the Pass Book laws which will include mass burnings of Pass Books."

He sees Mary shrug her shoulders as she continues working her needle and thread on the tear in the knee of John's pants.

"Well, the ANC still has Walter Sisulu, Oliver Tambo, and Nelson Mandela in charge. I'm sticking with them. And I don't think we should kick White people out of the organization," Charles says.

The rest of the news about the Prime Minister's legislation wrinkles Charles' forehead, especially about the law which might force Mary back to some Homeland in the hinterlands under the control of her father as the Zulu Chief.

Charles has no way to know what might be coming, but he is smart enough to figure that these Homelands will become little independent nations but always beholden to South Africa under the tutelage of the hereditary tribal chiefs and that Blacks will lose their South African citizenship and property. Those tribal chiefs would control their very existence.

But his fear flies away and he laughs at the thought because as long as Whites need Black workers inside South African towns and cities, those Blacks will not be transferred to these Homelands. As long as the Whites need Blacks in the White homes, in the White businesses, and in the White fields, no transfer of a Black will ever happen! The Whites won't stand for it.

Continuing to read the newspaper, Charles discovers that the ANC's boycott of potatoes over the mistreatment of Black farm workers has been successful, but Alfred J. Luthuli has been confined to his home for five years. He notes that dozens of Blacks have been killed amid the widespread rioting is still occurring over the enactment of more Apartheid legislation.

He reads that the government has finally completed the work on making Robben Island a prison, primarily for political prisoners. The newspaper predicts Robben Island will be more onerous than Poolsmoor.

Tired from his work today, Charles's newspaper slips to the floor as he enjoys a well-earned doze and begins a dream that eventually peace and racial equality will land in South Africa.

Chapter 37

In January, 1960, on his day off, Charles is reading the *Rand Daily Mail.*

He tells Mary, "The newspaper says that Alfred Luthuli has sent a warning letter to Prime Minister Verwoerd that the Natives' resentment is increasing about Apartheid. It reports that Prime Minister Verwoerd has ignored the warning, instead announcing that later this year the Prime Minister will call for a referendum for White voters only on whether South Africa should become a Republic."

Mary replies, "I'm getting more worried, because of the riots and the disturbances, although I know that the Pass Book law is the how the government detains and harasses all those against Apartheid."

"Yes, the paper says that there was more rioting near Durban with a least nine policemen killed and many more injured. The Commissioner of Police testified before Parliament that the intense civil resistance is cause for alarm."

"Oh?"

"At the last meeting of our local ANC Chapter, there's talk of the beginning of a nationwide anti-Pass Book campaign to begin at the end of March. As you know, now the ANC must compete with its rival, the Pan Africanist Congress. And, they are also considering the same kind of campaign against the Pass Book law, either by burning or surrendering Pass Books."

"What? How do you know that, Charles?"

"One of the PAC members revealed that to the ANC. Their idea is that people will assemble outside police stations without their Pass Books and challenge the police to arrest them. The ANC isn't considering anyone burning their Pass Book or giving them up, Mary. That's the PAC, as I understand their campaign."

Listening to the excitement in Charles' voice, Mary says, "Now, Charles, I don't want you taking part in any of that. I already made my own mistake by not carrying mine. Don't even think about burning or surrendering your Pass Book. We are very safe here with Frederick and Henrietta. Promise me, my dear!"

"I promise," Charles replies, knowing she is on safe ground.

* * *

Frederick Kruger is looking forward to the February 3rd speech by British Prime Minister Harold McMillan to the South African Parliament. McMillan has been on a tour of the British Colonies in Africa and now is meeting privately with Prime Minister Verwoerd. Of course, he wishes he could be that proverbial fly on the wall before McMillan's speech to Parliament.

Although witnessing Prime Minister McMillan's speech to a packed house in Parliament, Frederick is again enjoying reading parts of it published in *The Cape Town News*.

> "My Friends in this Parliament, I have some important news. Britain is separating from its South African colonies.

> "The wind of change is blowing through this continent. Whether we like it or not, this growth of national consciousness is a political fact.

> "As a fellow member of the Commonwealth, it is our earnest desire to give South Africa our

support and encouragement, but I hope you won't mind my saying frankly that there are some aspects of your policies which make it impossible for us to do this without being false to our own deep convictions about the political destinies of free men to which our own territories we are trying to give effect.

"I hope you will take heart at my message and continue to work for British values of freedom and human rights."

Frederick recognizes that the British Prime Minister is telling Black nationalists in South Africa to pursue their dreams for freedom and for racial equality.

However, he also knows that the Verwoerd government considers the speech as a telling abdication and abandonment by Britain of the White settlers in South Africa. He also hears Verwoerd's calling it 'a sell-out.' The government's propaganda machine will bring forth a strong reason for Whites, even the English speakers, to vote for the creation of a Republic, and eventually, Frederick thinks, a separation from Britain.

But, he can't give up hope.

***

On March 21, 1960, Father John O'Malley is driving his Humber from Pretoria to Johannesburg to meet in secret with Alfred Luthuli, Oliver Tambo, Walter Sisulu, and Nelson Mandela. The priest knows that the treason trial still continues with a few remaining defendants, including Walter and Nelson. Although Walter and Nelson must make an almost daily appearance at the courthouse, Father John will meet with the group in the evening to discuss working with its rival, the Pan Africanist Congress.

He is amazed that President Alfred Luthuli, confined to his house, somehow can sneak out without the authorities knowing it. Father O'Malley will be glad to see the old chief.

He suspects the Verwoerd administration will use divide-and-conquer tactics against the two political organizations, with the Pan Africanist Congress now believed to have over 70,000 members after splitting from the ANC.

The priest has read the circulars distributed by the PAC calling for a nationwide Anti-Pass Book campaign to start on March 21 when protesters throughout the country will march to local police stations and surrender their Pass Books to be arrested. He heard Robert Sobukwe say on the radio at a press conference on March 19th that there would be no violence by the PAC in their struggle for complete independence and freedom by 1963 from the South African government.

He hopes Sobukwe means that about no violence.

Father O'Malley understands together, both the ANC and the PAC will be stronger against Apartheid. He knows he'll have to soothe a few ANC egos to attempt any kind of reconciliation.

Eyeing the fuel gauge, the priest stops for petrol and after filling his tank, he enters the building to pay when the news pours from the radio. As he hears the exited English voice, he pictures the scene.

"Shortly after mid-day on this 21st of March in Sharpeville, the South African police fired on unarmed protesters who swarmed the police station. As of this moment, at least 69 Africans, including 8 women and 10 children, are dead and countless more injured, including women and children.

"Sharpeville is a Native town in the industrial area of Vereeniging, south of Johannesburg.

"First reports indicate the Sharpeville protestors (numbering between 5,000 and 20,000), and many more nationwide, were induced by the Pan Africanist Congress to turn in their Pass Books at the police station and face arrest.

"Although protests had occurred the night before, the police at Sharpeville were not well prepared. As the crowd increased, the original 20 policemen were joined by others, totaling 300. Soon, four armored cars were brought in. Additionally, the police were now issued Sten sub-submachine guns and Lee-Enfield rifles.

"As the crowd size increased to its estimated 20,000, the government had F-86 Sabre jets and Harvard Trainers fly within 100 feet over the crowd with hopes it would scatter. But, that didn't happen.

"Eye witness accounts reveal that as the protestors, singing freedom songs, pushed very close to the police station, one of the armed police lined in front of the station was pushed over and a small scuffle began.

"When a few rocks were thrown toward the British-made Saracen armored cars, one policeman atop the armored car fired at the protesters, without any warning, and his colleagues joined.

"Although the firing lasted barely 2 minutes, many of the protesters were shot in the back as they attempted to flee.

"The Police Commander in charge of the reinforcements at Sharpeville, Lieutenant Colonel Pienaar, excused the action. He told the press:

'After the stones were thrown, the men were jittery about the 9 policemen recently killed in the Durban riots and the men reacted swiftly. That was amazing since many had been on duty for over 24 hours without respite. Besides, my experience clearly demonstrates that Natives do not have the mentality to gather for a peaceful demonstration and any gathering by the Natives means violence. We expect a statement shortly from Prime Minister Verwoerd.'

"Stay tuned for more reports from this station."

Father O'Malley, stunned at the news, quickly pays the clerk and drives toward his meeting place in Johannesburg. Silently, he prays for the souls of the recently departed, for the quick healing of the wounded, for God's grace and support for their families, and for peace and justice for the surviving protesters.

As the car moves along the roadway, the priest's memory replaces with imagined pictures what he heard over the radio in the petrol station.

First, his imagination picks up a few bicycles among the twisted Black bodies; a woman in a bright skirt with a young girl in her blue and white blouse, bloody and about ten years old, crawling amid cries of anguish toward her; light gray smoke from the sub-machine guns shrouding the scene; and khaki-uniformed soldiers, with guns some shouldered and others poking at the Black bodies by turning them face up to check for life or to hide the bullet holes in their backs.

Then, his imagination, as if a camera, pans the scene to reveal the four huge camouflaged Saracen armored cars and a gun-toting soldier atop each vehicle; several ambulances and their nurses, clad in white with a Red Cross emblem, tending the wounded; and long after the onslaught, the Police Commander talking with the radio reporter with praise for the gallantry of his men.

Shutting his eyes, Father O'Malley wishes away what the unwanted gifts his imagination has placed inside his head.

While saddened because of the deaths and injuries, the priest understands that the radio report will play throughout the world, and perhaps in some places, on television. Although most of world has television coverage, that marvel doesn't exist yet in South Africa.

News in 1960 arrives in South Africa through radio or print or word-of-mouth, but not television.

The priest remembers that Prime Minister Verwoerd had considered television as undesirable and a danger to the people, following what the Minister of Posts and Telegraphs had said about the 'devil's black box' which would show films of race mixing and which would contain advertising lulling Blacks into dissatisfaction with their lives to foment revolution.

Father John remembers his thought, "I don't think I've heard a more xenophobic comment of hate."

He hopes important people in the United Nations, in Britain, and in America will hear or see what is

387

happening in South Africa because of Apartheid. Maybe, the priest hopes, some independent or freelance photographer shot some film, smuggled to the outside world to witness the slaughter

Father O'Malley also knows that the news of the Sharpeville massacre will produce massive demonstrations, protest marches, strikes, and riots throughout South Africa by people of all colors. Unfortunately, the priest recognizes that the South African police are indeed jittery and more police violence against the protesters will be forthcoming.

**

Charles is reading the March 23, 1960 issue of *The Cape Town News* as he breaks for lunch at the Kruger homestead.

He notes that yesterday, several protesters were killed by the police in another demonstration and that Robert Sobukwe and the PAC is calling for a nationwide strike because of the brutality of the South African police.

He can hardly believe what he is reading about Verwoerd's reaction to the Sharpeville incident in yesterday's speech to Parliament.

"The country need not be worried about the riots because those riots can in no way be described as a reaction against the Government's Apartheid policy and has nothing to do with Pass Books.

"Moreover, such disturbances are a periodic phenomenon and have nothing to do about poverty or low wages.

"My first duty is to thank the South African police for the courageous and efficient manner in which they handled the situation. Yes, at times the police found it difficult to control themselves, but they did so in an exemplary manner.

"Nonetheless, 132 Members of the Pan Africanist Congress and their leader, Robert Sobukwe, are held in Johannesburg and will be indicted for sedition and incitement to riot. We cannot and will not have this insurrection. All public gatherings of more than 12 persons are now banned."

Charles tells Mary, "I guess the Prime Minister must be asleep and doesn't know that, in response to the Sharpeville shootings, over 30,000 Africans peacefully marched in Cape Town on Parliament in spite of his banning more than 12 persons in a public gathering."

Mary says, "He doesn't have a clue."

Chapter 38

When Father John arrives at the safe house near Johannesburg, he pulls his Humber into the barn which also contains three other automobiles. Inside the house, he greets Nelson Mandela, Walter Sisulu, Oliver Tambo, Alfred Luthuli, Dr. Monty Naicker, Dr. Y. M. Daidoo, and several other ANC high ranking members.

When he sees that Ruth First, Joe Slovo, J. B. Marks are attending, the priest understands the Communists will play a big part in the campaign against Apartheid, even though the Communist Party is underground.

Father John has been invited because he has information from an informant, a plant inside the residence of the United States Ambassador. The spy had passed his information to Father John.

After getting permission to speak, Father John first announces, "Well, interestingly, today the Police Commissioner suspended the Pass Book law, not because of any appeasement to the Black protests and agitators, he says, but because the jails are full. He will restart it when he's good and ready, he says."

Nelson laughs, "Makes no difference because I'm going to burn my Pass Book when I talk to the press on March 28th in front of everyone. I've already lined up Ben Pogrund of the *Rand Daily Mail* to record my statement."

Alfred Luthuli says, "Well, I don't have any publicist but I'll be burning my Pass Book, too."

Walter Sisulu cautions, "Nelson, you and I are still on trial for treason. You burn your Pass Book before the press in public will be like rubbing dirt in Verwoerd's face. You will be surely arrested and jailed, without any trial, under these horrible laws."

Nelson replies, "I'm ready for it. Walter, whenever you're not required to attend the treason trail, you must keep speaking throughout the country to preserve the morale of our people. That is your calling."

Waiting for an opening, Father John continues. "My friends, the Verwoerd government very soon is going to shut down all forms of dissent by any political organization and now it doesn't need the approval of Parliament. My source declares that very, very soon, the government will declare as illegal the ANC as well as the PAC. Both the ANC and the PAC will be permanently banned, just like the Communist Party, and maybe others, too."

"That won't stop us," shouts Walter Sisulu as the priest continues.

"I suggest that you have every local chapter of the ANC to gather all important papers, especially membership lists or card files, and put those in safekeeping, protected from government hands. Make sure that vey trusted people have those records since the Security Police may infiltrate our ranks. We will have spies, my friends, and some turncoats."

Alfred Luthuli agrees.

The priest adds, "Not only will the ANC be outlawed, but Verwoerd will declare a State of Emergency, which means during that time, the country will really be governed by martial law. Nobody will have any rights!

There's talk that more and more regiments of the Citizens Force will be called up and activated to assist the Army and the Security Police."

Oliver Tambo jokes, "By the Citizens Force, you mean lots of White men prancing around in military formation on weekends and a few weeks of summer camp taking target practice, probably shooting at Black targets?"

Father John replies, "That's right, and it scares the hell out of me, even if I'm a priest, Oliver, because the Citizens Force increases the military power of the Apartheid regime. They already have the regular military, Army, Navy, Air Force, and the Security Police to outgun any dissent."

"That scares me, too, Father," Alfred Luthuli says.

"So, plans need to be made now if and when this more oppressive action becomes reality," Father John says.

The diverse group discusses the problem and possible solutions. The Communists favor immediate acts of sabotage, but Nelson says, "I'd like to avoid violence if possible and I don't want anyone injured or killed by so-called 'collateral damage,' especially innocent bystanders. However, I know situations may force us to change our tactics."

Alfred Luthuli says, "Here with us today is my friend, Manilal Gandhi, the Mahatma's son, and a prominent member of the South African Indian Congress. Like me, he is strongly in favor of non-violence as morally superior. Violence begets more and more violence, my friends."

Eventually, the group agrees to continue opposition without any violence, knowing however that operating in the dark will be difficult.

Nelson recognizes that the times require drastic decisions.

Nelson looks at Oliver Tambo and says, "Oliver, with the increase of these Citizens Forces, the ANC will be stymied and unable to operate. Alfred, I suggest that Oliver get out of South Africa and direct all ANC operations from outside the country. If we are arrested and jailed, we'll need someone to run the ANC. I think Oliver is our man."

Alfred Luthuli concurs and orders Oliver Tambo to leave South Africa and, when and if the time comes, to run the ANC in exile. He says, "Oliver, don't worry about getting permission from the government. Get a fake passport, now. Just get out fast!"

* * *

While the Kruger's daughter Robin, now 14, is attending school, Frederick and Henrietta have welcomed home twenty-two-year-old Hans from Witwatersrand University for the weekend. Hans has brought along his college roommate, Emil Dorbandt.

Just starting law school, Hans is anxious to share his freshman year with his lawyer-parents.

But first, his parents want information about the existence of any organized resistance to Apartheid among the students and professors.

Hans says, "Well, I suspected you'd want that kind of information. Emil, can tell you about that. While Emil is not a law student, he has been active in a large contingent of White students and professors who continue to protest Apartheid."

Emil says, "There are lots of students and professors against Apartheid, but the overwhelming number of White students and Professors side with the Government. Yet, we are constantly increasing our numbers against Apartheid, Mr. and Mrs. Kruger."

Frederick responds, "Emil, drop the formality, please. I'm Frederick and this charming woman is Henrietta.

"Now, is there violence? How do the Black students react? Henrietta asks.

"So far," Emil says, "there have been no violent clashes, although the arguments sometimes get very heated. You asked about Black students? Well, the few remaining Blacks don't mingle and, of course, don't comply with the Apartheid directives."

Henrietta asks, "Are the Black students treated fairly?"

"As fairly as one can expect under the circumstances, but certainly not by the administration officials," he answers.

Just then, Charles Washington enters, and after mutual introductions, Frederick asks him to join them.

Shaking hands, Emil says, "Glad to meet you Charles. You have a big fan here in Hans who has given me many praises about you. Glad you can join us."

Henrietta brings up the new law imposing separate education for Blacks. She asks Emil, "What's the reaction at Wits about that?"

"Well, when the *Bantu Education Act* was enacted, Verwoerd made a statement that angered all the Blacks at Wits and probably at every college."

She asks, "What was that, Emil?"

"He argued that the Natives have no place in the European community above slave labor. I can't remember his exact words but Verwoerd claimed that until now, the school system has misled Natives to the green pastures where Natives are not allowed to graze. Of course he's comparing Natives to cattle."

Charles frowns.

"Excuse me, Charles. I'm sorry you have to hear that disgusting remark from Verwoerd."

Charles says, "No need for your apology, Emil. We are used to being treated as animals. But thanks for your support against Apartheid. Someday, you young people will get our country straightened out. I'm very hopeful. Well, Hans, you are looking very fit. Good to see it. We'll talk later. I must be on my way. It was nice to meet you, Emil."

Emil says, "Yes, it was good to meet you, too, Charles. Excuse me, but I need to find the water closet."

Frederick says, "Down the hall, second door on your right, Emil."

As Charles leaves, Frederick says, "Well, tell us about your freshman year law professors, Son."

Giving his parents the complete lowdown on each of his professors, Hans now changes the subject and asks his father, "Are you going to stay in Parliament since the United Party is becoming more and more the very minority?"

"I'm thinking about it. But, I haven't yet decided. But, I'm leaning to get out since my voice and vote counts for nil."

Emil rejoins them.

After their chats about university life, Frederick says, "So glad you are enjoying Wits, Hans. And, Emil, please during the rest of your stay, consider yourself right at home."

Hans and Emil decide to take a walk on the Kruger homestead.

As the boys leave, Frederick says to Henrietta, "Here it is, March 31, 1960 and time seems to be just slipping away. Hand me the newspaper, please."

Frederick begins reading and says, "Yesterday, the government proclaimed a State of Emergency which suspends most civil rights. That means that a refusal to return to work can land an African worker in jail with a fine, Henrietta.'

"Oh."

"The newspaper says that over 18,000 people who oppose the government have been detained, with the Minister of Justice, John Vorster, using the Ninety-Day Detention law to hold them without facing any charges. Many of these people are already stuck away in detention camps"

Henrietta asks, "What's the news about the leaders of the ANC?"

"The paper says that both Alfred Luthuli and Nelson Mandela have also been detained and charged with burning their Pass Books. Because of his notoriety, Mandela has been transferred from the Johannesburg jail to a more secure one in Pretoria. Presumably, Mandela will be held in that hell hole until the State of Emergency is over. Oh, wait, because they will take him in chains each morning as his treason trial continues and return him to jail in the afternoon."

Henrietta asks, "How long will that be?"

"God knows, maybe months, whatever time Verwoerd considers as an emergency."

"What does the paper say about the new law you told me about?"

"The paper has it right. Parliament will enact the *Unlawful Organizations Act* on April 7th and that will outlaw several anti-Apartheid organizations, including the ANC and the PAC. And maybe even the Congress of Democrats, too. I think Verwoerd will go after Whites in any organized political organization opposed to the government."

"I agree."

"Verwoerd is setting himself as a target of hate."

Henrietta interrupts, "Are you saying what I think you are? That there's some kind of plot against the Prime Minister?"

"No, Henrietta, I'm just thinking out loud, that's all. But, I better tell Charles that membership in the ANC can now get him into trouble."

***

On April 1st, the United Nations Security Council votes 9-2 (with Britain and France abstaining) to adopt Resolution 134 deploring South Africa's actions and policies, which raise international friction and which result in loss of lives, and demanding South Africa abandon its policy of Apartheid and racial discrimination. The Resolution directs the Secretary-General to meet with South African Government to make arrangements which will adequately uphold the purposes and principles of the United Nations.

Needless to say, the Verwoerd government is not pleased, especially since the international community is isolating South Africa.

Chapter 39

Prime Minister Verwoerd on April 9th is opening the Rand Show in Milner Park in Johannesburg, part of the 50th year celebration of the Union of South Africa. After his speech, the Prime Minister inspects some prized cattle and takes his place in the VIP section reserved for honorary guests.

Seated nearby is David Pratt, a rich farmer who supports close ties with Britain and who is no fan of Apartheid. But, he also suffers from bouts of epilepsy and illusions of grandeur.

Suddenly, Pratt rises from his chair, walks toward the Prime Minister, and at point blank range, fires his .22 caliber pistol twice at Verwoerd's face, with the bullets perforating his right check and his right ear.

Another honorary guest knocks the gun from Pratt's hand and with the help of the Prime Minister's bodyguard overpowers Pratt.

Quickly accosted, David Pratt is hustled to the Marshall Square police station and because of his erratic behavior is taken to Forensic Medical Laboratory where a careful determination shows the man is unbalanced and not an anti-Apartheid terrorist.

The Prime Minister, rushed to a nearby Johannesburg hospital, where his condition is deemed satisfactory with no need for any surgery, is expected to obtain a full recovery within 60 days.

Naturally, everyone across the political spectrum condemns the attack and is thankful for the Prime Minister's eventual recovery.

Of course, not everyone is thankful for the Prime Minister's return to governing.

The outlawed South African Communist Party, now underground, relishes the idea that Prime Minister Verwoerd almost bought the farm, so to speak, and begins to plan how somehow, a more successful plan might cut short his rule. The Communists are no stranger to exercising a regime change in any government. Revolution is their watchword.

And, the Communists are not the only ones ever so hopeful to see Prime Minister Verwoerd's exit from his office.

Pratt's failed assassination attempt, later described in his mental health hearing by Pratt himself as shooting the 'Epitome of Apartheid,' certainly heightens the crisis created by the massacre of the Natives at Sharpeville by the South African Security Police and Army.

***

In June, Nelson Mandela is interviewed on South African radio and emphasizes unity of all Black people to fight the Apartheid government and for the entire world to join the fight against racial segregation.

He says, "If the government reaction is to crush with naked force our non-violent struggle, we will have to reconsider our tactics. In my mind, we are closing a chapter on this question of non-violent policy."

Mandela's statement awakens security concerns in London and in Washington.

Immediately after reviewing Mandela's interview, the British Foreign Office in London opens a file on Nelson Mandela.

And, after the Mandela radio interview plays in Washington, the Central Intelligence Agency in the Eisenhower Administration directs David Rickard, its secret CIA agent acting as the United States Vice-Consul in Durban, to keep a close eye on Nelson Mandela.

Twice, David Rickard reads his instructions from his CIA supervising contact in Washington, D.C.

"Because many of the former colonies in Africa have been either decolonized or have been or will be granted independence, these Nations are passing from a Western sphere of influence to one of non-alignment and are responding to the influence of Communist ideologies as opposed to those of Capitalism.

"South Africa is a stable ally opposed to Communism in spite of its Apartheid policies. America needs South Africa.

"Unfortunately, while the African National Congress and the Pan Africanist Congress appear to be working for equality and liberation of Blacks, both organizations are under the direct influence of Communists who maintain a direct line to the Soviet Union.

"At the moment uncertainty exists if Moscow is giving funding or material aid to these organizations, but future expectations of aid cannot be ruled out.

"You are directed to carefully watch Nelson Mandela who may be a Communist or a Communist sympathizer and, as such, a grave danger to the United States.

"Should you conclude that Mr. Mandela is such a threat, you are directed to assist in every possible way the South African authorities to control or eliminate that threat."

Even though the CIA now has plenty of the 'Company' operatives in South Africa, David Rickard knows he will need some local informants in order to carry out these orders. He phones his contact with the South African Security Police Commissioner's office.

"Colonel Spengler, this is US Vice-Consul Rickard and I need your help."

***

Anglican Bishop Ambrose Reeves, Bishop of Johannesburg, a vocal critic of the Verwoerd Administration and especially of the Sharpeville Massacre and an active opponent of the government's Bantu education program, refuses to sell the Anglican Church mission schools to the government. Anglican Archbishop of Cape Town, Joost de Blank, supports him.

From his pulpit, Bishop Reeves preaches, "Whatever the cost, we must make it plain to the Government, the members of our church, and to all the African people that we profoundly disagree with its education policy and we cannot and will not be a party to it in any shape or form."

Asked by Prime Minister Verwoerd that Bishop Reeves halt his tirades, the Bishop responds in a pastoral letter and in sermons from his pulpit that Verwoerd himself must halt his march to total racial segregation.

Needless to say, the Prime Minister is none too happy, particularly when he reads one of the pastoral letters. "Slanderous," he exclaims.

On September 12, 1960, the Security Police snatch Bishop Reeves from his residence right in front of his house keeper; and place him in handcuffs with a hood completely covering his head, Roman collar, and black coat. Then, they hustle him outside, hurry him to Jan Smuts Airport in an unmarked van, and secretly deport the bishop from South Africa through irregular procedures.

Leaning of Bishop Reeves' appearance at the Jan Smuts airport and of his disappearance, Archbishop de Blank recognizes the threat that priests, nuns, and all religious of every Faith who criticize the government are no longer safe. But he won't stop.

Later, *The Star* newspaper reports that "Although 23 passengers were listed by name on the seating manifest for DC7B Flight to London on September 12, 1960, one seat in the tourist section is listed as occupied but with no name on the seating manifest. Sitting in that seat was Bishop Ambrose Reeves."

***

In the United States of America, the 1960 Presidential Election between Vice President Richard Nixon and the Democratic challenger, Senator John F. Kennedy is set for the 2nd Tuesday in November.

A few weeks before the election, the Civil Rights activist, Reverend Martin Luther King, Jr. has been arrested because of a sit-in at an Atlanta department store and, because of an outstanding traffic warrant, is held, convicted, and sentenced to six months hard labor in the De Kalb County, Georgia jail. But when his wife attempts to visit him, she finds he has been secreted away over 200 miles to a maximum security prison in Reidsville, Georgia.

Discovering her anxious plight, Senator and candidate John F. Kennedy phones Ms. King and sympathizes with her, while his brother, Robert Kennedy, convinces the judge to grant bail to the Baptist minister, Dr. Martin Luther King, Jr. who is released.

Word spreads among the Black communities in the South and on Election Day, many Blacks vote for Kennedy, even though he is a dreaded Catholic, and help elect him as the President of the United States.

**

On August 31, the Verwoerd government lifts the State of Emergency but admits that over ten thousand Blacks opposed to the government are still detained and makes overtures to either ban, place under house arrest, or imprison known trouble makers.

Recognizing that the South African government intends to crack down on the leaders of the now banned ANC, Nelson Mandela decides to keep a lower profile, especially since he is still attending his treason trial in Pretoria. However, Nelson knows that Blacks under Apartheid already live a life between the darkness of secrecy and the light of openness and between legality and lawlessness. He will do his best to be unidentified to the South African authorities as he travels around the country when not attending his treason trial, now in its third year.

**

In preparation for the referendum for only White voters to make South Africa a Republic, the Verwoerd government floods the media with ads showing the benefits of the creation of a Republic and with ads downplaying any rupture from the British Commonwealth. Naturally, Frederick Kruger and his White allies will campaign and vote against the forming of a Republic.

The October 5th referendum results show that 52% of the White voters favor the creation of a Republic. Of course, no Black, Colored, or Indian voters are allowed to vote.

As promised, Prime Minister Verwoerd informs the British government that South Africa desires to remain in the Commonwealth. He proclaims to his country that the Republic of South Africa will begin May 31, 1961 on the fifty-first anniversary day of the Union's creation.

***

In July of 1960, the Communist Party of South Africa, still operating underground, announces that it is continuing under its new name, the South African Communist Party and will continue its work to end racial segregation by cooperating with all dissenting organizations, including the ANC, the PAC, the South African Indian Congress, the South African Colored Peoples Organization, the Congress of Democrats, and all Black Unions.

In December, the Communist Party invites Nelson Mandela to attend a secret meeting, but the meeting is not so secret as to escape the eye of the CIA agent, David Rickard.

CIA Agent Ricard has Mandela in his cross-hairs.

Discussions at the meeting center on the possible creation of an armed wing to attack government installations but not to endanger the lives of anyone. But, as of now, that's just in the early planning stage.

However, an infiltrated informer reveals to CIA agent David Rickard some of group's plans for sabotage of government installations.

On March 15, 1961, Prime Minister Verwoerd, addressing the nation, announces that South Africa is withdrawing from the British Commonwealth. The decision provokes a strong disagreeing reaction from English speakers and from the leaders of the industrial community.

Naturally, the Afrikaners are overjoyed, believing the country is better off outside of the 'Kaffir' Commonwealth, as they denigrate the British Commonwealth, now including India, Pakistan, and Ceylon.

The remaining British Commonwealth Ministers express dismay about South Africa's leaving.

About the same time, the Synod of 350 Delegates of the Dutch Reformed Church endorses the Church's current policy of racial separation and asks the Government to expedite the implementation of Apartheid. That all other organized religions in South Africa oppose Apartheid matters little to the Dutch Reformed Church.

When the High Court declares on March 29, 1961that all the remaining defendants are not guilty of treason, the Verwoerd government immediately extends the ban on the ANC and the PAC. Nelson Mandela and the ANC leaders decide to take the organization underground.

Nelson Mandela makes himself invisible to the Government as he travels throughout the country and preaches unified resistance to the Apartheid laws.

He is also planning to head an armed resistance campaign with proposed acts of sabotage against government facilities without any injury to people. But the plans remain in a state of flux.

Chapter 40

While Robin is doing her homework, Frederick is in his office working on their winery accounting ledgers. Nearby, Henrietta is reading the October-November, 1961 edition of *The Cape Town News Magazine.*

Interrupting her husband, she says, "I'm reading about the treason trial. The magazine says the remaining 28 defendants, including Nelson Mandela, Walter Sisulu, and Alfred Luthuli, were declared not guilty on March 29th. The magazine estimates to the trial cost over a million during the four years. Unbelievable, don't you think?"

Not getting any response from her husband, Henrietta flips the page and continues reading the article about the treason trial.

"The three judges on the High Court unanimously ruled that no evidence existed of Communist infiltration into the African National Congress, that no evidence existed that the ANC adopted any policy to overthrow the State by violence, and that no evidence existed to show that the ANC's Freedom Charter was communistic.

"No matter, said the Verwoerd government, because before the ink had dried on the High Court's decision, the Government retaliates by banning as illegal organizations both the African National Congress and the Pan Africanist Congress, placing a nation-wide ban on all meetings, and sending storm troopers to break up the African National Congress meeting in Pietermaritzburg.

"Recognizing that the prisons are now over-loaded, the Government has turned Robbin Island into a maximum security prison, because of the continued civil disorder, as shown by the strikes in May which cancelled all police leave and which forced the Government to enact defense legislation to enable the armed forces to help suppress any internal disorder."

Henrietta says, "Frederick, when you finish the bookkeeping, please look at this issue of *The Cape Town News Magazine* because there's lots of news in it." She continues reading.

"United Nations Condemns South Africa's Apartheid"

"In 1960, the United Nations Security Council adopted Resolution 134 deploring the policies and actions of the South African Government and called upon the Government to abandon its policies of Apartheid and racial discrimination, with France and Britain abstaining.

"But, in spite of conferences with Prime Minister Verwoerd by a United Nations delegation, South Africa persisted and ignored threats by several of its neighboring countries to cease trade with South Africa.

"On April 13, 1961 the United Nations General Assembly adopted Resolution 1598 (XV), spon-sored by India—which condemned Apartheid 'as reprehensible and repugnant against human dignity,' with the vote of 96 in favor, zero abstentions, and only Portugal and South Africa against.

"When the United Nations sent an eight-member delegation to investigate conditions in the UN Mandated Territory of South West Africa, the UN team is refused entry by the Minister of External Affairs who warns that farther intrusions will be considered as an act of aggression by the United Nations.

"Prime Minister Verwoerd says South Africa will not be pushed around by foreign states, including the United Nations, and tells the country that Ghana's import-export ban is insignificant. He also announces that South Africa will secure airline flight treaties in the near future with several nations, including France, Italy, Norway, and Sweden, and that South Africa has a favored-nation's treaty with Great Britain.

"With the participation of Britain and the United States, the General Assembly of the United Nations on October 11th voted a censure against South Africa because of Apartheid. When South Africa's Foreign Minister defended Apartheid with very offensive speech, immediately, the General Assembly censured him, with a vote of 67 in favor, 20 abstentions, and only South Africa's vote against censure."

Henrietta stops reading *The Cape Town News Magazine* to see if Robin has finished her homework. Returning, she continues her reading.

"Nelson Mandela: The Black Pimpernel"

"Throughout South Africa, Nelson Mandela is now recognized as 'The Black Pimpernel' (named after Baroness Orczy's 'Scarlet Pimpernel') because Mandela uses coins at a pay phone to ring up the press about his plans and the plans of the dissenters and to tattle tale about all of the gross ineptitude of the police in their many attempts to catch him.

"It's as if Mandela is an undercover reporter for the press.

"Since organizing the nationwide general strike on May 29th when over 40% of the Johannesburg Black labor force stayed home, over 50% of the Indian and Asians were out in Durban, and 25% of the Coloreds sat on their hands in Cape Town, Mr. Mandela has been moving easily around the country in spite of police and military dragnets, hoping to catch him.

"Obviously, he uses a myriad of disguises to continue the myth as 'The Black Pimpernel' and to escape the arrest warrants. He has been seen as a field hand in blue overalls. Sometimes, he appears studiously wearing those Mazzawati tea glasses. At other times, Mandela wears a pressed chauffeur's uniform and starched cap. Who knows what else?

"How he can move effortlessly to be in Johannesburg one evening, then the next night in Cape Town, and the next in Natal Province, and the next speaking with the dock workers in Port Elizabeth, is indeed a mystery. Yes, of course, the police have an identifying photo of Mr. Mandela with a handsome growth of a beard. But does he still have the beard?

"Needless to say, the Blacks, the Coloreds, and the Indians are rooting for Mandela's continued escape from the clutches of the Law. In the eyes of the young, Mandela has become one of South Africa's super-heroes.

"In some of the casinos frequented by Whites, one can find betting odds as to when Mandela will actually be caught.

"Naturally, rumors abound, such as the quiet warnings given Mandela by some Black policemen for him to avoid certain towns because of police roadblocks or because of police raids of known meetings.

"For this article, Mr. Mandela recollected the events before the May 29th stay-at-home.

"He says, 'Frankly, after Verwoerd declared that those supporting the strike were playing with fire and immediately before the protest day, the government staged the greatest peace time show of military force, exercised the largest call up of soldiers, cancelled police leaves, stationed military units at the entrances and exits of towns and with Saracen tanks rumbling through the dirt streets, and hovered helicopters—day and night, we at the ANC wondered if we should go forward with our plans. Plus, our rival, the Pan Africanist Congress, tried to sabotage our protest, even putting out handbills urging people not to join us. But we went forward with our plans. However, honestly the protest didn't achieve the desired success and I met with Benjamin

Pogrund of the *Rand Daily Mail* and told him the days of our non-violent struggle were over. The next day at a safe house in a White suburb I met with the local and foreign press, telling them that if the government was going to crush our non-violence with naked force, then we will reconsider our tactics and close this chapter of non-violent policy.'

"On June 26, Freedom Day, Nelson Mandela sent a letter to many South African newspapers informing everyone that he will never surrender to the police and this struggle for freedom is his life. He said, 'I will continue fighting for freedom until the end of my days.'"

Turning the page, she sees the dark block Headline: **Racial Relations in the USA**. Henrietta reads a very short feature.

"In the United States of America, the Kennedy-Johnson Administration is balancing racial relations on the tip of the proverbial pin. While President Kennedy has the support of Dr. Martin Luther King, Jr. and other leaders of the Blacks, the Head of the FBI, J. Edgar Hoover, is openly suspicious of Doctor King as a Communist.

"Yet, President Kennedy plans to introduce to the US Congress some 'civil rights' legislation, which is expected to go nowhere due to strong opposition from Senators and Congressmen in the South. Many observers rate racial relations as very tense in the USA, especially where the 'Jim Crow' laws prevail in the South and where

411

some Governors of southern States openly defy the federal government by barring Blacks' admission to schools and universities."

Henrietta flips the pages of the magazine and sees what she already knows has happened in South Africa. She skims the first sentence of the remaining articles in the magazine.

"On October 18, 1961, the National Party wins 105 Parliament seats and control of the government while the United Party takes 49 and, the Progressive Party and the National Union Party one each."

She notes that there is no mention that Frederick has resigned his seat in Parliament after long years of service to South Africa.

"Shortly thereafter, the Minister of Justice bans any protest against the arrest, trial or conviction of any person and issues the first house arrest confining the occupant for five years.

"Besides banning a person or an organization, the Minister of Justice can 'list a person' — meaning the person cannot be quoted, hold public office, or practice his profession (including law or medicine); or can produce 'banishment' — meaning the person can be charged and removed to an isolated place without trial.

"Is the Verwoerd government more and more determined to make South Africa a more secure State or something else? We shall see."

Reading that last two sentences again, she wonders how that line squeezed passed the censure's eraser. She's glad that the magazine can still produce unbiased news and opinion. Any more negative commentary might produce a complete ban *The Cape Town News Magazine.*

Henrietta says, "Frederick, I think after you read this magazine, we should talk because things are getting worse, much worse. If you can believe this article about Nelson Mandela and what he says, I think we are close to an armed insurrection and maybe a civil war. I'm worried, my dear."

Frederick gives her his full attention.

"I suspect many of our Black, Colored, and Asian friends are worried about which neighbor is trustworthy since any dissenters might be reported to the Security Police."

"Certainly; let me have the magazine."

***

In his slot where Frederick puts Charles' work orders, Charles finds *The Cape Town News Magazine* with a note from Frederick about Nelson Mandela.

Charles reads Frederick's note: "Read the article about Nelson Mandela. Looks like Mandela and the ANC will go underground and resort to violence. Be careful not to get involved. You might want to consider resigning. Let's talk when I return later in the week from the vine-yards."

Before beginning his gardener chores, Charles flips open the page to the article on 'The Black Pimpernel' and quickly reads it.

He knows that, a month ago, the local Cape Town ANC chapter, already meeting in secret, had a young man, a little over John's age, from Port Elizabeth speak that the time is at hand for the arrival of an armed struggle against Apartheid. He said his name was Victor Mhlaba and claimed to be a cousin of Raymond Mhlaba one of the higher ups in the ANC. The young man said the armed struggle should immediately begin. He seems to be signaling Port Elizabeth as an initial target.

Charles remembers the young man made an impressive and very believable speech, utterly amazing from a person so young. But, that the young man had also complimented the Pan Africanist Congress for stepping up its campaign of violence. That was worrisome.

But nothing about any violent actions from the ANC arose after Victor Mhlaba left the meeting. The group continued with the usual protests, bus boycotts, strikes, without any talk of violence.

Then, at the local ANC meeting last week, rumblings occurred that an armed struggle will begin soon. One man said the armed struggle would be called *Umkhonto we Sizwe*. Charles learns that means Spear of the Nation. But the man didn't reveal from whom or how he got that information, causing everyone to wonder if it came from Nelson Mandela or from one of the other leaders of the underground ANC.

Another man volunteered that his neighbor, a member of the banned Pan Africanist Congress, had told him that their rival, the PNC, had created *Poqo* to engage in acts of sabotage against the government. The man says, "In Xhosa, the word, *Poqo*, means independent or separatist."

One guy talked of the need for secret guerilla training to fight the increased regiments of the White Citizens Force, and, the government is thinking about conscription of all White men, age 18 and up.

Charles hopes this is just talk by a few of the local hot heads. But, what if it is true that an armed rebellion will come?

He remembers that his father abhorred violence and was a devoted follower of Gandhi. His father died, Charles remembers his mother's letter, because he engaged in a non-violent protest against 'The Ghetto Act'. Though he has rejected many of his father's Hindu beliefs, he has always held dear Gandhi's policy of non-violence as the true way to change ideas.

Charles isn't ready to engage in violence against the government.

Worse, Charles and his son, John, are having a few disagreements about the need for aggressive action, bringing back memories of his own disagreements about religion with his father.

**

Sixteen-year-old John isn't shy about asserting his admiration of 'The Black Pimpernel,' or an almost undying worship of Nelson Mandela, as Charles would term the boy's infatuation.

John says, "The Black Pimpernel every day makes fools of the Security Police and the entire Verwoerd Government. He will deliver us from this evil."

The nuns at John's school have fed John and his classmates with so much disgust over Apartheid. John has reported that his class discussions have ranged from a wait-and-see attitude of hope for equality and the end of racial segregation to talk about overthrowing the government through revolution and by acts of sabotage.

Of course, Mary and Charles have tried to tone down any talk of violence against the government by showing that violence really doesn't work in the long run.

Not to be deterred by his parents, John cites as evidence how successful violence can be. He reminds them of movie scenes involving the French, Danish, and Norwegian resistance in World War II against German occupiers.

Charles retorts that movies are just stories with a preretained point of view of the producer, the screenwriter, and the director that during the World War, violence had to be met with violence.

"Son, it was kill or be killed by the Nazis! That was different. It's not in South Africa," Charles says.

Although his son smiles agreement, Charles understands he hasn't fully convinced his son.

Charles fears that little Tyrone, listening to the arguments about violence, might be influenced by his idolized older brother.

During their last discussion, Mary and Charles learned that John has definite ideas about his future.

John says, "I don't want to be beholden to Frederick and Henrietta Kruger like you are. I want to be my own person. But, I will follow your advice and finish school this year. But, I may skip college and just get a job. I have a good brain and I am not afraid of hard work."

Now, with the new education law, Mary and Charles know John can no longer be admitted to any White college. And nobody knows which college will now accept Coloreds, even if John decided to go to college.

Thankfully, Mary convinces John to obtain and carry his Pass Book after he turns sixteen.

Since John is so enamored with Nelson Mandela, he wants to join the ANC's Youth League. Naturally, Charles drowns that wish since he knows that the Youth League masquerades as a religious or welfare front for the parent organization.

So far, John has agreed to abide by his parent's wishes not to join.

For this, Charles and Mary have thanked God. Charles doesn't want to see his son jailed by the Government forces, especially since change is appearing on the horizon from the United Nations' actions.

***

Charles vows to question one of the local leaders the next time a secret meeting is scheduled about an armed wing of the ANC, whether called Spear of the Nation, or something else. The wrinkles in his forehead have deepened with the news.

When he meets with Frederick, he'll ask him about the "Spear of the Nation."

Charles isn't ready to undergo military training and he isn't ready to engage in acts of sabotage. He realizes his family is immunized against much of Apartheid by working for Frederick and Henrietta and living in a safe and secure District Six. But he knows that like Sophiatown, bulldozed without any warning and turned in a segregated White enclave, the same government action also could happen to District Six with its unique biracial composition.

He can still picture from radio broadcasts the scenes showing government agents, with guns, forcing the occupants of Sophiatown out of their homes; showing women carrying children pleading with army soldiers who shoved them aside with rifle butts; and showing army trucks dumping the people's personal belongings and household goods in the dirt in a dusty tent city some distance away from their old homes.

He's heard the stories and is glad his family is safe, at least for now.

Entering the kitchen, Charles hands the magazine to Mary, "When you have a spare moment, read the part about 'The Black Pimpernel,' meaning Nelson Mandela. You know John's current hero. Then, tonight, let's talk about what's happening with the ANC."

"Yes."

"When Frederick returns from the vineyards later in the week, I want to talk with him about what's happening. I think he will want me to quit the ANC."

* * *

Frederick says, "Charles, this Spear of the Nation is the armed wing of the ANC and will, in my opinion, get this country much closer to a civil war."

He has Charles' full attention.

"How do you expect the government to react when government facilities are blown up? You know that the Security Police and the Army will never rest until every member is either killed or imprisoned! And, you are not a man of violence, from what you've told me. You are a peacemaker. You should not be associated with the ANC if they are turning to violence."

Charles says, "Yes, that is true that I don't condone violence.

"Frederick, remember my job in the ANC has been that of a block captain. Other than you, Mary, and the two

418

people I contact, nobody knows I'm in the ANC. I think I'm safe. What do you think?"

"No, you're not safe. I suggest you tell them tomorrow. The way things are going, my friend, we just can't risk it."

"I trust your judgment, Frederick. I'll resign from the ANC completely."

* * *

One of Prime Minister Verwoerd's aides enters the office with a handful of the November 11, 1961 South African newspapers and is glad the Prime Minister is busy with the Minister of Justice Vorster.

The aide nervously deposits them atop a credenza and quickly departs because he's already seen the front page.

Vorster grabs several of the day's newspapers to glance at the front pages.

"Oh, my God, Mr. Prime Minister, take a look at what's on the front page of every one of these newspapers!"

The Prime Minister saunters to the credenza where Vorster hands a few to the Prime Minister.

The redness blazes in the Prime Minister's face.

There, in black and white and a few in full color is Queen Elizabeth of the United Kingdom dancing with a Black man, Kwame Nkrumah, President of Ghana.

In the background stands the Queen's husband, the Duke of Edinburgh, smiling as the Queen of the British Commonwealth happily waltzes with the Black President in Accra.

Speed reading one of the papers, Verwoerd discovers that Queen Elizabeth's visit was to safeguard the

419

relation of Ghana in the Commonwealth even though some unrest, including explosions, had occurred in Accra.

And, the world—especially in Africa—is applauding the Queen of England.

Tossing the papers aside, Verwoerd comments, "Well, that is scandalous and a personal affront to South Africa. The woman better not think of every visiting South Africa and dancing with any Native. We won't allow it!"

Chapter 41

Nelson Mandela has never fired a gun at an enemy but now he is head of *Umkhanto we Sizwe* or The Spear of the Nation—MK in shorthand. Every day, he practices his marksmanship with his new-found pistol and rifle.

He has recruited several White members of the ANC, including Joe Slovo as one of the leaders of the MK High Command, and two additional Communists, Jack Hodgson and Rusty Bernstein, as explosive experts.

The MK people all are meeting near Johannesburg at Liliesleaf, a farm owned by Arthur Goldreich, a White member of the MK and of the Congress of Democrats. The place is deemed a safe house, unknown to the Security Police, who are still chasing 'The Black Pimpernel,' as Mandela miraculously appears throughout the country to speak to the multitudes opposed to Apartheid even as he serves at the leader of MK.

Nelson declares to his MK members, "Gentlemen, our goal is to frighten the National Party supporters, scare away foreign capital and weaken the economy to bring the government to the bargaining table. Now, if that doesn't work, then we must be prepared to move on to the next stage, meaning guerrilla warfare and terrorism."

For months, they have been refining their plans. Now, the time is at hand because the first acts of sabotage will occur during the night on December 16, 1961.

First, handbills are distributed in English and Zulu about what will occur in or near Johannesburg and Port Elizabeth to Post Offices, Government African Affairs Offices, and to electric power stations or grids.

While five bomb explosions damage properties without any injuries to people, the Security Police obtain enough information to foil three new attempts in and near Johannesburg and catch the bomb maker.

After a cruel but effective interrogation with the bomb maker, the Security Police link the explosions to MK with strong suspicions that Nelson Mandela might be involved. The Security Police step up all patrols to arrest Nelson Mandela.

When word filters to the underground ANC headquarters of the MK that Mandela's capture is foremost in the mind of the Security Police under strict orders from the Prime Minister, the MK leadership council recommends Mandela leave South Africa.

In January of 1962, Nelson Mandela secretly travels to attend in Ethiopia the Pan-African Freedom Movement Conference hosted by Oliver Tambo.

Afterwards, Mandela studies war manuals of revolutionaries and obtains training in demolition, guerilla, and mortar firing tactics in a number of African countries all opposed to South Africa. He is welcomed by the leaders of each African country.

In Ethiopia, Haile Selassie supplies Mandela with a fake passport so that Mandela can later return to South Africa under the name of David Motsamayi, one of the ex-clients of the law firm of Mandela and Tambo.

Eventually, Mandela flies to London to meet the leaders of the Labor Party and the Liberal Party and seek military and financial assistance from those opposed to Apartheid.

When he returns, MK will increase its campaign of sabotage.

Not to be outdone by the ANC's MK, the Pan Africanist Congress has created *Poqo* (or Pure in English) as the armed wing of the banned PAC to begin its own reign of terror by killing several Whites in the Cape Province.

The PAC now proudly excludes Whites from its membership and wants war on all Whites as the oppressors of the tribes of Africa.

***

An angry Prime Minister Verwoerd is beside himself and seeks ideas from his advisors. He has some ideas himself, but wants some input, especially from his Minister of Justice, B J. Vorster.

Verwoerd and Vorster, fans of the Nazis, both opposed allowing Jewish immigrants into South Africa from Nazi Germany. They still remain as soul mates.

Before the War, with a doctorate in psychology from Stellenbosch University, Verwoerd visited Germany in 1927 and developed much of his dogmatic, intolerant, and domineering xenophobia in public life in admiration of Nazism.

The Smuts Administration during World War II interred Vorster because he was a General in the extra-paramilitary *Ossewa Brandwag* (Oxwagon Sentinel) siding with Germany in the war and is believed to have engaged in suspected sabotage of British supply depots.

Vorster says, "Mr. Prime Minister, if I may suggest, I think we should adopt the tactics Hitler's Gestapo used to uncover saboteurs in occupied villages."

"Oh?"

"If the perpetrators were not revealed, one or more of the townspeople faced a firing squad. And, if the saboteur was not given up, not only was the saboteur killed, but members of his family succumbed. I tell you, Mr. Prime Minister, the rates of sabotage decreased exponentially!"

"Well, yes, thank you, Mr. Vorster, but I don't think the world is ready for shooting innocent people by firing squad. We are more civilized than that."

"Certainly."

"But I do like your idea of vesting some punishment upon a perpetrator's family members who undoubtedly possessed knowledge of the planning of the act of sabotage. It wouldn't be death, of course. Instead, under certain circumstances, it would be banning, deportation, or imprisonment."

"Thank you, sir."

"Yes, I like that very much to make people think twice before acting. It will definitely put the fear of God into their very soul that a family member may pay the costly price of their trespass."

After several conferences, the Prime Minister is ready to address the nation.

The radio stations grant his request for free time. They also make available plenty of promotional advertising concerning the date and time of the Prime Minister's address to the nation, twice—first in Afrikaner and then in English.

Just an hour before Verwoerd speaks, the press aide releases his speech to the newspapers. The Prime Minister listens to the announcer and begins his speech.

"Ladies and gentlemen, here is Prime Minister Verwoerd.

"Good Evening, Fellow South Africans!

"Tonight I speak with you about a matter of grave concern to all of us who value a stable and peaceful society where we can raise our families, earn a decent living, and go about our daily affairs without the threat of looming and dreadful terror.

"You have seen in the press the pictures of several of the Nation's Postal Offices, the Offices of the Government's African Affairs, and electric power stations. Fortunately no loss of life or of human injury has resulted from these cowardly and dastardly acts of violence. But that is our good luck, which may not continue in the future.

"But, in the rural areas of the Cape Province and in other parts of our country, innocent Whites—men, women, and yes, even children—have been brutally murdered by tribal gangs of cowardly thugs hiding behind masks.

"You have read or heard or seen that several other attempts of sabotage of Government facilities in Johannesburg have been thwarted and the perpetrators arrested, tried, and convicted.

"Obviously, these acts of sabotage at the dock facilities in Port Elizabeth, Durban, and Cape Town are intentionally designed to hurt our economy by limiting imports and exports.

"These acts of terror are also intentionally designed to scare away multi-national businesses from locating in South Africa and from adding more jobs to their factories already here. As an example, there have been serious fires in the Natal Province as a result of arson. And, I could go on and on.

"To stop these horrible acts of terror, I have instructed the Minister of Defense to build up our Defense Forces to make South Africa self-supporting in military equipment, and until that happens, our country will be purchasing arms and military equipment from Britain, from the United States, from Israel, and from France. But, I will not reveal exactly what that will be, but it shall put the fear of God into our enemies hearts and minds.

"We will find and bring to justice all those terrorists belonging to these illegal organizations. "Let me warn you terrorists: You can run but you cannot hide from South African justice! We will dig you out from your holes, you vermin!

"You know that Parliament in June has enacted 'The Sabotage Act,' which gives the Government increased power to impose more restrictions on organizations and individuals.

"Under 'The Sabotage Act,' any person who willfully injuries another person; or who obstructs, tampers with, or destroys the health or safety of either the public, or the maintenance of law and order, or the supply of water, electricity, fuel, foodstuffs, sanitary, medical or fire extinguishing services, is guilty of sabotage, which can be punishable by imprisonment for life or by death.

"That's right, punishable by life imprisonment or punishable by death.

"I have also instructed the Commissioner of the Security Police to use every available means to locate and arrest anyone suspected of sabotage. I have also instructed the Commissioner of the Security Police to use every available means to halt these acts of terror, including appropriate and just punishment of the family of any person committing acts of sabotage.

"Yes, you heard me correctly! The Government will consider all family members of any saboteur as co-conspirators who will be justly and accordingly punished.

"So, my fellow citizens, your Government stands ready and able to safeguard our beloved South Africa. We will not succumb to terrorist threats and shall defeat every enemy of our beloved country, whether from within or outside of our borders. We shall prevail!

"Thank You! May God Bless each of You! And May God Bless South Africa!"

**

Frederick and Charles are discussing the Government's crackdown on saboteurs and how that campaign has curtailed freedom, of movement among all Non-Europeans, especially Blacks.

"Charles, in my travels to and from the vineyards, I've seen hundreds of cattle trucks pulling trailers packed not with cows but with shirtless men—all Black—and with both legs shackled together and daisy-chained to one another. I dare not stop to discover the reason for their confinement since my mere inquiry will definitely subject me to interrogation by the Security Police, even though I once served in Parliament. That should tell you how worried I am about these draconian measures Verwoerd is taking to fight these acts of violence."

The image of the men in cattle trucks is bothersome to Charles.

"The new Sabotage Act also restricts our right of freedom of speech. Before long, we may not even have freedom of thought."

Not realizing, Frederick is frightening Charles, but nonetheless, continues.

"Here we are at the start of August of 1962 and we have the PAC crazies of *Poqo* murdering Whites and the saboteurs of MK using guerilla tactics to damage the country's economy. In my humble opinion, even if the Security Police and the army catch the leaders, these two organizations will continue to wage war from outside the borders of South Africa. And that means, South Africa will necessarily conduct raids across borders to wipe out these camps of terrorists."

Charles is paying close attention and releases his fears.

"Frederick, it's getting very scary for me to take Tyrone to Catholic school and for Mary and me to walk to and from work. We have been stopped numerous times for Pass Book inspections. Almost every day we see or hear the rumble of tanks or armored vehicles in the streets in District Six and the next day we hear that some people have been snatched from their homes. Just getting groceries can give you the shakes."

"I understand, Charles."

"You may remember that in our last chat, I expressed my concern that John is becoming more and more radical, even making slurs against Whites. Just yesterday, he says that when he turns 17 in October, he will be leaving home and looking for work, preferably work on the docks, like his grandfather, but not here in Cape Town."

Frederick says, "Your son has already told me, quite politely I might add, that he doesn't want to work for us in the vineyards or the winery. Where does John think he can find work?"

"Someone told him there's plenty of work in Port Elizabeth because many people are shying away because of more possible sabotage."

"What does Mary say?"

"We both have tried and tried to set him straight, but he says he'll leave one way or another, which means, I guess, he'll run away if we push him. Having done that myself when things weren't going my way, I can understand how the boy feels. Your suggestions?"

"I guess my talking with him will just cement his thoughts. I suggest that you let your son decide on his own that now, of all times, is not the time to be facing the world alone. That means, Charles, that you and Mary tell him in a loving and caring way, that if and when he leaves, he will be truly be on his own and totally in charge of his own life. It's what the psychologist call 'tough love.' But, it works."

"Yes, I will talk with Mary. I hope you are right, Frederick."

Chapter 42

Nelson Mandela is ready to return to South Africa, having completed his guerilla training.

On July 24, 1962, Mandela uses his fake passport and travels with his old driver, Cecil Williams, through Botswana and, near Lobatse, crosses the South African border just after midnight.

By using unmarked dirt roads along the border and by changing drivers in Cecil's Austin, the men push themselves all night to meet with the MK High Command for a strategy session at Liliesleaf Farm.

On arrival, he's overjoyed to see Walter Sisulu, J.B Marks, and Joe Slovo.

Reporting to the ANC High Command that the leaders of the African countries are more enamored with the Pan Africanist Congress then with the ANC because the ANC cooperates with Whites, Coloreds, and Indians in a common cause, Mandela wants to slightly reshape the ANC to continue receiving the monetary and military assistance from these African countries.

He considers the supposed change a mere façade which will not harm the necessary cooperation of all groups opposed to Apartheid. He understands that Whites can be, and are, allies, not enemies. But several in the MK High Command think no change is needed and the ANC should not itself become racist.

The discussion results in the necessary consultation by Mandela with Alfred Luthuli in Groutville near Durban, meaning Mandela wearing his chauffeur's uniform and ferrying Cecil Williams must risk traveling there.

One man warns that his presence and travel plans might be leaked because the ANC contains many disadvantaged Blacks looking for a way up. "Yes," he says, "we do have informers."

Mandela heeds the warning and vows to be extra careful in traveling to meet Luthuli in Groutville.

Alfred Luthuli does not agree with Mandela's plan because the ANC's policy of non-racialism is the very core of the ANC's reason for existence. He says, "The ANC need not change its policy to suit foreign politicians. The ANC is not making war on Whites, Nelson. We are at war with Apartheid!"

Agreeing, Mandela will think about a solution to remaining true to the ANC ideals and continuing to receive military and monetary assistance from African countries. He knows it will be a balancing act.

Later that evening, Mandela briefs the Durban High Command of MK and travels to a friend's house for a welcome home party. There, he meets old friends, including Father John O'Malley, G. R. Naidoo, and Dr. Monty Naicker, enjoying his time.

On the next day, a Sunday, in the afternoon of August 5th, he and Cecil Williams will start the long drive to Johannesburg.

In talking with Father John O'Malley, Mandela says, "No, Father, I haven't become a Communist but I have accepted their assistance in our common fight against Apartheid. At heart I'm still a Methodist and while I accept Capitalism, I get truly angry when the rich treat the poor like dirt. My struggle is not to make all classes of workers equal, but instead, Father, my struggle is to ensure equality among the races."

Father John is satisfied with his answer.

**

CIA operative and US Vice-Consul David Rickard is about to have Sunday brunch at his favorite Durban restaurant, when he is approached by a well-dressed Black man, today's brunch companion. The Black man says, "Good Day, Mr. Vice-Consul, but before we select our food, we need to talk because I have some very important and valuable information for you."

"Fine, follow me to this ante-room, where we can talk in private," the Vice-Consul whispers to the man.

Quickly, the Black man divulges his information.

"And, sir, you are certain that this housekeeper was actually present at the house of G. R. Naidoo, the photojournalist, and that Nelson Mandela spent the night there? She is sure that the man was Nelson Mandela?"

"Vice-Consul Rickard, my source says the woman arrived at the house on Saturday morning to prepare for a party that night. She told my source that when Mandela arrived later she recognized Mandela from his pictures as 'The Black Pimpernel.' She swears on her mother's grave the man was Mandela!"

"And your source says the housekeeper says that later this afternoon, Mandela and a White man will be leaving for Johannesburg, but we don't know exactly when, or their route, or their car, or the specific destination there."

"That's right, but we can plot their probable route of travel from Mr. Naidoo's house to the road to Johannesburg," the man suggests.

"Yes, we can. That we can do. We can determine all the possible ways to get there."

The Black man nods.

"So, you say that the housekeeper left Naidoo's house about nine o'clock on Sunday, met some friends with this news, overheard by your source, who telephoned you with this news and here we are a noon. That's hard to believe that happened so fast!"

"My source says the woman was so impressed that she couldn't stop talking about it. That's how my source got this information and he called me right away. So immediately, I hurried to my meeting with you at noon."

"And, you can trust your source?"

"Vice-Consul Rickard, every piece of information from my source about the plans of the MK has been absolutely correct. So, yes, I do."

"And, you think I should believe this?"

"Yes, sir, I do."

"Okay. If it's true and we catch Mandela, I will approve your and your family's immigration to America, just as was promised. I don't forget my friends and I repay for good information.

"Now, excuse me while I telephone Colonel Spengler to see if we can catch Mandela on his way to Johannesburg. If the Security Police catch him, you and your family will be on your way to America, my man. Pack your belongings."

***

As Nelson Mandela and Cecil Williams leave G. R. Naidoo's house, Mandela dons his white dust coat and chauffeur's cap, but Cecil insists on driving first, with Mandela in the front passenger seat.

As they pass through Durban and its industrial areas, Cecil decides to take the main highway from Durban to

Johannesburg. Looking out the window as Cecil winds the Austin over the hills. Nelson relaxes and absorbs spectacular views of the Indian Ocean

They have been discussing plans for projects to sabotage when Mandela notes that since the main rail line from Durban to Johannesburg parallels the main road, he says, "Well, Cecil, this rail line would be an easy target. I'll put that in my notebook."

Their discussion continues after they pass through Pietermaritzburg and hurry through Howick, finally entering the small town of Cedara.

Suddenly, zooming passed their trusty Austin is a large unmarked Ford with several White men inside.

Turning around to the rear, Nelson sees two more speeding cars with White men inside.

Cecil says, "That car ahead is blocking our path and the men have guns pointed at us and are signaling us to stop!"

Although Nelson tries passing himself as David Motssmayi by showing his fake passport, he doesn't fool the South African Security Police, many of whom have previously dealt with him.

Somehow, Mandela ditches his tell-tale notebook without its discovery.

After an appearance before a local Magistrate, the Security Police take Mandela and Williams to Johannesburg.

The next day, Mandela appears in handcuffs before a Senior Magistrate, hears he is charged with leaving the country without valid travel documents and inciting Blacks to strike, and to his relief, hears nothing of his link to *Umkhonto we Sizwe*.

Thinking of himself as a symbol of Justice in the court of the oppressor, Mandela announces that he will represent himself in the trial, with Joe Slovo as his legal advisor.

As Mandela leaves the courtroom to be taken in a sealed van to the Johannesburg Fort, he hears crowds cheering a popular ANC Bantu chant of "Power" and its response "The Power is ours!" That uplifts his spirit.

Instead of being returned to his prison cell, Mandela is placed in the prison hospital because of its impregnable walls and four massive locked gates since rumors abound in the press of a rescue attempt.

For further safekeeping, Mandela, with another prisoner believed to be a planted police informer, will be taken later in a dirty van to Pretoria.

Mandela decides he will not seek bail, considering himself as the public symbol of rebellion and struggle, though his trial is not scheduled until October 15, 1962, months away.

Chapter 43

Charles, Mary, John, and Tyrone are listening to the August 4th radio broadcast of a soccer match.

Appreciative that John has finally agreed to attend college next year but also unaware that their son aspires to join the banned Pan Africanist Congress, they're enjoying some family time.

Hoping to stay on her son's good side, Mary says, "Your father brought this old copy of *The Cape Town News Magazine* from Frederick. I know it's the May-June, 1962 edition, but turn the page to page 35 for a big surprise."

After reading the featured story that 'The Black Pimpernel' had secretly returned to South Africa from his travels abroad, John says, "If this is true, I can hardly wait for the newspapers to publish more reports of my hero outwitting the Security Police. But, the newspapers have been silent, maybe because he was still out of South Africa."

Two days later, John can hardly believe his eyes as he reads in the *Rand Daily Mail* that Nelson Mandela has been arrested by the Security Police and charged with two serious crimes and is in the Johannesburg jail awaiting trial. The newspaper has learned that Mandela's trial will probably be held either in Johannesburg or Pretoria, but is unsure of the exact date or location for security reasons.

John says, "Mom, do you think the Sisters would organize a trip to see the trial? I would certainly like to go. It would be the thrill of my life. You know—a trip for our senior class to attend the trial? What do you think, Dad?"

"Well, John," his father says, "I don't know if there would be room in the courthouse seats because there will be a lot of others there. Besides, you know the seats are segregated for Europeans and for Non-Europeans. But, I guess the Sisters can deal with that."

Charles looks at Mary for help.

Mary adds, "Well, we'll see. Certainly, if the school will sponsor such a school trip, I think that would be a wonderful experience for everyone to see the trial. John, why don't you talk with the good Sisters to see if it's possible?"

After thinking how helpful his mother is, Tyrone asks, "Well, can I go if the school sponsors the trip?"

John answers for his parents, "Tyrone, you're too little and I know the school won't take you and your class mates on this trip."

"Well, that's not fair! It's not fair at all!" Tyrone exclaims.

Looking at each other, Mary and Charles reluctantly agree that if the school sponsors such a trip, then John may go. Of course, they explain to Tyrone the reasons for the school not to allow a trip out-of-town for young-sters, which satisfies their younger son.

Then, they extract a promise from John to be careful and avoid trouble if the school does indeed schedule any trip to the site of the Mandela trial in October.

"Yes, I will behave myself," John says as he figures how he can finagle the Sisters to arrange a trip to Mandela's trial for a few in his class.

***

For those Whites who deplore the violence throughout the country but who have long opposed racial segregation and especially Apartheid, the government's reactions to safeguard against indiscriminate violence and acts of sabotage presents Whites with an impossible choice.

Long a champion against racial segregation and Apartheid, Frederick deplores the violence, especially the Pan Africanists Congress' campaign of murdering Whites under the auspices of its armed wing of *Poqo*. He senses his beloved country is ebbing toward a full-fledge race war and realizes the government must not allow this kind of lawlessness.

But, he won't surrender his own values and ideals in exchange for safety and security.

Recognizing now that he has zero influence with the Verwoerd administration, Frederick has written his contacts among the nations on the African Continent for support against Apartheid. Several countries have imposed import and export bans on South African goods and cancelled South African airplane landing rights in their countries.

Frederick has also written his contacts in the United States, especially Robert F. Kennedy the US Attorney General, who connected Frederick with Dr. Martin Luther King. Frederick invited Kennedy to visit South Africa to see for himself about Apartheid.

Thrilled that the famous civil rights leader actually wrote him and urged his non-violent opposition to Apartheid, Frederick realizes this is one way to oppose this evil.

The Verwoerd administration not only continues its self-preservation campaign against saboteurs and murderers to safe guard the country, but also increases it restrictions on freedom of speech and freedom of assembly through house arrests, banning, detention, deportation, and imprisonment.

Worse, Frederick believes, the government's strict censoring of any anti-Apartheid publications is effectively driving underground any opposing views. Even the news on the radio is slanted toward the government.

Immediately after Mandela's arrest, the Minister of Justice bans the White Congress of Democrats, under the *Suppression of Communism Act.* The Congress of Democrats' National Vice-President is placed under house arrest for five years.

And, fearing an increase in demonstrations, the Minister of Justice bans until April 30, 1963 any more demonstrations protesting the arrest, trial, or conviction of any person. Frederick says, "So, now if I openly protest the arrest or trial of anyone, I can be banned and placed under house arrest. Unbelievable!"

Verwoerd's promise to increase the military budget has been realized, with some government officials suggesting small arms should be distributed to Whites, especially because of the Pan Africanist Congress armed wing's activities against Whites.

Frederick's face reveals the worry of an approaching race war. People, good and bad people, Blacks and Whites will be killed simply because of skin color.

***

After learning of Nelson Mandela's arrest, Father John O'Malley hurries to The Fort in Johannesburg, but finds his friend has been moved to a more secure location, namely into the prison hospital.

Eventually the priest gains entry to hear Mandela's confession by fooling the guards into believing that Mandela, a Methodist, is Catholic. With Mandela playing alone, the priest goes through the ruse with the Sacrament of Confession, asking the guards for privacy.

Now, out of earshot, Father John whispers several plans for Mandela to escape. He's even smuggled in a hacksaw inside his coat.

But Mandela says, "Father John, I've already vetoed one plan as unworkable and, while I'm thinking about the other that Joe Slovo brought me, I probably won't try any escape. Take your hacksaw with you when you leave and be careful, Father because the Security Police will now be watching you."

The priest's eyebrows rise. "Did you say Joe Slovo?"

Mandela responds, "Yes, while I'm representing myself, I've picked Joe as my legal adviser. Later, I may get Bob Hepple, too."

Father John says nothing, but sees that Mandela is surrounding himself with more and more Communists. He wonders if his friend is becoming a Communist.

"Quite correctly, Father John, by refusing bail and by no considerations of escape, I will be charged in the Court of the Oppressor as a symbol of Justice. That will be uplifting to our followers."

"Yes, of course, but you have no defense against the charge of leaving the country without the proper documents. And, as to the other charge of inciting Blacks to strike, well, the government will produce tons of documents and witnesses who the judge will accept as credible. You will go to prison!"

"Yes, that may happen, but I intend to continue this fight as long as I have breath in my lungs, Father!"

Chapter 44

Mandela's trial is scheduled in Johannesburg for Monday, October 5, 1962, but on Saturday, he is secretly moved to Pretoria because the intense publicity in the press has crowds and crowds of people lining the route from The Fort to the courthouse. The authorities fear riots, especially since a newly organized "Free Mandela Committee" has the crowds along the route shouting, "Free Mandela! Free Mandela!"

Worse for the authorities, the "Free Mandela" campaign is resonating outside of South Africa, especially in the United States and Britain.

Even though Mandela cannot notify his supporters that his trial has been moved, nonetheless word of his transfer leaks out so that when his case begins Monday morning in the Old Synagogue in Pretoria, the courtroom is jam-packed with his supporters.

When Mandela appears in the courtroom dressed in his Xhosa leopard-skin *kaross* instead of in a suit and tie, the crowd in one voice repeatedly cries out the Bantu words for "Power!" with the return chant in Bantu, "Power to the People!" causing Mandela to turn, fist raised, to the upstairs crowd.

Naturally, the prosecutors, the Magistrate, and the Security Police understand the reasons for Mandela's traditional dress of the *kaross.* As Mandela is enjoying the adulation of the crowd, the Prosecutor quickly whispers to the Magistrate out of Mandela's earshot and while his two legal advisors, Joe Slovo and Bob Hepple, are reviewing papers.

Prosecutor Bosch says, "Your Worship, his wearing the stupid leopard skin signifies Mandela's disdain for the White man's court and his contempt for White justice.

The more he does that the more difficulty we will have with these crowds."

Magistrate Van Heerden replies, "Yes, I recognize that Mr. Mandela wants the world to see that he is carrying on his back all of the Black cultural values and that his leopard skin is a veiled threat to all Whites of a wild animal's imminent attack.

"I will ask Colonel Jacobs, the commanding officer of the police, to have Mr. Mandela voluntarily surrender his leopard skin, but if he won't, then I'll allow him to wear the leopard skin in court but not to and from the court since that might incite other prisoners and stir up the crowds of his supporters.

"Under no circumstances will I have these people make a mockery out of this South African Court"

Turning his attention to Mandela, the Magistrate says in a loud voice, "Mr. Mandela! Mr. Slovo, and Mr. Hepple! Please approach. I see that you and your two legal advisors have requested a two-week delay because of the Government's failure to promptly notify you and your advisors of the change of venue. I find some merit in their request and it is ordered the trial will start in one week. You are excused until next Monday."

***

John, angry that his Catholic school wouldn't schedule a school trip for Mandela's trial, hears Charles announce that the trial is now scheduled for Monday next but not in Johannesburg but instead in Pretoria.

Charles says, "Before you ask, no I cannot take off work to go with you to Pretoria. I'm sorry, son. I just can't do that. But, I'll get Mr. Mandela's address and you can write him. I'm sure he will be glad to receive your letter."

John says, "I understand, but I still would like to go. I know, I know, I can't. But I do want to keep up with what is happening to him."

Charles says, "That we can do over the next several weeks."

***

Over his breakfast on November 8, 1962, Frederick opens the *Cape Town News* and begins reading the featured story.

> "The trial of Nelson Mandela has now lasted almost 4 weeks and the government has called over 150 witnesses from various sites throughout the country.
>
> "Although having two legal advisors, Mandela is essentially representing himself throughout the trial.
>
> "Mandela proclaimed that he 'would call as many witnesses as the State, if not more,' but when the time to present the case for the defense, Mandela arose from his chair and told the Court he was not calling any witnesses.
>
> "This reporter heard a gasp from the spectators, both from European and from Non-European spectators, and heard a very surprised Prosecutor Bosch cry out, 'Lord, Lord!'
>
> "When questioned by Magistrate Van Heerden, Mandela said he was guilty of no crime. Then the prosecutor moved to find Mandela guilty as charged. The trial was adjourned until the next day for Mandela to address the Court in what is called a 'Plea in Mitigation.'

443

"The next day found hundreds of Mandela's supporters blocks and blocks away from the courthouse. Inside, none of the 150 Non-European seats were empty, nor were any of the European seats. It was standing room only, even for the press. Some foreign correspondents waited outside.

"That Monday, wearing the traditional Xhosa *kaross* instead of a suit and a tie, Mandela, eyes upward toward the balcony, raised his fist and in Bantu, shouted Power!' and his supporters answered in Bantu, 'Power to the People!'

"In the balcony, his wife, Winnie, and his Tribal relatives, all attired in the *kaross* (the leopard-skin like blanket) continued to stand and shout, causing Magistrate Van Heerden to repeatedly pound his gavel and cry for order in the court.

"Quieting, the audience listened as the Magistrate read the charges and informed Mandela to speak his piece.

"In his hour-long speech, Mandela did not seek any judicial appeal for mitigation. Instead, he explained the reasons for his existence and the reasons for his actions. More importantly, Mandela promised if again he had his freedom, he would act the same way.

"(Unfortunately space limitations prevent us from publishing the complete text of Nelson's Mandela's speech in his Plea in Mitigation. Hereafter is a summary of his thoughts. If you wish to purchase the complete text, please contact the paper's administrative office.)

"Mandela stated, 'I joined the African National Congress because its policy of democracy and non-racialism reflected my own deepest convictions and as a lawyer. Your Worship, I was forced to choose between compliance with the law and accommodating my conscience. The law designed and written by the Nationalist government is an unjust, intolerable law and our consciences dictate opposition, protest, and alteration, because people of good conscience cannot sit idle and do nothing. Our grievances have been and are still ignored by the government which provoked violence by employing violence to meet our non-violent actions.'

"Mandela completed his thoughts by saying, 'Your Worship, for whatever sentence you impose, rest assured that when I've completed my sentence, I will still be moved, as all men are moved by their conscience and I will still be moved by my dislike of race discrimination and will, as best I can, again take up the struggle for the absolute and final removal of those injustices. Sir, I have done my duty for my people and for South Africa and am not a criminal. Instead, the criminals who should be brought before this court are the members of this government.'

"After a ten-minute recess, Magistrate Van Heerden pronounced Mandela's sentence of two years for the passport violation and of three years for inciting strikes—five years total, with no possibility of parole. There was a slight gasp from the upstairs gallery.

"As the Magistrate arose to leave, Mandela turned to the upstairs gallery, with clinched right fist raised and shouted in Bantu, 'Power!' and the return chant in Bantu, 'Power to the People!' filled the courtroom.

"Suddenly, without any cue, the Blacks began singing their beautiful anthem, *Nkosi Sikelel iAfrika.* The words mean 'God Bless Africa!'

"The Prosecutors allowed Mandela a brief visit with his wife, Winnie who held her head high and who shed no tears. As Nelson Mandela left the courthouse in an unmarked police van for the Pretoria Local, a red-bricked prison, the departing crowds of Blacks were still singing in their language, 'God Bless Africa.'

"Interviews with several Whites demonstrated general satisfaction with Mandela's sentence and the hope for less violence in the future.

"However, a Catholic priest, Reverend John O'Malley, OMI, completely disagreed, saying 'Mr. Mandela is correct when he says that the criminals are the members of this government and the struggle will continue until these injustices are finally removed, hopefully before this situation worsens.'

"None of the Blacks, other than the self-confident Winnie Mandela, would go on record and agree with what Rev. O'Malley had to say."

"At the moment, whether Mandela will remain in Pretoria Local or be moved to the prison on Robben Island is uncertain."

Frederick sets the newspaper on his desk for a moment to absorb the news. He isn't surprised that Father John attended the trial and spoke to the reporter. But, Father John has put himself in the crosshairs for the government's aim for dissenters. He'd better be very careful and remember what happened to that deported Anglican Bishop, Frederick thinks.

Now, he turns the page and continues reading.

"On November 6, the 17th Session of the United Nations General Assembly adopted a Resolution deploring South Africa's racial policies and created a Special Committee to review South Africa's failure to abandon these racial policies.

"The Resolution favors diplomatic and economic sanctions against South Africa and asks the Security Council of the UN to expel South Africa from the Council.

"A movement is rumored that certain African and Asian delegations want the Trusteeship Committee to install a United Nations presence in South West Africa to assure the people in the territory of their inalienable right to be a free and independent nation from South Africa.

"Meanwhile, the Prime Minister of Uganda announced a boycott on all South African goods.

"Prime Minister Verwoerd had no comment on either development, other than to say that South Africa under Apartheid had speeded up its program of separate development to allow the races their individual freedom and would in the next year grant Transkei, a Bantu Homeland, its own self-government, as a showcase to the world of how Apartheid truly works.

"However, notes (supposedly from the saboteurs) carefully left in obvious places after the acts of sabotage in Port Elizabeth and in Durban celebrated the actions of the United Nations General Assembly, to the utter disgust of the Minister of Justice.

"The Minister of Justice, B.J. Vorster, announces that if these acts of sabotage do not cease, then, next year, he will seek new legislation waiving the long held right of Habeas Corpus and enacting other iron-fisted laws to protect the safety of the citizens of South Africa.

"Paraphrasing the Prime Minister, Mr. Vorster warns every dissenter, especially saboteurs, that the government intends to punish not only the saboteurs but also all family members and their business or profession. The Minister of Justice warns, 'Parents and spouses and children of any saboteurs will be punished just like the saboteur will and this will also be true for any person and his family members for any act of violence.'

"Mr. Vorster reports that since September, more than 23 attempts of horrible sabotage have been thwarted and over 60 Blacks have been arrested, including some family members.

"He also says that some leaders and at least 437 listed members of the Communist Party have been banned. Additionally, at least 36 other organizations have been ordered to cease membership and to disband immediately.

"The Minister of Justice hints that more arrests of the saboteurs will be forthcoming."

Frederick, stunned by the news in the *Cape Town News,* folds the newspaper and pushes his unfinished breakfast plate aside and turns to his wife.

"Henrietta, I guess we should ramp up our own security. At the time we resigned from the Congress of Democrats, I felt terrible in abandoning our White friends and simultaneously felt glad to avoid out and out confrontation with the Verwoerd government."

"I heard that Helen Joseph, the National Vice President of the Congress of Democrats, has been banned by Vorster for five years. And she is only the first," she reports.

"Now, after what is happening, our resignation was the best thing. We can still be opposed to the government and Apartheid, but not so damn openly. What do you think, Henrietta?"

"Well, Frederick, I haven't yet read the paper which apparently has soured your mood, but nonetheless I agree. I have a lot on my mind."

"Go ahead, dear."

"If we were still members of the Congress of Democrats, now banned, and with some of its officers under house arrest, the government would definitely be after us, especially you, a former Member of Parliament always opposed to the National Party."

"True."

"I don't like to think about it, but, my dear, they'd shut down our winery by revoking all our permits and move our workers to the Homelands. The way things are going, maybe even bar you from practice as a lawyer. I suspect we get a tax audit, too."

"Perhaps."

"They'd hurt us and our family—Hans and Robin—in every way possible, even take away our livelihood. I suppose they could stop Hans from working on his law degree."

"That's a possibility."

"I hope Charles has followed your advice and disassociated himself from the ANC and has not engaged in any demonstrations. Please check with Charles about that, dear."

"Yes, I will."

"Oh, you better ask him about John since the boy has been very livid in expressing his opinions about Mandela.

"So, yes, we should keep a lower profile and keep our opinions close-knit. I don't like it, but that's the way it is."

***

450

Charles and Mary are about to talk with John as Tyrone plays outside their District-Six home.

Mary says, "John, your father and I want to talk with you about some important things. Go ahead, Charles."

"Well, John, we need to talk about how we can keep our family safe, especially since the government is cracking down on all forms of dissent and especially against people who are opposing it. That means we all need to be careful what we do and what we say, especially here in District Six because we can't be sure which of our neighbors may be hidden government informers. That means also that we cannot be going around Cape Town and giving our opinions."

John's face undergoes a makeover from serenity.

"Now, son," he continues, "we are safe in talking inside this house, I think because there are no hidden microphones, and we are safe with Frederick and Henrietta but other than that, we are not safe in giving our opinions about the government, and so on."

John looks first at his mother and then turns to his father, but hears his mother speak.

"Yes, John, we all must be careful in these days and times."

Before his father can continue, John says, "Look, Dad and Mother, I'm now seventeen and ready to attend college. I've received a good education and I understand completely what our government has done.

"Don't you think I should be entitled to my own opinions about Nelson Mandela and what he stands for against this oppressive government? Don't you think I should be able to choose my friends and who I can hang out with? You know, I'm not a child anymore!"

Charles tries to soft peddle what he wants to say. "Look, son, I admire Mr. Mandela, too and agree that the government is terrible and is oppressive. No one is arguing that is not the case."

John looks away.

"And, as I have explained to you countless times before, you cannot associate with the ANC or any part of it. You cannot be involved with them in any way. Because if you are, the government will assume that your mother and I are also involved. And that means even your little brother. We might all be shipped to the Homelands or somewhere more terrible!"

John is now paying attention.

"I asked for your promise not to be involved with the ANC. You gave me that promise and I believed you. And, now, I find out from others that you are working with the fake charities that the ANC Youth League is behind. You have lied to your mother and I, John, and I don't like that!"

Charles watches John's face for a reaction.

"I know you are smart enough to understand that our security and safety are dependent on staying out of the government's sight and not raising any kind of ruckus."

John just looks at his father.

"You know I resigned from the ANC when they decided to form the MK to engage in acts of violence, even sabotage. And yes, I know you are familiar with the MK."

John is surprised to hear his father knows about the MK.

"Thank goodness we are completely connected to Frederick and Henrietta Kruger who have been very, very good to us."

John says, "Yes, I understand all that, but I'm not a child and I should be able to decide who my friends are and what I do!"

"Look, son, we provide you with shelter, with food and water, and with love and protection. We ask very little of you, other than you do certain menial chores around the house. But, as long as you live in this house, son, you must obey our rules.

"If you don't believe me, ask your mother."

Tearfully, Mary says, "John, you must obey our rules."

John replies, "And if I don't, then you are kicking me out! Is that it? I can't believe you would really do that, just because I want to have my own friends and just because you don't want me to express my political beliefs!"

His mother interrupts, "John! John! That is no way for you to behave and to shout at us! Now, we don't want you to leave home! But, we want your promise you will get out of the ANC Youth League before you get into real trouble. And, John, if you get into trouble, then, from what the government is saying, we will be in trouble. That means all of us, even little Tyrone. Is that what you want? I hope not!"

Charles says, "Look, John, your actions will jeopardize your family's welfare and safety. Understand that your mother and I firmly believe in the concepts of racial equality and human dignity for all people and we remain absolute against this government and against the Apartheid. You understand what I'm saying?'

Shaking his head affirmatively, John hears his father's voice.

"Look, son, even Frederick and Henrietta are keeping a low profile against the government. Frederick just told me that he and Henrietta are worried that they might lose their permits to operate the winery and have all their workers sent to the Homelands. He says they could even suspend his license to practice law and keep Hans from continuing at the law school at Wits. They resigned from the White people's organization—the Congress for Democrats. So, yes, they are avoiding openly criticizing the government."

John notices his mother is still teary-eyed and decides he needs to hold his tongue, because he will never win this argument. He'll tell his parents that tomorrow he'll resign from the ANC Youth League. And that will be the truth.

But, he's planning to get involved with the Pan Africanist Congress because he's convinced that they have the answer to destruction of the South African government—get rid of the White purveyors of Apartheid. But that will remain his secret.

Before he agrees to his parent's demands, he remembers that his father had once compared total passivity to the moderates in the 1930s in Nazi Germany. He can see in his memory almost exactly what his father had said, as if the words were written in indelible ink.

> "The world, and especially South Africa, is a dangerous place, but becomes much more dangerous when good men do nothing and look the other way when evil men take over."

John thinks he would like to throw those words back in his father's face, but he understands those fiery words would become embers and burn a long time in his father's heart. That wouldn't be good.

And, deep, deep down, he knows his father is not a total passivist and that his father, like Frederick and Henrietta oppose Apartheid.

As his father takes a breath, John says with a straight face, "Okay, I hear what you are saying and I will go tomorrow and resign from the ANC Youth League. I don't want to do anything that will hurt this family. I love all of you!"

Mary's face beams.

"And, I will do my best to keep my criticism of the government to myself, because, as you said, we do have informers in the neighborhood."

Both parents quickly embrace John, as little Tyrone comes inside, surveys the situation, and says, "Can I have a hug, too?"

Chapter 45

Reverend Martin Luther King, Jr., the U.S. Civil Rights Leader, teams up with Alfred Luthuli, ex-president of the African National Congress and the winner of the Nobel Peace Prize in 1960, to issue on December 10, 1962 a joint "Appeal for Action against Apartheid."

The Declaration asks all men of good will to take action against Apartheid by declaring December 10th as 'Human Rights Day' and by getting Churches and other organizations to protest Apartheid on this day.

It asks that each person urge the person's government to support sanctions against South Africa; to urge each government's United Nations' representative to isolate South Africa; and to urge each government to avoid the export or the import of South African goods.

The Declaration also asks each person to transfer public opinion to public action until an effective Quarantine of Apartheid has been established.

Over a hundred prominent Black celebrities, entertainers, and politicians sign the "Appeal for Action against Apartheid."

Without a doubt, the joint Declaration causes a big stir throughout the world but especially in the United States where the protests and marches against racial segregation are increasing in the South, forcing President Kennedy to employ federal armed marshals to allow a Black military veteran into the segregated University of Mississippi.

But afraid that France will sell South Africa French planes, the Kennedy administration authorizes Lockheed to sell seven C-130 Cargo planes on September 29, 1961to South Africa. Since that date, the

Kennedy administration has been allowing other sales of military equipment to South Africa.

With the sale of military planes and equipment, the U.S. finds itself as a supporter of South Africa's Apartheid in spite of the 1962 "Appeal for Action against Apartheid" from Dr. Martin Luther King, Jr. and especially since many countries in the United Nations are pushing for an arms embargo against South Africa.

***

On December 18, 1962, Joseph C. Satterthwaite, the U.S. Ambassador to South Africa, sends a top secret air-gram to the State Department in Washington outlining what he thinks should be America's secret 'Internal Defense Plan' for South Africa.

He's been working with the large host of CIA people in the country, especially Vice-Consul David Rickard who assisted in Nelson Mandela's apprehension.

Rickard has played a big part in the formation of the Ambassador's determination of U.S. policy.

The Ambassador recalls David Rickard's words that "Mandela is completely under the control of the Soviet Union, an absolute toy of the Commies and was ready to incite the Indian population of the Natal Province to rebel and to also to lead the Blacks in an armed insurrection which would open the door to Russian intervention."

Ambassador Satterthwaite notes that U.S. policy does not favor repression of the legitimate claims for Black equality. But, if subversive Communists, financially and militarily backed and funded by Russia, should sponsor a revolution by Blacks and/or Indians, or, if the national security of the United States is directly threatened, then U.S. military intervention into South Africa may be necessary.

He adds that while Apartheid is a liability, nonetheless the South African government remains an important ally due to its strong opposition to Communism, due to its strategic location of its naval ports and airfields, and due to its granting of rights for U.S. tracking stations for NASA and for ballistic missile ranges in South Africa.

The Ambassador points out that the racial policy of Apartheid encourages the spread of Communism and the U.S. must continue to criticize the Apartheid policy to avoid the loss of America's goodwill in the rest of Africa, where many former colonies are now independent nations. He encourages an increase in cultural exchanges, an increase in non-White student exchanges, and an increase in African visits by several American Black entertainers, such as Harry Belafonte and Louis Armstrong.

But, of course, Ambassador Satterthwaite understands the Kennedy Administration is walking a tightrope between the civil rights campaign in the U.S. and between strategic concerns about Communism in South Africa.

He also knows that South Africa to prevent a revolution organized by Communists needs America to sell South Africa arms, airplanes, submarines, and other military equipment, but the Kennedy Administration dawdles, unable to make up its mind.

***

Frederick runs into the kitchen to tell his wife that on May 2, 1963, Parliament has enacted what is now known as the 'Ninety-Day Detention' law.

458

"Henrietta, under this law, any commissioned police or military officer now can detain, without a warrant, anyone suspected of committing a political crime and hold the person for 90 days without access to any lawyer. When the 90 days, expires, the person can be immediately be detained and held for another 90 days, and that can be illimitable!"

"Verwoerd and his crew are going wild! Due process of law is out the window! What else is in this dictatorial law, Frederick?"

"It's what has been termed the 'Sobukwe Clause,' named after Robert Sobukwe, the former president of the Pan Africanist Congress, who's being transferred to the prison on Robben Island. You may remember that he surrendered his appellate rights. Now, a person convicted of political offenses can be detained for a further 12 months. Plus, there's more."

"More?"

"The Act allows the Government to declare unlawful any organization or group of people originating or banding together after April 7, 1960—the date when *Umkhonto we Sizwe* and *Poqo* commenced—and extends the ban again to the ANC and the PAC."

"I can hardly believe it."

"They already partly control what we read and what we hear. Before long, if we don't think like the National Party, we'll be arrested!"

Henrietta says, "Frederick, we must walk very, very softly, because Verwoerd is shutting down every kind of open dissent from any and every opposition. We need to caution all of our employees, especially Charles and Mary, to be careful what they say in front of others."

"Why do you single out, Charles and Mary? I don't see any threat from them toward openly engaging in any acts or words of dissent."

"Not them, my dear, but their son, John. I have some information that he was active with the ANC charity. Father Vincent told me John helped out in packing some food bags for the needy."

"Oh? I think that was a long time ago, Henrietta, but I will check that with Charles."

***

Prime Minister Verwoerd and Defense Minister J.J. Fourche are commiserating over the delay by the United States to authorize the sale of more military arms and equipment.

Defense Minister Fourche hesitates but finally reveals that several countries are boycotting the import of any South African goods.

"Worse," he reports, "the United Nations Special Committee on Apartheid has published a report that several Member States will sever diplomatic relations with South Africa."

Prime Minister Verwoerd says, "The United Nations is trying to get the whole world against us and isolate us. Now, that Committee even wants to place an embargo for arms and ammunition as well as petroleum. Some of our African neighbors, especially Ethiopia and Angola, both of whom are giving aid and military training to the ANC and the PAC, would like to take over our country."

"I don't like to hear that, Mr. Prime Minister."

"By the way, I'm telling our representative to the Economic Commission for Africa that we will withdraw because of the hostility shown to South Africa by certain other African States. We need to get the necessary arms and military equipment to combat these Communists, stop these acts of sabotage, and to scare any kind of invasion from anyone."

"That's great, Mr. Prime Minister."

"What the hell is the United States of America thinking in promising arms and military equipment and then putting everything on hold?"

Defense Minister Fourche says, "Mr. Prime Minister, I've talked with Ambassador Satterthwaite about the hold up and he says that the Kennedy White House fears allowing the sale of arms to South Africa because the American Civil Rights groups are raising a big stink in the American press and the backlash is causing the Kennedy administration to retract its promise to us."

"The United States needs to control those Blacks."

"I've explained to the Ambassador that without those arms and military equipment, we may come up short against these rebels. He says he'll contact the State Department."

Prime Minister Verwoerd replies, "Doesn't that idiot know that even the Truman Administration recognized that America could not trust the Blacks and the ANC against their love affair with Russia and Communism? What are they thinking?"

"Only God knows, sir."

"I'm sure the American CIA knows that this racial strife is intended to extend Russian and Communist influence throughout Africa and especially here into South Africa."

"Yes, they do."

"The idiots in the Kennedy Administration keep crowing and crowing about the so-called domino effect in South Viet Nam but, for the life of me, they can't see that can happen right now and right here in Africa! Their intervention into Viet Nam will end up just like the French conflict did, I predict. The US will declare victory and leave, just like the French."

"You are right about that, Mr. Prime Minister."

"Tell Satterthwaite that if the United States doesn't want our business, we have no qualms about seeking a deal with the French who are ready to sell us more planes, submarines, arms, helicopters, tanks, armored cars, and what have you."

"Yes, Mr. Prime Minister."

"And, if that doesn't put a burr under him, then remind him that South Africa is one of America's best friends in the Cold War. Tell him that America needs our ports for their navy and that America needs our country for their NASA tracking stations in the space race."

"I'm on it, sir."

"Yes, and remind the fool that we have many, many American businesses in South Africa."

Chapter 46

After hearing what Frederick had to say about John's still engaging with the ANC's Youth League, Charles arrives home and immediately confronts his son.

"Dad, I was merely helping Father Vincent in packing those bags of food for the poor, but I already told the Youth League local president that I was no longer a member."

Charles questions, "Well, you knew those food bags had been paid for by the ANC or by its Youth League, didn't you!"

"Yes, but I was just helping Father Vincent. I wasn't wearing anything that would show I was a member of the Youth League. I was just helping out, that's all," John stresses.

"Well, I want you to cut all contacts, since Frederick Kruger is worried that the Verwoerd Government has passed another law to seriously punish all people in opposition. When Mr. Kruger gets worried, son, I get worried. Your mother and I just want to keep you safe."

"I understand your concern, but don't you think we should all try and help the poor—people less fortunate than we are? I don't think it is right for us to slink on by and kind of hide in the shadows, just because we have Frederick and Henrietta to protect us."

Charles says, "Don't criticize Frederick and Henrietta! They have been very good to us, especially to you, paying your and Tyrone's Catholic school tuition and helping your mother and me in so many ways."

John decides not to retort.

"We are not hiding. We live openly here in District Six. The Security Police come into District Six every day.

They patrol right passed our house and when I'm home, I even wave to them. Every day, we take John to school. We go to Mass every Sunday. We shop in the stores. Sometimes we go to the picture shows. Sometimes we go fishing in the bay. We travel almost every day to work at the Kruger's homestead. You have freedom to travel around Cape Town. We are not hiding, John."

John remains silent.

"Yes, I agree that we should help the poor and people less fortunate, but we don't need the ANC or its Youth League to do that."

John is not going to argue with his father about that.

"I'm glad you cut the ties with the ANC Youth League. Thank you. Now, we don't need to have any more arguing about it. Let's go help your mother get supper on the table."

Charles would like to tell John that he used to be a block captain for the ANC, but such a revelation, Charles thinks, would just cement John's desire. He keeps the old news to himself, although he wants his son to know he has never been a coward.

Thankful that his father has accepted his explanation, John smiles because in the next few weeks, he will attend a secret assembly of the Pan Africanist Congress. He hopes someone there will reveal some information about his hero, 'The Black Pimpernel', now serving a five-year sentence and having been transferred to the dreadful prison on Robben Island.

***

During 1963, Walter Sisulu, as Secretary of the African National Congress, has been traveling around the country to rally the ANC's followers, even though the ANC has been banned.

Out of the country, Oliver Tambo is running the ANC.

Sisulu is always one step ahead of the Security Police, carefully entrusting his schedule to faithful ANC people since he is cognizant of the existence of ANC informers ready to further their own ends through government cooperation.

But, somehow, word of where and when Sisulu will appear gets out to the ANC followers, especially those in the Youth League.

At many stops, Sisulu brings information to local ANC apostles about possible strategic targets for sabotage.

At one January meeting, he met a dynamite expert and was given the necessary ingredients and instructions for bomb making. Of course, he passes on the information and materials to certain local ANC chapters, now all underground.

Although Sisulu has been arrested five times without a conviction, finally in March of 1963 he is convicted of furthering the aims of the banned ANC and of organizing the illegal stay-at-home protest in May of 1961. He receives a six-year prison sentence but is allowed bail. To prevent any escape, Sisulu is placed under a twenty four-hour house arrest, since newly discovered evidence indicates Sisulu holds an office in MK—the Spear of the Nation.

Not surprisingly, Sisulu jumps bail on April 20 and disappears from view of the Security Police and the Department of Justice. One newspaper reports that Sisulu has fled supposedly to Bechuanaland.

On June 26, from an underground ANC radio station at the ANC's secret hideout at Liliesleaf Farm in Rivonia,

Walter Sisulu broadcasts on 'Freedom Radio' high hopes to the ANC listeners that MK—the Spear of the Nation—will continue the fight against Apartheid though acts of sabotage and urges all people of good will to join in the fight.

Sisulu makes a special appeal to Black youngsters to join the fight and continue the struggle for freedom.

Some of those listeners in Cape Town are a group of young Blacks ranging in age from 17 to 21 years of age in the African National Congress. One of them carries Sisulu's message to John Washington and urges him to stay in the ANC.

But John Washington won't be one of them. After quitting the ANC, he has joined the Pan Africanist Congress. The PAC not only opposes the ANC for support from Whites but also intensifies the PAC's campaign against Whites.

Just like Walter Sisulu of the ANC, the PAC has a dynamite expert traveling around the country and teaching its members about sabotaging government facilities, with one target being the railroad tracks leading into Port Elizabeth.

To obtain the PAC information, John tells his parents that he is attending a college counselor's meeting at his Catholic school. Instead, he is meeting with a group of PAC members learning the ins and outs of sabotage.

***

In late May of 1963, Frederick Kruger is reading a copy of a letter written by Dr. Martin Luther King, Jr. when the Reverend was incarcerated in the Birmingham, Alabama jail on April 11, 1963. The sender of the letter, Father John O'Malley, had received a copy from Roy Wilkins, Executive Secretary of the NAACP.

Since Father O'Malley wants Frederick to especially pay attention to what Dr. King says about White moderates, he's highlighted that part of the letter.

Although Frederick has read the entire letter, his eyes return to the high lightened parts.

"I must confess that in the past few years, I have been greatly disappointed with White moderates. I have almost reached the regrettable conclusion that the Negro's great stumbling block in his stride toward freedom is not the White Citizens' Council or the Ku Klux Klanner, but the White moderate, who is more dedicated to 'order' than to justice; who prefers a negative peace which is the absence of tension to a positive peace which is the presence of justice; who constantly says: 'I appreciate you in the goal you seek, but I cannot agree with your methods of direct action;' who paternalistically believes he can set the timetable for another man's freedom; who lives by a mythical concept of time and who constantly advises the Negro to wait for a 'more convenient season.'

"Shallow understanding from people of good will is more frustrating than absolute misunderstanding from people of ill will. Lukewarm acceptance is much more bewildering than outright rejection.

"I had hoped that the White moderate would understand that law and order exist for the purpose of establishing justice and that when they fail in this purpose they become dangerously structured dams that block the flow of social progress. I had hoped that the White moderate would understand that the present tension in the South is a necessary phase of the transition from an obnoxious negative peace, in which the Negro passively accepted his unjust plight, to a substantive and positive peace, in which all men will respect the dignity and worth of human personality."

Frederick recalls the last line in the priest's letter. "You, my friend, are no moderate, but use this to motivate your White moderate friends."

That he will gladly do.

Chapter 47

The Kennedy Administration's Under Secretary of African Affairs, G. Mennen Williams, on June 12, 1963 sends a secret memorandum to the U.S. Secretary of State, Dean Rusk, advising that Apartheid has now reached a new and decisive phase due to a strong condemnation at the meeting of independent African States in Ethiopia.

Mennen suggests the United States condemn Apartheid because racial discrimination in the United States and in South Africa is an interrelated issue. He recommends a total embargo of all arms and military equipment to South Africa to prove especially to these African nations that the Kennedy Administration seriously opposes Apartheid.

But, on the same day, the Deputy Secretary for Political Affairs, U. Alexis Johnson, sends a contrary memorandum to the Secretary of State, advising against a total arms and military equipment embargo on South Africa. He argues that although Apartheid will eventually prove disastrous, the United States needs aircraft landing rights, naval ports, and tracking stations, now more important because of Egypt's closing the Suez Canal.

He points out that unless other Western nations also embargoed South Africa, a U.S. embargo would have very limited effect on South Africa and he doesn't see that happening.

He adds that many American businesses are now located in South Africa and will need the protection of the South African Defense Force and the Security Police.

Secretary of State Dean Rusk decides that the South African policy of Apartheid is not necessarily more repugnant than that of other authoritarian regimes and that a deep distinction exists between Apartheid and racial discrimination in America. He concludes that the United States will not assist South Africa to enforce Apartheid but will assist South Africa as America's ally to confront forces which also affect the life and death of America, too, namely Communism and Russia's attempt to dominate the world.

Both the military leaders in United States and in Britain agree with the Commandant General of the South African Defense Forces that South Africa is the only fixed point offering modern naval bases, harbors, airfields, developed industrial complexes, and a stable government in the entire ocean between Australia and South America.

South Africa holds one-fourth of the world's supply of manganese and chromite and all of the world's supply of amosite asbestos, plus plenty of corundum, antimony, gold, and industrial diamonds. America is most interested in South Africa's uranium.

American companies, such as Coca Cola, General Electric, General Motors, Ford Motor Company, Motorola have huge investments—factories and many employees living in South Africa.

Britain, too has many citizens living in South Africa and receives much gold from South Africa

For the present the United States will not impose any arms embargo on South Africa and, like Britain, will continue to trade with South Africa, in spite of any suggested action by the United Nations.

Chapter 48

On July 11, 1963 at Liliesleaf Farm in Rivonia the entire high command of *Spear of the Nation* except for Nelson Mandela already imprisoned on Robben Island, is meeting in a strategy session.

However, when Father John O'Malley hears that the leaders are planning Operation *Mayibuye,* a plan for guerrilla warfare throughout South Africa, the priest says, "Well, gentlemen, I apologize, but my Faith will not allow me to take part in any indiscriminate killing of people, even those of the Security Police. So, I ask that you reconsider that strategy. I can stomach sabotage without injury to people. But, I cannot condone killing someone except in self-defense."

Walter Sisulu tries to dissuade the priest, "Father John, you have served with us for such a long, long time. We all appreciate your service. But the government is killing our people in the ANC practically every day. We have no choice but to defend our people against this horrible atrocity called government. The South African Defense Forces are even going across the borders and tracking down our people. They either kill them there or later after capture. This is our self-defense. Please stay with us, Father John."

The priest says, "I understand where you are coming from, Walter, but I cannot agree with what you are planning with these guerrilla tactics, which to me means bombing police stations or other government offices and killing bystanders, people who just happen to be at the site of the explosion. That strategy violates God's Commandment and what my Church stands for."

"But, Father John, we…"

"I've seen the proposed plans for Operation *Mayibuye,* which are sitting right there on the dining room table. I'm sorry but I cannot be involved in that."

Walter says, "Well, if you must go, just keep silent about the plan and continue helping our cause as you have in the past."

Father John says, "Of course, of course. By the way, be careful in broadcasting on the radio station, because I heard that the South African Defense Force has a way to pinpoint with accuracy the location of our transmitter."

After a blessing by the priest and hugs and handshakes, Father John leaves and drives to the exit gate where the security guard waves him through.

As he leaves the dirt road for the highway, he sees a dry cleaners' van turn onto the dirt road. Strange, he thinks, that a dry cleaner is coming to the Farm.

Driving farther, the priest sees two more vans, both unmarked, coming toward him, two White men in the front seats.

Then, Father John sees Arthur Goldreich's approaching car on the highway. He waves to him but Goldreich's car doesn't stop and continues toward Liliesleaf Farm.

***

Father John has driven to Durban to meet with his superiors for guidance and support about his stand against guerilla warfare. After the two-day conference, he returns to his room and begins reading yesterday's edition of a local newspaper.

"POLICE RAID ANC HIDEOUT IN RIVONIA"

"On July 11, the Security Police with German Shepherd or Alsatian police dogs raided the hideout of the African National Congress in Rivonia and captured what they say is the entire High Command leaders of 'Umkhonto we Sizwe' or 'The Spear of the Nation.'

"Unnamed sources report that boxes of incriminating evidence, including plans for guerrilla warfare and additional acts of sabotage, were also confiscated and said to be a 'treasure trove' which will enable government prosecutors to seek the death penalty of these leaders.

"Acceding to security requests of the government prosecutors and the Security Police, this newspaper will not publish the names of those arrested to avoid tipping off any additional co-conspirators to flee the country to avoid additional arrests and prosecutions. However, those detained include alleged members of the High Command of the ANC and of the Communist Party of South Africa.

"After an appearance before the Magistrate and initially denied counsel, all those arrested were charged with sabotage and detained under the Ninety Day Law.

"For security reasons, all the defendants were taken to Robben Island and joined Nelson Mandela, who now also will be charged with sabotage, since his name is linked to certain plans discovered on a table.

"All defendants will be allowed counsel.

"Our unnamed sources predict that the trial for all the defendants will be scheduled for October 9, 1963 in the Palace of Justice in Pretoria."

Setting aside the newspaper, Father John realizes that his name and thousands of others will now be in the hands of the Security Police. He must meet with the superiors of his religious order, the Oblates of Mary Immaculate, for advice to flee or stay.

His superiors suggest that Father John talk with Archbishop Denis Hurley and be guided by the Archbishop's decision about his fate.

**

Archbishop Hurley, a long-time opponent of the Apartheid government, in 1951 blasted Apartheid in a pastoral letter read in all Catholic Churches as "blasphemy and intrinsically evil." Since then, he has continued his fight with the Apartheid Government, even though other religious have been ousted from the country.

After Father John explains what happened and how he almost was captured in the police raid at Liliesleaf Farm, the Archbishop offers, "Sit here, Father John and slow down."

"Your Excellency, I'm afraid I may end up as part of the inner circle and that could be tragic. I fear I must leave South Africa."

"Father John, you've been a valuable asset in our struggle with Apartheid. I cannot put your life in danger. Yes, you should leave. And yes, you must leave at once."

"Yes, thank you, Your Excellency."

"You will have the chance to return when things are safe. My son, you are in my prayers and you always will be."

Father John remembers the ANC Executive Committee had discussed an emergency plan if escape from South Africa became necessary. He explains the plan to Archbishop Hurley.

"First, I would travel in my car with some priests to Swaziland, not that far from Durbin. Then, catch a flight to some safe haven since we know the Security Police conduct raids into Swaziland and even some of the other neighboring countries."

The Archbishop doesn't concur. "No, Father, if you are correct about your name associated with the High Command arrested in Rivonia, the Security Police will be hunting for anyone looking like a priest at all border crossings, especially into Swaziland, surrounded by South Africa. Plus, they may already have those escape plans you mentioned."

Father John shakes his head in agreement.

"Take one of the new Fords. Discard all your priestly give-a-ways. I'll have Father Vandervalle prepare you a new passport. Drive slowly to the border with Bechuanaland and in Lobatse you will be safe. I will send you further information after you are out of South Africa. You can still work to help the ANC from a neighboring country."

"Yes."

"You can be true to your moral principles by working as a medic for these guerilla fighters. Now, go pack your things and see Father Vandervalle to get your photo for your new passport."

"Yes. Thank you Archbishop Hurley!" as he receives another blessing and some money.

Father John begins packing in a small black suitcase what meager possessions a Catholic priest is allowed under his vow of poverty.

As he leaves the building, Father John recognizes that he is not alone in this predicament. The Security Police now have the names and the addresses of anyone ever a member of the African National Congress or any of its affiliates, such as the Youth League.

All current members and former members of the ANC are now in jeopardy.

***

Frederick hands Charles a copy of the August-September, 1963 edition of *The Cape News Magazine* and says, "Charles, look what's happening in America about racial segregation. Read the article on page 42. You'll love that!"

"Sure," he says and flips open the magazine.

"American Civil Rights Activists March on Washington."

"On August 28, 1963, more than 200,000 people of all colors under the rainbow marched on America's capitol to convince the Kennedy Administration to initiate a strong Civil Rights Law to protect freedom and jobs. Someone nicknamed the group as the 'Rainbow Coalition.'

"According to unnamed sources, President Kennedy tried to convince the leaders of the sponsoring organizations to cancel the march because the march would upset many in

Congress and forestall, maybe permanently, the Kennedy push to enact any Civil Rights legislation.

"The goals for the march included enacting laws for the protection of voting rights, to end segregated accommodations, for redress of violations of constitutional rights, for desegregation of all public schools, for a massive federal works program, for workers' training, and for a federal law banning employment discrimination.

"Organizations participating included the National Association for the Advancement of Colored People; the National Urban League; the Negro American Labor Council; the Congress of Racial Equality; the Student Non-violent Coordinating Committee; the Southern Christian Leadership Council; the National Catholic Council for Interracial Justice; the National Council of Churches of Christ in America; the American Jewish Congress; United Auto Workers Union; and many others.

"Additionally, many people of prominence and entertainers appeared and spoke, such as Bob Dylan and Joan Baez.

"But the main speaker, at the high point of the event, was Dr. Martin Luther King, Jr.

"The Reverend King had given at least parts of this speech at past events, but today his voice boomed out across not just Washington, D.C., but to all of America and, perhaps to the whole world.

"Some of what Dr. King said: 'I have a dream this afternoon. One day, justice will roll down like waters, and righteousness like a mighty stream. Every valley shall be exalted, and every hill and mountain shall be made low. I can imagine the day when all of God's children, Black men and White men, Jews and Gentiles, Protestants and Catholics, will be able to join hands and sing with the Negros in the spiritual of old: Free at last! Free at last! Thank God Almighty, we are free at last!"

Charles says, "Well, you think Verwoerd will see what's happening in America and soften up, maybe just a little, Frederick, now that many of the ANC leaders have been arrested?"

"I wish you were right, but I doubt it.' You won't hear any of this about America on the radio and in the newspapers favoring the government, maybe just a small paragraph."

"You are right about that."

"Even the fact that the United Nations seems to be ganging up on South Africa and that other countries are either boycotting our exports or banning South African airplane overflights or landing rights doesn't seem to bother the man."

"Frederick, what's going to happen to those ANC leaders arrested in Rivonia, and now, I understand, that Nelson Mandela is the leading defendant in this trial where each one of them could get the death penalty? I see there's not a lot of news in this magazine about that."

"Well, Charles, the judge has granted all the defendants a three-week postponement to allow their lawyers to get more involved. As you probably know, all of them were taken to Robben Island and now are in Pretoria for the trial. The judge is an old United Party appointee and I believe they will get a fair trial."

"Who is the judge?"

"The judge is Quartus De Wet, and as I said, he is not a government lackey and will accept no foolery from the prosecution which is led by Percy Yutar, a deputy attorney general. De Wet was one of the last appointed judges from the old United Party. I know him and he's a good and honest man."

"That's very good news."

"I suspect the trial of these defendants will take months, and with Nelson Mandela as the lead defendant, the government will have extra security in and around the court. And, even though the defendants don't enter the courtroom from outside the building but come in underneath the courtroom, to get this many defendants and their lawyers and all of the prosecution's witnesses and documents, the trial will be slow going."

"Thanks for the information. See you tomorrow, Frederick."

Chapter 49

Having once been the target of an assassination attempt, Prime Minister Verwoerd is recoiling from the shock that President John F. Kennedy has been assassinated on November 22, 1963 by a sniper hiding in a building along a parade route in Dallas, Texas.

To the Minister of Justice Vorster, the Prime Minister says, "B.J. let me tell you how thankful I am that we finally captured those leaders of the MK, the so-called 'Spear of the Nation.'

"Frankly, I suspected there always has been a plot or a campaign by these crazy Communists and revolutionaries to kill me. They all hate Apartheid and the good we are doing for our country. We need to keep all of them imprisoned if we don't give them their ultimate reward to the hereafter."

"Mr. Prime Minister, I'll make sure each and every one of our prosecutors does everything to make that happen. I can tell you, sir, that we've an ironclad case against Mandela and his henchmen. The idiots actually left all sorts of incriminating documents in the house, including their plans for guerilla warfare."

"They must be brain dead!"

"And, sir, I'm pleased to report that the Minister of Defense recently informed me that our forces have traced many of these dissenting no-counts into our neighboring countries and are secretly putting them out of their miseries. Several of those terminated are known Communists."

"Thank goodness for that, Vorster."

"Sir, to put the fear of God into these revolutionaries, I've expanded our warning and message on posters and billboards and even on the radio that anti-government protests can put their family members at risk of arrest and long prison sentences."

"Good to hear that. But, to be honest with you, I still worry about another attempt, another try at assassination. There's no telling what hatred has been instilled in some of the Blacks for our attempt to keep our country stable and safe. I suppose that can include some misguided Whites, too."

Vorster says, "No need to worry, sir, because you are well protected!"

"Honestly, I always wondered whether crazy Mr. Pratt faked insanity or really intended to shoot me because of Apartheid."

"Pratt was declared nuts, sir."

Prime Minister Verwoerd muses, "The newspapers speculate on why Kennedy might have been killed. Some say it was an ultra-right-wing group called the John Birch Society, while others think Fidel Castro of Cuba ordered it because of President Kennedy's Bay of Pigs invasion, which the Cubans completely repelled."

Vorster adds, "Maybe it was Khrushchev. Remember, Kennedy backed him down in the Cuban missile confrontation. Kennedy was a strong anti-Communist."

The Prime Minister rubs his chin.

"I suppose that Lyndon Johnson could have been behind it because rumors indicated he and his backers didn't like Kennedy and the Kennedy people didn't like that hick from Texas."

The Prime Minister says, "Is that right? I understood Johnson and the president's brother didn't get along."

"Yes, sir. Or, Mr. Prime Minister, as I heard from American Ambassador Satterthwaite last month, the politicians in the Southern states had railed up all those people who don't like Negros and don't like or appreciate what President Kennedy was doing with civil rights and forcing Negros into their schools and universities."

The Prime Minister says, "Now, that makes more sense to me."

"A lot of those people in the South, I think they're called red necks, have plenty of guns to do the job. From what I understand, they've already killed several of these so-called 'freedom riders,' Blacks and Whites in the South. You know, the American Constitution lets people have guns—the right to bear arms."

"Well, to me, that seems more believable because the enactment of any of that civil rights legislation will threaten all those 'Jim Crow' laws in the South and probably threaten the lives and livelihood of lower class Whites in the rest of the country. A pocketbook issue can overrule any kind of morality."

"That's a sure probability, Mr. Prime Minister."

"Yes. Well, I've sent our condolences to the new US President, Lyndon Johnson, to Kennedy's widow and family, and also to Ambassador Satterthwaite."

"Excuse me, Mr. Prime Minister, before I forget. I've learned that in America some company has discovered a way to lighten skin color so that a person can get White skin. They're even trying the product on a person's teeth, too."

"What, did you say, Vorster? That's preposterous, making Blacks into Whites!"

"Yes, sir, American business has a way to make a Colored or even a Black look like a White. Well, trials show it doesn't work most of the time. They call it bleaching. But, I suggest we ban the importation and sale of any such product and make it a felonious crime to even possess it."

"Of course, see to it at once, Vorster!"

***

Charles and Mary have made arrangements, thanks to the intercession of Frederick Kruger, for John, now 18, to enroll in the government college approved under the 1959 "Extension of University Education Act" for Colored students. The government has clamped down on all schools mixing the races, although several religious schools are still resisting since they don't receive any government funding.

Because of the new law, John really has one choice: Western Cape University for Coloreds.

John says, "I've checked out Western Cape University. The school was established in 1960 in the Bellville suburb of Cape Town. The first rector is an Afrikaner. Most of the courses are conducted in Afrikaans. In fact, it's not yet even considered a university because it's not autonomous and is operated under the auspices of the University of South Africa, a wholly White and Apartheid school."

Charles says, "Yes, I understand all that, John, but you've taken courses in Afrikaans in school. You realize that the government has closed all the decent schools for Blacks, Coloreds, and Indians. They set up these schools for each race, Blacks, Coloreds, and Indians."

"Dad, I know all that. But, a few Black friends in school got special permits to attend the U of Cape Town or to go to Wits. I don't see why I can't. After all, Robin is already at Wits; she'd look out for me."

"Son, your mother and I tried, with Mr. Kruger's help, but we just couldn't get you any permit. I'm sorry but that's it. We can't compare you to Robin for obvious reasons."

"Dad, Western Cape trains students for mid-level jobs in education or in civil service. I don't want that kind of education. Isn't there some way I could attend the school you did? St. Charles College in the Natal Province, wasn't that it?"

"Well, if you want to be a priest, John."

John laughs, "No, I don't want to be a priest, but I can act like it. Couldn't you at least try? Can you contact Father John and see? I can't go to Western Cape and I won't!"

Perplexed, Charles looks at Mary because hearing his son lie about wanting to be a priest raises some doubts about his son's veracity and credibility. It's becoming more and more difficult for Charles to accept his son's declaration disassociating himself from the ANC and its Youth League. Some clues have been disturbing. But, he doesn't comment.

Mary says, "Yes, we'll see what we can do."

**

But, after several attempts to contact Father John, Charles finally learns that his mentor has fled the country in fear of his life.

Explaining the problem to Frederick and Henrietta, Charles is almost beside himself.

Henrietta says, "I'll be glad to home school John, if that will help."

Shaking his head negatively, Charles says, "Thanks, but no, John won't go for that, not in a million years, Henrietta."

Frederick volunteers, "I've known Archbishop Hurley a long time. I'll phone him for advice and hopefully, the Archbishop will solve our problem by getting Charles into some Catholic institution. He won't let the government tell him who can and who can't attend a Catholic college. He's just that stubborn."

**

After several unsuccessful attempts by Frederick to reach the Archbishop, Henrietta answers the phone to find Archbishop Hurley wanting to speak to Frederick. She hands him the phone and Frederick explains the problem to his old friend.

Hanging up, Frederick tells Henrietta, "He's going to call Bishop Ernest Green in Port Elizabeth. He'll call us back."

Ten minutes later, Henrietta answers and gives Frederick the phone.

After several minutes of conversation, Frederick hangs up and declares, "Wonderful, Henrietta! John will be going to a Catholic school in Port Elizabeth at the start of the new school year in January, 1964!

"The Archbishop convinced Bishop Green to take a more forceful stand against Apartheid. Hurley convinced him to use his influence to get the Marist Brothers to accept a Colored and a Black student as a protest against Apartheid."

"Wonders never cease, Frederick. I'll tell Mary and you find Charles. John is going to college in Port Elizabeth!"

Frederick runs out the door.

Chapter 50

David Rickard, United States Vice-Consul and CIA operative, is meeting with Colonel Spangler of the Security Police.

"Colonel, I've just received a secret air-gram that several hundred men from the African National Congress, MK branch, have landed in Odessa, Ukraine. Also a large contingent of rebels has also landed in Minsk, Belarus—obviously in Soviet Russia—for guerrilla training. Sources say that the men arrived from Ethiopia and other friendlies in Africa."

"Is your intelligence accurate, Mr. Rickard?"

"Absolutely! But, Colonel, as you pass on this information to your Defense Force contact, remember, to keep the CIA and my name out of it. We do not want Russia or its agents to have any inkling that we have assets in the Ukraine or in Belarus or in Ethiopia. We do not want to endanger or compromise those assets."

"Yes, of course. And thanks for the information."

"I suspect we'll be conducting another nighttime operation across the borders against these camps of damned rebels. Naturally, we don't crow about these operations, which, I'm rather proud to say, have been very successful. Why, just last week we killed several of them and captured almost a hundred very near Lobatse."

***

A camouflaged Father John O'Malley, lying in the dense brush, hears the rata-tat-tat of machine gun fire as the South African Army overwhelms the camp of ANC rebels. He crawls away from the nearby path until he is completely hidden and hopefully not in some poisonous snake's home. He figures all the gunfire and noise has scared away the creatures of the jungle.

Father John, still opposed to guerrilla warfare and the killing of civilians, has nonetheless given his services as a priest and as a medic to these revolutionary soldiers of the ANC.

He doesn't carry any weapon for protection, thinking his life is in God's Hands.

A commanding voice yells in Afrikaans, "Over here! We've them penned down in that gully! You men, circle around to your right. We'll have the whole bunch surrounded!"

Closing his eyes, Father John hears a different voice, again in Afrikaans, but he can't see anyone.

"No, we're not taking prisoners as we did in Lobatse a few weeks ago. We just have to bind their wounds, feed them, and cart them back to Johannesburg or to Pretoria for a trial.

"If they're not convicted, we end up having to fight them all over again. So, this time, no prisoners! Don't worry—orders from Headquarters!"

The priest silently prays for the souls of his comrades as he hears more gunfire amid cries for mercy. Not moving, he closes his eyes. Eventually, all is quiet, but he still remains in his place of safety, afraid to discover outside what he knows cowers inside his head.

Finally, perhaps an hour later, the priest emerges and crotches toward the camp. He can hardly keep from vomiting as his eyes capture the immorality to humanity.

Gathering his thoughts, at first he thinks of getting his Extreme Unction kit, but realizes he doesn't need any holy oil to anoint on the bodies of twenty-five dead comrades lying in various states of repose in the jungle.

Finished with his administrations of the Sacrament, Father John finds a working radio tossed into the jungle overgrowth. He reports the tragedy to the ANC command and receives the location of another ANC camp and begins a long hike to a place of refuge.

***

In December, the Rivonia trial begins. Nelson Mandela as the lead defendant is accused of two charges of sabotage. The prosecutor, Percy Yutar, expertly lists the details of explosives to be used in the plan and carefully outlines the guerrilla activities to be followed by a wide spread military invasion.

He points repeatedly to the discovered plans, which, he argues, clearly demonstrate the intentions of all the accused.

Percy Yutar intends to not only put the fear of sabotage into the mind and heart of the judge, but by and through the reporting words on the radio and words in the newspapers to scare the public.

Since the Verwoerd government still maintains its boycott on television, the news is delivered nationwide only through radio and newspapers or word of mouth.

Shocked by the revelation of indiscriminate killing of civilians and the threat of an invasion by a foreign power, namely Russia, the majority of Whites grit their teeth in show of patriotic solidarity.

Most Anti-Apartheid Whites silently engage in denial by disbelieving the news, while most Blacks and Coloreds certify their beliefs that the news is just more government propaganda to scare them into submission.

Because of the large number of witnesses for the prosecution, the trial is expected to last for months, maybe all the way into October of 1964.

And the trial goes on and on.

Chapter 51

Early one January morning in 1964, Charles, Mary, John, and Tyrone get into Henrietta's Ford sedan after loading John's two suitcases so she can drive them to the bus depot. John will catch the long haul coach to Port Elizabeth.

When they arrive at the bus terminal for Non-Europeans, Henrietta stops for the unloading and says to Charles, Mary, and Tyrone, "I'll park over there and wait for you there."

She points to the parking lot a block away, for European customers, close to the terminal for European travelers.

As Charles pays for the coach fare and hands John the ticket, they see that John's bus will depart in fifteen minutes.

John doesn't play down his excitement about attending the Marists Brothers College because he has a secret agenda.

Once he received the news that he would attend college in Port Elizabeth, John contacted a local PAC leader that he was ready to work against Apartheid in Port Elizabeth. A couple of days later, John received instructions and directions how to contact a PAC member who would put him in touch with a contact in Port Elizabeth.

Tearfully, Mary hugs her son. "John, I'm so happy for you that I'm crying tears, but they're tears of joy. Yes, tears of joy for you!"

Hugging his mother, John says, "Yes, me, too, because I'm happy and sad at the same time."

Mary says, "Now, study hard, respect your teachers, say your prayers, and for goodness sakes, don't get in any trouble, and I expect to receive a letter from you every week. And don't forget to eat your veggies and brush your teeth. You promise?"

"Yes, I promise."

"Now, John, if you don't, God will send me a sign. You know that, right?" she laughs.

"Mother, I promise. I promise."

Charles says, "John, we are so proud of you. We know you will be successful in college. I'm very pleased you have gotten your anger against the government under control. You know, my son, these times are very dangerous, so please be careful."

He hands John a copy of 'The Cape Town News' to read on his journey.

"Yes, I will," John says as he turns to his little brother. "Tyrone, you must listen to Mother, do all your chores, study hard in school, and obey your teachers and especially Mom and Dad."

Tyrone responds, "Okay, I will. Now how far is it to Port Elizabeth?"

Charles says, "I think it's about 800 kilometers. How far is that in miles, Tyrone?"

"That's easy. Point Six times 800 is 480 miles. How long will it take to get to Port Elizabeth?"

Charles answers, "Well, with a few stops here and there, I'd guess about seven or eight hours, maybe more."

Mary says, "Well, we need to go to your bus because it's time for boarding."

After kisses and hugs and several good-bye waves among the family, John's coach leaves the terminal. The remainder of the Washington family walks toward the parking lot for Europeans and Henrietta's Ford sedan.

When Henrietta sees them, she keys the ignition and drives toward them.

**

As the coach leaves the suburbs of Cape Town, John begins reading the front page of *The Cape Town News*.

"Prime Minister Verwoerd says that the South Africa stands shoulder to shoulder with America in opposing all governments sponsoring Communism and champions America's fight in South Viet Nam against a possible attempt by North Viet Nam and its Chinese and Russian operatives to take over South Viet Nam.

"The United States now has almost 17,000 military advisors in South Viet Nam after the leaders of the Diem regime have been assassinated and a military coup has left the country in a power vacuum. Now South Viet Nam is totally dependent on the United States which, reportedly in 1963, poured over $500 million into the country now controlled by the Viet Cong in over 40% of the rural areas.

"US Secretary of Defense Robert McNamara says that Viet Nam has the complete and unending support of the United States to defeat the Communists insurgents. He vows that the

United States will not let the Communists Viet Cong and the military regulars of the North Vietnamese take over South Viet Nam, Cambodia, or any country in South East Asia under the so-called 'Domino Effect.'

"Unnamed sources say that the United States under the new president, Lyndon Baines Johnson, is planning to drastically increase not only the funding but also the military presence of army, marines, navy, and air force troops in the country.

"Rumors abound that the United States will begin bombing North Viet Nam and mining its harbors.

"Senator Barry Goldwater of Arizona, an arch-conservative and virulent anti-Communist, is planning on opposing President Johnson in the 1964 presidential election, meaning that President Johnson must play his cards that he is not 'soft on Communism' and yet is not 'a warmonger.'

"Prime Minister Verwoerd says that South Africa stands with America and will continue its fight to make South Africa a stable and safe country against all revolutionaries, either from within or from outside our beloved country.

"Reports from the Defense Minister show that South Africa has increased the numbers in the Defense Force and in the Security Police to combat these acts of terror and sabotage. He also says that the government's efforts to establish a

South African production of certain military equipment are proceeding nicely, especially in the manufacture of the Belgian F N rifle."

John stops and thinks that he must be very careful when he is in the classroom not to be too bold in his views. Obviously, he doesn't want to reveal that he is a revolutionary and now an active member of the Pan Africanist Congress. He turns the page and continues reading.

"The Rivonia trial continues, with no end in sight.

"After the Court dismissed the first indictment on legal technicalities and the defendants had been re-indicted, Prosecutor Yutar presented his Opening Statement that the banned but underground African National Congress had proceeded with a plan of violence and sabotage by means of guerrilla warfare designed for an invasion by a foreign power's military to overthrow the government.

"When Justice de Wet asked the defendants for their response, guilty or not guilty, each defendant followed the lead of Nelson Mandela, who said, 'My Lord, it is not I, but the government that should be in the dock. I plead not guilty.'

"The prosecutor has so far presented 173 witnesses, thousands of documents and photographs, Marxist books, maps, blueprints, treatises on guerrilla warfare, Mandela's escape notes, his other damaging writings, and his fake passport issued to David Motsamayi, his alias.

"The most damaging witness has been Bruno Mtolo, a Zulu from Durbin and a leader from the Natal region of MK—the Spear of the Nation. Mr. Mtolo testified in ghastly detail how he had blown up a municipal office, a power station, and electric lines. He explained precisely the mechanics of bombs, grenades, and land mines. Mr. Mtolo also testified that 'Operation Mayibuye,'—the guerilla operation that would spark a military invasion and internal revolution— had the approval of the MK High Command, including Mandela.

"But what severely damaged Mr. Mandela was Mtolo's startling testimony that Mandela and the MK were instruments of the Communist Party, with Mandela instructing the MK cadre that each one to be a success must first be a good Communist.

"Although the defense disclosed Bruno Mtolo owns convictions for petty theft, this unfavorable evidence didn't seem to sway Justice de Wet, at least in the view of this reporter.

"Now, it appears that the government's case is almost finished and should wrap up in late February of 1964. Then, the world will discover what defense, if any, will be offered, since from the beginning, the defense has never, ever denied responsibility for acts of sabotage, instead using the trial as a show for their continuation of the struggle for racial equality.

"Of course, exactly which defendants will actually testify and submit to cross-examination or simply read a statement is unknown.

"In the meantime, a movement is afoot—even in the United Nations—for the government to free all the defendants, especially Nelson Mandela.

"And, daily, outside the courtroom, the crowd chants, 'Free Mandela! Free Mandela! Free Mandela!' And, every day, the chants grow louder."

Setting the newspaper on the vacant seat next to him, John Washington's spirit is filled with admiration for Nelson Mandela and his own necessity to continue in the struggle for racial equality. The newspaper account has hardened his resolve.

After he checks in at the Marist Brothers College, he will receive instructions to meet someone who is supposed to connect him to another man, the explosive guy.

John wonders if these men are members of the Pan Africanist Congress, rather than the ANC because, like him, they are tired of the appeasing and the get-along-with-Whites attitude of the ANC. John thinks that South Africa should become 'pure' again and separate itself from control of the Whites.

Maybe *Poqo* is the way to get there.

John now has his mind filled with thoughts that his new tribe, *Poqo,* is good and its enemy, the Whites, is necessarily evil. That tribal division engenders purpose in his young life. He is embolden with significant meaning and now, as an innocent victim, can mass his hatred against Whites, the oppressors. How easy it is to become worthy and fault free!

Now, he is ready for a nap on the long bus ride to Port Elizabeth.

Chapter 52

Finally, John has arrived at the Port Elizabeth Non-Europeans bus terminal. Lugging his two suitcases, he reaches the ticket office for local transportation to the Marists Brothers College.

Since his bus leaves in about an hour, John uses the toilet, never leaving his suitcases from his sight. He accepted the warning that thieves and pickpockets frequent the bus stations.

The bus ride to the college reveals that its location is not in the seedy part of town but ensconced in a pastoral setting, not too far from downtown. He begins the long walk to the administration building, finds his way to the registrar's office.

After registration is completed, Brother Thomas says, "Well, John, we're glad to have you and hope you have a wonderful stay. As you may know, except for you and one other new student, all the boys here are White. But, you will find that we preach, preach, and preach tolerance since we are all God's children."

John's face raises a question.

"Yes," Brother Thomas says, "you will be rooming with a Black student, a beginning freshman like you. He's already here—been here for a week. I hope that's acceptable, John."

John shakes his head affirmatively, as the two descend into the basement and pass several closed doors on both sides of the hallway. He asks, "Excuse me, Brother Thomas, these rooms along the hall, are they rooms for other students?"

"Oh, not now, those rooms are just for storage. Before the government's new laws, they were rooms for students."

"Where are the rooms for the other students, Brother Thomas?'

Stuttering, he says, "Well, those are dormitories on the second floor for the White students. I hope you understand that the culture, the government, the parents would cause a lot of trouble, if we ..."

Ever the diplomat when necessity calls, John says, "Oh, I understand. Brother, that's South Africa."

But beneath his diplomacy, he seethes.

"Yes, thank you. Well, here we are at your room, John. Come in and have a look around. You will see that it's comfortably furnished and you share a wash basin and water closet, and a shower. This room used to be our maintenance man's room, but now one of the Brothers takes care of that."

John asks, "Is the outside door locked at night, Brother Thomas?"

"Yes, but it can be opened from the inside. Just push on the bar. You know, in case of fire. But, it can't be opened from the outside, so nobody can break in to steal or hurt someone."

John's mind is spinning with plans to work on the PAC's agenda, but he doesn't reveal any of that. He can leave through the door, put a stick underneath to keep it from locking and be back inside. But he'll have to invent some kind of cover since he has a roommate who is Black and maybe not a friendly.

John says, "It is my understanding that all freshmen must live at the college. Does that mean we cannot leave when we want to, Brother Thomas?"

"Oh, heavens no! You are not in prison. When you want to go off campus, you just sign out at the front desk upstairs. That's so we know where you are in case we need to contact you in some kind of emergency. I mean if your parents got really sick or something like that. And, after your freshman year, any student is welcome to live off campus if he wants to."

"Well, that's seems fair. But, do you have to tell where you are going, Brother?"

"Yes, in case we need to contact you. I mean, if your mother got sick or something like that, you would want to know about it, right? When we have extended holidays, some students will go camping or rent a bungalow near the beach."

John smiles and shakes his head affirmatively. He can always leave a fake whereabouts when he leaves by the front door. But no need to, though, at night out the basement door, he silently smiles.

John thinks, "Go to the parks or the beaches? Of course, we can go only to the Non-European beaches, usually trashy. Ditto the parks."

Hearing the religious say, "rent a bungalow" causes John to almost slap his knee with laughter—a bungalow for Blacks? Ha!

Shaking John's hand, Brother Thomas says, "Well, please let me know if we can help you in any way, John. And, again, welcome to Brothers College."

Alone, John is arranging his things, when a tall and muscular Black boy about John's age enters and says, "I'm your roommate. I'm Kevin Fazzie from East London, just up the road from Port Elizabeth. I've got the bed by the window."

Introducing himself, John says, "I'm from Cape Town. Tell me about this place since Brother Thomas told me you have been here for a week."

Kevin quickly gives John the straight skinny about the college.

"The Marist Brothers and Priests preach and practice tolerance but the students don't follow through with real tolerance. At least, I've yet to meet any student who wants anything to do with me. In the halls, they look away and avoid any meaningful conversation. In the dining hall, I usually sit alone because if I sit next to some Whites, they ignore me unless one of the Brothers is nearby."

John says, "Well, Kevin how'd you get here? I understand that the Archbishop of Durbin pulled some strings for me. What about you?"

"Yes, that's the same ticket for me. But, I'm glad to be here. I know I'll get a good education here and I'm used to Whites snubbing me 'cause I'm Black. I can take it, John."

"Oh, I'm glad to be here, too. You know, Kevin, when I finally got it through my thick skull that without a college education, I'd be one poor Colored sucker in this country. I sure wasn't going to the Colored college to be some low-paying slave of a civil servant."

Kevin agrees, "Yes, but at least you are not one hundred per cent Black. You must be part White, right? You are lucky because your do get some White privileges as a Colored, right?"

John laughs, "Not a bit White, but part Indian and part Black and part Colored. My mom is pure Zulu, my father is part Zulu and part Indian. Hey, man, I get the snubs from Whites, too. I think many Whites dislike me more because my skin, my hair, and my features demonstrate what mixing the races will look like."

Kevin puts on an understanding smile.

"And it scares the shit out of some of them."

Kevin says, "Well, hopefully one day, we'll see racial equality."

John likes that statement but decides to hide his views fostered by the speeches from his mentors in the Pan Africanist Congress that the White Apartheid govern- ment must be taken down. He almost showed Kevin the issue of 'The Cape Town News' about the Rivonia trial.

In the next few days, he'll wait for his PAC contact in order to move South Africa toward racial equality and the end to White domination. How fortunate the location of his room has an open door for him to sneak out at night. And, when he's not in class, an open front door for him to leave during the daytime is a plus.

Already, he's created an imaginary girl friend to visit as his excuse for sneaking out at night. He thinks Kevin will buy it, and, he hopes, will keep mum.

In the meantime, John will study and do his best to get along with the White students because he certainly doesn't want to spill his cover. It's just perfect.

***

Finally after several weeks, John receives a note in his message box to meet his PAC contact at a small café. The man will be wearing a red and blue shirt and will give him a phone number to contact a man named Victor Gwala. John is told not to give Victor his real name and that Victor will later give John new identifications. He'll keep silent his real name.

John suspects that Victor Gwala is also a fake name.

After a few meetings, John discovers that Victor is very secretive and careful in not disclosing too much about himself. He warns John that should either of them get caught by the Security Police, then, neither will have much information about the other.

Victor says, "Here is your new identification card and pass book. When we are together, leave your real ones and just carry these new ones."

John does find that Victor was once a member of the ANC but is also tired of the tactics of the ANC and, like John, has embraced the more aggressive tactics of the PAC and he also doesn't like Whites.

Victor has been keeping up with the progress in the trial and says, "If they convict Mandela and the others and sentence them to death, all hell will break loose in this country. We will avenge them till the last of us is dead, too. The PAC will rise up even in solidarity with the ANC, John. We will become like black panthers in the wild jungle!"

After getting down to business, they agree that on each Sunday afternoon on the edge of town to meet at a hidden cabin Victor has rented. There, they will began their bomb making and build up a supply.

The local PAC leadership has designated that these bombs are for several electrical grids as potential targets.

Victor says, "When we have the right number of explosives, I will leave a message at the college from your cousin. The message will say that I'm in town. We will then meet at our pre-arranged spot the next night at our usual time at the cafe. Got it?"

"Yes."

"Have any questions, John?"

"No. Oh, wait—how do you get the message to the school?

"I phone from a pay phone."

***

Over the next several weeks, John is sneaking out of the basement on designated nights, with the excuse for his roommate that he is visiting his new girlfriend and will be returning before daylight. Kevin smilingly has shouted encouragement with the hope John's girlfriend has a sister or a friend.

So far, Victor and John have exploded two bombs without any injuries but with severe damage to the electric grids.

Now that Easter Week is approaching in late March of 1964, the local PAC leaders have more extensive plans to move their bombs from electrical grids to other targets. They plan to explode bombs each night during Easter Week. On Good Friday and Easter Sunday they plan to plant bombs near train stations.

Of course, since the Security Police and the Army are guarding places where people congregate, all these plans are changed and Victor is given an easier target during Easter week.

***

On March 23, John reads the note in his box. He tells the Brother at the sign-out desk that he will be off campus until the Monday after Easter because he is going camping with his cousin. John is relieved when the Brother at the sign-out desk doesn't ask for the location of the camp ground or for any contact information.

John doesn't want to give him any information.

The College will not be able to contact John for almost a week even after checking the Non-European campground.

Chapter 53

During the Easter recess from Tyrone's Catholic school in Cape Town, Mary is walking with Tyrone near the edge of the Kruger homestead. Tyrone is enjoying the myriad of brown and yellow leaves on the ground, intermittently kicking them into the air.

Far away from his wife and son, on the other side of the property, Charles is hard at work cutting brush in a thorny thicket. After he told Frederick that he needed one of those new gasoline powered saws, Frederick had purchased a Stihl chain saw imported from West Germany. The machine is a dream in cutting tree limbs although it makes a very loud racket.

When Frederick returns this evening from the vineyards, he will express his gratitude for making his job easier.

Suddenly, Charles sees Tyrone running toward him and shouting. He can't understand what his son is yelling. He cuts off the machine.

Tyrone is screaming, "Father, two snakes bit Mother! She stepped on this long puff adder in the leaves! We couldn't see it! It bit her on the leg and she fell down on top of another snake. It bit her on the other leg!"

Charles drops the chain saw and runs with his son to where Mary lay on the ground. He sees a snake bite on her right calf and also one on her left thigh. The snakes are nowhere in sight.

"Tyrone, you're sure they were puff adders?"

His son shakes his head yes and says, "They made that puffing sound."

Charles says, "Run as fast as you can and get Ms. Kruger. Hurry! Go, son. Run as fast as you can."

Charles recognizes his wife is in a state of shock and quickly lifts her and calls her name. She looks at him with fear in her eyes, but just groans. He kisses her check and tells her, "It'll be all right."

He begins the task of carrying a now unconscious Mary toward the house when Henrietta and Tyrone drive up in Henrietta's car.

Henrietta is out of the car and says, "Those bites look bad. I've brought some crepe bandages but I couldn't find any splints to keep the legs straight. Charles, tie this crepe bandage above the bite on her thigh while I tie one on her calf. Tie it as tight as you can. Put her in the car with her head on your lap; and stretch her legs out on the back seat to keep them straight. This will keep the poison localized. We'll get her to the hospital where they have anti-venom."

Looking at the shaken child, she says, "Tyrone, you sit in the front with me. Your mother will be okay. We're taking her to the hospital. So, don't worry!"

Henrietta sees Mary's skin is pale and bluish and is covered with sweat. She is unconscious.

As Henrietta drives to the Non-European hospital, she tries not to show worry and again tells Tyrone that his mother will be all right. But, she knows that with two bites perhaps twenty or thirty minutes ago, the poisonous venom has already put Mary into anaphylactic shock. Her respiratory nerves have been compromised. She's hardly breathing.

Henrietta has seen pictures of a puff adder's wide mouth open with two hypodermic needle-like fangs. She decides to say nothing about how fast the cytotoxic venom will destroy tissue. With two envenomations, that venom can be deadly to a human.

Arriving at the Non-European hospital, Henrietta runs into the Emergency Room. Immediately, two Black technicians hurry a gurney to Henrietta's car and remove Mary to the Emergency Room. A nurse quickly takes her vital signs.

When the doctor on duty sees the bites, listens to Mary's heart and reads the nurse's notes. Listening to her heart again and feeling her pulse, his face saddens. "I'm so sorry, but she is gone. We're just too late."

Henrietta hollers, "Can't you give her the anti-venom?"

Apologizing, the doctor says, "Madam, the anti-venom won't do any good. It's too late. It's just too late! Two bites! She is gone. She is gone. I'm so sorry."

***

Throughout the country, more and more arrests by the Security Police are occurring, because the sabotage is not stopping.

The Security Police and the Army are raiding Black neighborhoods and burning the homes of suspected saboteurs and, if there's resistance, shooting indiscriminately. Reports show many Natives, even children, killed or injured in these raids.

During rush hour in the Johannesburg train station, a bomb injures hundreds and kills a White woman. Quickly apprehended, the culprit is severely beaten by the Security Police and is certain to receive the death sentence in his showplace trial.

J.M. Vorster, the Minister of Justice, warns family members to dissuade anyone in the family who might be thinking of sabotage. He figures that these threats against the family members of any saboteur, used extensively by the Gestapo in Nazi Germany during World War II, will do the trick.

In a nationwide radio address Vorster threatens.

"Mark my words, because any person committing an act of sabotage will not only be arrested and punished, but so will all of the family members of such terrorist. And that includes the parents, the spouse, the children, and even the grandchildren, because we will not suffer these atrocities!

"The very existence of our beloved country is a stake. We must stand strong against these vicious attacks on innocent people.

"As Minister of Justice, it is my sworn duty to apprehend these terrorists and I will use every available means to bring these saboteurs and their family members to Justice!"

Throughout the country but especially in the population centers, Vorster has installed billboards with a message threatening long term prison sentences for all family members of suspected saboteurs.

When another time bomb explodes during rush hour in the Johannesburg train station and injuring hundreds, J. M. Vorster, the Minister of Justice, is incensed.

Vorster announces the he will not lift the Ninety-Day Detention Law because of these acts of sabotage. He claims that the Communists are regrouping in spite of the Rivonia trial.

Vorster orders an amended message to the billboards already containing the message threatening long term prison sentences. Now, the new billboards threaten the forfeiture of property, licenses, and permits for all family members of suspected saboteurs.

Chapter 54

John Washington finally receives notification from the Brothers at the college about his mother's death and, after a phone call to his father, is on his way from Port Elizabeth to Cape Town.

Arriving, he takes a Non-European taxi from the bus terminal to the District-Six home to meet his father and little brother.

Frustration covers Charles' spirit because of his failed efforts to notify John of Mary's death and of her funeral, even though the funeral was delayed for two days. But he greets his son with a smile, and then, with a hug.

After a few words, Charles says, "Let's walk to the Kruger's homestead. There, we can see your mother's grave and say some words. You can speak to her. I think she'll like that, John."

John says, "Apartheid even demands burials in separate cemeteries among the races. I guess they believe Heaven is also segregated. I guess we owe Frederick and Henrietta for burying mother here instead of in some pauper's field."

Charles nods, wondering what to speak to both of his children about their mother's death.

"Well, Dad, she was a very good mother to me and to Tyrone. I will miss her dearly. You know how sorry I am that I missed her funeral."

"I know. That's all right."

John gently places a bunch of her favorite flowers by the small wooden headstone, to be replaced next week with a stone one. John gives a brotherly hug to Tyrone, who wipes a falling tear from his cheek.

"Son, your mother was always very proud of you and prayed that you would get a good education. I know you won't let her down."

"No, I won't. The college is good and I'm learning a lot. I don't want to miss out on my school work. So, I'll leave tomorrow."

Of course, John is not revealing what he is really doing in Port Elizabeth. He and Victor have already blown up two electrical power stations while he was on his 'Easter Vacation.'

They are being groomed for more dangerous assignments. John knows that if Nelson Mandela, Walter Sisulu, and the remaining defendants receive the death sentence, then he and Victor will be targeting places where Whites congregate. That's what the local leader of *Poqo* has promised, according to Victor.

"We'll kill some of those Whites," Victor crowed.

His thoughts are interrupted by his father's voice.

"Yes, I'll ask Henrietta to drive us to the bus terminal tomorrow. Come. Let's walk back to our house. You can tell me more about the college."

Again John says, "Sure. You know I'm very sorry to have missed Mother's funeral, right? I told the school we'd be camping but didn't say where."

"Certainly, but don't worry. It's not a problem. We'll have supper and talk some more about your mother and my dear and wonderful wife. I fixed some of your favorites for supper."

"Thank you, Dad."

"Come on, Tyrone, I think John wants to tell you about college with the Brothers and how much fun it is."

During the evening, Charles is doing his best to connect with John. With little Tyrone, Charles has assured the young boy of his love, caring, and devotion as a father. But, Charles senses a wall between him and John.

On many nights after Mary's death, Charles has asked God why Mary was taken instead of him. He's suffered with extreme doubts that he will be able to take care of his sons and give them an ordinary life, without their mother. He'll keep trying to be a better father.

The next morning, after goodbyes, John is on his way in the long haul coach for Non-Europeans to Port Elizabeth.

And Charles still senses the wall remains between he and the boy.

***

A few weeks later, on April 20, 1964, Charles and Tyrone have walked to have an early breakfast with Frederick, Henrietta and Robin after they have paid a devotional visit with them to Mary's gravesite on the Kruger estate. Now, Mary's grave is adorned with Mary's favorite flowers planted alongside, the work of Charles' loving hands. And the grave has a real headstone.

At the gravesite, they recite the rosary and sing Mary's favorite hymn. Then, the five each recount a loving conversation with Mary or a funny story about her.

Afterwards, they walk to the Kruger's house, where Henrietta prepares breakfast of eggs, bacon, and giant pancakes. The pancakes are Tyrone's favorites because she puts bananas in the batter.

Robin is already at the table, seated next to where Tyrone will sit.

When Charles and Tyrone are seated and ready to be served by Henrietta, Frederick says, "Let's join our hands as we say the Blessing and thank Our Lord for each other's love."

When breakfast is finished, Frederick says, "Excuse me, but I want to hear the news" and turns on the radio for the Cape Town radio station delivering the morning's news, as everyone grabs a nearby chair.

"Before we begin the news today on April 20th, we bring you the currents from the Rivonia trial.

"The defendants began their defense today, with Nelson Mandela as the lead defendant choosing to read a statement rather than submit to cross examination by the Prosecution. Legal experts opine that Mandela's tactic is legally permissible. Whether Justice de Wet will give much credibility to Mandela's statement is unknown but unlikely, legal experts opine.

"Since the trial is just now getting underway and the lawyers for both sides are jousting over legal technicalities, we do not have the substance of Mr. Mandela's statement. Of course, he would not want to give the press an advance copy so as to give the Prosecution a sneak preview. Better to keep them off balance.

"Later, we will at least present the substance of Mr. Mandela's defensive statement since we assume it will be lengthy.

"Now, here is some other news.

"Minister of Post and Telegraphs Hertzog re-affirmed his early decision in March that the government will not allow the introduction of television into South Africa, no matter that most of the entire civilized world enjoys television programs. He says South Africa need not march lockstep with other countries.

"Now, here is some other news occurring in the last several days throughout South Africa and throughout the World.

"A few weeks ago, the American radical fire-brand, Malcolm X, called on all African Americans to reconsider the policy of non-violence. He said, 'it's time for Negros to defend ourselves.' He urged Negroes to go out and buy guns and rifles, which would be, in America under their Constitution, 'within their rights.' Malcolm X then departed for a pilgrimage to Mecca.

"Prime Minister Verwoerd said Malcolm X is not welcome in South Africa and would be denied a visa if he wanted to come.

"Vatican City has become a non-voting member of the United Nations General Assembly and expresses its disfavor of Apartheid.

"There was no comment from South Africa's Foreign Minister about the Vatican's new role; it is expected that the Government will not be pleased.

"The United Nations Group of Experts on South Africa has presented its report to the

United Nations Secretary-General and recommends that 'all the people of South Africa should be brought into consultation and should thus be able to decide on the future of their country at the national level.'

"Prime Minister Verwoerd, who refused entry by the United Nations Group of Experts into South Africa, says that the United Nations should cease and desist entry into the affairs of our country and should mind its own business.

"In Hollywood, the American movie, 'Tom Jones' won the Best Picture award; Patricia Neal won the Best Actress award, and Sidney Poitier, a Black actor, won the Best Actor award for his role in *Lilies of the Field*. This is the very first time a Black actor has won any Academy Award in the United States of America.

"There is little chance that *Lilies of the Field* will be shown legally in South African cinema theaters.

"Simultaneously, the American President Lyndon B. Johnson and the Soviet Premier Nikita Khrushchev announced from each country agreed plans to reduce the production of matters for the manufacture of nuclear weapons.

"Prime Minister Verwoerd issued a statement that he expected no reduction in America's need for South African uranium. He vowed that South Africa and America are strong foes of Communism.

"Well, ladies and gentlemen, that is your news update at this hour. Stay tuned for more news on the hour."

Before the commercial begins, Frederick flips off the radio. He says, "Later, we'll be able to hear the substance of Nelson Mandela's defense statement. Then, in tomorrow's newspapers, they'll print the full speech. I can hardly wait."

Chapter 55

In John's class on government, Brother Timothy is urging the students to listen this evening to the radio which will carry the substance of Nelson Mandela's defense statement.

That evening, John and Kevin are listening, as are practically the whole country and much of the whole world.

The radio announcer begins.

"Today, April 20th Nelson Mandela began his defense statement from the dock of the Supreme Court in Pretoria on charges of sabotage.

"First, Mandela gave some personal information. Then, he admitted that he was a convicted prisoner for leaving the country without a permit and for inciting people to strike, and was serving his sentence on Robben Island.

"Emphatically, Mandela denied that the struggle in South Africa is under the influence of foreigners or Communists. He pointed out that some accusations in court are untrue. Nonetheless, he admitted that he planned sabotage but not in a spirit of recklessness or in any love for violence, but instead only because of the political situation after many years of tyranny, exploitation, and oppression by Whites.

"Mandela also admitted that he helped form *'Unkhonto we Sizwe'* but denied that 'Spear of the Nation' was responsible for a number of acts outside of the organization's policy.

"He said that because all lawful modes for expressing opposition to the principle of White supremacy had been blocked by legislation and would leave Blacks, Coloreds, and Asians in a permanent state of inferiority, the government and the law must be defied. But, when any law was broken, it was so as to avoid violence. Yet, when the government foreclosed this path and resorted to force to crush any opposition to its policies, only then did the ANC resort to violence.

"Mr. Mandela said that the African National Congress for 37 years had adhered to a strict constitutional struggle but when the White government remained unmoved and enacted Apartheid, the ANC engaged in peaceful protests and demonstrations which the government declared as unlawful. More than 8,500 people were imprisoned even though not a single act of violence had occurred.

"Mandela pointed out that although he and 19 others were convicted of organizing the stay-at-home campaign, all sentences in that early trial were suspended because of their non-violence.

"He said that later, the government enacted laws with harsher penalties for protests, but still there was no violence. When 156 leaders of the ANC were arrested and charged with violence, the court justly decided in rendering the defendants five-year sentence that there was no policy of violence.

"After Sharpville's shooting, the ANC was declared unlawful, forcing the ANC underground rather than dissolve. Mandela explained that since the African people were not part of the government, the ANC would continue its fight.

"The 1960 referendum to establish a Republic for South Africa denied 70% of the people in South Africa the right to vote or even be consulted, Mandela stressed. Protests and demonstrations, though illegal, were met with harsher laws, with Saracens, armed vehicles, and solders into the towns in a massive show of force designed to intimidate people, Mandela said.

"Mandela opined that there was no choice but to fight because the government had chosen to rule by force alone. A government which uses force to govern teaches the opposition to also use force, he said.

"Mandela explained that force could be sabotage, guerilla warfare, terrorism, or revolution. But *Umkhonto we Sizwe* chose sabotage, without loss of life, because they hoped by the widespread destruction of power plants, rail and bus lines, telecommunication towers, and empty buildings would discourage foreign capital and force the government to make democratic government a reality.

"But the White response clearly showed that a civil war between Whites and Blacks might happen, especially when the newspapers reported that sabotage was punishable by death and when the government ordered all Whites to undergo military training.

"Mandela admitted that he left the country to tour certain African nations, united against South Africa, and admitted that he did receive military training to make himself ready if necessary. He also sought funds in London.

"On Mandela's return, he found no alteration in the political situation and the death penalty for sabotage was now a fact.

"Mandela explained that the aims and goals of the ANC and Communist Party never were the same. Communism, Mr. Mandela said, stands for the establishment of a state based on the principles of Marxism and to emphasize class distinctions, while the African National Congress believes in racial harmony between Whites, Blacks, Coloreds, and Asians.

"He freely admitted that there has been close cooperation between the ANC and the Communist Party, but that cooperation was in pursuit of a common goal, the removal of White supremacy. Mandela said he had never been a member of the Communist Party.

"Mandela said that Communism thinks the parliamentary system is reactionary and disdains democracy, but Mandela emphasized he is, and always has been, an admirer of democracy, especially democracy in the United States.

"He pointed out that he and the ANC have been fighting against the hardships suffered by the African people at the hands of Whites, who live at the highest standard of living while Africans live in poverty and misery, suffering malnutrition, tuberculosis, pellagra, and scurvy. He said that Africans cannot escape poverty because education has been thwarted and worker skill has been blocked by White legislation through Apartheid and by reserving the good jobs for Whites.

"Mandela said that 40% of African children between age 7 to 14 do not attend school and to those children who do, very few obtain their certificates or diplomas. Children without school wander the streets without parents, the father away in the mines or the sweatshops and the mother working faraway in the urban areas.

"And, these townships or shanty towns can be dangerous because of daily stabbings or assaults.

"The Pass Laws render a person liable to police surveillance at any time, with thousands thrown into jail each year for not carrying an identification card.

"Mandela said that Blacks, Coloreds, and Asians want equal political rights because without them, the disabilities and the suffering will be permanent.

"He said that the African struggle is a struggle for the right to live.

"Nelson Mandela, eloquent as always and once touted as the Black Pimpernel, concluded his statement with these stunning and challenging words, and we quote:

'During my lifetime, I have dedicated myself to this struggle of the African people. I have fought against White domination, and I have fought against Black domination. I have cherished the ideal of a democratic and free society in which all persons live together in harmony and with equal opportunities. It is an ideal which I hope to live for and to achieve.

'If needs be, it is an ideal for which I am prepared to die.'

"Mr. Mandela' speech lasted for almost four hours until after four o'clock in the afternoon, but Justice de Wet did not recess for the day, even though there was a very loud commotion in the courtroom. Instead, the Justice waited for calm and asked for the next witness, apparently hoping to reduce the impact of Mandela's stirring speech.

"Ladies and gentlemen, now the Rivonia trial will continue with each of the remaining defendants to testify and be subject to cross examination unless choosing, as Mr. Mandela, to merely make a statement.

"According to Prosecutor Yutar, the trial is not expected to end until sometime in May, with Justice de Wet not passing sentence until June.

"We now return you to our regular broadcast after this commercial break."

**

After listening with Kevin, his roommate, to the radio station's reporting of Nelson Mandela's statement of his defense, John cements in his memory Mandela's words that he is ready to die for his ideals of racial equality.

Kevin interrupts his admiration, "John, do you think they will give Mandela the death penalty? And, if they do, what does that mean for our country?"

"If they do, there will be widespread outrage and more and more acts of insurrection. Many government facilities will be blown to kingdom come. And, eventually we will have civil war against the Whites! And that will be good, I think."

Kevin says, "I agree if he gets the death penalty, but I don't think they'll make Mandela a martyr. They'll give him a life sentence, and the rest of them, too. But like the radio said, the judge won't decide until the trial ends, maybe in June."

John makes no comment, but he will keep his pre-arranged meeting with Victor for tomorrow night to continue their campaign.

**

Throughout South Africa and even to neighboring countries, radios are broadcasting the substance of Nelson Mandela's statement of his defense.

In the outskirts of Lobatse, Botswana in a rebel camp, the African National Congress revolutionaries are listening to the radio broadcast of Mandela's statement.

Suddenly, gunfire from carbines carried by an invading but illegal force of the South African Army and Security Police drowns out the sound of Mandela's statement, replaced by cries and groans of anguish.

All the ANC rebels and followers of MK are killed either initially or later as the wounded are examined.

The invaders gather the identification cards from the bodies, what money remains in their pockets or wallets; pile the bodies in a heap; and torch them before pulling out and returning to South Africa, completely ignoring protests from the now lately-arriving investigating Botswana authorities.

＊

In District Six, Charles and his son, Tyrone, listen and also hear his neighbors' radios record the substance of Nelson Mandela's statement. Remembering how much hero worship John had for the 'Black Pimpernel,' he wonders if John is also listening.

Now, he explains to Tyrone what all this means, but he avoids any talk of a civil war between Whites and Blacks.

＊

Frederick and Henrietta have mixed emotions about the broadcast. Without any doubt, they are firmly behind the ideals championed by Nelson Mandela. But they fear Mandela and his MK co-defendants' convictions, a certainty, will—no matter whether the sentences are life in prison or death—will stir up more hatred between the races.

Prime Minister Verwoerd and Justice Minister Vorster have already proved they will stop at nothing to preserve South Africa for Whites. The increased

Security Police, now joined by the Army, have more and more weapons to enforce the law to control Blacks, Coloreds, and Asians.

Henrietta says, "Of course, if Mandela receives and suffers the death penalty, there will be no stopping the insurrection, the carnage, the property destruction, and the loss of lives. The government better hope that Mandela and the others get life."

Frederick agrees, but says, "What will our neighbors say?"

"Of course, the Herzogs and the Vandenbergs will hope they all get the death penalty for certain. I've completely given up trying to convince Anna and Rebecca of the evils of racial segregation. It's a hopeless case, Frederick, with them."

"I guess that's not so surprising."

"At Robin's school, most of our friends think like we do. And that goes double for many of our old friends in the United Party. You know, Frederick, I think we should stop trying to convince our friends like the Herzog's and the Vandenberg's, who accept and appreciate White privilege. We are never going to see eye to eye with them. Some of our friends are guilty of self-delusion and cannot admit what is happening."

"That's for sure."

"I don't see these people ever agreeing that racial segregation is against the law of God that all humans are created equal. Instead, I think we should do more preaching to the choir, because we need to keep together the people who think like we do. It makes more sense to help each other stay together in our beliefs than it does to try and persuade our friends who have different core beliefs."

"What do you think?"

"Yes, that makes sense to help all of us cement our beliefs and make us stronger together. We can motivate those who agree with us and reinforce our beliefs.

"That's a great idea, Henrietta.

"Hopefully we can still remain friends though we disagree. I understand that some of them do not want to risk defiance and opposition, fear of being ostracized through public shame and humiliation. Although sometimes, I wonder if we will remain friends."

"What do you mean, Frederick?"

"In fact, a couple of days ago in talking with Samuel Vandenberg, he made a joke that he might have to report us. It would be false of course, about us harboring banned Blacks and not hiring Whites to replace Blacks. He laughed that would give him an opportunity to bid on some of our vineyards if the government confiscated them. He thought it was very funny. I didn't laugh."

"Really?"

"I know he's several times made references that we are 'kaffir' lovers because we have helped Charles and Mary. Each time, I've ignored his digs. Now, I'm biting my tongue about criticizing in front of him about Vorster and his Gestapo tactics of punishing the family members of law breakers. So, be careful around the Vandenbergs."

Henrietta says, "Now that I think of it, Anna Herzog is very proud that Vorster has used the Suppression of Communism law and the Criminal laws to detain people without a trial. She's not a lawyer but one would think an arrest doesn't automatically prove guilt. That seems so basic."

"She really said that?"

"Yes and I tried reasoning with her but, as you might suspect, that proved absolute fruitless. I could not make any headway. We better watch our backs, Frederick. Some of our old friends may not prove trustworthy."

Frederick says, "Yes. I have it on good authority that several of our opposition friends have suffered through tax audits and multifarious building inspections."

"Who?"

"You remember Tommy O'Dell in the Harbor Master's office? He complained too often about racial segregation preventing his advancement. Now he's completely out of a job. And in his place is a White man with little experience, simply because of Apartheid."

Henrietta adds, "If one reads between the lines, one can see that the Verwoerd government is trying to de-legitimatize the press printing opposing news. Yes, we must be very, very careful in our continued opposition."

***

The *Rand Daily Mail* prints Mandela's speech word for word even though Mandela's words were banned by the government. The speech makes headlines in newspapers throughout much of the world and buttresses organizations in their campaigns 'To Free Mandela,' especially in Britain and the United States.

In America, Martin Luther King, Jr. is in the forefront of the campaign "To Free Mandela."

In the United States, Congress is considering Civil Rights legislation with Representatives and Senators feeling the arm-twisting ability of President Lyndon Johnson.

As the Rivonia trial continues into May and into June, world opinion rests in favor of Mandela and his co-defendants.

On June 9, 1964 the United Nations Security Council passes Resolution 190 urging South Africa to release all persons convicted or being tried for their opposition to Apartheid, seven favoring, none against, and Brazil, France, Britain, and the US abstaining.

Chapter 56

On June 11, 1964, all of South Africa and much of the world is listening to the broadcast of the Rivonia trial. The radio announcer begins.

"Good Morning, Ladies and Gentlemen. We are here in the Palace of Justice in Pretoria and are awaiting Justice Quartus de Wet to pronounce his verdict.

"Earlier, during legal arguments by both sides, Justice de Wet pointed out to Prosecutor Yutar that the government had failed to prove the defendants had ever decided on guerilla warfare although they had talked about the plan known as 'Operation Mayibuye.'

"Certainly, the Justice's assertion gave the defendants and their supporters hope.

"In case you're wondering about what the gamblers think, the betting among them is that Nelson Mandela, Walter Sisulu, and the other four main defendants will earn a guilty verdict from Justice de Wet. For the remaining defendants, except Rusty Bernstein, the odds for a guilty verdict are mixed.

"Justice de Wet had already dismissed charges against defendant James Kantor, leaving just nine defendants.

"The Justice found the main defendants guilty on all four charges; found defendant Ahmed Kathrada (aka Kathy) guilty on one count; and found defendant Rusty Bernstein not guilty.

"Justice de Wet announced that he would not deal with the question of sentence today and the government and the defense will be given opportunities for any submission tomorrow morning at ten o'clock.

"Court was then adjourned.

"As an aside to the Rivonia trial, anonymous sources report that Minister of Justice John Vorster hopes for the imposition of the death sentence on all the defendants. It is rumored that Vorster once remarked that former Prime Minister Smuts' greatest blunder in dealing with him was failing to execute Vorster for treason during World War II. Vorster is reported to have said he won't make the same mistake in dealing with these treasonous saboteurs.

"That concludes this special broadcast and we return you to a commercial break. Now, be sure to tune in tomorrow at ten o'clock for the sentencing phase of the Rivonia trial."

Throughout South Africa and the world people can hardly wait for tomorrow to arrive. Would all of the defendants be sentenced to death as the government has requested?

The gambling houses are giving odds with the punishment as life in prison as the underdog.

The pleas for leniency from people of many nations inundated the South African justice system.

In Britain, fifty Members of Parliament marched in protest in London and the British Foreign Secretary works behind the scenes to overturn the verdict.

In America, some Members of Congress protest. Adlai Stevenson as the US Ambassador to the United Nations acknowledges that the United States would do everything to help the accused avoid a death sentence.

Many International Trade Unions protest the trial.

Many dockworkers throughout the world threaten to not handle any South African goods if the verdict results in death.

Soviet Russia's Leonid Brezhnev wrote Prime Minister Verwoerd requesting leniency for all of the accused.

Prime Minister Verwoerd boasted to the usual newspaper reporters assigned to cover the Prime Minister, "Every last one of these damned telegrams and letters is taking up residence underneath my desk. I trust Justice Quartus de Wet is not swayed by any of this crap and he recognizes how dangerous these rebels are!"

Of course, all these publicized entreaties cannot be avoided by Justice de Wet since the newspapers and radio broadcasts never stop revealing the names of the senders.

Finally, June 12, 1964 arrives.

Since the South African government still refuses to authorize television in the country, radio is the only real means of instant communication to the public.

And people in South Africa and throughout the world are ready for the broadcast.

> "Good Morning, Ladies and Gentlemen. Today
> is the day! Today, Justice Quartus de Wet will
> announce his sentence for the remaining defend-
> ants in the famous Rivonia trial.

"As we arrived near the Palace of Justice in Pretoria, we heard sirens conveying a covey of Security Police vehicles through the streets and saw that all cross streets had been blocked for all other traffic. As we parked, we could see that anyone within a mile of the Palace of Justice had their identity validated. The Police are taking no chances.

"In spite of the extra security, at least three thousand people are lined up for blocks and in front of the courthouse. Some carried banners or signs which demanded, 'Free our Leaders' or 'We Stand by our Leaders' or 'Free Mandela.'

"Of course, none of the assembled people outside viewed any of the defendants who entered the courtroom from the basement.

"Inside, the courtroom overflows, with the local and the foreign press confined to standing room only positions. Naturally, the spectator's seats are full, Europeans on the first floor and Non-Europeans in the upper galley.

"As the defendants enter the courtroom from the basement, a loud murmur emits from the upstairs gallery. Nelson Mandela looks up and waves to his mother and second wife, Winnie, who returns his greeting.

"Now, all is very quiet in the courtroom as Justice de Wet takes his seat. The registrar calls the name of the case, with Nelson Mandela as the lead defendant.

"First, there are two Pleas in Mitigation for the defense, both very reasonable to our ears, but Justice de Wet doesn't seem to be listening since he is taking no notes and never looks up.

"When the Pleas in Mitigation are completed, Justice de Wet nods for the defendants to rise to hear his verdict. He appears to be looking directly at Nelson Mandela, but his face is a mystery.

"Quickly, he says, 'I have recorded the reasons for the conclusions I have come to.'

"Justice de Wet seems pale and is breathing heavily. These signs telegraph what must be the death sentence from this normally calm man.

"Finally, Justice de Wet speaks:

'I have heard a great deal during the course of this case about the grievances of the Non-European population. The accused have told me, and their counsel have told me, that the accused who all were leaders of the Non-European population were motivated entirely by a desire to ameliorate these grievances. I am by no means convinced that the motives of the accused were as altruistic as they wish the court to believe. People who organize a revolution usually take over the government and personal ambition cannot be excluded as a motive.

'The function of this court as is the function of the court in any other country is to enforce law and order and to enforce the laws of the state within which it functions. The crime of which the accused have been convicted, that is the main crime, the crime of conspiracy, is in essence one of high treason. The state has decided not to charge the crime in this form.

'Bearing this in mind and giving the matter serious consideration, I have decided not to impose the supreme penalty which in a case like this would usually be the proper penalty for the crime, but consistent with my duty that is the only leniency which I can show.

'The sentence in the case of all the accused will be one of life imprisonment.'

"A huge gasp comes from the assembled. A smiling Nelson Mandela looks upward toward his mother and wife, raises his hand with a thumbs up—a sign of the salute of the African National Congress.

"Police are trying to quiet the shouting crowd and push them from the courtroom as the handlers of the accused are herding them from the dock to the door leading underground where they will be placed, handcuffed in cells, until the outside crowd had dispersed.

"We are told by the authorities that Dennis Goldberg, who is White, will be taken to a different facility.

"Outside, the crowd in unison is shouting in Bantu, 'Power,' and then comes the reply in Bantu, 'Power to the People,' over and over. Then people are singing, 'God Bless Africa,' or in their native tongue, *'Nkosi Sikelil iAfrika.'*

"According to our sources, the defendants will remain in the local Pretoria jail and eventually will all be moved to the prison on Robben Island.

"Thanks for listening to this special broadcast. That complete our broadcast and we now turn you to our commercial break."

**

John can hardly wait to see Victor tonight in celebration. Their celebration will culminate with a bomb at an electrical grid leading into the dock area at Port Elizabeth.

**

Frederick and Henrietta, joined by Hans and Robin, are overjoyed since none of the defendants received the death sentence, but are sad with the life in prison sentence.

Henrietta says, "Of course, this won't be the end of the protests against the government, especially since most of the rest of Africa and the civilized world is criticizing Apartheid. And with Prime Minister Verwoerd in control with men like John Vorster in charge as Minister of Justice, we will still have more and more people rounded up as if they were cattle and thrown in prison."

Frederick's head shakes affirmatively as he says, "Well, we'll continue to keep a lower profile since I hear that a few of our friends have found their business permits are under siege. They're putting the squeeze on them."

**

Charles bows his head as radio announces that none of the defendants have received the death sentence. He again explains to Tyrone what Nelson Mandela had done, what he said as the reason for his actions, and what he believed.

He adds, "Tyrone, Mr. Mandela and his kind never abandoned the struggle to change these laws by non-violent means. I firmly believe that non-violence will win. This will take time, but in the end, goodness will always prevail over evil. So, yes, son, eventually this madness will end. Now, it's time for bed. Say your prayers and tell Mother how much you love her and miss her."

"Yes, I will, Dad."

Still missing Mary, Charles smiles that he has successfully provided structure, connection, and love for his son to ease the boy's loss and grief over his mother's death.

* * *

Eventually, word of the sentence reaches Father John O'Malley now working in another ANC camp in Botswana. He isn't surprised that none of the defendants, especially Nelson Mandela will appeal the verdict or the sentence of Justice de Wet. He remembers Nelson telling him that any appeal would appear disillusioning to their cause, the struggle for freedom.

Kneeling, the priest thanks God for sparing their lives and asks Him to make their prison sentences less burdensome. He ends his prayer with the Sign of the Cross.

Before he arises from kneeling, gunfire erupts in the camp from another over-the-border raids by the South

537

African Security Police aided by the Army and without the invitation or knowledge of the Botswanan authorities.

Father John O'Malley dies with the rest of his comrades in a final escape from Apartheid.

***

On June 13th, the day after the sentencing, a new law extends the death penalty to anyone undergoing sabotage training within South Africa and renews the 'Twelve-Day-Without-Bail' detention law.

Under the new law, Minister of Justice Vorster is now allowed to indefinitely detain anyone even after a person's prison sentence has been completed.

Although Parliament ended its one hundred three days by enacting 150 new laws to secure the nation, acts of sabotage continue throughout the country.

Bombs explode near bus and train stations. High line pylons are damaged or destroyed. And, near the docks at Port Elizabeth, a switch engine derails not because of any sabotage.

But, nearby an electrical grid leading into the Port Elizabeth dock area is destroyed.

Chapter 57

Frederick is finishing reading the July 5, 1964 edition of *The Cape Town Guardian* to see what's happening in America when, on the last page, he spies this article:

"On July 2, 1964, US President Lyndon B. Johnson signed the 'Civil Rights Act.'

"The new law outlaws discrimination based on race, color, religion, sex, or national origin in and at all public places, such as parks, courthouses, restaurants, theaters, sports arenas, and hotels. The federal courts now have power to rule on complaints of discrimination.

"The law also bans such discrimination by employers and unions and creates a federal agency known as the Equal Employment Opportunities Commission to enforce this part of the new law.

"Famed Civil Rights leader, Dr. Martin Luther King, Jr. termed the new law as the 'second emancipation.'

"With the exception of Senator Ralph Yarborough, Democrat from Texas, every senator from the States of the old Confederacy, known as the South, voted against the new law.

"President Johnson remarked that while he was overjoyed with the new Civil Rights law, he feared that the Democratic Party would now lose the majority of votes from people in the South. Nonetheless, he said that Congress would now begin work on a Voting Rights Law.

"Former presidential candidate Richard M. Nixon, rumored to be considering the next presidential race in 1968, declared that the Republicans now have a fighting chance in the next election. He explained that most Americans worry about safety and security, especially for their children, and he promised to crack down hard on drug use and crime.

"Some left-wing pundits suggested Mr. Nixon was race-baiting against Blacks because of his code words, 'drug use and crime'. Of course, Mr. Nixon said that interpretation was 'ludicrous.'

"Prime Minister Verwoerd commented, 'Well, what's going on in America isn't going to happen in South Africa, because we have a stable and well-ordered country where everyone is benefiting from our terrific economic growth, our rising stock market, low interest rates, and the Blessings from God.'

"Minister of Justice Vorster declined any comment on this story, but used the time to say, 'I have no intention of lifting the Ninety-Day Detention Law because I have solid evidence that at least four, and possible five, countries outside of South Africa are providing training places for saboteurs for their evil work inside our country.'

"Mr. Vorster declined to identify those countries as giving away information to the enemies of South Africa."

Putting aside the newspaper, Frederick wonders whether racial segregation will truly end in America even if and when Blacks are guaranteed the right to vote. At least, he sighs, there's hope and that hope may extend someday to South Africa. Eventually, that hope will rest in the hands of the younger generation, such as Hans, Robin, and Tyrone.

Thinking of his son, he's a little sad that Hans chose to open his own law practice instead of partnering with a friend of Frederick's. But he understands that his son needs to make his own mark in the world and not because he is the son of Frederick Kruger, a former Member of Parliament, attorney, prominent winemaker, and the like.

The boy doesn't need his father's connections.

A smile crosses his face as he recalls how proud Hans was to show off his new law offices near the Cape Town courthouse.

Hans was also proud to tell his father of his success in reconciling his first client with the client's wife and saving their marriage.

While his son would never violate the Code of Legal Ethics to reveal the name of his first client, Frederick thinks he has accidently stumbled upon the man's identity. Waiting in his son's reception room for their luncheon date, who should exit from Hans' office but a muscular man wearing the uniform of the Counter Insurgency Section of the Security Police with the rank of Lieutenant?

Immediately, Frederick recognized the man as Emil Dorbandt, a college classmate of his son and a frequent visitor on holiday to the Kruger's home.

Frederick shook hands with Emil and they reminisced over several of Emil's visits. Emil commented about how much he enjoyed meeting Charles and Mary during his visits, even expressing condolences over Mary's death.

When the Lieutenant left Hans' office, he nervously mentioned to Frederick that he was there just to congratulate Hans in opening his law office.

But a suspicious Frederick connected the dots that Emil was his son's first client, although he wouldn't tell that to his son.

At lunch, without telling his father that Emil was the client, Hans mentioned that his first client had promised to repay Hans' good work with some favor in the future.

After an enjoyable lunch, most of the conversation focused about the new Civil Rights Law in America, especially since the Verwoerd government is more aggressively curtailing civil rights, even threatening to punish innocent family members.

Frederick is glad that his son is following his advice to stay in low key in opposing Apartheid and paying heed to some advice from an old lawyer.

He reminded Hans, "Never forget, son, paying clients are overwhelmingly White and most will not appreciate any words against Apartheid. That's basic economics."

Hans agreed.

"We Whites, yes you, me, Hans, and all of us, whether we know it or not, are all living in the privileged class and are benefiting from just having White skin. And that's true whether or not we oppose Apartheid. We must hold on to our beliefs, of course, but we are still the beneficiaries of having White skin."

Frederick smiles as he recalls him and his son embracing and kissing each other's checks with their goodbyes.

"Well, maybe someday," Frederick muses as he folds the newspaper "that Lieutenant's promise to help Hans will pay off, especially if he's in the Counter Insurgency Section. But, you know, one can never be sure about these promises from happy clients, who, with the passage of time, somehow forget the good work of their lawyer."

He laughs as he repeats his last sentence and mutters, "And that's the God's truth!"

Chapter 58

Months later, John picks up his make-believe cousin's note from the registrar's office. It tells him where and when to meet, but since the note is in code, the Brothers at the college cannot determine the where and the when.

A few nights later, the time has arrived.

After sneaking out the college basement door, John catches a local bus to meet Victor. John's back muscles tense as he views from the bus window the billboard threatening family members of a saboteur.

A few stops later and he has arrived to meet Victor outside the little café several kilometers from the docks at Port Elizabeth, but Victor is nowhere in sight and very late in the darkness of the night.

John looks at the slip of paper he received from the Brother at the college message desk to make certain he is present at their new meeting location and at the appointed time. He decides to get a coffee and takes a window seat.

Victor is supposed to bring the necessary explosives and the detonators and whatever.

Worried, John checks the date on one of the newspapers lying on the table. It's August 23, 1964, a Sunday, their appointed meeting date.

Glancing at the paper, he sees that the South African Police now number almost 18,000 and that the Army Reserves are now attached to every police station. That's a signal for him and Victor to be very alert.

John is already on his second coffee when he sees Victor emerge from a car on the perimeter of the parking lot. He sees Victor hesitates before leaving the car and look around as he stands beside the car, waiting for John. Obviously, Victor doesn't want to enter the café.

Since the Black waitress has already dropped the check on his table, John leaves some coins, including a tip, and hurries to Victor's car.

Victor quickly gets behind the wheel and John hops in the passenger's seat.

John comments, "This is a different car than the other one. What happened?"

Victor says, "Yes, like the other one, it's stolen."

"Is that why you're late?"

Victor shakes his affirmatively and explains the delay and gets right to tonight's mission.

Victor says, "This will wake up the dead with the noise. They've given me extra, extra explosives, wiring and fuses. John, tonight we will make history. We are blowing up a train!"

"Wow! You're fooling—a real moving train?"

"Well, actually we're just blowing up the trestle under the bridge."

"Oh."

"I'll drive to a few blocks from the spot, park the car, and then we'll hike to the train tracks and the trestle. You ready for some action, John?"

"Yes, you bet!"

"Okay, let's go," he says, putting the car in gear and driving from the parking lot.

When they near the area where the explosives will be placed, Victor drives onto a dirt road which parallels two sets of railroad tracks. He pulls into the bush, parks, and says, "John, we'll leave the car here and hike down these tracks to a viaduct or bridge and climb underneath where I will place the explosives in the trestle framework. We'll have about sixty minutes before a train is supposed to come. But we won't be there then."

John asks, "What am I supposed to do?"

"You will help me carry this stuff down the tracks to the trestle. Then, you hand me what I tell you I need, because I'll be down in the trestle fixing the charge."

John is a little put out that he won't be actually assembling the explosives.

As Victor and John are putting the explosive materials on the ground near the bridge, several Security Police come up from beneath the trestle, with their guns pointed at the boys.

One shouts first in Afrikaans and then in English, "Hands up or I'll shoot!"

Since Victor is the closest to the policeman, he complies as the policeman hollers in Afrikaans, "Over here! I've got two of them!"

John hears footsteps banging across the tracks atop the bridge and sees another group of Security Police, with guns drawn, running toward them.

Scared, John puts his hands straight up and doesn't move.

He hears one policeman say something in Afrikaans to another carrying a radio. He suspects that they've called their commander to report their capture.

Asked in English for their identification cards, Victor reaches for his wallet and says, "Here's mine. I'm Victor Gwala, from Port Elizabeth."

Victor's secret is that his real name is Victor Mhlaba and his cousin is Raymond Mhlaba, one of the Rivonia defendants and, more importantly, he wants his mother's name and his home address undisclosed.

John immediately pulls out his fake identification card and pass book. Today, John is known as John Haron and he's also from Port Elizabeth. He says convincingly, "My name is John Haron and here are my cards."

Quickly the policemen handcuff Victor and John with their hands behind their backs. Two others grab the explosives.

They roughly push Victor and John across the top of the railroad bridge to the other side where their vans are parked.

Even though neither has struggled, both John and Victor have a few cuts on their faces, with Victor owning a black eye.

In English, the policeman in charge orders both boys into the back of a van.

"You, sit on this side of the van. Give me your legs," the policeman says to John.

As John complies, around each ankle, the policeman clips a leg iron which he attaches to a short chain coming from a metal ring in the side wall of the van. John notices there is no carpet or mats on the van's floor.

To Victor, the policeman points to the other side of the van. He secures Victor with a leg iron chained to a metal ring in the side wall of the van.

Then, to silence them, a policeman sticks tape over the mouth of each prisoner.

The vans, blinking lights and sirens wailing, speed to the Walmer police cells in Port Elizabeth.

At the booking desk, a Lieutenant asks in Afrikaans to several of the arresting Security Policemen, "I see that they have some facial cuts and bloody noses. One even has a black eye. How did that happen, gentlemen?"

In unison, the Security Police answer, "Well, they fell on the tracks while handcuffed. You know how rough those tracks are, sir."

"Well, next time, be more careful with your prisoners. We don't want the press to show people that we are inhumane, now do we?"

"Oh, no sir," they answer as if only one voice is responding.

"Very well," the Lieutenant says.

After Victor and John have been fingerprinted and photographed by the police, the Lieutenant .turns to Victor and says in English, "You say you are Victor Gwala, but this doesn't check out with our records. Would you like to give me your real name?"

Suspecting bluffing by the Lieutenant, Victor says, "That's my real name. There must be some mistake or some mix up with your records, sir."

To John, the Lieutenant says, "Your card has a lot of smudges on it. Why is that?"

"Sir, I don't know, but maybe the office clerk had dirty hands or some ink on his hands. That could be it," John lies with confidence.

Noticing the enterprising reporter working the police beat, the Lieutenant waves him to come inside.

When the reporter raises his camera, the Lieutenant says, "Sorry, but no photographs at this time, since their accidental fall on the railroad tracks over the bridge will give the wrong impression to the public. We don't want that, do we?"

The reporter lowers his camera and casts a big smile.

"But, here is a press release about the capture of two terrorists, Victor Gwala and John Haron, with the names of the Security Policemen responsible.

"But, for security reasons, we don't want this information immediately released. You understand, sir, we want to keep the public safe from these terrorists. But, I'll let you know when we can allow a release later this evening. So, don't notify the newspaper or anyone else before I give you the okay."

Naturally, the reporter complies. The public will get the news through radio and the newspapers when the Security Police is ready. It could be later tonight or tomorrow.

The reporter steps outside the office.

The Lieutenant returns to John and Victor and says, "So far, you both are very uncooperative, even though we haven't pressed you for much information."

Victor smiles while John's face remains mute.

"And your memories are faulty. You can't remember who gave you the explosives. You can't remember who your contacts are. You can't remember the names or addresses of any of your contacts."

The Lieutenant smiles as he waits for any reply.

Their silence prods the Lieutenant.

The Lieutenant says in his clipped English, "Fine. In that case, Mr. Gwala and Mr. Haron, you both are being transferred to the Sanlam Building where the Counter-Insurgency Section boys can interrogate you. The sixth floor is very famous for that. I hope you enjoy it."

He orders in Afrikaans, "All right. Strip both of them and put those medical gowns on them. Handcuffs and shackles, too. Take both of them in the vans to Sanlam, Room 619. They will decide who goes first. Then, wait there for further orders."

Chapter 59

After a speedy ride in the back of a van, naked underneath the hospital gown, handcuffed, mouths taped, and in leg irons chained to the side wall of the van, Victor and John arrive at the Sanlam Building. They are accompanied by four handlers of the Security Police.

The prisoners' shackled legs barely leave enough space for them to walk with a shuffle from the vans to the building lobby. As the guards pass the security desk, they hurry their prisoners to an elevator and all six zoom to the sixth floor.

Suddenly, one of the guards rips the tape covering each prisoner's mouth.

Since none of the guards say anything to the prisoners, Victor asks, "What's up here on the sixth floor?"

The question immediately produces a deluge of laughter. When all the guffaws subside, one tall and beefy policeman says, "Oh, you'll find out! Yes, you'll find out soon, little man!"

Outside, a guard says in Afrikaans, "They want Mr. Gwala first. Park the other terrorist on that chair by the door."

The two Security Police sit John in a chair and one says in English, "Keep your mouth shut but keep your ears open!"

Seeing the questions on John's face, one policeman volunteers, "Sometimes they use the 'helicopter' in there. That's where they spin you around upside down with your feet manacled from the ceiling and your hands cuffed behind your back. It's a scream!"

The other policeman adds, "But, that's not as much fun as when they can practice the 'airplane' flight. That's where they have your feet cuffed at the ankles and your hands cuffed behind your back; then a broom stick is inserted between your cuffed ankles and your cuffed hands. You're picked up and the broom stick now rests on two desks with you up in the air. What fun, but the fun is for us!"

He can barely contain his laughter.

The first policeman says, "Hopefully, you will survive these and other tricks, because if you're just barely alive, then to save on medical and burial expenses, we'll have to get rid of the body. That means dumping the barely alive body in the crocodile hole. If you ask me, I'd say that's a tasty way to die! And, you'll be helping Mother Nature feed her charges!"

John sees a big grin on his face.

The other policeman adds, "I don't know if that's an easier way than being roasted on an iron spit over a wood burning fire to get rid of a body to save those medical expenses and funeral expenses, too. What do you think?"

The first policeman answers, "Well, in my experience, it takes a very long time for even a hot fire to turn thigh bones and butt flanks to ashes so that they can't be traced. In my humble opinion, the crocodile hole is much quicker and less troublesome, too."

Then, both policemen can't stop laughing as they point to John's face, now full of anxiety over what is happening to Victor in the other room.

And, he'd like to erase the picture in his mind of people still alive dropping into a crocodile hole.

Looking around, John notices the room has been freshly painted a stark white and the concrete floor is clean. On the wall, hangs wall clock. John marks the time as ten o'clock.

***

Entering Room 619, Victor sees a wooden chair and a small table in the middle of the room. Beneath the chair, he sees two rings protruding from the concrete floor. At the edge of the room, he sees a few Security Police, including his two handers. They are all talking around a table with a few chairs. Nearby is a tall chest of drawers.

Taken to the wooden chair in the center of the room, he is told to sit while his leg irons are shackled to two rings in the concrete floor. Now, if he stands, he can barely shuffle, but just in place. When he glances at the concrete beams above, he spies two metal rings and chains.

Looking at the small table, Victor sees a small metal box with an open metal lid, a pair of plyers, some electric wires, and an old-timey crank telephone with two keys.

A tall and smartly dressed uniformed man, not very muscled, approaches Victor, walks behind him, and zips open the strings holding Victor's hospital gown over his nakedness.

The gown finds its way to the floor as Victor sits naked in the wooden chair before all these White Security Police. To cover his genitals, he tries crossing his legs, but his legs won't remain in place to protect his dignity.

When one of the policeman points that Victor is not circumcised, another remarks, "That won't prevent the electric current from doing its job."

Then, the man who untied his hospital gown stands facing him.

In a friendly voice, the man says in English, "Hello, young man, I'm Major Harold Snyman. I'm in charge of this special section of the Security Police. We are the Counter Insurgency Section and we deal exclusively with terrorists. And, what is your real name, since we know you are not Victor Gwala? And, before you answer, let me tell you we have ways to find out. So you can save yourself and us a great deal of trouble by just giving your real name. We can start there."

Victor looks at the major.

"But, if that doesn't work, then, we'll use some helpful tactics to get your memory working."

"Well, sir, there must be some mistake or some mix up because I am Victor Gwala. You can see it on my papers. Yes. I am Victor Gwala."

Major Synman responds, "All right, Victor, in that case since you want to play games with us. That's not very good. Now, I could hit you with my fists or with my open hand in a slapping motion, but I won't. I'll save myself the trouble."

Victor seems relieved.

"I noticed that you glanced at the tools we have on the small table. No, we don't use the plyers to tighten or loosen bolts. Instead the plyers are used to either extract fingernails or extract teeth."

Victor gasps.

"The other helpmates, well, we'll see about those. But, I see curiosity in your eyes."

Victor realizes the man is already torturing him.

"Now about the metal box with the open metal lid, we politely request that you place your privates in the box. But if you refuse, we gently assist you in placing your privates in the box and then we close the metal lid. Slam! Yes, it's very dramatic, Victor. Most of our invitees are not fond of the sound when the metal lid closes."

The major watches Victor's eyes to discover if his words are creating any images in Victor's mind.

He continues, "But don't worry, Victor. I hope you don't mind if I call you by your first name."

Victor is too scared to reply.

"Good, I didn't think so. I didn't think so. I'm not going to use those helpmates right now, Victor. Instead, I'm turning you over to Detective Gideon Nieuwoudt, who has a way, a method, or a means to help with recall. You might call him a memory expert.

"He's all yours, Gideon."

Victor sees the Detective open the top drawer in the chest of drawers and retrieve what looks like a stiff green hose as long as his arm. As the man approaches, Victor determines that a metal pipe hides inside the green hose.

The Detective strikes the hose upon the concrete floor with a loud bang in whip saw motion.

Victor can only imagine what that metal pipe hose will do to his body and imagines what sound will exit from his mouth. But before even a shriek can escape, the Detective walks behind him. Without any warning, the green hosed pipe slams across Victor's shoulders and neck.

Detective Nieuwoudt says, "Before I swing again, tell me the names of the people who gave you these explosives!"

Too stunned with the awful pain across his neck and shoulders, Victor's mouth opens a gap but no sound emits. A tingling runs from his neck down his spine.

Victor expects another blow, but sees his tormentor walk around him.

Detective Nieuwoudt faces Victor and reaches for the electric wires attached to the crank telephone. He says nothing as he clips the other ends of the wires first to one of Victor's nipples and then to Victor's uncircumcised penis.

Smiling, he begins to crank the phone as the electric current speeds through the wires to Victor's body parts.

Victor's body shakes violently but his voice box cannot immediately respond with a scream. A minute later the electric current stops and Victor's voice box emits a chilling scream.

The detective says, "Ready to talk? Or, shall I give you a little more juice? The juice is like jazz, don't your think?"

Victor appears to lose consciousness.

Major Synman says, "Okay, we don't want to kill him, Gideon. We've plenty of time to get the necessary information. You men, take him to the other room, keep him naked, and put a hood over his head. Then, bring in the other one. Maybe we won't have to wait. Actually, I'd like a spot of tea."

The Major hears the men laugh at his remark.

***

Already shaken after hearing Victor's screams, John freezes when he sees the men coming for him, a substitute for Victor, now hooded, naked, dragged across the floor, and dropped as if he was the proverbial rag doll—all right in front of John.

Looking at Victor's naked body, John gasps, as if in his last breath of air, when he sees the blackened marks around one of Victor's nipples and his foreskin.

John looks around, but knows there is no escape as the men yank him from the chair.

A last glance at the wall clock tells John the time is now eleven o'clock.

Chapter 60

Charles Washington is trying to put Tyrone to bed after their usual disagreement as to why the youngster cannot stay up since he's not ready for sleep. He suppresses a giggle because Tyrone is improving at putting up rational arguments to avoid bed. Finally, Tyrone surrenders to his necessity for sleep.

Charles kisses his son's forehead and says, "Sleep well, my son, and let the angels give you wonderful dreams. I love you."

Now, at last, Charles turns on the radio for some relaxing music, especially since tomorrow, Frederick wants a lot of the garden area reworked. Since Mary's death, Charles uses the ten o'clock program to reminisce.

He still wonders why God took Mary instead of him, especially since she was much closer to the two boys than he. Yet, he's diligently pushed himself to be close to Tyrone, give him loving guidance as a parent and to be part of the boy's life.

Henrietta has given him tips in handling his own and Tyrone's grief, especially in keeping Mary's memory alive by celebrating Mary's birthday and their wedding anniversary.

Now, Charles is closer to his son than he ever imagined. The two share their everyday episodes of life, Charles' workday and Tyrone's school day.

Not thinking about tomorrow's work, Charles twists the radio dial to his favorite station and settles in for a little solitude.

As the music plays, an announcer interrupts at eleven o'clock:

"Good Evening this Sunday Evening. This just in from the South African Security Police!

"In Port Elizabeth tonight, two young terrorists were captured as they were attempting to blow up a wooden trestle holding a bridge which carried trains near the dock area.

"The Security Police identified them as Victor Gwala, a Black, and John Haron, a Colored. Both young men are from Port Elizabeth.

"Of course, the Security Police are interrogating the two suspects to secure more information.

"Minister of Justice Vorster announces that not only will the government seek the full measure of the law against these two terrorists, but also the government will also seek against their family members, detention at the very least and at the maximum, long term prison sentences, including life.

"Vorster says he will never rest until these acts of sabotage cease.

"That's the news for now. We return you to music you can relax by. We wish you a most pleasant evening."

Charles listens through a few songs, turns off the radio, and says a prayer of thanks that his son, John, isn't involved and a prayer for each family of the two accused young men.

***

On Monday afternoon, Henrietta is reading the *Rand Daily Mail* and sees that John Vorster, as the Minister of Justice, is carrying out his Gestapo threats to punish family members of saboteurs.

As a lawyer, she is very concerned that even in these extraordinary times of attacks on government property, whether the South African courts will sustain punishment on family members, not only of saboteurs but also on anyone outwardly dissenting.

Right now, the government has so many tools to quash dissent, starting with banishment, house arrest, and detention without any trial and without any bail.

Her imagination selects as candidates the Washington family, Charles and Tyrone, if John had ever carried out his open antagonism against the White government.

Fortunately, John's open antagonism has dissipated, she smiles.

**

Over a week has passed since Victor and John were apprehended and undergone interrogation by the Counter Insurgency Section of the Security Police.

Beaten into submission, Victor has given away the store to his interrogators. The names and addresses of some local PAC members are now out in the open.

Yet, to protect his mother from family punishment, Victor intentionally misleads the Security Police about his real name, real address, and his mother's full name. Of course, he does surrender John's attendance at the Brothers College. But, Victor is still alive, with all of his teeth and the full use of his tongue, but he doesn't know what has happened to John.

Taken to a nearby office for medical treatment, Victor sees a wall calendar showing today as the first day of

September. Victor realizes he has been held captive for eight days.

A man in a white smock begins to treat his bruised body and bandage his cuts. Victor thanks God the Black nurse gave him some salve to put on his penis and on one of his nipples. He cringes when the nurse places the salve on his thumbs before each is carefully bandaged.

But both thumb nails are missing.

The Security Police in Port Elizabeth cannot validate information as to his true identity because his fingerprint record supposedly on file with the local magistrate's office has been apparently misfiled. They will need to compare his fingerprints with the ones on file in Pretoria.

That means tonight Victor will be riding some eleven-hundred kilometers in the back of a Police van to the Security Police's Compol Offices in Pretoria.

***

But, John Washington doesn't fare as well as Victor, because he can truthfully answer only a very few of the questions from his tormenters since he truly doesn't know the answers. Victor had never shared any of that information with him.

Naturally, Major Synman and his crew didn't believe John and his torture continued. He received multiple electrical shocks to his nipples and penis. All of John's fingernails are missing. His nose is broken and his jaw is broken. A few teeth are gone. His face bears a blue-black and reddish color. Both eye sockets are swollen. Welts of black and blue ride on his chest and kidney areas. Judging from the hang-down angle of his left wrist, it appears fractured.

Not only does John reveal his true name, and that he is a student at Brothers College, but he also names his father and brother and their home address in District Six in Cape Town. Fortunately, he doesn't mention Frederick and Henrietta Kruger.

Naturally, the Security Police record his family revelations in line with the protocol from the Minister of Defense. Major Synman orders that information be radioed to the Counter Insurgency Section of the Security Police in Cape Town for immediate action.

Major Synman hopes his prompt action will net him an award of merit and a deserved promotion in rank and pay.

When he later discovers the information has been misplaced for several days and the transmission has been delayed, Major Synman is pissed.

On the first of September, John has been moved to the prisoner's hospital wing for Non-Europeans. A thorough examination reveals John's vital signs signal serious heart trouble, kidney failure, and pneumonia. John's prognosis is extremely poor. In fact, the Black doctor predicts he won't last the night.

And he doesn't.

To avoid any more witnesses to his beating, John will not receive the Last Rites from any Catholic priest, even if he were conscious enough to ask.

Nonetheless, the cause of John's death will be disguised as either from pneumonia or from tuberculosis because of his stay with other infected prisoners in the Walmer Police cells, known to be damp and crowded.

The Black doctor and nurse will so certify on John's death certificate and that information, including a copy of John's death certificate, will be released to the press.

All of John's hospital records will be carefully doctored in confirmation with his death certificate, with the actual hospital records destroyed as a space-saving measure.

And the Black doctor and nurse will play along if either values their own privileged life during Apartheid.

The government will waste no money for a funeral or a burial and John's body will be cremated without any religious ceremony.

When terrorists strike a nation and threaten its security and very existence, then many in the South African Security Police will believe that the ends can indeed justify the means so that the means equals acceptable moral behavior.

***

Major Synman says to Victor, "They want you in Pretoria for questioning. I suggest that you cooperate because if you don't, the men in Pretoria will beat it out of you."

Victor just looks at him.

The Major directs, "First, strip him naked. Re-shackle him. In the van, chain him face down to the metal floor, with his hands cuffed behind his back. No stopping for him to piss outside the van, you understand. Tape his mouth. And don't give him anything to eat or drink. This little terrorist can drown in his own piss. Get this piece of shit out of my sight!"

A Security Policeman tapes Victor's mouth and ties a hospital gown over Victor as his handlers lead him out of Room 619.

***

Down the elevator and outside the Sanlam Building in an alley, a Security Policeman removes the hospital gown, exposing Victor's nakedness. Victor shivers with his hands handcuffed behind his back, as a hood now covers his head. The policemen push him inside the rear of the van, order him to lie face down on the metal floor, and then chain his shackled legs to hooks in the sidewall of the van.

Victor counts four Security Policemen who are making the long trip with him to Pretoria, two in the front and two in the back by the wire cage. He closes his eyes and is thankful to be able, finally, to just lie down and sleep during the 1,100 kilometer trip even though his injured penis is rubbing and bouncing against the metal floor.

***

The next day in Pretoria, a naked Victor is taken to a fire hydrant in an alley outside of the Compol headquarters. Still handcuffed and leg-ironed, a blast of cold water hoses him, but the stink of stale urine remains. Given a blanket for drying and covering, Victor stands shivering among the White Policemen.

Now, five policemen guard Victor as they ride the elevator to the tenth floor. Inside, the tape over is mouth is removed and he is again photographed and fingerprinted; then taken to a room reminiscent of Room 619 in the Sanlam Building in Port Elizabeth.

As a black hood is placed over his head, one of the policemen says, "Sit there and wait while your fingerprints are compared to what's on file at central. Soon, you'll be asked some questions and I suggest you give truthful answers. I'd hate to see you accidently fall out of this tenth floor window, little man!"

Chapter 61

In Cape Town on September 1st, Lieutenant Emil Dorbandt telephones, "Hi, Hans. It's Emil. Can you meet me for lunch? I need to talk with you about my case. I can take off for an hour."

Hans Kruger asks, "You mean there's more talk of a divorce?"

"No. It's nothing like that with the wife. But, something has come up about the agreement. And, I don't want to share that with all these gossips here in the police office," the Lieutenant says, with a little laugh. He smiles at someone nearby.

"Emil, I'm really, really pressed this Tuesday. I'm in the middle of preparing a time-sensitive document. My document is due tomorrow, the second of September! They want to close this deal before the end of 1964!"

"Hans, this is very, very important. I really, really need to see you about this!"

Emil glances at some of the onlookers and says, "I need a break and can meet you at our old spot in twenty minutes. It's important, Hans."

"Emil, can't it wait till tomorrow?"

"Hans, no it can't wait. Damn it, Hans, it can't wait!"

Hans says, "All right, Emil. Don't get so excited. I'll be there in twenty minutes."

Telling his secretary to stall, Hans hurries to his car.

Emil arrives first and quickly secures a private booth, orders a beer for each of them, and, seeing Hans enter, waves to Hans to join him.

"Okay," Hans asks, "what's so important, my friend?"

Whispering, Emil explains that John Washington, captured and an admitted saboteur, has been interrogated by the Counter Insurgency Section in Port Elizabeth and that orders will be given soon to arrest and detain both John's father and brother under Vorster's directives as the Minister of Justice.

"What? When did this happen? Are you sure?"

Emil details what he knows and says, "Somehow, we didn't get the word that one of the captured terrorists was John Washington until today. That is a very lucky."

"Is this for real?"

"Yes. Now, we are so busy complying with all of Vorster's orders. Our office will receive detention orders probably tomorrow morning at the latest to grab Mr. Washington and his son. Plus, I see that Mr. Washington owns a criminal record for assaulting an Afrikaner and that some informant in District Six thinks he is an ANC contact."

"Arrest and imprisonment or deportation to the Homelands—that's terrible news," Hans murmurs so as to prevent anyone nearby from hearing.

"Hans, they've got maybe tonight to get out of the country!"

"You think Vorster is really going to do that—punish the innocent family members?"

"Yes, it's already happening, Hans. I don't agree that innocent people should be punished simply because they are related to a criminal. That's not what I learned in even grade school.

"While I don't know everything about Charles Washington, I know from talking to him many times at your

566

house that he is an honorable and intelligent man and doesn't believe in violence."

"Emil, you are right about Charles. He doesn't believe in violence. What happened to John?"

"The official records say that died from either pneumonia or tuberculosis exposure from the other prisoners in the jails cells in Port Elizabeth. His body was cremated according to procedure. I say the official records because whenever any prisoner is killed during interrogation, that's what is put on the record, usually"

"What do you mean by usually?"

"Don't look so alarmed, Hans. I don't condone all police actions. I do know that sometimes a prisoner's death is labeled as a suicide or sometimes a prisoner's disappearance is labeled as an escape but in reality the prisoner has been disposed of in some way. But, the records will never say that a prisoner died because of a police beating or torture. Claiming tuberculosis or pneumonia as the cause of death can also hide the truth."

"Does that happen often, Emil?"

"Hans, it happens more than I'd like to admit. Not everyone in the Security Police is an ogre or a monster, but—sad to say—some of the Security Police have swallowed the government's Apartheid bullshit. Some of them have become so very hardened. They have lost their humanity."

"So, you think John may have been tortured until he died?"

"I didn't say that's what happened, because I honestly don't know. I suggest that we spare the boy's father of my suspicions, Hans. His son's death will be hard enough to deal with. And that's true for the little brother, too."

"Good God, Charles and Tyrone will be crushed about John's death, no matter how he died!"

"Yes, they will."

"But are you sure about that they'll be coming to arrest them?"

"Yes absolutely. But, since the message doesn't contain a high priority code, it will be tomorrow in all probability. Go and phone your father! They need to get out of the country tonight. When it appears in a day or two that they have fled, the borders will be locked."

Hans thanks Emil. But rather than use the public phone in the tavern, Hans returns to his office.

As Emil hurries back to the Counter Insurgency Offices of the Security Police, he is thankful he may have saved Charles and his son from injustice.

**

Receiving the news from Hans, Frederick Kruger is momentarily dumbstruck, but quickly springs into action.

First he tells Henrietta the terrible news and asks her to retrieve Tyrone from school. She leaves immediately.

Then he runs from the house to where Charles is working and hollers for him to come to the house.

There, he breaks the sad news of John's death and cremation and explains the immediate need for Charles and Tyrone to escape from South Africa.

"When Henrietta returns with Tyrone, she'll drive you to the house. No, that won't be good, because the neighbors will see her and tell the police. You take

Henrietta's car. When the police investigate, we'll say you stole the car and we think you are headed for the border."

Charles says, "Yes, I'll tell our neighbors that I've stolen her car and Tyrone and I are driving to the border."

Frederick says, "Tyrone can stay here with us until you return. Pack any keepsakes you want. Put your clothes in no more than a suitcase and a duffle bag. Pack Tyrone's clothes in a suit case or a bag he can carry. And get all important papers, especially your id cards, and Tyrone's school records, and the like."

"Okay"

"Then, come back here. By then, I hope I'll have everything arranged."

As he finishes, Henrietta walks in with Tyrone. She hasn't told him what has happened. Charles hugs his son and tells him that Henrietta is fixing him a snack.

He says, "Tyrone, I need to get some things at home. I'll be back shortly. Save some of that snack for me."

***

At the District Six house, Charles packs pictures of Mary, John, and Tyrone. He grabs an envelope containing legal documents such as birth certificates, Pass Books, Reference Books, and Tyrone's school report cards. Naturally, he pockets all the money he has hidden. Quickly, he throws his own clothes into his suit case, realizing he'll have to straighten them later.

Hurrying into Tyrone's room, he's scattered about what to take, but finally selects winter and summer clothing and stuffs it into a duffel bag. Looking at his son's toys, he realizes he cannot take his soccer ball, games, or most of his books. Finally, he stuffs a few books atop the clothes in the duffel bag.

Charles makes two trips to the car with his cargo.

Running next door, he knocks repeatedly and when Susan opens the door, Charles says, "Is Harold home? No, let me in, because I've something important to tell you."

After explaining and getting her calmed, Charles says, "When the police come, just say you saw me leave and I said you can have our things because Tyrone and I are leaving the country in Henrietta's car. I've already got fake papers."

Quietly he prays forgiveness for his lie.

When she seems to understand, Charles says, "Thanks for all your friendship and Harold's too," as he opens the door and heads for Henrietta's car.

As fast as he can without arousing suspicion, Charles drives to the Kruger estate and waves a friendly to the two hired Kruger security guards, one Black and one White.

**

Frederick has made arrangements with the Captain of a freighter carrying several thousand wooden boxes of the Kruger Pinotage and the Kruger Chardonnay to Brazil and to the United States.

The wine is already on board, but Frederick has three extra-large crates of a special Reserve which still must be loaded on the ship. Frederick already has export permits for these three extra-large crates. The crates rest in the back of Frederick's truck.

In one of the crates, Charles and Tyrone will replace the ten wooden boxes of wine, each box containing twelve bottles; in the other, their luggage will replace the boxes of wine.

He agreed to pay passage for Charles and Tyrone to the United States and Frederick will bring the money for the Captain.

With Tyrone listening, Frederick explains his plan to Charles.

"I've already unloaded the boxes of wine from two crates on the back of the truck. You and Tyrone will hide in one crate and your luggage in another. And, I've drilled some air holes in the crate for you and Tyrone. It's big enough to hold you both."

Charles can't believe this is happening.

"Henrietta and I will drive the truck with the crates near Table Mountain where it's dark and meet you there. You know the spot where we once had lunch. After we leave, you and Tyrone will leave in Henrietta's car and meet us there. We will tell the police that you stole Henrietta's car. The guards at the front gate will verify that when the police come to investigate."

Charles says, "Wait a minute. When will we get inside the crates?"

"Good question. When you meet us near Table Mountain, you and Tyrone will get inside the crates on the truck. Henrietta will then drive her car and drop it at an alley near the bus depot. She'll get in the truck and ride with me to the docks."

"Okay, that makes sense, Frederick."

"When we get to the docks, after the export permits are examined, the three crates will be lifted by a crane and placed on the ship's main deck."

"Okay. But won't the guard want to examine the crates?"

"The guard usually just stamps the papers and never looks at the crates."

"I hope that's what happens today, Frederick."

"After the ship is out of South African waters, you will be released from the crates and will be safe. When we get home, we'll report that you stole her car and have disappeared. And, your neighbors will verify..."

Before he can finish, Tyrone asks, "You mean, Mr. Kruger, we are leaving tonight on a ship? Why?"

Since Charles realizes that nobody has informed Tyrone what has happened to create this emergency, he motions for Tyrone to come with him to Frederick's office.

After both have a heartfelt cry, Charles says, "Tyrone, Mother and I loved John and we tried to keep him safe, but he disobeyed us and got himself into trouble."

Tyrone brushes away the tears.

"You know that I don't like this government and I don't like its policies of racial segregation. But, unlike your brother, I don't believe in violence that may kill innocent people."

Tyrone is listening to his father.

"Nonetheless, in my heart of heart, John will always reside and I pray that his soul is in heaven with God and the angels. Your brother died for what he believed in and he is a hero. I hope you understand, Tyrone."

Brushing away tears, Tyrone says, "So, we are leaving because the government wants to punish us for what John did?"

"Yes, that's it exactly."

"And we are leaving tonight. What about my things? My soccer ball?"

"Well, Tyrone, I've got what I could in such a hurry. Sorry, I couldn't get it. But, we can replace those things when we get to America. It'll be all right, I promise."

Still sniffing but accepting his father's words, Tyrone returns with Charles to where Henrietta and Frederick are sitting.

Charles says, "I have a few thoughts. Won't the police think you helped us? And if they do, what's going to happen to you?"

Henrietta says, "That is so like you, Charles, to think about us. No wonder we love you so much! You don't need to worry about us."

"That's right. Nobody will have a clue because we are being very careful. We'll say you stole the car. Your neighbors will tell them you had her car and loaded up some things. The guards at the front gate will verify the story that you and Tyrone left in Henrietta's car. Hand me the suit case and the duffel bags and I'll put them in this crate."

"Okay."

"The police will find Henrietta's car near the Non-European bus terminal and conclude you are on the run to the border. By then they'll have your picture at every border stop. They'll conclude you and Tyrone escaped."

Charles adds, "Well, that makes sense. How will I ever thank you, Frederick and Henrietta? You've been just like family to us!"

Frederick responds, "No need for that, because you are family to us. Now, wait a few minutes before leaving in Henrietta's car. We'll be waiting for you at the spot near Table Mountain. You know, where we stopped one day for lunch. It's very dark and deserted at that spot. There, you'll get in the crate on the truck. We will pray no one sees us."

***

Everything is following Frederick's plan. He's already removed the lid on one crate and is ready to nail it shut after Charles and Tyrone are safely inside. Driving Henrietta's car, Charles pulls up behind the truck. He and Tyrone climb into the truck bed.

Frederick says, "Charles, this envelope contains a letter from me and documentations which should help you obtain political asylum because of the government's policy to punish family members and because of Apartheid. Since you and Tyrone don't have a visa to admit you into the United States, you will need to ask the immigration or custom officials for political asylum. I will write Dr. Martin Luther King, Jr. and some others to assist you."

"So, I show this to the officials when we land in America?"

"That's right, but you retain the documents and my letter until you meet with higher ups over the border controllers."

"Got it," he says and he and Tyrone lay down in the crate.

"Good. Charles, this second envelope should tide you over during the trip and when you reach America. No, don't get up and there's no need to thank us because we owe you so much. We should be thanking you! Okay, one last handshake! And, Tyrone, you are sailing away on a great big wonderful adventure!"

"Yes, I know, Mr. Kruger, and thank you, sir."

He hears his father.

"Frederick, there's so much I want to say to you. But, since time is precious, I'll just say thank you for treating my family as equals. Thank you for treating me as a man."

Frederick can hardly keep his eyes from welling-up and says, "Get out of here." He quickly nails the crate shut, gets inside the truck, and follows Henrietta as they both drive to the drop-off alley.

She parks her car in an area without lights, makes certain the area is deserted, and quickly slides into the truck's passenger seat.

At the dock area, Frederick shows the export permit for the three crates. The policeman, already tired from his long and boring shift and familiar with the Kruger's wine shipments, stamps the papers and doesn't even bother to check the crates.

Driving from the fenced area to the loading area, Frederick parks, leaves Henrietta in the truck, and walks to the crane operator's cab.

"Good evening. I've got three crates of very expensive wine to load on the freighter, 'Majestic Sea' of Liberian registry. Here's a little extra for a very careful and gentle load."

Smiling and accepting the bills, the crane operator says, "Thank you, sir. I can do!"

As the load swings upward, Frederick walks toward the gang plank of the freighter and continues up to the ship.

There, a uniformed crew member asks, "Mr. Kruger?"

"Yes. And here is the envelope for the Captain. And the export permits for the three extra crates."

"Thank you, Mr. Kruger. Now, you'd be wise to leave because we are upping anchor very quickly after awaiting you. It's already half passed midnight. "

Frederick Kruger says, "Right, and bon voyage." He quickly returns to the dock.

***

Inside the crate, Charles and Tyrone feel the crate swaying and finally plunking onto the ship's deck.

In a few minutes, Charles says to Tyrone, "You hear that bull horn? You feel that motion? That means we are underway. The ship is moving out to sea. We will remember this day, September 1, 1964 for the rest of our lives!"

"When are they getting us out of this crate, Dad?"

"Very soon, son," Charles says, as the movie in his memory replays his own escape from this father's abuse some twenty odd years ago.

Hugging his son and kissing his forehead, even in that tight space, Charles realizes they are making good their escape from Apartheid.

The End

EPILOGUE

Facing the five other Grievance Committee Members, Tyrone Washington says, "Well, I hoped you enjoyed the story and that the history wasn't too boring.

"As you guessed, my father and I were granted political asylum thanks to the able assistance of Dr. Martin Luther King, Jr. and several others, particularly Congressman Henry B. Gonzalez from San Antonio.

"After high school, college, and law school in Houston, I accepted a job here in San Antonio. But that's enough about me."

Tyrone looks at the five faces, and says, "Yes, I see lots of questions on your faces.

"I'll try and answer the obvious ones. Yes, my dear father died just before I moved to San Antonio.

"As Frederick and Henrietta Kruger became more vocal against Apartheid, they had their wine export license suspended, faced a vineyard tax only applicable to their vineyards, and were threatened with detention. But the Security Police never discovered they helped my father and I escape. They both died before Apartheid ended.

"Hans also more openly opposed Apartheid. He had his law license suspended. He was placed under house arrest for six months. Now, Hans is practicing family law in a multi-racial law firm in Cape Town.

"Robin became a nurse and married a physician. Both worked openly against Apartheid and both had their licenses to practice suspended and placed under house arrest for over a year.

"Emil Dorbandt rose in the ranks of the Counter-Insurgency Police and clandestinely assisted many Blacks and Coloreds to escape the oppression of Apartheid.

"After my father and I left South Africa, the government continued with more and more oppressive Apartheid laws from 1964 onward.

"Unbelievable numbers of Blacks and Coloreds either were deported to the Reserves, were killed, or were imprisoned under Prime Minister Verwoerd, who was assassinated in 1966. B. J. Vorster and P. W. Botha, as Prime Ministers, continued the oppression.

"Because of Botha's more intolerance of any dissent over Apartheid, the entire civilized world isolated the country and damaged its economy. In 1986, the US Congress overrode President Reagan's veto of an act which blocked US banking, new investments, exports, imports, air flights, and military assistance to South Africa. That put the fear of God into them.

"Finally, when the country was about to explode into a race civil war, Prime Minister de Klerk took office, recognized that the entire civilized world was against South Africa, and knew that South Africa needed a sensible solution.

"De Klerk met with Nelson Mandela and ultimately freed him from Robben Island. After months of long and difficult negotiations, de Klerk and Mandela found the obvious answer.

"Using the US Constitution and its Bill of Rights as a basis, South Africa adopted a new Constitution in 1994.

"Nelson Mandela was elected as the new President and along with Bishop Desmond Tutu created a Reconciliation Commission to move the country away from revenge for wrongdoing.

"Now, the country is making great strides although evidence exists of government corruption and evidence exists that not all White inequality has disappeared.

"In many ways, South Africa is similar to our dear United States of America because we still have corruption and simmering racial segregation or hatred and distrust among the races.

"Today, our beloved country reveals greater disunity, much of it race-based and much of it political party-based. Just like South Africa's Apartheid from 1948 onward, our current government has exploited differences and divisiveness and fused both with oppression.

"The result breeds animalistic hate among the separated groups, not just hate within the separated groups for others with differences, but also hate and distrust for the government itself.

"When the leader of the government, Prime Minister or President, and his cabinet, uses the big stick of fear of Blacks or fear of the opposite political party to capture the hearts and minds of ordinary people, then any reasonable dissenting discourse is silenced.

"This is the playbook used by every totalitarian government and by oppressive regimes throughout the ages.

"I hate to say it but in our country, the President and his supporters have legally seized control of the government, in spite of the President losing the popular vote yet winning through an archaic but legal voting system.

"Some people argue that the Electoral College eliminates mob rule, but by awarding the total of a State's electoral votes to one candidate instead of dividing a State's electoral votes proportionally, it disenfranchises the popular votes of a State's minority.

"By awarding the total Electoral vote to one candidate in a State (winner take all) completely abdicates the one-person-one-vote theory of equitable government.

"That's exactly how the Apartheid government was elected to Parliament in South Africa by a minority of the voters.

"In South Africa, the overwhelming majority of the people were disenfranchised, marginalized, and separated into groups.

"But unless one is blind, one can see how the political party in power in the United States is restricting the rights of the minority to vote by installing more and more roadblocks to exercise that right to vote. And, slowly but surely, those in control are dismantling the governmental agencies protecting our health, safety, and our very livelihood."

Tyrone sees the group affirmatively shake their heads.

He continues, "Before long, even the truth will be suspended if good people don't come to the aid of their country. People must be willing to speak up to save our democracy and its institutions.

"Unless people awake and act by voting and by speaking out, then, from tyranny, there will be no escape."

ACKNOWLEDGEMENTS

Creative writing, difficult per se, becomes easier when the author has loving support and competent assistance. Fortunately, my wife**, Dr. Linda R. Southers, PhD.** has given important guidance and psychological assistance and urged me onward.

And, **Ralph Bussard of Informa.net** has provided competent technical assistance with his expert knowledge of computer software.

To Linda and Ralph, you have my eternal gratitude.

***

To the talented volunteers serving on lawyer disciplinary Grievance Committees everywhere, thank you for working diligently to provide real justice both for complainants and for accused lawyers, we all owe you.

***

In the beginning pages, I've listed those Historians and Sources from whom I've borrowed many parts of their outstanding research as a basis for this novel. Thank you for your dedication in educating all of us.

***

I accept sole responsibility and I apologize for any typos, goofs, inaccuracies, mistakes, or flaws and beg your forgiveness.

Frank R. Southers

AUTHOR-CREATED CHARACTERS

Betty Sue Meadowlake

Alice & Sol Washington; Charles & Mary Washington; and John & Tyrone Washington

Father John O'Malley; Father Sean

Jim Wright

Daniel Reitz

Albert & Josie Simpson

Father Vincent

Tabo Jabayu

William Meer; Maggie & Ruthie Nair

Frederick, Henrietta, Hans, & Robin Kruger

Ophelia Jones

Susan & Harold Langho

Sergeant Vanderwaal & Officer Piet Aarde

Anna Herzog; Rebecca & Samuel Vandenberg

Brother Thomas; Brother Timothy

Tommy O'Dell

Father Vandervalle

Kevin Fazzie

Victor Mhlaba aka Victor Gwala

Emil Dorbandt

THE AUTHOR

To contact: email frs@southers.com

FRANK R. SOUTHERS, a Texas Attorney, served on the San Antonio, Texas Grievance Committee for 10 years, the last six as Chairperson, and thereafter, has represented Complainants, Witnesses, and Accused Lawyers in the Texas legal disciplinary process.

He served for 20 years as an Adjunct Professor of Law at St. Mary's University School of Law in San Antonio, Texas.

Listed in Texas Monthly Magazine and voted by his peers as a 'Super Lawyer,' Mr. Southers has also been certified as a Personal Injury Trial Specialist by the Texas Board of Legal Specialization.

Having been trial counsel in well over 50 jury trials, Mr. Southers holds the rank of "Advocate" in the American Board of Trial Advocates, a national bar association.

He has held many attorney leadership positions, to name a few, Chair of the Litigation Section of the State Bar of Texas; President of the San Antonio Trial Lawyers Association; Director of the Texas Trial Lawyers Association.

Mr. Southers has written numerous articles on Legal Malpractice, Torts, Trial Tactics, Personal Injury, Evidence, Civil Procedure, Medical Malpractice, Mediation, and Grievance Law. He co-authored a legal treatise, *The Texas Workers' Compensation Desk Book.*

Turning to fiction writing, Mr. Southers' legal thriller novels, besides *Escape from Apartheid* are:

The Grievance Committee—Book One,

A Serious Mistake,

To Get Even, a Novel,

Lawyer Magic,

Senator White.

All novels are available in paperback or kindle at Amazon.com or on order from your favorite Book Seller.

Raised in San Antonio, Mr. Southers has lived in Austin, Texas and now lives with his wife and their two dogs in Carmel By-the-Sea, California.

CPSIA information can be obtained
at www.ICGtesting.com
Printed in the USA
LVHW020215120620
657890LV00017B/2001

9 781985 622067